The Ethics of ABORTION

Contemporary Issues

Series Editors: Robert M. Baird
Stuart E. Rosenbaum

Other titles in this series:

Affirmative Action: Social Justice or Reverse Discrimination?
edited by Francine J. Beckwith and Todd E. Jones

Animal Experimentation: The Moral Issues
edited by Robert M. Baird and Stuart E. Rosenbaum

Are You Politically Correct? Debating America's Cultural Standards
edited by Michael E. Bauman and Francis J. Beckwith

Cloning: Responsible Science or Technomadness?
edited by Michael Ruse, Ph.D., and Aryne Sheppard

Cyberethics: Social and Moral Issues in the Computer Age
edited by Robert M. Baird, Reagan Ramsower, and Stuart E. Rosenbaum

Drugs: Should We Legalize, Decriminalize, or Deregulate?
edited by Jeffrey A. Schaler, Ph.D.

The Ethics of Organ Transplants: The Current Debate
edited by Arthur L. Caplan and Daniel H. Coehlo

Euthanasia: The Moral Issues
edited by Robert M. Baird and Stuart E. Rosenbaum

Generations Apart: Xers vs. Boomers vs. the Elderly
edited by Richard D. Thau and Jay S. Helfin

The Gun Control Debate: You Decide
edited by Lee Nisbet, Ph.D.

Hatred, Bigotry, and Prejudice: Definitions, Causes, & Solutions
edited by Robert M. Baird and Stuart E. Rosenbaum

Homosexuality: Debating the Issues
edited by Robert M. Baird and M. Katherine Baird

Immigration: Debating the Issues
edited by Nicholas Capaldi

The Media & Morality
edited by Robert M. Baird, William E. Loges, and Stuart E. Rosenbaum

Morality and the Law
edited by Robert M. Baird and Stuart E. Rosenbaum

Pornography: Private Right or Public Menace?
edited by Robert M. Baird and Stuart E. Rosenbaum

Punishment and the Death Penalty: The Current Debate
edited by Robert M. Baird and Stuart E. Rosenbaum

Sexual Harassment: Confrontations and Decisions
edited by Edmund Wall, Ph.D.

Smoking: Who Has the Right?
edited by Jeffrey A. Schaler, Ph.D., and Magda E. Schaler, M.P.H.

Suicide: Right or Wrong?
edited by John Donnelly

The Ethics of
ABORTION

Third Edition

Pro-Life vs. Pro-Choice

edited by

ROBERT M. BAIRD

and

STUART E. ROSENBAUM

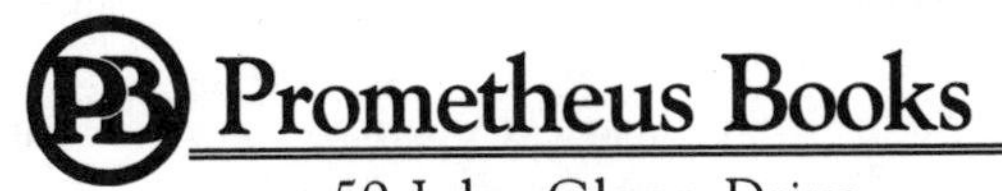

59 John Glenn Drive
Amherst, New York 14228-2197

Published 2001 by Prometheus Books

Inquiries should be addressed to
Prometheus Books
59 John Glenn Drive
Amherst, New York 14228-2197
VOICE: 716-691-0133, ext. 207
FAX: 716-564-2711
WWW.PROMETHEUSBOOKS.COM

05 04 03 02 01 5 4 3 2 1

Library of Congress Cataloging-in-Publication Data

The ethics of abortion : pro-life vs. pro-choice / edited by Robert M. Baird and Stuart E. Rosenbaum.—3rd ed.
p. cm. — (Contemporary issues series)
Includes bibliographical references.
ISBN 1-57392-876-3 (pbk. : alk. paper)
1. Abortion—Moral and ethical aspects. 2. Abortion—Law and legislation. I. Baird, Robert M., 1937- II. Rosenbaum, Stuart E. III. Contemporary issues (Amherst, N.Y.)

HQ767.15 .E84 2001
363.4'6—dc21 2001031860

Printed in the United States of America on acid-free paper

CONTENTS

Part Two. Abortion and the Constitution

Part Three. Abortion and Feminism

Part Four. Abortion and Christianity

INTRODUCTION

Robert M. Baird and Stuart E. Rosenbaum

For almost thirty years the issue of abortion has grown increasingly difficult. Few issues have more thoroughly fragmented contemporary America. Operation Rescue and Rescue America, large antiabortion organizations, have organized thousands of actions against clinics that perform or refer for abortions, against physicians who perform abortions, and against organizations even indirectly supportive of the practice of abortion. The people in these organizations act with the fervor of absolute moral conviction. Likewise, women and men with equal fervor vow they will not allow abortion again to become a "back alley" activity requiring women to risk their lives to obtain what should be a safe and simple surgical procedure. So far as one can estimate such things apart from ones own convictions, sincerity and integrity appear in equal measure on both sides.

Sometimes, however, the judgment that comparable integrity moves activists on both sides seems confounded by the facts. When Michael Griffin, an antiabortion activist, murdered Dr. David Gunn, an abortion provider, at a clinic in Pensacola on March 17, 1993, he set the stage for successive acts of violence against abortion providers. In 1994, John Salvi killed two receptionists and a security guard at abortion clinics in Massachusetts. Dr. Barnett Slepian, an abortion provider, was killed by a rifle shot through his kitchen window in the Buffalo suburb of Amherst, New York, in 1998. The moral and religious integrity Michael Griffin avowed as his defense seemed strangely to endorse murder; according to news reports, Griffin vowed to provide his own legal defense and to make the Bible its cornerstone. The circumstances surrounding many other abortion provider "incidents" confirm the typically felt moral rectitude of those who attack abortion providers. However much we find Michael Griffin's action baffling, the man himself apparently felt morally and religiously comfortable with his action. Furthermore, public statements offered by those commenting about Griffin's offense on behalf of Operation Rescue and Rescue America, while regretting Griffin's action, did not neglect to mention the millions of babies abortion providers like Gunn kill every year in America. They did not *say* Griffin was justified in killing Gunn, but they obviously thought Griffin's murder of Gunn was no worse morally than Gunn's regular abortion of living fetuses. The perspective of these antiabortion organizations is reinforced by specific Web sites emphasizing the belief that abortion is straightforwardly murder and that abortion providers are murderers; see, for example the "Nuremburg files" Web site, a site founded on the idea that just as Nazi war criminals were found guilty for crimes against humanity in their killing of Jews, so one day abortion providers will be brought to justice for their similar crimes.[1] Was Michael Griffin morally justified in murdering David Gunn? Was Gunn even more disreputable than Griffin because he regularly dispatched living fetuses? Was Gunn so blind, morally, that killing him was the only morally responsible recourse? Or was Griffin's idea of moral and religious integrity badly misguided? The deep perplexity many people feel about these and related questions motivate this collection of essays.

The society Margaret Atwood describes in *The Handmaid's Tale* looks like one in which Michael Griffin and other antiabortion activists might feel at home. Atwood's imaginary society of the future is an orderly, authoritarian society founded on the Bible, a society in which women are slaves to the men who use them only for pleasure and reproduction, a society in which abortion is forbidden on penalty of death. Would contemporary societies be better if they were more like Atwood's society to the extent of being more "biblical" and more respectful of life? Or would they be worse because less tolerant of divergent understandings of the "biblical," and less tolerant of diversity in individual efforts to put together meaningful lives? In particular, are contemporary societies better or worse to accord women free choice in all aspects of their reproductive lives, including free choice about unplanned pregnancies?

An interesting analogue of Atwood's imaginary antichoice society appears in contemporary Communist China. Communist Chinese society is also antichoice, but instead of requiring women to reproduce as much as possible the Chinese require women to reproduce no more than once. The one-child mandate is rigidly enforced, and women who become pregnant a second time face mandatory abortion. Most women in contemporary Western societies likely find Communist Chinese society no more desirable than Atwood's imaginary society. Most women want control over their own reproductive powers, control systematically denied in both of these antichoice alternative societies.

"Pro-choice" individuals who argue for abortion rights might naturally find Atwood's imaginary society more objectionable than Communist China. "Pro-life" individuals who argue against abortion rights might naturally find Communist China more objectionable than Atwood's imaginary society. What those alternative societies have in common is the requirement that women accept external control of their reproductive powers.

Different sorts of rationales seem to authorize external control of women's reproductive powers. A biblical rationale for an antichoice position differs from a population control rationale for an antichoice position. Michael Griffin, with his staunch biblical perspective, would certainly not be tolerant of the Chinese one-child-per-family policy mandating abortion. Likewise, Communist Chinese planners would find Griffin's biblical perspective, at best, oddly unrealistic. Most women in contemporary Western societies would find both Griffin's and the Communist Chinese positions to be objectionably paternalistic.

These antichoice positions, in their endorsement of external controls of women's reproductive powers, are the antithesis of pro-choice positions. Pro-choice positions characteristically seek to leave reproductive decisions with the women who must bear the consequences of those decisions. In the cultural context following *Roe* v. *Wade*, women's reproductive choices have included the decision whether or not to abort their fetus. Since 1973, many women have chosen to exercise their constitutional right to choose abortion, and they have done so for many different reasons. In recent years, however, American women are attempting to exercise reproductive choices outside the parameters established by the *Roe* decision.

An increasingly common occurrence in American cities is young women's abandonment of infants. Sometimes young women have left their newborn infants in restrooms, sometimes even in toilets; sometimes they have abandoned them in the snow; sometimes they have thrown them into rivers; and sometimes they have simply tied them inside plastic bags and thrown them into dumpsters. In 1998, Mobile, Alabama, began a program allowing mothers to abandon their newborns at hospitals with no questions asked; the rationale for the program was that leaving babies at hospitals was better than leaving babies in dumpsters. In Houston, billboards appear along highways urging mothers not to abandon their newborn babies. Texas, California, and New York, along with several other states, are considering legislation that might encourage mothers to leave their infants in safe places—hospitals, welfare agencies, fire stations, or police stations—rather than throwing them into dumpsters or otherwise disposing of them.

This phenomenon of baby abandonment is relatively recent and is deeply shocking to middle-class American families that have always valued children and sought to nurture them to maturity. Many pro-life thinkers see this phenomenon of baby abandonment as simply a natural extension of the "culture of convenience" expressed constitutionally in the *Roe* v. *Wade* decision. Americans, these pro-life thinkers may suggest, have become accustomed to thinking of other lives as expendable to the extent that those lives interfere with their own convenience or happiness. According to this line of thought, Americans have become constitutionally and culturally accustomed to "having their own way," and expect not to be inconvenienced even by their own children; some will even discard their own children in their commitment to "having their own way."

Pro-choice thinkers—those who support the *Roe* v. *Wade* decision—in contrast to these pro-life thinkers, may believe that more complex social and cultural factors are at work in cases of baby abandonment. The women who abandon their own children are typically little more than children themselves. Such women are typically high-school students; they may be living in a local culture in which abortion, though legal strictly speaking, is not readily available or is available only at great cost of personal embarrassment and shame. Such women are not ready to take on the responsibilities of rearing a child and they frequently have no means of support even for themselves. As their pregnancies continue, their embarrassment increases and they have few if any natural means of emotional support. When the day of delivery comes, as it must, these women-children are overwhelmed by the fact of their responsibilities and by the fact of their inadequacy to meet those responsibilities. The way out some of them choose—abandoning their babies or disposing of them—may be a culmination of shame and embarrassment in the knowledge that they are unprepared to satisfy the responsibilities of motherhood.

For these pro-choice thinkers, the problem of abandoned babies is not a symptom of the fact that Americans live in a "culture of convenience" anchored by the *Roe* decision; it is rather a symptom of the fact that Americans live "in the closet" about their own and their children's sexuality. Facing the fact of their own and their children's sexuality would mean, for these pro-choice thinkers, endorsing and encouraging the kind of sexuality education that would make problem pregnancies like those leading to abandoned babies extremely rare, and would also make abortions extremely rare. For such pro-choice thinkers, the fact of women-children abandoning their own babies is a strong indictment of the American cultural disposition to avoid facing the facts about human sexuality. To face those facts and to accommodate them by enacting wise and appropriate social policies, in the view of these thinkers, will both eliminate the phenomenon of abandoned babies and minimize recourse to abortion.

A kind of pro-choice thinking that bears some resemblance to that of the women-children who dispose of their own infants appears in the practices of some cultures as different from American culture as is the Chinese antichoice culture mentioned above. Throughout India, for example, abortion is commonly practiced in order to avoid female children. Where sonograms are readily available and affordable, Indian families seek abortions after using sonograms to confirm the female gender of the fetus. Where sonograms are either not readily available or not affordable, Indian families frequently practice female infanticide. Their need to provide a costly dowry to secure the marriage of a female child motivates these families to kill, or to have their midwives kill, female infants. Poorer sections of India commonly practice female infanticide as a means of avoiding the impoverishment that comes with female children.

These Indian practices of infanticide appear, from most moral perspectives of Western culture, barbaric. Although the practices themselves are undoubtedly rooted in local cultural conditions, this fact does not relieve their barbaric appearance. The traditional Indian practice of female infanticide, as well as the incipient trend in America to dispose of infants, seems a profound affront to conventional American moral and religious sensibilities.

The antichoice perspectives represented by Margaret Atwood's fictional society and by Communist Chinese society are at the other end of a spectrum of possibilities from the pro-choice perspectives represented by the incipient trend in America toward infant abandonment and the Indian practice of female infanticide. The antichoice perspectives seek external control of women's reproductive choices, while some pro-choice perspectives seek to extend women's control of their reproductive lives well beyond anything envisioned in the *Roe* v. *Wade* decision authorizing women's choice of abortion. In this cacophony of competing possibilities of control and choice, the *Roe* v. *Wade* decision may take on the appearance of a moderate and even reasonable middle ground.

In any case, we are compelled again to raise this question: Where on this confusing spectrum of alternatives does one find the view richest in moral integrity, the wisest view, the view most worthy of allegiance? This is the question that motivates this collection of essays.

This collection of essays and opinions about abortion is our third. The issue is increasingly divisive and disheartening. Since our first edition of this collection, murders of abortion providers have become unsurprising, if still shocking. A new fragmentation of opinion and a new rigidity of "abortion politics" have become a customary part of our cultural landscape. We regret these cultural developments and we hope reasonable people on every part of the spectrum of opinion about abortion will seek to understand those with whom they differ.

We have segmented the collection into groups of essays, each addressing a distinctive aspect of the issue. An ideally balanced collection of essays on this topic, along with an ideally balanced introduction to the collection, is probably an impossible ideal. Anyone picking up a collection like this one will inevitably have predispositions and will look to see how the editors and authors handle and react to those predispositions. We, the editors, do have our moral, political, religious, and professional perspectives. We do confess that those perspectives as a whole have guided our choices about what to keep from earlier editions of this collection and what to add to it to make up the present volume. In our opinion the selections included here are incisive and informative, and anyone who hopes to think coherently about the topic of abortion needs familiarity with them.

The first group of essays presents a series of "snapshots." Richard Selzer focuses on the horror of the killing in abortions; Ellen Messer and Kathryn May, as well as Anna Quindlen, focus on the horrors of life without safe, legal abortion. The Rick Hampson and Miriam Jordan essays raise the extended pro-choice issues about infanticide and infant abandonment. The Jack Hitt essay raises the question of how American women will be able in the future to exercise their constitutionally guaranteed abortion rights when current providers leave the American scene, whether through death or retirement.

The second set of essays concerns the constitutional issue of abortion. Whether or not *Roe* v. *Wade* was a legitimate use of judicial authority is a question judges and scholars have debated extensively. We offer here edited versions of each of four major Supreme Court decisions dealing with abortion: *Roe* v. *Wade*, *Webster* v. *Missouri*, *Planned Parenthood of Southeastern Pennsylvania* v. *Casey*, and the *Stenberg* v. *Carhart* decision concerning Nebraska's effort to outlaw the D&X ("partial birth abortion") procedure. The selections by Michael McConnell and Melvin Wulf engage the question whether or not the *Roe* v. *Wade* decision was constitutionally legitimate or was unwarranted "judicial activism." The selection by Paul Simmons is a careful reflection about how the Court's decisions about abortion cohere and also about how they affect women.

The third group of essays focuses on issues about abortion and feminism. Many believe that feminists must be pro-choice, that opposition to abortion is inconsistent with feminism. Sidney Callahan, however, an avowed feminist, argues on feminist grounds that abortion must be legally proscribed. The selection by Naomi Wolf is a reflection on her own personal experience with the aim of seeing more clearly into the heart of the abortion controversy as it bears on women who naturally have reproductive destinies.

The fourth group of essays focusses on abortion and Christianity. The first two essays, by Gary Leber and Daniel Maguire, address the issue of organized obstruction of abortion clinics. Leber sees in the practice of abortion a holocaust of killing that no morally reputable persons, especially Christians, can tolerate. Maguire, a Catholic theologian, sees Leber's perspective as almost heartlessly "principled" in its refusal to take notice of the complexity of women's lives and the decisions they must make. The essays by Paul Simmons and Richard Schoenig address the issue of how Christians, as Christians, ought to see abortion. Paul Simmons, a Baptist theologian, offers a biblical perspective on questions about abortion. Richard Schoenig urges Christians to greater consistency with their own creedal traditions. Finally, Roger Paynter, a Baptist minister, concludes with a thoughtful sermon about abortion.

The last set of essays offers more distinctly philosophical treatments of the issue of abortion. Judith Thomson's classic essay remains a challenge to those who would limit access to abortion on purely moral grounds. Since the essay's appearance in 1971 (even before the *Roe* v. *Wade* decision) it has attracted much attention. John Wilcox's essay, in our judgment, is among the more interesting and creative responses to Thomson's challenge. Mary Anne Warren's essay is typical of many philosophical approaches to the issue of abortion in setting out necessary conditions of personhood and finding that fetuses fail to meet those conditions. Since Warren's essay is typical of this approach, we have not included many other fine essays of the same type. Harry Gensler offers a Kantian-style argument against abortion, suggesting that an obvious principle of morality precludes abortion. Joan Callahan believes that the approach typical of much philosophy—including, in this collection, Warren's essay—must be inconclusive and offers an alternative approach to the issue. Don Marquis' 1989 essay has generated much discussion and controversy within the philosophical world and is newly included in this current collection. Also added is a selection from Jeffrey Reiman's 1999 book, *Abortion and the Ways We Value Human Life*, along with his critique of Marquis' pro-life perspective.[2] The final essay by Greg Easterbrook brings to bear on the abortion controversy relevant scientific research that he believes supports the basic wisdom of the *Roe* v. *Wade* decision.

We hope this collection will be useful to all who are concerned about the issue of abortion.

Waco, Texas
September 2000

NOTES

1. www.christiangallery.com/atrocity. For a more detailed account of these and related abortion provider occurrences, see Sharon Lerner, "Blight to Life: Antiabortion Extremists and Another Murdered Doctor," *Village Voice*, October 28–November 3, 1998. This essay is reprinted in Robert M. Baird and Stuart E. Rosenbaum, *Hatred, Bigotry, and Prejudice* (Amherst, N.Y.: Prometheus Books, 1999), pp. 31–33.

2. We regard Reiman's book, *Abortion and the Ways We Value Human Life* (Lanham, Md.: Rowman & Littlefield, 1999), as a useful addition to contemporary literature on abortion; it provides succinct access to the history of abortion practices as well as analysis of traditional philosophical approaches to abortion.

PART ONE

Abortion

Finding the Issue

1

ABORTION

Richard Selzer

Horror, like bacteria, is everywhere. It blankets the earth, endlessly lapping to find that one unguarded entryway. As though narcotized, we walk beneath, upon, through it. Carelessly we touch the familiar infected linen, eat from the universal dish; we disdain isolation. We are like the newborns that carry immunity from their mothers' wombs. Exteriorized, we are wrapped in impermeable membranes that cannot be seen. Then one day, the defense is gone. And we awaken to horror.

In our city, garbage is collected early in the morning. Sometimes the bang of the cans and the grind of the truck awaken us before our time. We are resentful, mutter into our pillows, then go back to sleep. On the morning of August 6, 1975, the people of Seventy-third Street near Woodside Avenue do just that. When at last they rise from their beds, dress, eat breakfast, and leave their houses for work, they have forgotten, if they had ever known, that the garbage truck had passed earlier that morning. The event has slipped into unmemory, like a dream.

They close their doors and descend to the pavement. It is midsummer. You measure the climate, decide how you feel in relation to the heat and the humidity. You walk toward the bus stop. Others, your neighbors, are waiting there. It is all so familiar. All at once you step on something soft. You feel it with your foot. Even through your shoe you have the sense of something unusual, something marked by a special "give." It is a foreignness upon the pavement. Instinct pulls your foot away in an awkward little movement. You look down, and you see . . . a tiny naked body, its arms and legs flung

---

From *Mortal Lessons: Notes on the Art of Surgery* by Richard Selzer (New York: Simon and Schuster, 1976), pp. 153-160.

apart, its head thrown back, its mouth agape, its face serious. A bird, you think, fallen from its nest. But there is no nest here on Seventy-third Street, no bird so big. It is rubber, then. A model, a . . . joke. Yes, that's it, a joke. And you bend to see. Because you must. And it is no joke. Such a gray softness can be but one thing. It is a baby, and dead. You cover your mouth, your eyes. You are fixed. Horror has found its chink and crawled in, and you will never be the same as you were. Years later you will step from a sidewalk to a lawn, and you will start at its softness, and think of that upon which you have just trod.

Now you look about; another man has seen it too. "My God," he whispers. Others come, people you have seen every day for years, and you hear them speak with strangely altered voices. "Look," they say, "it's a baby." There is a cry. "Here's another!" and "Another!" and "Another!" And you follow with your gaze the index fingers of your friends pointing from the huddle where you cluster. Yes, it is true! There *are* more of these . . . little carcasses upon the street. And for a moment you look up to see if all the unbaptized sinless are falling from Limbo.

Now the street is filling with people. There are police. They know what to do. They rope off the area, then stand guard over the enclosed space. They are controlled methodical, these young policemen. Servants, they do not reveal themselves to their public master; it would not be seemly. Yet I do see their pallor and the sweat that breaks upon the face of one, the way another bites the lining of his cheek and holds it thus. Ambulance attendants scoop up the bodies. They scan the street; none must be overlooked. What they place upon the litter amounts to little more than a dozen pounds of human flesh. They raise the litter, and slide it home inside the ambulance, and they drive away. You and your neighbors stand about in the street which is become for you a battlefield from which the newly slain have at last been bagged and tagged and dragged away. *But what shrapnel is this? By what explosion flung, these fragments that sink into the brain and fester there?* Whatever smell there is in this place becomes for you the stench of death. The people of Seventy-third Street do not then speak to each other. It is too soon for outrage, too late for blindness. It is the time of unresisted horror.

Later, at the police station, the investigation is brisk, conclusive. It is the hospital director speaking: " . . . fetuses accidentally got mixed up with the hospital rubbish . . . were picked up at approximately eight fifteen A.M. by a sanitation truck. Somehow, the plastic lab bag, labeled HAZARDOUS MATERIAL, fell off the back of the truck and broke open. No, it is not known how the fetuses got in the orange plastic bag labeled HAZARDOUS MATERIAL. It is a freak accident." The hospital director wants you to know that it is not an everyday occurrence. Once in a lifetime, he says. But you have seen it, and what are his words to you now?

He grows affable, familiar, tells you that, by mistake, the fetuses got mixed up with the other debris. (Yes, he says *other*; he says *debris*.) He has spent the entire day, he says, trying to figure out how it happened. He wants you to know that. Somehow it matters to him. He goes on:

Aborted fetuses that weigh one pound or less are incinerated. Those weighing over one pound are buried at a city cemetery. He says this. Now you see. It *is* orderly. It *is* sensible. The world is *not* mad. This is still a civilized society.

There is no more. You turn to leave. Outside on the street, men are talking things over, reassuring each other that the right thing is being done. But just this once, you know it isn't. You saw, and you know.

And you know, too, that the Street of the Dead Fetuses will be wherever you go. You are part of its history now, its legend. It has laid claim upon you so that you cannot entirely leave it—not ever.

I am a surgeon. I do not shrink from the particularities of sick flesh. Escaping blood, all the outpourings of disease—phlegm, pus, vomitus, even those occult meaty tumors that terrify—I see as blood, disease, phlegm, and so on. I touch them to destroy them. But I do not make symbols of them. I have seen, and I am used to seeing. Yet there are paths within the body that I have not taken, penetralia where I do not go. Nor is it lack of technique, limitation of knowledge that forbids me these ways.

It is the western wing of the fourth floor of a great university hospital. An abortion is about to take place. I am present because I asked to be present. I wanted to see what I had never seen.

The patient is Jamaican. She lies on the table submissively, and now and then she smiles at one of the nurses as though acknowledging a secret.

A nurse draws down the sheet, lays bare the abdomen. The belly mounds gently in the twenty-fourth week of pregnancy. The chief surgeon paints it with a sponge soaked in red antiseptic. He does this three times, each time a fresh sponge. He covers the area with a sterile sheet, an aperture in its center. He is a kindly man who teaches as he works, who pauses to reassure the woman.

He begins.

A little pinprick, he says to the woman.

He inserts the point of a tiny needle at the midline of the lower portion of her abdomen, on the downslope. He infiltrates local anesthetic into the skin, where it forms a small white bubble.

The woman grimaces.

That is all you will feel, the doctor says. Except for a little pressure. But no more pain.

She smiles again. She seems to relax. She settles comfortably on the table. The worst is over.

The doctor selects a three-and-one-half-inch needle bearing a central stylet. He places the point at the site of the previous injection. He aims it straight up and down, perpendicular. Next he takes hold of her abdomen with his left hand, palming the womb, steadying it. He thrusts with his right hand. The needle sinks into the abdominal wall.

Oh, says the woman quietly.

But I guess it is not pain that she feels. It is more a recognition that the deed is being done.

Another thrust and he has speared the uterus.

We are in, he says.

He has felt the muscular wall of the organ gripping the shaft of his needle. A further slight pressure on the needle advances it a bit more. He takes his left hand from the woman's abdomen. He retracts the filament of the stylet from the barrel of the needle. A small geyser of pale yellow fluid erupts.

We are in the right place, says the doctor. Are you feeling any pain? he asks.

She smiles, shakes her head. She gazes at the ceiling.

In the room we are six: two physicians, two nurses, the patient, and me. The participants are busy, very attentive. I am not at all busy-but I am no less attentive. I want to see.

I see something! It is unexpected, utterly unexpected, like a disturbance in the earth, a tumultuous jarring. I see a movement—a small one. But I have seen it.

And then I see it again. And now I see that it is the hub of the needle in the woman's belly that has jerked. First to one side. Then to the other side. Once more it wobbles, is *tugged*, like a fishing fine nibbled by a sunfish.

Again! And I *know*!

It is the *fetus* that worries thus. It is the fetus struggling against the needle. Struggling? How can that be? I think: *that cannot be*. I think: the fetus feels no pain, cannot feel fear, has no *motivation*. It is merely reflex.

I point to the needle.

It is a reflex, says the doctor.

By the end of the fifth month, the fetus weighs about one pound, is about twelve inches long. Hair is on the head. There are eyebrows, eyelashes. Pale pink nipples show on the chest. Nails are present, at the fingertips, at the toes.

At the beginning of the sixth month, the fetus can cry, can suck, can make a fist. He kicks, he punches. The mother can feel this, can *see* this. His eyelids, until now closed, can open. He may look up, down, sideways. His grip is very strong. He could support his weight by holding with one hand.

A reflex, the doctor says.

I hear him. But I saw something in that mass of cells *understand* that it must bob and butt. And I see it again! I have an impulse to shove to the table—it is just a step—seize that needle, pull it out.

We are not six, I think. We are *seven*.

Something strangles *there*. An effort, its effort, binds me to it.

I do not shove to the table. I take no little step. It would be . . . well, madness. Everyone here wants the needle where it is. Six do. No, *five* do.

I close my eyes. I see inside of the uterus. It is bathed in ruby gloom. I see the creature curled upon itself. Its knees are flexed. Its head is bent upon its chest. It is in fluid and gently rocks to the rhythm of the distant heartbeat.

It resembles . . . a sleeping infant.

Its place is entered by something. It is sudden. A point coming. A needle!

A spike of *daylight* pierces the chamber. Now the light is extinguished. The needle comes closer in the pool. The point grazes the thigh, and I stir. Perhaps I wake from dozing. The light is there again. I twist and straighten. My arms and legs *push*. My hand finds the shaft—grabs! I *grab*. I bend the needle this way and that. The point probes, touches on my belly. My mouth opens. Could I cry out? All is a commotion and a churning. There is a presence in the pool. An activity! The pool colors, reddens, darkens.

I open my eyes to see the doctor feeding a small plastic tube through the barrel of the needle into the uterus. Drops of pink fluid overrun the rim and spill onto the sheet. He withdraws the needle from around the plastic tubing. Now only the little tube protrudes from the woman's body. A nurse hands the physician a syringe loaded with a colorless liquid. He attaches it to the end of the tubing and injects it.

Prostaglandin, he says.

Ah well, prostaglandin—a substance found normally in the body. When given in concentrated dosage, it throws the uterus into vigorous contraction. In eight to twelve hours, the woman will expel the fetus.

The doctor detaches the syringe but does not remove the tubing.

In case we must do it over, he says.

He takes away the sheet. He places gauze pads over the tubing. Over all this he applies adhesive tape.

I know. We cannot feed the great numbers. There is no more room. I know, I know. It is a woman's right to refuse the risk, to decline the pain of childbirth. And an unwanted child is a very great burden. An unwanted child is a burden to himself. I know.

And yet . . . there is the flick of that needle. I *saw* it. I saw . . . I *felt*—in that room, a pace away, life prodded, life fending off. I saw life avulsed*—swept by flood, blackening—then *out*.

"There," says the doctor. "It's all over. It wasn't too bad, was it?" he says to the woman.

She smiles. It is all over. Oh, yes.

And who would care to imagine that from a moist and dark commencement six months before there would ripen the cluster and globule, the sprout and pouch of man?

And who would care to imagine that trapped within the laked pearl and a dowry of yoke would lie the earliest stuff of dream and memory?

It is a persona carried here as well as a person, I think. I think it is a signed piece, engraved with a hieroglyph of human genes.

I did not think this until I saw. The flick. The fending off.

Later, in the corridor, the doctor explains that the law does not permit abortion beyond the twenty-fourth week. That is when the fetus may be viable, he says. We stand together for a moment, and he tells of an abortion in which the fetus *cried* after it was passed.

What did you do? I ask him.

There was nothing *to* do but let it live, he says. It did very well, he says. A case of mistaken dates.

---

*torn away—Eds.

2

THE BAD OLD DAYS

Ellen Messer and Kathryn E. May

CAROLINE

Caroline is a forty-four-year-old woman who is a librarian at a college in a small rural town.

For a long time I think I drank to avoid the feelings. And it wasn't until quite recently, five years ago, after I had stopped drinking for a while, that I went through a whole period of really reliving the terror of this experience. It was in the summer, between my junior and senior years of college. I was going to college in Cleveland, living there for the summer. And somehow I just knew I was pregnant.

It was the first and only time that I was ever sexually intimate with this man. He was a young artist whom I had been seeing for some time. I wasn't particularly physically attracted to him, but he was pressing me, and I just finally got to the point where I couldn't struggle with it anymore. So I gave in. Somehow I immediately had the sense that I was pregnant.

I really didn't know what to do. I knew, though, that having a baby would ruin my whole life. The man involved felt responsible and wanted to marry me, but I thought it was a very weak reason for getting married. I spent a lot of time just seeing my life in a shambles. Things at that time in Cleveland were very tight. There had been several incidents reported in the paper. An abortion ring had been broken up. It was 1963, and when I followed up on the few leads there were, it seemed that it was absolutely the worst possible time in about five years to have an abortion in Cleveland.

From *Back Rooms: Voices from the Illegal Abortion Era* (New York: St. Martin's Press, 1988), pp. 3–10, 20–22, 131–33, 147–49, 179–80. Reprinted by permission of the authors.

In the meantime the weeks were going by and I was more pregnant all the time and it was really getting to the point that if I didn't do something soon it was going to be too late. Being raised a good Catholic girl, abortion was not a thing that I was very comfortable thinking about. But I didn't feel that I had any other option. I was getting pretty desperate by this time because I was nine weeks pregnant. I finally located an abortionist in Youngstown, Ohio.

This so-called doctor was a bookie and he was an abortionist. He was an elderly man in a ramshackle little house in a disreputable, shabby part of Youngstown. It in no way fit my image of a doctor's house and office. I think there was some actual gambling going on while we were waiting.

He had a room with a chair and stirrups set up. The money, one hundred dollars, had to be in cash, in certain denominations, and it had to be given to him in an envelope. He checked it very thoroughly to make sure it wasn't marked. He explained he was doing a saline injection and that there should be some cramping and the abortion would happen within twenty-four hours. Nothing happened.

I don't know how many days passed; I did a lot to block out this experience. But I do know that when I finally aborted I was alone in my room in the dormitory at school. I went through at least twelve hours of labor alone in my room.

It was more terrible than I ever imagined, partly because I was alone, partly because I was scared. I was timing the contractions and I just didn't think I could bear anymore. I didn't feel I could cry out for help, and I just remember thinking, "I'm going to get through this." I remember noticing that the contractions were getting more and more frequent, five minutes, then four minutes, then three minutes, and then there was a lot of blood and there was a fetus. I was really beside myself, and terrified. I didn't know what to do. There was more blood than I ever imagined. I used one of these metal wastebaskets we had in the dorm rooms and I remember it being filled up. I think I had gone through a whole night and it was now midmorning, and there weren't many people around. I managed to get to the bathroom, very surreptitiously. I was terrified of someone discovering me, of being arrested.

I remember taking this fetus and not knowing what else to do but flush it down the toilet. And I was terrified that it wasn't going to go down, that they'd have to call a plumber and then there would be this hunt to find out who did this terrible thing in the dorm, and I'd be tracked down and prosecuted. Somehow I thought then it would be over, but it wasn't over. It went on and on. I kept hemorrhaging and it just wouldn't stop.

I had become pregnant in August, and the abortion was in early November. I remember going home for Thanksgiving and my mother kept saying, "I think you're anemic." And I remember being very drained and wiped out.

Early in December, I became friendly with a very gentle, brilliant but quite crazy college student who had been hospitalized while he was suicidal. I found myself confiding in him that I'd had this abortion, and was still bleeding. He talked to the rector of the Episcopal church in Shaker Heights, and the rector, to whom I shall be forever grateful, called one of the doctors in his congregation. He was so appalled at my condition that he said, "Do you realize you could have killed yourself?" He admitted me to the hospital.

After they built me up they did a D & C. I wasn't yet twenty-one, so the doctor called and spoke to my mother and said there was nothing to be concerned about; the D & C was just a routine procedure and would help. He said that I was quite anemic.

I must have been in the hospital five days. The Episcopal church paid my hospital bill and the doctor never charged. I was very thankful, and totally done in at the end of that ordeal.

I didn't feel guilty. I was determined once I made the decision to go through with it, and I did.

NORA

Nora is a historian and educator.

There was a doctor who did surgical abortions in Virginia, in the early fifties. He was ultimately arrested and, I believe, sent to prison.

I went to him, to that place in Virginia, in the spring of '52. He was recommended by a doctor in Washington, D.C., who I think may have gotten a cut of the money.

Preparations for doing this were very complicated and anxiety-filled. I had to stand on a street corner in Washington, D.C., holding a copy of *Time* magazine. A woman was supposed to approach me and ask me if I had a problem, and I said, "Yes, I have a problem," and, "Can we discuss it?" She said, "No, this is only the first stage." Then I had to make a phone call and this time I was told to be in a hotel lobby with a copy of the Washington *Post*, which I thought was kind of funny, since most people carried the Washington *Post*. The next stage happened a week later. I was picked up by a car, on still another street corner, by someone who took me to a place where there was a long black limousine waiting. I think there were three or four other young women in the limousine when I got in. I can remember that the radio was on, and Rockefeller was trying to get the presidential nomination, in preparation for the '52 election.

Then we left Washington, and the car stopped, and the driver said, "And now, for fun, we're going to put these little goggles over your eyes." And so we all wore masks. But the limousine had opaque windows, so no one could see that these people were sitting there wearing masks. And then we arrived at a farmhouse. It was very well staffed. There were a lot of guards, strong, tough-looking men. The limousine was put in a garage and we walked from there into the house. There were guards standing around with guns, three or four nurses, and a staff of maybe ten. The procedure itself was a D & C with local anesthesia, which meant that there was not too much pain, but it was scary as hell.

I couldn't see the doctor because he was all done up for surgery. He talked as he worked, because I think he sensed that I didn't want the routine: "Who are your favorite movie stars?" So he said, "You know the things people talk about are interesting. I have had movie stars on this table, I've had doctors, lawyers. . . ." The doctor did have a somewhat reassuring quality.

This cost four hundred dollars. It was well done. I had volunteered to be first, not wanting to see or hear anything else, but I found out later that I wouldn't have seen or heard anything because there were television sets all over the house, playing very loudly, and in addition, the toilets were calibrated to flush every half-minute or so, so there was a lot of noise. If anyone had freaked out and yelled, I don't think you would have heard it.

When it was over, I was taken into a bedroom and laid down with white sheets.

LILA

Lila is a successful businesswoman and has recently earned a doctoral degree.

I had been dating Joseph almost a year. I didn't want to be a married student with a baby trying to finish up college for two years. I really couldn't imagine having a baby by this guy. What I first did out of my own naïveté was to ask people, "What can I do?" I only remember one remedy—very hot baths and gin. To this day I can't stand the smell of gin. I must have tried that about three or four nights. It didn't work.

I decided to ask my stepmother in Des Moines if she could help me. Now, my stepmother's a real meddling and involved lady—she knows everything about everybody everyplace. So I told her I was pregnant and that I didn't want to have the baby, I wanted to finish school, and she says, "Come to Des Moines this weekend." I said, "How much will it be?" and I think she said one hundred dollars. I felt nothing. I didn't feel anxious. I think I was stupid. No, I was not stupid, I think I was overcontrolled. I just got on the train. Not only did I not think about the moral or ethical implications, but I didn't think about the physical possibilities. Maybe I didn't know. Maybe I knew and just blocked it out.

But I said, "I'm going to go have this thing and I'll be back to school on Monday."

We must have done it on a Friday night. I think she picked me up from the train station. We went to the poor section of town. Now, I'm the daughter of a well-known man in our town, not to mention my stepmother. Whenever I saw these townspeople I saw them as my father's daughter. They were renters of his apartments and frequenters of his pool hall. So now that I'm going to this house where everybody knows there's an abortionist that has an apartment in the back, I was even more self-conscious. And my stepmother greeted everybody and she just walked me through the door.

It was a kitchen table, coat-hanger abortion. It took maybe six minutes. I got on the kitchen table. I think my stepmother gave me a drink of brandy or something, and she said, "Now this may hurt a little bit." She held my hand and this woman stuck a piece of coat hanger into my vagina. She stuck the coat hanger in, a piece that had been sterilized or whatever the hell she had done, and then my stepmother said, "Okay, now you get dressed." And what you were supposed to do was leave that in there until you started to abort. And then I left. I remember walking out with this coat hanger between my legs. I went back home to my father's house.

That evening I started bleeding and I remember I had cramps, and my stepmother put me to bed. I remember her giving me a drink, and giving me aspirin, and I went to sleep and to me it was fine, because it was better than I would do with my menstrual cramps. I got up very early in the morning and went to the bathroom and there was just this passage of blood and a clot that was slightly bigger than the clots I usually passed during my menstrual period. I realized that that was the fetus passing. I felt a little mixed then because it seemed like I should have done something at that moment. The next month my period came on time.

HEATHER

My first abortion was approximately one month before abortion became legal. I had become pregnant on what was called the sequential birth-control pill, which was given to me by a gynecologist because I was not ovulating.

When I went back to my gynecologist, who was the head of ob-gyn at a large metropolitan hospital, he yelled at me. He asked me what kind of birth control I was on, and I told him "sequential birth-control pills," and he said, "Who was the idiot who gave you those?" and it was him! So he tried to cover that whole thing up and dragged my husband into it. We were young kids in our twenties, and newly married, and he said he wanted one thousand dollars cash—to "pay off the hospital board"—in a paper bag! So I had to go take the money out of the bank and pay him cash, and see two psychiatrists that he gave me the names of and pay them each one hundred dollars in cash to get them to type a letter saying that I was suicidal. It was as if my husband and this doctor were on the phone like cronies, consulting each other and that sort of thing. My husband's screaming, "We can't have this child. . . . " It was like a full moon or something, and I was the victim.

I should also mention that my husband was checking places for me to go. He had me ready to go to Haiti when the revolution broke out in Haiti, so I couldn't get an abortion there. He was going to fly me to England, because you could obtain an abortion there. So the process was something that seemed to take weeks of the most incredible and ridiculous effort involved in booking flights and travel agents and everything else, just to do what people now go to a local clinic for.

Finally, I went to the hospital and had the abortion. It was just a terrible mess. I was just there overnight—I got home and went into labor! I had terrible pain, and tried to call the doctor. We finally tracked him down at a restaurant. He told my husband that I was just being a big baby, but he agreed to give me a prescription. John went to get it, and while he was gone, a fetus came out of my body, which freaked me out. It was one thing to have an abortion and go through all this process, but to have to deal with the fetus! It was supposed to be a D & C, but he did not remove the fetus. Later he insisted that I must have had twins and he had missed one. It really affected my mind, and the doctor just tried to cover it up, and he didn't recommend that I receive any help, and was constantly saying to my husband, "Oh, she's just being crazy."

During the follow-up examination, this doctor was on the phone with one of his colleagues and said, "Oh, hi, yeah, I'm here with all the girls with their legs up. You know me, I'm just a glorified plumber." I just got up off the table, and put my clothes on and walked out the door and went home. He called my house and wanted to know why I had left, and I said, "Look, I just decided I'm not a glorified sink," and I just would never go back. . . .

DR. WHITE

Dr. White's medical practice has spanned more than forty years.

Early on in my practice, a friend's sister found out she was pregnant. At the time she was unmarried, in her midthirties, and already had two children. She became so desperate that she jumped in front of a subway train at Forty-second Street and Broadway in an effort to commit suicide. She survived the accident with a fractured skull, fractured shoulder bones, and fractured pelvis, and spent four months in the hospital. Her child was delivered about three months later—a perfectly normal child. I thought if a woman was willing to go to that length to avoid a pregnancy she didn't want, then something really ought to be done, and I became an active advocate of abortion from that time on.

After that, when a woman came to me for help, and she was a patient I knew, I would be willing to go out on a limb. What I did was to examine her and try to initiate bleeding. This was done by gently inserting the instrument that I would normally use for taking endometrial biopsies. And then after starting a little bleeding I'd tell her to go home and call me back within twentyfour hours to let me know if the bleeding continued. If it did, which I expected that it would, I would then admit her as a threatened abortion and complete the process in a legitimate way. In reality, I was performing an illegal abortion. But it was under controlled circumstances, in a hospital with proper backup, anesthesia, and so forth.

I recall what happened to me when I was an intern. I was very much in love with a nurse, and she became pregnant. And when it happened, we looked at each other and I said, "This can't be, I'm earning twelve dollars a month." She was doing a little better—something like fifty or seventy-five a month. And we agreed that we should have an elective abortion. I was referred to a doctor whose office was on West End Avenue, and I remember to this day—that was the summer of 1940—going to West End Avenue, on the subway from Brooklyn where we both were working. We walked into this office and an older gentleman, surely in his sixties at the time, greeted us, took my nurse friend into the office. I sat in the waiting room like any other anxious partner. About an hour later, he came out and said that she would be all right, and I could take her home. I shall never forget that ride on the subway going back to Brooklyn, because of my concern that she might have been harmed in some way. She was feeling kind of beat from the ether, and she was obviously exhausted and upset by the whole experience. And that personal experience was enough to make me think women shouldn't have to carry children they don't want.

3

THE ABORTION ORPHANS

Anna Quindlen

The photograph on the postcard is of a Gibson girl, hair piled atop her head, lace on her rounded shoulders, and a face in profile that is not so much pretty as soft and very young. Beneath the picture are these words: Clara Bell Duvall was a 32-year-old mother of five when she died of an illegal abortion in 1929.

On the other side is written in a strong, slanting hand, "My mother in her wedding picture at 18 years of age."

"The image of her in her casket is seared in my brain," said Linn Duvall Harwell, who had just turned six when her mother died.

The hospital listed the cause of death as "pneumonia."

She used a knitting needle.

She had a son and four daughters.

"She was a beautiful mother," says Mrs. Harwell. "That must be understood. She was loving and affectionate. We were poor and it was 1929 but we were cared for. The minute she died, it all changed."

"I can't help but think how my life would have been different," says Gwendolyn Elliott, who is a commander in the Pittsburgh Police Department. She was five when Vivian Campbell, her mother, died in 1950; she and her brother were raised by their grandparents. When she was eighteen and ready for college, she tried to cash in some bonds her mother had left her and was told she needed a death certificate. And there it was, under cause of death: the word "abortion," followed by a question mark.

The abortion orphans may be the shadow of things to come. Those of us who believe that abortion must remain legal are flailing about for a way

---

to make vivid what will happen if it is banned once more. We have had the right so long that we have forgotten what the wrong is. Meant to evoke bloodstained tables and covert phone calls, the term "back alley" does not resonate for women who grew up with clean clinics and licensed doctors.

But there is indeed a kind of endless alley in the lives of Linn Harwell and Gwen Elliott, the dead end in your heart when you grow up without a mother. They tell us something about banning abortion that is both touching and chilling, these two little girls who grew up to become activists because of what happened to them. Which likely means many little girls, and boys, too, who do not know, who still believe pneumonia did it, or who are ashamed, who keep the secret.

This is the shadow of things to come. Someone's mother will die. That's not how we commonly think of this. We usually think of children having children, even though statistics show more than half of the abortions performed in the United States last year were performed on women over the age of twenty-five.

We think of cases like the horrific one unfolding in Ireland right now, in which a fourteen-year-old girl who says she was raped has been forbidden by the courts to travel to England to have an abortion. Her parents made a critical mistake: They were good citizens. They asked police about having fetal tissue tests done as evidence. The attorney general stepped right in to enjoin the girl's planned abortion.

She says she was raped by a playmate's father.

She says she wants to kill herself.

A judge ruled that the risk of suicide "is much less and of a different order of magnitude than the certainty that the life of the unborn will be terminated."

It is a great mistake to believe that if abortion is illegal, it will be nonexistent. Ireland has the most restrictive abortion laws in Europe, and still several thousand of its citizens travel elsewhere to end their pregnancies each year.

Some kind of douche, some kind of drug, some kind of tubing: women will do it themselves. They always have. They become desperate for reasons we know nothing of, reasons not as easily quantifiable as being raped by a friend's father at age fourteen. Linn Harwell's mother had had five children, eight pregnancies. Gwen Elliott's mother had two small children and had just separated from her husband. Their reasons died with them. What lived on were their motherless children.

"My father said that when they took me to the cemetery somebody told me she was sleeping," says Commander Elliott, "and I thought that any time he wanted he could go get her. My father says I used to ask, 'Why don't we go get Mommy?' But I don't remember it."

That is the shadow of things to come.

4

Saving Babies Left to Die

States Providing Safe Landing for Abandoned Infants

Rick Hampson

A girl with a newborn she didn't want phoned a hospital in Mobile, Alabama, on the day before Christmas. She had heard that the hospital took babies; what should she do?

Bring it in, replied Terri Little, emergency room supervisor at Springhill Hospital.

I don't have to sign any papers? The girl asked. No, Little recalls telling her. Just bring it in.

Springhill is part of a national movement to solve a disturbing problem with a less disturbing solution: Encourage mothers who want to abandon their babies to drop them off at a hospital instead of throwing them in the trash.

A few hours later, a teenager in jeans carrying a boy wrapped in a white blanket came in the ER. No diaper bag, no purse. She walked to the counter where Little was sitting and nonchalantly handed over the boy "like he was a bag of groceries," Little thought.

Did she have any medical information to pass along? Little asked.

No, the girl said. She turned and walked out through the double doors. She didn't look back.

Her son still had his umbilical cord. To Little, he looked "healthy as a horse and cute as a button."

It was less than twelve hours to Christmas. The nurses named him Nick.

"It's sad, but this is how the program is supposed to work," Little says today. "I don't want to read about any more babies thrown in the trash."

Trash-can babies are a problem that Americans literally can't ignore.

In the first month of this year, a couple in Paterson, New Jersey, spotted something in a pile of debris along the railroad tracks that looked like a doll. A Denver supermarket clerk saw something moving on a shelf behind the disposable diapers. A boy in Minneapolis heard cries from the bathroom and later saw his sister go outside with a garbage bag and dump it, oddly, in the neighbors' trash.

In each case—and in at least eight others last month—a baby had been left to die, or perhaps to catch the eye of a stranger.

Each year, hundreds of young women secretly bring babies to term—fooling relatives, friends, and sometimes even themselves—only to bury them in shallow graves, throw them in Dumpsters, leave them in alleys or woods or, in one infamous case in New Jersey two years ago, a restroom at the senior prom.

In the past twelve months their bodies have been discovered in the Mississippi River, in a trash bin behind a Texas high school, in a field in Richmond, California, in a gas station rest room in Los Angeles. It's a crime that smacks everyone in the face. In greater Houston, where thirteen babies were abandoned in a ten-month period ending in September, billboards plead, "Don't Abandon Your Baby!"

On Long Island, a paramedic started a group that "adopts" infants who have been abandoned and died. The child is given a name—always with the surname "Hope"—and a funeral. In southern California, a housewife claims the bodies at the morgue. Her father builds small caskets and volunteers knit blankets for each tiny body. Then the woman lovingly buries them in a private cemetery plot she calls "The Garden of Angels."

A surprising number of discarded babies survive, despite being sealed in plastic or left out in freezing cold. In the past year they have been found alive in a flower bed outside a Houston hospital, on a front porch in Galveston, under a bush near a school in Sunnyvale, California, and under a tree in Kiwanis Park in Rahway, New Jersey. In greater Pittsburgh, hundreds of families have put baskets out on their porches for unwanted babies; so far, none have been dropped off.

No one knows how many babies are thrown away or abandoned, or even how many cases are reported. A computer search of major daily newspapers found 65 reports of discarded newborns in 1991, and 105 in 1998. But experts estimate that half are never discovered.

States Stepping In

The number of babies thrown away or abandoned in public is relatively small. But it's so shocking that localities in several states have made it easier and safer for mothers who want to abandon their newborns to do so.

Although programs vary, most promise that if the mother drops off her infant at a hospital or similar facility, she'll face little or no risk of prosecution if the baby is unharmed, and few or no questions.

Local programs have been started in Alabama, Texas, Minnesota, and Florida, and legislation has been or is to be proposed in California, Kentucky, and several other states. Texas congresswoman Sheila Jackson Lee is drafting legislation to keep federal statistics on the problem.

The movement to save newborns by making it easier for their mothers to give them up started two years ago in Mobile, when a young television reporter named Jodi Brooks decided she had seen too many stories about discarded babies.

In most places, authorities try to find the mother and prosecute her. Even one who drops off her unwanted baby at a hospital can expect some pointed questions and a call to the police (although criminal charges are unlikely).

To change this, Brooks brought together the local prosecutor, social service agencies and hospitals. The result was a heavily publicized program called "A Secret Safe Place for Newborns." The baby must be brought in within seventy-two hours of birth to a designated hospital, where everyone down to the groundskeeper is supposed to be ready to accept a baby. A mother has six months to reclaim her child if she changes her mind.

Since the Mobile program began in November 1998, only one infant has been discarded that authorities know of, a baby who was found alive in the woods. Four babies have been turned in; two were later reclaimed by their mothers and the others are in foster homes, including the Christmas baby named Nick.

But the program has critics. "I'm not for anything that makes abandonment easier," Judy Hay of Harris County (Texas) Children's Protective Services. "I want questions asked, so the child won't wonder some day, 'What's my medical background? Am I at risk for sickle cell? For breast cancer?' You're condemning someone to the lifelong question 'Who am I?'"

In the case of Nick, Terry Little got nothing out of the mother, not even when he was born. "It's Catch-22—get information without asking too many questions," Little says resignedly. "You don't want to spook 'em."

"Something to Get Rid Of"

Will a young mother who is isolated, scared, and possibly in denial of her pregnancy—in such denial that she neither has an abortion nor makes plans to formally hand the baby over for adoption—come to a well-patrolled, camera-scanned emergency room?

After talking to several girls who abandoned their babies, "I've gained new respect for the power of denial," Judy Hay says. "To them, this wasn't even a real human being. It was just something to get rid of." And perhaps not even worth a trip to the hospital.

The Safe Place approach also is opposed by an organization called Project Cuddle, which has a national hotline (1-888-628-3353) and volunteer network. In the past three years, it has counseled 190 girls who, it claims, might have otherwise abandoned their babies.

"These girls don't want anything to do with the system, including a hospital," Project Cuddle's Laurie Larson says. "They want a connection with a person who will help them, and we give them that." She notes that three of the thirteen Houston-area babies were abandoned after a state law took effect that gave legal protection to mothers who turn unwanted babies over to medical personnel.

Michael McGee, education director for Planned Parenthood, says the real problem is a society that sends powerful but mixed messages: Sex is glorious, sex is shameful. The result is pregnant teens who can't even acknowledge that they are pregnant. He says a program like Mobile's may help some girls, "but it's a Band-Aid after the fact."

An Unexpected Pregnancy

Tywana Davis knows how it feels to be young, pregnant and scared.

She was a high school senior in Columbus, Ohio, living with her grandparents. If they found out, she told herself, they'd make her go back to her mother—to a home that often had no heat, no electricity, and no food. Just drugs.

So she said nothing, started wearing baggy clothes and hoped she'd miscarry. She hadn't by graduation, nor by the time she went off to Ohio Dominican College. Finally, on the day before Thanksgiving, on a comforter on the floor of her dormitory room, she gave birth to a girl.

"I thought, 'What can I do? How can I bring this baby home to my grandparents?' The only thing I could think to do was get rid of her."

She wrapped the sleeping infant in a T-shirt and sweater, put her in a plastic grocery bag and carried her down three flights of stairs. She stepped out into the cold November night, walked to a trash bin in back of the dorm, and laid her baby inside.

But when the girl got back to her room, she realized she couldn't just leave the baby down there. So she used a pay phone in the hall to call campus security with an anonymous report: Something was making noise in back of the dorm.

She watched from her window as an officer arrived and found her baby. Then she lay down and waited for her ride home for Thanksgiving.

Trail of Abandoned Newborns
Among cases in one month in 2000:

- Paterson, New Jersey, January 1: A newborn boy's body is found in debris on railroad tracks. Police say a fourteen-year-old mother threw the baby out of second-story window before leaving it on the tracks. She is charged with murder.
- Denver, January 2: A newborn girl is found alive behind packages on a supermarket shelf.
- Monroe, Louisianna, January 3: A live newborn girl is found on lawn chair in carport. The mother, a juvenile, is released to her parents.
- Shelbyville, Kentucky, January 10: A newborn boy is found alive in a trash bin outside a pawnshop. A twenty-year-old woman is charged.
- New York, January 10: A newborn girl's body is found by police outside a public housing project in the Jamaica section of Queens. The mother's identity is unknown.
- Minneapolis, January 12: A newborn is rescued from a garbage can after a boy sees his teenage sister drop a bag into the neighbors' trash. The mother is charged as a juvenile.
- Allentown, Pennsylvania, January 18: A woman, twenty-one, who said she found a baby in the trash outside her family's home and did not know whose it was is charged with leaving the infant there herself.
- Santa Cruz, California, January 19: A baby is found alive in a diaper bag in a thrift store parking lot. The mother, twenty-three, who was identified on surveillance tapes that showed her leaving a hospital earlier in the day, told police she had no interest in the child. She could face charges of child endangerment.
- Fort Worth, January 25: A week-old boy is found alive in an unheated laundry room of an apartment complex. The parents' identity is unknown.
- Germantown, Maryland, January 26: A newborn girl is found in a trash bin outside an apartment complex in freezing temperatures. The mother, nineteen, is charged with attempted murder.
- Indianapolis, January 26: A boy, about five days old, is found frozen to death in a snow bank outside a hospital. The mother's identity is unknown.

Investigators checked a list of students who had not left the dorm. They came to her grandparents' door on Thanksgiving.

Tywana Davis pleaded guilty to child endangerment and was sentenced to a year's house arrest. But her grandparents stood behind her, and raised the child while their [grand]daughter finished college.

Today Davis is twenty-three, with a job in marketing and custody of a four-year-old Danielle. She also counsels pregnant teens. She hears in their voices the fear, panic, and ignorance that once crippled her.

Can the Safe Place approach penetrate the consciousness of girls who won't even face the fact that they're pregnant?

Yes, she says, "but you got to spread the word. Otherwise, forget it. These girls are in their own world."

5

Brief Lives

Miriam Jordan

Dewa, India—Inside a bamboo shed in this poor village, a midwife named Sanjha presided over the brief labor of Ramkali Sah, an illiterate woman with wide eyes and a coy manner. Sanjha ushered a newborn out of Ramkali's womb and announced a girl.

The midwife knew then what the family would want. She would be told to murder the girl.

Despite India's big steps toward economic growth and integration into the global economy, the age-old practice of female infanticide still flourishes here. There's a growing effort to eliminate the practice by educating the midwives that perform the killings. But in India's poorest villages, that work faces deep-rooted cultural and financial obstacles.

A Sliding Scale

The village of Dewa lies in Bihar state, where fully 10 percent of India's one billion inhabitants live. It is the country's poorest state, with a dearth of doctors in remote areas and thousands of midwives. The midwives earn about fifty cents and a sack of grain for each live delivery of a girl, twice as much plus a sari if it's a boy. Getting rid of a newborn female fetches as much as five dollars.

The female-to-male ratio in India, always lower than the global average, consistently declined in the past century, though it's impossible to link that trend conclusively to female infanticide. The 2001 census is expected to report a ratio of 900 women to every 1,000 men. That would be down from 927 in 1991, the latest complete census, 941 in 1961, and 972 in 1901.

Part of the imbalance, nationally, comes from abortions. In towns, it's common to see signboards advertising ultrasound services that often lead to terminated pregnancies—although the use of ultrasound to determine gender was banned in 1996. The Indian Medical Association estimates that three million females fetuses are aborted each year, generally after sex-selection sonograms and mostly in urban areas. Other estimates put the number at five million.

In poor and backward places such a Bihar, however, where sonograms are still a rarity, it's cheaper to kill a newborn girl than to travel to a city and pay for a gender test and abortion. And Bihar's gender ratio is among the most lopsided in the country. The 1991 census in Bihar showed 912 women for every 1,000 men, down from 1,054 women in 1901. In the district where Dewa is located, the ratio in 1991 was 819 women to 1,000 men.

In some pockets of Bihar and Rajasthan, another poor state, the female-to-male ratio is a meager 600 to 1,000. Last August, one village in Rajasthan witnessed its first Hindu wedding procession to a bride's home in 110 years, because no other girl had been allowed to survive.

South Asia has a long history of violence against females; besides infanticide, there also are acid attacks and killings sparked by dowry disputes. According to the National Crime Records Bureau, dowry deaths jumped nearly 26 percent between 1996 and 1998, to 6,917 from 5,513. The bureau recorded 114 cases of infanticide in all India in 1998, compared with 107 in 1997 and 113 in 1996. But such deaths usually go unreported, and the bureau's executive director, Sharda Prasad, says that any crime is likely to be grossly underestimated. "It's anybody's guess" what actual figures are, he says.

Mr. Prasad believes that "modernization has contributed to an increase in dowry deaths, . . . because there are more demands for goods. People want a TV, a fridge. If they can't purchase these things with their own money, they should come with a girl." And one corollary to this may be contributing to the persistence of female infanticide: As aspirations outpace rises in income, a daughter represents an even bigger potential drain on her family's finances.

Well before Ramkali Sah was born in the fall of 1998, the extended Sah family already knew the math. They had married off a daughter the previous year, and it had cost them a dairy cow, farm tools, a bicycle, and $575 in cash—all told, about a year's income. Another girl would be crippling.

Some Indians regard a daughter not merely as a liability but as a traitor: She switches loyalties when she is married off, usually in her teens, and moves in with her in-laws. "Raising a daughter is like watering your neighbor's plant," says a south Indian proverb. Women are subordinate to men in Hindu scriptures; a Hindu goes to heaven only if a son lights the funeral pyre.

"If a boy is born, he will be a breadwinner," says Asherfi Sah, the patriarch of the Sah family and the father of five sons and one daughter. One of his sons, Prakasj, is the husband of Ramkali.

Prakash Sah is among the village's fortunate men who have managed to leave behind the farm work and get one of the more lucrative factory jobs that have become available with economic reforms. A visit to one of the extended family's huts reveals a new radio inside and a new bicycle parked outside.

But the Sah clan wasn't feeling flush in the fall of 1998, when the family was still recovering from the previous year's marriage of Prakash's sister. Moreover, Prakash and Ramkali already had two girls. The last thing the Sashs needed was a new baby girl.

So, they turned to the able hands of the midwife Sanjha, who reckons she is about forty-five. Her wiry arms are covered with tattoos, which is common among the tribal and low-caste women in north India, as is the single name. She knows many ways to kill: snap the baby's spine; shove rock salt down her throat; force her into a clay pot and seal it.

Sanjha won't discuss how many infants she had killed before she abandoned the practice three years ago. But she is more forthcoming about why she stopped killing and what happened when she was hired to deliver Ramkali's daughter.

The change of heart came when Sanjha began to receive rudimentary training from an organization called Adithi. Founded in 1988 by Viji Srinivasan, a development worker who had been with the Ford Foundation for six years, it aims to improve the lot of poor Biharia, providing informal education for girls and women, and small loans to support cottage industry. It gets funds from international organizations, such as the Britain-based Plan International and Action Aid, as well as aid organizations of foreign governments.

Dithi started holding village meetings in the early 1990s to teach midwives about prenatal care and hygiene. Traditional birth attendants deliver nine out of ten babies in Bihar, and Adithi had identified a need to teach some basics: cut the umbilical cord with sterilized scissors, for instance, rather than with a scythe that was used on grass and weeds.

"I used to deliver a baby on a heap of straw—not even a mat," Sanjha says.

Over time, Adithi staff won the confidence of the midwives in Dewa and other villages, and the instructors began to grasp the extent of infanticide committed by their students. The revelations led Adithi to try conducting a structured survey on infanticide, but there was almost no cooperation in the communities. So the organization turned back to the midwives, who quietly came out with their own appalling estimates.

There are about 535,000 traditional birth attendants in Bihar for a population of 100 million. In several districts of the state, Adithi found that each midwife killed as many as five newborn girls a month. The study, released in 1995, was an informal exercise, but Ms. Srinvasan believes that "if anything, the survey underestimated infanticide."

She sent the findings to Bihar's welfare commissioner, the most senior civil servant in the state welfare ministry, but got no response. In fact, the national government and most state governments officially deny that infanticide takes place. Infanticide "was true in the past, but no longer," says A. K. Choudhary, formerly Bihar's health commissioner and now secretary of rural development.

Adithi began a grassroots campaign against infanticide at the source: the midwives. It wasn't easy. At early sessions, the midwives—some of them holding their own baby girls—questioned the notion that girls have an equal right to live. They said they need money; they noted that the families didn't want the babies anyway. Over and over, Adithi counselors urged the women to think of newborn girls as if they were their own daughters.

Most challenging still was getting the midwives to resist their employers. Most midwives are *dalits*, those on the lowest rung of Indian society, and have almost no stature in their communities because the job involves blood and so is considered impure. Midwives are only one step above people who collect human waste.

It took Sanjha two years to absorb Adithi's message. Before the encounter with the Sahs, however, she kept silent about her change of heart, for fear of losing potential clients. During that time, to save the girls she delivered, she would try to persuade families to keep them. On several occasions, families she served agreed to spare the child, but later Sahjha would hear the infant had died of "natural causes," which usually meant the family had let the infant starve.

Ramkali Sah gave birth in a bamboo shed where firewood was stored. Sanjha recalls that it was a crisp night bright with stars that dimly lit the rice paddies and wheat fields around Dewa. When the Sahs learned that their third child was a girl, judgment was swift, Sanjha says. "The mother-in-law said, 'Kill her or abandon her somewhere so that she'll freeze to death.'"

Sanjha resisted, and the Sahs raised the stakes: an extra eight kilograms, or about eighteen pounds, of rice to dispose of the child. Extra rice is like extra cash. Sanjha delivers five to six babies a month and has a sharecropping arrangement with a landowner in the village. Her husband, a mason, brings home about two dollars per job. All told, they live on less than forty dollars a month. Rice would free up cash to repair the straw roof on their half-brick hovel.

Still she stood firm, asking the Sahs to give her the child with the idea of handing it over to Adithi for adoption. The Sahs wouldn't budge.

Hours later, Sanjha finally returned home, leaving the child behind in the arms of the furious mother-in-law. For three days, the midwife kept an eye on the baby from a distance. Publicly, the child remained nameless, although rumors in the village said that she had been called Mantorni, which is Hindi for someone who breaks your heart. On the fourth day, Sanjha heard that the Sahs were not feeding the infant.

Unable to do more herself, she contacted a nearby Adithi office. A counselor named Asha came and called an impromptu village meeting. Asha and the Sahs recall the scene.

More than two dozen women villagers gathered near a well where clothes are washed, sitting on straw mats beneath an oak tree to escape the noonday sun. Asha began by congratulating the Sahs on the birth of their baby girl. Then, she got right to the point: "I hear there might be a problem with the child's health. Can we help?"

Sampatia Sah, Ramkali's mother-in-law, reacted angrily: "I know why you've come," she snapped. Beside her, Ramkali cradled the five-day-old Mantorni.

Asha began a Socratic dialogue with the group on the value of daughters. Who returns to visit you more—your married sons or daughters? How many of you believe that girls deserve to be educated? So, how many of you think a daughter is as valuable as a son? Thus prodded, several women agreed that girls can be an asset and more loving than boys.

Asha turned to the Sahs, who had sat silently though this exchange. "If you don't want your baby," she said, "let Adithi put her up for adoption."

The mother-in-law remained defiant. Asha warned her that she would face prosecution if anything happened to the child. As the meeting broke up, many of the women agreed that they would watch over the Sahs' daughter.

The next day, Asha returned with a photographer. The message was clear: A snapshot would be proof that Mantorni had once been healthy.

It's hard to gauge Adithi overall effectiveness. In this pocket of Bihar it has trained 400 or so of the midwives, who serve about 190,000 people. These 400 have all told Adithi they have stopped killing.

In fact, emboldened by their training some midwives have taken great risks to save babies. At least fifteen newborns have been spirited away to Adithi headquarters without their parent's consent. All those girls have been adopted.

A year after her birth, the Sahs have come to terms with their new daughter. "We're keeping the child," Sampatia declares. She has nineteen grandchildren, and boy or girl, she says, "I love them all equally." But, she adds, "the world knows that when a son is born, the status of a family increases."

As grown-ups talk outside their shack under a blue sky, the girl first known as Mantorni—now a bubbling one-year-old—sits on Sampatia's lap and giggles as her cheek is stroked. The Sah family has given Mantorni a permanent name now: Rani, which means "Queen."

6

Who Will Do Abortions Here?

Jack Hitt

On a cold Minnesota morning, the abortion doctor and I pushed his six-seater plane out of the hangar and onto the runway. We removed the leather nose cozy (handmade by his wife), cranked the prop, and minutes later were aloft above the linear plats etched along the Laurentian Divide. We were heading west to Fargo, where the doctor singlehandedly keeps North Dakota's last abortion clinic open every Wednesday.

Alexander Nicholas is part of a growing trend among abortion providers. (Alexander Nicholas is not his real name; it's a pseudonym he uses because, he said simply, "my life is in jeopardy these days.") At one point last year, he was touching down in Minnesota, North Dakota, Wisconsin, and Indiana. In the trade, these new frequent-flier docs are called "circuit riders." They are proof of two things: that the medical infrastructure undergirding the right to an abortion is strained to the breaking point and that the practical reality of abortion is retreating into a half-lighted ghetto of pseudonyms, suspicion, and fear

"I really don't see a solution to this problem," Nicholas said, "until medicine is presented with a crisis." He may not have long to wait.

Twenty-five years ago this week, the Supreme Court legalized abortion with its decision on *Roe* v. *Wade*, and since then, the legal and moral contests surrounding *Roe* have achieved a kind of odd stability. The most conservative Supreme Court in half a century has embraced the principles of the 1973 landmark decision. And the moral debate plays out like an unending episode of *Crossfire*, almost reassuring in the way antiabortion and abortion rights positions rerun on a continuous tape loop.

In recent years, the number of women terminating a pregnancy has remained fairly constant, about 1.5 million a year. The doctors who serve the system are another matter. Today, 59 percent of all abortion doctors are at least sixty-five years old. That's not a typo: nearly two-thirds are beyond legal retirement age. Most doctors who perform abortions specialize in obstetrics and gynecology; according to a study done three years ago, the percentage of OB-GYNs willing to perform abortions dropped from 42 percent in 1983 to 33 percent in 1995. (Doctors going into what's called family practice medicine were thought by some to be part of the next generation of abortion providers, but a study published in October revealed that only 15 percent of chief residents doing family practice had any experience with the simplest abortion procedure.)

OB-GYNs learn the surgeries and procedures associated with abortion during their hospital residency programs. A 1991 study showed that only 12 percent of these programs now routinely teach abortion, and, according to Philip Darney, a professor at the University of California at San Francisco's medical school, all indications are that the percentage is "still trending down."

One factor in this is the growth in hospital mergers. Many bring together institutions with no religious affiliation and Catholic hospital chains like the Sisters of the Sorrowful Mother. The Catholic Church is, of course, firmly against abortion, and typically, one immediate result of this sort of merger is the elimination of abortion training and birth-control counseling.

Few medical schools dare to even mention, much less teach, the mere facts of abortion. My wife finished medical school last year. She never heard the word "abortion," uttered in a classroom. Which medical school was it that neglects to expose students to what is one of the most common surgeries among American women? Yale.

"I am training a young woman right now in Duluth," Nicholas explained as the plane zipped across a landscape of infinite fleece. "She's doing it as part of a family practice residency at the clinic, but she had to request it and is training on her own time." He spoke in a measured way, like nearly everybody in the Coen brothers' movie *Fargo*, and his blue eyes were friendly beneath his winter muskrat hat.

"It's very different for people like her," he added. "A lot of doctors don't want partners who perform the service." This is one of the reasons nearly nine out of ten abortions are done not in doctors' offices or in hospitals but in clinics like those Nicholas regularly visits. This phenomenon has played a concrete role in moving abortion off the main street of prestigious American medicine toward the half-hidden back alley from where it once emerged.

Nicholas knew that old world. In the hospitals of Chicago, where he was a resident in the 1960s, survivors of botched abortions regularly limped in or were carried in to receive his care. "They were bleeding, had foreign bodies in their vagina, or came in with temperatures of 106," he said.

"The younger doctors especially don't have the history we have with the procedure," he went on to say. "They don't know how women were affected in the old days. They're out of the loop because they never had to go through what we did. They have no experience."

If the right to an abortion seems here to stay, the medical system that has provided the safe, legal abortions can no longer be taken for granted. The medical schools and hospital residency programs that have stopped teaching abortion are responding, in part, to the argument that abortion is immoral. But mostly they are responding to the same fears that keep providers like Nicholas from allowing their real names to be used. This fear pervades every aspect of abortion, and has driven it increasingly into a kind of medical netherworld, where doctors wear bulletproof vests and students learn what they can where they can and research is relatively rare. This shadow world, in turn, makes the providing of abortions less and less appealing even to those doctors who consider themselves "pro-choice."

The murders in 1993–94 of five abortion doctors and clinic staff members have changed every aspect of the abortion debate. The militant antiabortion group Operation Rescue, which denied responsibility for the murders, nonetheless collapsed. Its fifty state chapters now number eight. Still, by wrecking itself on its own increasingly violent rhetoric, the radical wing of the antiabortion movement did win an important battle. It made the abortion procedure a dangerous, undesirable, and even somewhat illegitimate thing to do: *among doctors*.

Once upon a time, Nicholas was greeted by women with gratitude. Now he is often met on the tarmac by gangs of mostly men screaming curses at him. He has received phone calls in which cold voices ask menacingly, "How's your plane flying, Alex?" Just three weeks before I met Nicholas in Minnesota, an abortion doctor just over the border in Canada was shot through the window of his house while he ate dinner. A photograph of Nicholas's plane circulates among antiabortion Internet sites.

The overwhelming majority of abortions are performed by a small group of doctors. (Some 2 percent of OB-GYNs carry the burden, performing more than twenty-five per month.) "Most doctors love it that someone else is performing the service," he said, "because they don't have to worry about the hate mail and the harassment. But I'm not going to keep doing this until I have one foot in the grave." Nicholas, one of the younger pups in this field, is sixty. He said he plans to be hunting moose full time when he's sixty-two.

"I'm not going to do this forever."

Lost History, or What a Young Doctor Doesn't Know

In any society, the terms of a particular debate have a way of shaping the outcome, and this is very much the case with abortion. In a sense, abortion medicine is being undermined rhetorically as much as any other way. These days it has become impossible to talk or think about abortion in any terms other than those of moral revulsion. It's either pure evil (the "pro-life" view) or a necessary evil (the "pro-choice" view). Even feminists have, in recent years, engaged in a discussion to redefine abortion in terms of transgression and mourning.

But in the plane with Nicholas, and later in other interviews with doctors whose early careers predated *Roe*, I discovered a theme I hadn't anticipated. None of them could speak about abortion as a moral issue because their initial encounter with abortion was not as an argument, but as an emergency.

Their histories date back to women who had back-alley abortions that resulted in internal infections and other, more disturbing complications. Legalization has largely eliminated these things, as well as the estimated five thousand annual abortion-related deaths in the years before *Roe*. The dichotomy for these doctors is not legal or illegal, moral or immoral, but safe versus unsafe.

"It's one thing to remove the uterus of a woman who had had children," said David Bingham, a fifty-seven-year-old OB-GYN who has been doing abortions since his residency in the years just prior to *Roe*. "What was really hard was to remove the uterus of some sixteen-year-old because of gas gangrene, and to know that she would never have a family."

The belief that abortion is a form of preventive medicine is prevalent among older doctors. As such, many of the sentiments I heard from them are all but unvoiced today, opinions out of some 1973 time capsule.

"I save lives," Bingham said.

"What?" I asked. I assumed that I had misheard him.

"I save lives," he repeated, his tone desperate. "I respect these people who have picketed outside my office for twenty-five years, in and out of snowstorms. Obviously they believe in what they are doing and are very persistent. At the same time, I have taken care of many of their wives and children and even some of the people on the picket line who suddenly find themselves in a way different situation than they ever thought possible. I know what would happen if they were successful politically—a lot more tragedy, a lot more deaths. I saw what it was like when it was illegal. Look—we have saved tens of thousands of lives, maybe hundreds of thousands."

I heard this again from Richard Hausknecht, a sixty-eight-year-old Park Avenue OB-GYN who helped open the first New York clinic in 1970 at Seventy-third and Madison. "You are preserving a woman's life," he said, "by not forcing her to take the extreme measure of a life-threatening illegal abortion or having a child when it's totally inappropriate to do so."

This kind of talk about abortion, unheard on the political talk shows and the floor of Congress, is, strangely, just as rare among those studying to become doctors who perform abortions. I interviewed a number of OB-GYN residents in the fall, and among the questions I asked was why had they learned the procedure. They answered that "I am pro-choice" and it's "a matter of privacy" and "women's rights," but never "I save lives." Hausknecht, who also teaches at Mount Sinai Medical School, detected a similar change during a recent lecture he gave to students on abortion history.

"I showed them slides of death rates due to abortion prior to Roe," he said. "It didn't have any impact. It was as if I were talking about tuberculosis"—by which he meant something that was eradicated years ago.

The passage of *Roe* v. *Wade* did not erase a medical history in which "abortionist" was an insult worse than "quack." Abortion is the only procedure singled out by Hippocrates for inclusion in the oath, which strictly forbids it (and which is why modern doctors recite an edited version of Hippocrates's original words).

The history of abortion isn't widely known for the simple reason that almost none of abortion's past serves either side of the contemporary debate very well. For example, abortion was legal in America from 1607 to 1828. The drive to outlaw it in the nineteenth century had little to do with morality. Doctors were beginning to professionalize, so they pushed for a ban on abortions as a remedy for the bad medicine they saw being practiced by profiteering charlatans and well-intentioned midwives.

Unfortunately, their successful effort to make abortion illegal simply drove it into the back alley, where, according to some estimates, as many as 2 million abortions a year were performed—a number that if even half accurate should sober up today's Victorian nostalgists. The movement to legalize abortion in the 1970s was motivated by the same medical logic that had led to its ban: to eliminate botched abortions. To that extent, *Roe* has been successful. Deaths at the hands of self-taught abortionists virtually disappeared after 1973. And other statistics began to change. Bingham, who served as a case reviewer in Detroit for the Centers for Disease Control in the early '70s, said the impact of the first states to legalize abortion was immediate.

"The day abortion became legal in New York State," he recalled, "was also the day that we—in Detroit—noticed that the number of patients coming into the hospital with 'miscarriages' plummeted."

Because residents have no knowledge of abortion history before *Roe*, they see their choice to perform abortions as a political one. And they are often disturbed to discover that the women they serve, more often than not young or poor or both, don't speak the language of constitutional rights.

"For some it is definitely a kind of birth control," said one weary OB-GYN resident I spoke with in a hospital not far from Manhattan. She believes in abortion rights and does abortions, but like all such residents I interviewed, she spoke only on the condition of anonymity, fearing harassment or worse by abortion foes. "These women are on their sixth one. They have a troubled family situation, and you feel it's in the best interest for the possible future child." Her voice grew slow and sad. "In some ways I do feel that—but it doesn't make it any more pleasant."

The chief resident at the same hospital said: "Some days you just want to shake these people. 'Why didn't you take your birth-control pills? Why didn't you get your Depo-Provera shot?' "

These OB-GYN residents seemed to get little satisfaction, as doctors, in doing abortions—the satisfaction, however sober, that they saved a life by carrying out the procedure in a medical setting. For any doctor, there is pride in performing a technique well and seeing a patient on the mend—that's what the doctors who remember the horrors of the back alley say they feel. This is lost on the residents I spoke with. Some of them have the kind of revulsion you expect to find among abortion protesters.

"If you do twelve in a row, it can make you feel bad," the chief resident said. "No matter how pro-choice you are, it makes you feel low." Another resident said: "I guess I never realized I would find it as unpleasant as I do. I really don't enjoy it at all. It's not a rewarding thing to do."

She went on to say that, truth be told, she preferred doing second-trimester abortions—a more difficult surgery—to the simple first-trimester abortions.

"Why?" I asked.

"Because the patient is asleep," she said. Many of the women who come in are drug addicts, who often have exceptionally low pain thresholds. "They look at you as an evil person who is deliberately putting them through a painful procedure. I just feel like explaining to them that this is not something that I am going out of my way to do. It's their whole attitude that bothers me. I feel like a simple thank you is in order instead of 'Why are you doing this to me?' "

Among OB-GYN residents willing to perform abortions, there is also, oddly enough, disparaging talk about those doctors who perform many abortions, particularly those, like Nicholas, who travel from clinic to clinic, working long hours at great risk. One resident referred to the clinics as "factories." Another said, "That whole world is a mystery to me." Finally, one OB-GYN who supports abortion rights but has chosen not to perform abortions said bluntly what the others were probably thinking: "It's seen as the dirty work of our field. The sad truth is that the people who moonlight at the clinics are grade-B doctors. They're not the cream of the crop. And it's not because they're committed. It's because they can't find steady work."

When I raised this with Dr. Hausknecht, he grew annoyed, but acknowledged that the prejudice is very much alive in medicine. "It's true that abortion providers are perceived as not very good doctors—that they have no alternative so they do abortions, that they cannot earn a living any other way," he said. The fear of getting too much of an abortion reputation preys on the minds of residents and influences their career decisions.

"I was thinking of doing a study last year," one resident said. "I wanted to look at different gestational ages and then compare them to outcomes among different types of abortion. But then I started to think, well, gosh, wait a minute, I don't want to end up being known as the abortion person—do you know I mean?"

THE ABORTION ELECTIVE, OR WHAT A DOCTOR IS NOT REQUIRED TO LEARN

"My wife," said William Rashbaum, an OB-GYN in a large East Coast city, "told me I owe it to women before I die to make sure others have my skills." But training is slow. He said that he can't devote as much time as he would like to since, at age seventy-one, he still shuttles full time between his private office and several hospitals to help with current demand.

While few OB-GYN residency programs routinely teach abortion procedures, many do allow residents to learn it as an outside elective—at, for example, Planned Parenthood, which arranges for residents in programs that don't teach abortion to rotate through a clinic nearby. But for residents who typically work between eighty and one hundred hours a week, the offer of taking an elective course in their "spare time" constitutes a cruel joke.

In every residency program that does teach abortion, anyone can opt out on moral grounds, and many do. Those who want to learn the procedure know they are, in a sense, being penalized—working even more hours, often feeling cheated. "Residents who do abortions know they are being pulled from learning other procedures," said the chief resident I interviewed, "because they are the only ones doing abortions. What else are they missing? I know that among some residents there is a little bit of resentment."

From day one, said one resident, the issue of just who will and will not perform abortions is a topic that just hangs in the air. Eventually folks "just kinda know," he said, who will be doing the procedure. "And it's hard not to suspect that some people opt out because they are looking for any way to lighten the load." In his program—ensconced in a liberal Northeastern teaching hospital—only half the OB-GYN residents are learning the technique.

"Abortion is the only procedure you can choose not to learn," another resident said. "I can't say I don't believe in hysterectomy or I don't believe in tubal ligation and therefore won't learn the procedure. Abortion's the only one you can opt out of learning for whatever reason. It can be real or unreal. You just might want to get out of work. It sounds cynical, but in a residency? Absolutely."

Few residents would have encountered abortion in medical school. Efforts to remedy the curricular absence of abortion training have been led by the American Medical Women's Association. The organization has developed a full course on birth control, including abortion, and has been pressing the medical schools to add it to the curriculum. But the going is slow. Of the 160 medical schools in America, only 5 offer the course, and in each case it is an elective.

To combat the sense of isolation among the students who want to learn how to perform abortions, a group was founded three years ago called Medical Students for Choice. One of its members described being scolded by an OB-GYN professor for mentioning abortion in a casual conversation on the wards. When she lobbied to start up a chapter at her medical school, faculty pressure was applied to change the name to Students for Reproductive Health and Freedom—anything to avoid that protest-inducing word "choice."

In 1995, the Accreditation Council for Graduate Medical Education decided to get tough and explicitly mandated that all OB-GYN residency programs must provide abortion training (although individual residents could still opt out for moral reasons). This was met in Congress by the Dan Coats Amendment, which ensured that any residency programs unaccredited because of abortion training would continue to receive the federal financing that underwrites all accredited residency programs. In the end, the "mandate" became a recommendation not to impede "elective" training. No school has been unaccredited.

A Lack of Research and Innovation, or What No One Knows about the "Partial Birth" Procedure

The one area of abortion medicine that appears to be thriving is research. From time to time, the news media relate some new procedure that holds out the promise of removing abortion from doctors and the clinic, and thus, the thinking goes, from the antiabortion movement. You might get the impression that research laboratories remain unaffected by the strains felt by other aspects of abortion medicine. But evidence of abortion's marginality can be found even here.

Take, for instance, the new form of first-trimester abortion that uses the drug methotrexate. Like the procedure utilizing the better-known drug RU-486, the methotrexate abortion requires an initial visit to a doctor for a shot of the drug; the patient then follows up by taking four pills of a different drug at home.

The man who pioneered this technique and who achieved the rare distinction of publishing a full study in the *New England Journal of Medicine* under a solo byline was Dr. Hausknecht. During a grand rounds lecture at Mount Sinai one morning in the fall, he was lauded by his peers as a "pioneer" and a "hero."

Then, during the question-and-answer period, one doctor put it bluntly: "Is this the panacea long sought by certain feminist groups so that women can bypass the physician?"

Hausknecht shook his head no. All methotrexate abortions had to be supervised by a doctor and the patient had to have ready access to an abortion facility. In the event of failure, an old-fashioned surgical abortion must be performed. And because methotrexate can involve several doctor visits and often has side-effects lasting on and off for weeks—bleeding, vomiting—the procedure introduces a new problem to the issue: an ongoing awareness of the abortion process. How many women would choose methotrexate over the immediate physical and psychological resolution of the surgical method?

In an interview with Hausknecht in his office, I discovered that the rare occurrence of having only his name on the article was not, it turned out, a badge of honor. Actually, it simply meant that his own department at Mount Sinai—once headed by the famous reproductive-health pioneer Alan Guttmacher—wouldn't put up its money or prestige for the study.

"I had to charge my patients," Hausknecht said. "The research was self-funded. It's difficult to write good scientific research by your lonesome. It would be nice to have a biostatistician to help you. Nice to have colleagues tear it apart and put in their two or twenty cents' worth." The reason Hausknecht is a "pioneer" has as much to do with merely pursuing abortion research as it does with his results.

"You can look at any medical meeting of any kind in recent history," said Dr. Jane Hodgson, an abortion pioneer who will turn eighty-three the day after *Roe*'s anniversary later this week. "You will not find a single paper given on abortion."

Consider the contributions American researchers have made in other areas of reproductive medicine: in vitro fertilization, ultrasound, superovulation, birth control—American know-how is deeply involved in all innovations. But abortion? When Americans have been involved, abortion's ambiguous history is never far off. The soft tube, or cannula, used to penetrate the uterus was developed by Harvey Karman, hence the "Karman cannula" still found in any medical catalogue. Karman was not a doctor, but he performed abortions pre-1973, if you get my drift.

Almost all developments in abortion medicine have happened elsewhere. The suction-curettage procedure dates to work done years ago in Communist Hungary. Prior to some abortions the cervix must be dilated, typically by inserting sticks fashioned from twisted seaweed, which when wet expand—a process perfected centuries ago by the Japanese. The use of prostaglandins, the compounds used to terminate second-trimester pregnancies, originated in Sweden.

RU-486—which operates a lot like methotrexate—is French. It was once predicted to be widely available in the United States by mid-1997, but it remains all but impossible to get. It is being tested in secret locations and manufactured by a secret company; the plan was to have it eventually shipped by a secret middleman. However, one result of this furtive distribution apparatus, created to avoid antiabortion "action alerts," is that the pill's American patent-holder, the Population Council, managed to unknowingly hire a disbarred lawyer (he was convicted of forgery) to serve as the business manager. So the entire RU-486 procedure is currently tied up in the courts.

"RU-486 is no closer today to being available than it ever was," Hausknecht said.*

New abortion procedures or techniques tend to emerge slowly, and from a kind of half-light—a fact overlooked during last year's battle over late-term abortion. Interestingly, the furor concerned terminology, with abortion-rights advocates maintaining that conservatives' use of "partial birth" was a loaded description, and one never used by doctors. The proper medical term, they said, is "intact dilation and extraction," or "intact D & X." But most OB-GYNs I spoke with had never heard that term before the controversy. Few knew how, or where they could learn, to do one.

So I called a few doctors who performed this procedure. One said he taught it, and not long after, I found myself in the deepest shadows of abortion medicine, dressed in one of those blue paper surgical outfits with shoe coverings and tissuey snood. I had been smuggled into an operating room and was watching a resident watching a doctor in order to learn the procedure.

The patient, whose life was not endangered by her pregnancy, lay sedated on her back on the operating table; her ankles dangled in the air, gently held by loops of cloth tied to high steel poles. At the tap of a button, the bed rose, bringing her womb up to working level, and the doctor lowered a clear plastic face mask, like an arc welder's. The doctor inserted his gloved right hand deeply into the patient's vagina until only his thumb protruded.

"I am looking for a foot," he said to the resident standing beside him. I stood directly behind them. He pulled out a foot, a bit longer than an inch.

"There is the foot," he said. "Now you pull the one leg and then you reach in and flex the other one like this." He reinserted a single forefinger into the vagina and suddenly two legs, froglike, appeared. The skin was translucent, membranous. The feet quickly turned a dark purple. Within minutes, so did the legs. The doctor gripped each leg as if holding hedge clippers.

---

*Mifepristone, widely known as RU-486, was approved for use by the United States Food and Drug Administration on September 28, 2000.—Eds.

"Place each thumb on the buttocks," he instructed. The pads of his thumbs and the fetus's buttocks were perfect matches in size and shape. "Then turn and twist like this." He pulled firmly. A back appeared, then with the flick of a forefinger, a small arm fell out and then another. The anesthesia had relaxed the natural paisley curl of the fetus into something linear and flaccid. A 10-inch homunculus, its head locked into the cervix hung in full view, motionlessly toward the floor, its long, tapered legs disturbingly elegant.

It happened quickly. The back of the fetus's skull was punctured. There was a tiny spurt of blood into the stainless-steel waste can that sat on the floor beneath. A curette was inserted, a hose was attached and the deep rumble of the suction machine near me kicked on. Into a clear plastic jar at my feet there appeared instantaneously about a half-inch of pinkish fluid marked by tiny whitish-gray globules. On some animal level, deep in my own brain stem, I knew what it was and leapt back in fear. The periphery of my vision went gray, and a minute later, when my equilibrium returned, I found myself standing amid an ancient medical ritual.

The doctor was excoriating the resident for giving too many wrong answers to hard questions he had posed during the procedure. This particularly humiliating variation of the Socratic method is a form of hazing that medical students call "pimping."

"What are the three most important words in medicine?" the doctor yelled.

The resident was speechless. The doctor seized the student's cheeks with both hands and pulled his face as close as a boot-camp sergeant's.

"What are they?" the doctor roared.

"I don't know," the resident said meekly, his chin digging into his chest in abject humility. The doctor smiled the smile of a man who had set this verbal trap a hundred times before.

"Precisely," he said. "I . . . don't . . . know. Learn to say them." After the resident left, I asked the doctor what else the young doctor would have to do to learn about an intact D & X. He looked at me oddly. Else? There was nothing else.

Most young surgeons learn procedures via hands-on experience, but they are also required to take classes, read books, attend meetings of their peers, and keep up with the improvements found in the periodical literature. But none of this support exists for the intact D & X. In fact, it's not just the phrase "partial-birth abortion" that can't be found in the medical books; neither can "intact dilation and extraction."

Why? Because much of the "continuing education" in abortion technique occurs in quickly arranged opportunities, on the fly, by word of mouth.

"When you get caught in the middle of an abortion that is further along than anticipated," Dr. David Bingham said, "you have a tremendous motivation to find out what to do. So that's when we would just discuss with each other what worked to get out of that situation."

The channels of communication among abortion doctors more closely resemble the oral tradition from the pre-electronic bush. The doctors dwell in relative isolation in their offices or clinics. There is not a lot of chance for conventioneering. The local manager of the Holiday Inn isn't really eager to arrange the plastic letters on the roadside sign to read, "Welcome Abortion Providers!" So they talk among themselves. The late-term-abortion controversy broke out only after the very first draft paper describing the procedure was leaked in 1993 to the National Right to Life Committee.

Even though there are OB-GYN periodicals willing to disseminate information about new techniques, getting information out is not the problem.

"It's not that they won't publish research," Hausknecht said. "It's that they have no research to publish." And what little there is arrives at a sluggish pace. "We would have had RU486 and methotrexate fifteen years ago if weren't for the politics," Bingham said.

The Internet is a help. Probably more professionals have learned about methotrexate from a Web site (www.medicalabortion.com) devoted to Hausknecht's work than from the original *New England Journal of Medicine* article. But the normal organizational conduits of medicine just aren't operative for abortion. I asked Hausknecht when the last time was that the American Medical Association (AMA) had anything to say about abortion. "They came out in favor of the partial-birth ban," he replied darkly. "That's about it."

The job of clearing information and maintaining standards—something the AMA traditionally does for medicine—has fallen to abortion's own private organization, the National Abortion Federation (NAF). The NAF is a Washington-based association of abortion providers, but it does much more than any other typical guild of like-minded professionals. As if to underscore just how remote abortion is from mainstream, prestigious medicine, the NAF is perhaps best understood as a kind of mini-AMA. Abortion is the only field in medicine to have one, or need one.

Living a Life in the Shadows, or How Abortion Shapes One Heartland Life and May Someday Affect a Lot of Others

Dr. Alexander Nicholas is an observant Catholic father of three, which is not everybody's idea of an abortion provider. I first met him at his home, a modest one-story house of aluminum siding and brick on an average American street. He invited me there because he wanted me to see that it "was no Cadillac deal."

His wife, Amelia, dressed in slacks and a sweatshirt boasting the name of her curling club, showed me to the breakfast table for a snack. Her silver napkin ring had a black plastic tag glued to it that read "Grandma." The kitchen was overrun with evidence of Christmas chores. Bonbons cooled on two baking sheets nearby. I was invited to sample her most prized confection, a blend of green and pink miniature marshmallows, Rice Krispies, and peanuts held together by almond bark.

"They got more 'bark' than bite, don't they?" the doctor commented as we munched.

Not knowing what else to do, I just ground the gears and rudely shifted the conversation from marshmallows to abortion—more specifically, to how he and his wife go about their lives in the abortion netherworld. Their cheery Midwestern can-do-ism never faltered.

"Oh, it hasn't been so bad," Amelia said. "Except 1993, when members of Operation Rescue surrounded the house day and night for a week of candlelight vigils. That was no good."

"Some good came of it," Dr. Nicholas leapt in. "That couple down the street—we'd never really done anything with them. Son of a gun, he brings us a pie."

The town also held a rally, arguing that Nicholas's right to a regular life in his home with his family was as important as the moral debate about abortion. Nicholas's insistence on finding the good in what has happened is not just a product of his Midwesternness. It's now a part of his mental survival. Most of his days are filled with a constant low-grade foreboding.

After Nicholas landed the plane in Fargo that morning, we were met by one of the clinic staff members. We drove through town and pulled up to the clinic, a small blue-trimmed house next to the Holiday gas station. A man and a woman in thick parkas paced back and forth across the driveway. The man was holding a sign that read "Never to Laugh," leaving a new visitor uncertain about whether the sentiment applied to him.

"Oh, gosh," Nicholas groaned, "I see we got Timmy and Cathy today," referring to the protesters. The staff member pulled the car around back behind a high fence. She looked at me and mouthed the words, "Bring yourself to Christ." As I got out of the car, the exact same words came droning over the fence, like a rote response in a litany: "Bring yourself to Christ."

The woman driving rolled her eyes at me again and then in a singsong voice said, "Alex, you were born a Catholic."

Immediately, like the refrain from a dirge, "Alex, you were born a Catholic" floated over the top of the fence.

The entire moment was comical and creepy, reminding me of nothing more than that Warner Brothers cartoon of the sheep dog and wolf who punch a clock every morning just outside the herd of sheep. *Morning, Ralph. Morning, Sam.* Then they spend the day merrily going through the same circular motions—comical because at their core they are potentially violent.

Legalized abortion has become the most hashed-over political and theological debate in a nation devoted to debates. The pro and con exchanges are as rehearsed as *The McLaughlin Group*. The national animosities break out continuously, along old lines, repeating in almost mythic cycles.

Today, we watch as RU-486 sets off protests, but most of us have forgotten that the reason no company would openly manufacture the drug is that corporate executives remember the protests staged against Upjohn in the 1970s when that company agreed to produce prostaglandins. Likewise, the national disgust at the harrowing late-term-abortion procedure is very similar to the horror following the arrest and conviction of Dr. Kenneth Edelin in 1975 for manslaughter. (His conviction was eventually overturned.) His crime was performing a rare procedure called a hysterodomy. Bingham explained that the procedure entails "delivering the fetus by C-section—it was moving but was unable to breathe at this point and it was allowed to expire."

According to the polls, public opinion swings back and forth between revulsion at the procedures of abortion and insistence on a woman's right to one. We are nothing if not conflicted. In a 1990 Catholic Conference poll—typical of dozens of polls—60 percent of Americans believed that every "unborn child" has a right to life. At the same time, 69 percent believed that abortion should be legal

The same polls that show Americans deeply conflicted also show that when the national conversation is focused on the fetus, the squishy middle tends to express more antiabortion sentiments. But when the debate turns to women being harassed and deprived of the fundamental American right to make up one's own mind, the pendulum lumbers over to the other side. Political tacticians know this and try to engineer media controversies to work one way or the other at election time. That is why Jesse Helms stood in the well of the Senate and detailed over and over the visceral mechanics of a late-term abortion.

The procedure is profoundly upsetting. The image of that limp suspended fetus has not left me. By the time I traveled back home—two days later—I had trouble holding my eight-month-old daughter. That fetus appeared in my dreams, but then so did another arresting picture that surfaced, unbidden, from my mind's archives. It was the cover, I believe, of an issue of the *Village Voice* in the early 1980s. In black-and-white, it showed the hall of a hotel where illegal abortions were performed. On the floor lay a white woman, unnaturally pale—and naked. What made it especially scary to look at was that the normal length and elegance of her adult body were curled into a fetal ball, as if she were cold. But she and her fetus were dead.

The older doctors believe that a legal abortion has two benefits beyond eliminating such horrors. It gives poor women the same access to a safe procedure as middle-class women (who always had it, long before *Roe*, and, because they can afford a plane ticket or can find a friendly family doctor, always will). And because, these doctors believe, the existence of a safe, available procedure reduces the suffocating sense of desperation an unexpectedly pregnant woman feels, and heightens overall awareness of birth control, legalization actually results in fewer abortions.

There is good evidence to support this latter view. Chile, for example, has banned abortion, and the penalty can be stiff: up to five years in prison for the mother. Chile also has one of the highest per capita abortion rates in Latin America. Ireland, the only large Western European country to prohibit access, is thought to have an abortion rate higher than the Netherlands, where laws governing access have long been liberal.

The distinction between poor and well-off patients seeking abortions is another issue that tends to be discussed only among providers. "The problem in training doctors to perform abortions," Dr. William Rashbaum said, "is that the commitment to performing them has as much to do with the poor as with women." He described a certain doctor he had recently trained and then said: "He's a good doc, but he'll never stick with it. He doesn't have the commitment to the poor. I just don't see a lot of that these days."

To serve poorer women was why abortion clinics were developed nationwide in the first place, right after *Roe* became law. Hospitals charged up to $1,000 back then, which was too much for many women, particularly those still in school or in the inner cities. One consequence of the rise of these clinics (where abortions still cost only a few hundred dollars) was that the abortion procedure began to slip away from prestigious medical institutions into free-standing clinics. Today, for example, 7 percent of abortions are performed in hospitals, 4 percent in doctors' offices. The rest are performed in clinics.

"The institutions lost control and interest," Hausknecht said. "Academic physicians of major institutions had started doing abortions after *Roe* because they were the ones with access to new techniques. But if you look at them today, academic physicians are the most uninvolved group."

Now the clinics—cut off from medicine's protection, prestige, and research—have become part of abortion's problem. It's easy for doctors to think of the procedure as something outside medicine because the surgery is literally not happening around them. Many of these clinics are also being segregated into poor neighborhoods because terrified landlords in middle-class areas won't rent to them or because they need cheap rent to compensate for increased security costs. In many ways, the clinics are returning to a kind of back alley.

The vision of a new procedure or cutting-edge technology alleviating the problem is a chimera. What kind of patient will opt to have Hausknecht's methotrexate, RU486, or the new technique out of Houston that allows for an abortion within ten days of conception?

"They will be popular with educated women who have definite opinions about what they are doing," Rashbaum said. Few poorer women, he added, will be among the first to embrace these new, more private, more high-tech procedures. "The poor don't think about medical care until they are very uncomfortable," he said. "And pregnancy isn't that uncomfortable." The poor and the uneducated, his experience leads him to conclude, are the most likely to procrastinate, forcing themselves to consider abortion later, when finding a doctor willing to perform a second-trimester procedure is most difficult.

And if more and more middle-class women do choose pills, that would leave abortion clinics and abortion politics to our system's most politically enfeebled constituency—single, largely minority women. It is a bleak scenario, one in which abortions for the poor and abortion providers would be pushed even further into the shadows.

The passage of *Roe* v. *Wade* was a signal event for OB-GYNs practicing in 1973. But the watershed moment for a new generation of doctors was the spree of fatal shootings that began in 1993. Praise for saving women from illegal abortionists has been replaced by fear of helping another person exercise a constitutional right. Medicine has yielded to politics.

Rights are meant to be exercised in a clear light, in all towns and neighborhoods and cities, without fear of ostracism or physical harm. Antiabortion forces insist that abortion should be the exception. The medical establishment has been scared off, leaving the practical day-to-day work of abortion overwhelmingly to the same doctors who first pioneered it twenty-five years ago. Now these doctors are growing old, and there is the prospect of their not being replaced.

Should this happen, Americans would face a political conundrum, one we haven't really wrestled with in a long time. We're a little rusty at considering questions like this: Can people be said to possess a right if they're too afraid to exercise it?

PART TWO

ABORTION

and the Constitution

7

Roe v. Wade

The 1973 Supreme Court Decision on State Abortion Laws

Mr. Justice Blackmun delivered the opinion of the Court. . . .

We forthwith acknowledge our awareness of the sensitive and emotional nature of the abortion controversy, of the vigorous opposing views, even among physicians, and of the deep and seemingly absolute convictions that the subject inspires. One's philosophy, one's experiences, one's exposure to the raw edges of human existence, one's religious training, one's attitudes toward life and family and their values, and the moral standards one establishes and seeks to observe, are all likely to influence and to color one's thinking and conclusions about abortion.

In addition, population growth, pollution, poverty, and racial overtones tend to complicate and not to simplify the problem.

Our task, of course, is to resolve the issue by constitutional measurement, free of emotion and of predilection. . . .

Jane Roe,[1] a single woman who was residing in Dallas County, Texas, instituted this federal action in March 1970 against the District Attorney of the county. She sought a declaratory judgment that the Texas criminal abortion statutes were unconstitutional on their face and an injunction restraining the defendant* from enforcing the statutes.

Roe alleged that she was unmarried and pregnant; that she wished to terminate her pregnancy by an abortion "performed by a competent, licensed physician, under safe, clinical conditions"; that she was unable to get a "legal" abortion in Texas because her life did not appear to be threatened by the continuation of the pregnancy; and that she could not afford to

---

From *United States Reports*, vol. 410, pp. 113–178. Cases adjudged in the U.S. Supreme Court during the October Term, 1972.

*Here, the State of Texas—Eds.

travel to another jurisdiction in order to secure a legal abortion under safe conditions. She claimed that the Texas statutes were unconstitutionally vague and that they abridged her right of personal privacy, protected by the First, Fourth, Fifth, Ninth, and Fourteenth Amendments. By an amendment to her complaint Roe purported to sue "on behalf of herself and all other women" similarly situated. . . .

The principal thrust of appellant's* attack on the Texas statutes is that they improperly invade a right, said to be possessed by the pregnant woman, to choose to terminate her pregnancy. Appellant would discover this right in the concept of personal "liberty" embodied in the Fourteenth Amendment's Due Process Clause; or in personal, marital, familial, and sexual privacy said to be protected by the Bill of Rights. . . .

It perhaps is not generally appreciated that the restrictive criminal abortion laws in effect in a majority of States today are of relatively recent vintage. Those laws, generally proscribing abortion or its attempt at any time during pregnancy except when necessary to preserve the pregnant woman's life, are not of ancient or even of common-law origin. Instead, they derive from statutory changes effected, for the most part, in the latter half of the nineteenth century. . . .

It is undisputed that at common law, abortion performed *before* "quickening"—the first recognizable movement of the fetus *in utero*, appearing usually from the sixteenth to the eighteenth week of pregnancy—was not an indictable offense. . . .

Whether abortion of a *quick* fetus was a felony at common law, or even a lesser crime, is still disputed. . . . A recent review of the common-law precedents argues, however, that . . . even post-quickening abortion was never established as a common-law crime. . . .

It is thus apparent that at common law, at the time of the adoption of our Constitution, and throughout the major portion of the nineteenth century, abortion was viewed with less disfavor than under most American statutes currently in effect. Phrasing it another way, a woman enjoyed a substantially broader right to terminate a pregnancy than she does in most States today. At least with respect to the early stage of pregnancy, and very possibly without such a limitation, the opportunity to make this choice was present in this country well into the nineteenth century. Even later, the law continued for some time to treat less punitively an abortion procured in early pregnancy. . . .

Three reasons have been advanced to explain historically the enactment of criminal abortion laws in the nineteenth century and to justify their continued existence. It has been argued occasionally that these laws were the product of a Victorian social concern to discourage illicit sexual conduct. Texas, however, does not advance this justification in the present case, and it appears that no court or commentator has taken the argument seriously. . . .

---

*Roe's—Eds.

A second reason is concerned with abortion as a medical procedure. When most criminal abortion laws were first enacted, the procedure was a hazardous one for the woman. This was particularly true prior to the development of antisepsis. Antiseptic techniques, of course, were based on discoveries by Lister, Pasteur, and others first announced in 1867, but were not generally accepted and employed until about the turn of the century. Abortion mortality was high. Even after 1900, and perhaps until as late as the development of antibiotics in the 1940s, standard modem techniques such as dilatation and curettage* were not nearly so safe as they are today. Thus, it has been argued that a State's real concern in enacting a criminal abortion law was to protect the pregnant woman, that is, to restrain her from submitting to a procedure that placed her life in serious jeopardy.

Modern medical techniques have altered this situation. Appellants and various *amici*† refer to medical data indicating that abortion in early pregnancy, that is, prior to the end of the first trimester, although not without its risk, is now relatively safe. Mortality rates for women undergoing early abortions, where the procedure is legal, appear to be as low as or lower than the rates for normal childbirth. Consequently, any interest of the State in protecting the woman from an inherently hazardous procedure, except when it would be equally dangerous for her to forgo it, has largely disappeared. Of course, important state interests in the areas of health and medical standards do remain. The State has a legitimate interest in seeing to it that abortion, like any other medical procedure, is performed under circumstances that insure maximum safety for the patient. This interest obviously extends at least to the performing physician and his staff, to the facilities involved, to the availability of aftercare, and to adequate provision for any complication or emergency that might arise. The prevalence of high mortality rates at illegal "abortion mills" strengthens, rather than weakens, the State's interest in regulating the conditions under which abortions are performed. Moreover, the risk to the woman increases as her pregnancy continues. Thus, the State retains a definite interest in protecting the woman's own health and safety when an abortion is proposed at a late stage of pregnancy.

The third reason is the State's interest—some phrase it in terms of duty—in protecting prenatal life. Some of the argument for this justification rests on the theory that a new human life is present from the moment of conception. The State's interest and general obligation to protect life then extends, it is argued, to prenatal life. Only when the life of the pregnant mother herself is at stake, balanced against the life she carries within her, should the interest of the embryo or fetus not prevail. Logically, of course,

*Expanding the opening of the uterus and detaching the fetus from the uterine wall.—Eds.

†Legal briefs submitted by parties viewing themselves as "friends of the Court." These are often designed to provide valuable background information.—Eds.

a legitimate state interest in this area need not stand or fall on acceptance of the belief that life begins at conception or at some other point prior to live birth. In assessing the State's interest, recognition may be given to the less rigid claim that as long as at least *potential* life is involved, the State may assert interests beyond the protection of the pregnant woman alone.

Parties challenging state abortion laws have sharply disputed in some courts the contention that a purpose of these laws, when enacted, was to protect prenatal life. Pointing to the absence of legislative history to support the contention, they claim that most state laws were designed solely to protect the woman. Because medical advances have lessened this concern, at least with respect to abortion in early pregnancy, they argue that with respect to such abortions the laws can no longer be justified by any state interest. There is some scholarly support for this view of original purpose. The few state courts called upon to interpret their laws in the late nineteenth and early twentieth centuries did focus on the State's interest in protecting the woman's health rather than in preserving the embryo and fetus. . . .

The Constitution does not explicitly mention any right of privacy. In a line of decisions, however, going back perhaps as far as *Union Pacific R. Co.* v. *Botsford* (1891) . . . the Court has recognized that a right of personal privacy, or a guarantee of certain areas or zones of privacy, does exist under the Constitution. In varying contexts, the Court or individual Justices have, indeed, found at least the roots of that right in the First Amendment, . . . in the Fourth and Fifth Amendments, . . . in the Ninth Amendment, . . . or in the concept of liberty guaranteed by the first section of the Fourteenth Amendment. . . . These decisions make it clear that only personal rights that can be deemed "fundamental" or "implicit in the concept of ordered liberty" . . . are included in this guarantee of personal privacy. They also make it clear that the right has some extension to activities relating to marriage, . . . procreation, . . . contraception, . . . family relationships, . . . and child rearing and education. . . .

This right of privacy, whether it be founded in the Fourteenth Amendment's concept of personal liberty and restrictions upon state action, as we feel it is, or, as the District Court determined, in the Ninth Amendment's reservation of rights to the people, is broad enough to encompass a woman's decision whether or not to terminate her pregnancy. The detriment that the State would impose upon the pregnant woman by denying this choice altogether is apparent. Specific and direct harm medically diagnosable even in early pregnancy may be involved. Maternity, or additional offspring, may force upon the woman a distressful life and future. Psychological harm may be imminent. Mental and physical health may be taxed by child care. There is also the distress, for all concerned, associated with the unwanted child, and there is the problem of bringing a child into a family already unable, psychologically and otherwise, to care for it. In other cases, as in this one, the additional difficulties and continuing stigma of unwed motherhood may be involved. All these are factors the woman and her responsible physician necessarily consider in consultation.

On the basis of elements such as these, appellant and some *amici* argue that the woman's right is absolute and that she is entitled to terminate her pregnancy at whatever time, in whatever way, and for whatever reason she alone chooses. With this we do not agree. Appellant's arguments that Texas either has no valid interest at all in regulating the abortion decision, or no interest strong enough to support any limitation upon the woman's sole determination, are unpersuasive. The Court's decisions recognizing a right of privacy also acknowledge that some state regulation in areas protected by that right is appropriate. As noted above, a State may properly assert important interests in safeguarding health, in maintaining medical standards, and in protecting potential life. At some point in pregnancy, these respective interests become sufficiently compelling to sustain regulation of the factors that govern the abortion decision. The privacy right involved, therefore, cannot be said to be absolute. In fact, it is not clear to us that the claim asserted by some *amici* that one has an unlimited right to do with one's body as one pleases bears a close relationship to the right of privacy previously articulated in the Court's decisions. The Court has refused to recognize an unlimited right of this kind in the past. . . .

We, therefore, conclude that the right of personal privacy includes the abortion decision, but that this right is not unqualified and must be considered against important state interests in regulation.

We note that those federal and state courts that have recently considered abortion law challenges have reached the same conclusion. . . .

Although the results are divided, most of these courts have agreed that the right of privacy, however based, is broad enough to cover the abortion decision; that the right, nonetheless, is not absolute and is subject to some limitations; and that at some point the state interests as to protection of health, medical standards, and prenatal life, become dominant. We agree with this approach. . . .

The appellee* and certain *amici* argue that the fetus is a "person" within the language and meaning of the Fourteenth Amendment. In support of this, they outline at length and in detail the well-known facts of fetal development. If this suggestion of personhood is established, the appellant's† case, of course, collapses, for the fetus's right to life would then be guaranteed specifically by the Amendment. The appellant conceded as much on reargument. On the other hand, the appellee conceded on reargument that no case could be cited that holds that a fetus is a person within the meaning of the Fourteenth Amendment.

The Constitution does not define "person" in so many words. Section 1

---

*The State of Texas—Eds.

†Roe's—Eds.

of the Fourteenth Amendment contains three references to "person." The first, in defining "citizens," speaks of "persons born or naturalized in the United States."The word also appears both in the Due Process Clause and in the Equal Protection Clause. "Person" is used in other places in the Constitution: in the listing of qualifications for Representatives and Senators, Art. 1, § 2, cl. 2, and § 3, cl. 3; in the Apportionment Clause, Art. 1, § 2, cl. 3; in the Migration and Importation provision, Art. 1, § 9, cl. 1; in the Emolument Clause, Art. 1, § 9, cl. 8; in the Electors provisions, Art. 11, § 1, cl. 2, and the superseded cl. 3; in the provision outlining qualifications for the office of President, Art. 11, § 1, cl. 5; in the Extradition provisions, Art. IV, § 2, cl. 2, and the superseded Fugitive Slave Clause 3; and in the Fifth, Twelfth, and Twenty-second Amendments as well as in §§ 2 and 3 of the Fourteenth Amendment. But in nearly all these instances, the use of the word is such that it has application only postnatally. None indicates, with any assurance, that it has any possible prenatal application.

All this, together with our observation, *supra*,* that throughout the major portion of the nineteenth century prevailing legal abortion practices were far freer than they are today, persuades us that the word "person," as used in the Fourteenth Amendment, does not include the unborn. . . .

We need not resolve the difficult question of when life begins. When those trained in the respective disciplines of medicine, philosophy, and theology are unable to arrive at any consensus, the judiciary, at this point in the development of man's knowledge, is not in a position to speculate as to the answer.

It should be sufficient to note briefly the wide divergence of thinking on this most sensitive and difficult question. There has always been strong support for the view that life does not begin until live birth. This was the belief of the Stoics. It appears to be the predominant, though not the unanimous, attitude of the Jewish faith. It may be taken to represent also the position of a large segment of the Protestant community, insofar as that can be ascertained; organized groups that have taken a formal position on the abortion issue have generally regarded abortion as a matter for the conscience of the individual and her family. As we have noted, the common law found greater significance in quickening. Physicians and their scientific colleagues have regarded that event with less interest and have tended to focus either upon conception, upon live birth, or upon the interim point at which the fetus becomes "viable," that is, potentially able to live outside the mother's womb, albeit with artificial aid. Viability is usually placed at about seven months (28 weeks) but may occur earlier, even at 24 weeks. The Aristotelian theory of "mediate animation," that held sway throughout the Middle Ages and the Renaissance in Europe, continued to be official Roman Catholic dogma until the nineteenth century, despite opposition to this

---

*Common reference term in legal briefs. It means "cited above."—Eds.

"ensoulment" theory from those in the Church who would recognize the existence of life from the moment of conception. The latter is now, of course, the official belief of the Catholic Church. As one brief *amicus* discloses, this is a view strongly held by many non-Catholics as well, and by many physicians. Substantial problems for precise definition of this view are posed, however, by new embryological data that purport to indicate that conception is a "process" over time, rather than an event, and by new medical techniques such as menstrual extraction, the "morning-after" pill, implantation of embryos, artifical insemination, and even artificial wombs.

In areas other than criminal abortion, the law has been reluctant to endorse any theory that life, as we recognize it, begins before live birth or to accord legal rights to the unborn except in narrowly defined situations and except when the rights are contingent upon live birth. For example, the traditional rule of tort law denied recovery for prenatal injuries even though the child was born alive. That rule has been changed in almost every jurisdiction. In most States, recovery is said to be permitted only if the fetus was viable, or at least quick, when the injuries were sustained, though few courts have squarely so held. In a recent development, generally opposed by the commentators, some States permit the parents of a stillborn child to maintain an action for wrongful death because of prenatal injuries. Such an action, however, would appear to be one to vindicate the parents' interest and is thus consistent with the view that the fetus, at most, represents only the potentiality of life. Similarly, unborn children have been recognized as acquiring rights or interests by way of inheritance or other devolution of property, and have been represented by guardians *ad litem*.* Perfection of the interests involved, again, has generally been contingent upon live birth. In short, the unborn have never been recognized in the law as persons in the whole sense.

In view of all this, we do not agree that, by adopting one theory of life, Texas may override the rights of the pregnant woman that are at stake. We repeat, however, that the State does have an important and legitimate interest in preserving and protecting the health of the pregnant woman, whether she be a resident of the State or a nonresident who seeks medical consultation and treatment there, and that it has still *another* important and legitimate interest in protecting the potentiality of human life. These interests are separate and distinct. Each grows in substantiality as the woman approaches term and, at a point during pregnancy, each becomes "compelling."

With respect to the State's important and legitimate interest in the health of the mother, the "compelling" point, in the light of present medical knowledge, is at approximately the end of the first trimester. This is so because of the now-established medical fact . . . that until the end of the first trimester mortality in abortion may be less than mortality in normal

*For the duration of a legal proceeding.—Eds.

childbirth. It follows that, from and after this point, a State may regulate the abortion procedure to the extent that the regulation reasonably relates to the preservation and protection of maternal health. Examples of permissible state regulation in this area are requirements as to the qualifications of the person who is to perform the abortion; as to the licensure of that person; as to the facility in which the procedure is to be performed, that is, whether it must be a hospital or may be a clinic or some other place of less-than-hospital status; as to the licensing of the facility; and the like.

This means, on the other hand, that, for the period of pregnancy prior to this "compelling" point, the attending physician, in consultation with his patient, is free to determine, without regulation by the State, that, in his medical judgment, the patient's pregnancy should be terminated. If that decision is reached, the judgment may be effectuated by an abortion free of interference by the State.

With respect to the State's important and legitimate interest in potential life, the "compelling" point is at viability. This is so because the fetus then presumably has the capability of meaningful life outside the mother's womb. State regulation protective of fetal life after viability thus has both logical and biological justifications. If the State is interested in protecting fetal life after viability, it may go so far as to proscribe abortion during that period, except when it is necessary to preserve the life or health of the mother. . . .

To summarize and to repeat:

1. A state criminal abortion statute of the current Texas type, that excepts from criminality only a *life-saving* procedure on behalf of the mother, without regard to pregnancy state and without recognition of the other interests involved, is violative of the Due Process Clause of the Fourteenth Amendment.

(a) For the stage prior to approximately the end of the first trimester, the abortion decision and its effectuation must be left to the medical judgment of the pregnant woman's attending physician.

(b) For the stage subsequent to approximately the end of the first trimester, the State, in promoting its interest in the health of the mother, may, if it chooses, regulate the abortion procedure in ways that are reasonably related to maternal health.

(c) For the stage subsequent to viability, the State in promoting its interest in the potentiality of human life may, if it chooses, regulate, and even proscribe, abortion except where it is necessary, in appropriate medical judgment, for the preservation of the life or health of the mother.

* * *

The decision leaves the State free to place increasing restrictions on abortion as the period of pregnancy lengthens, so long as those restrictions are tailored to the recognized state interests. The decision vindicates the right of the physician to administer medical treatment according to his professional judgment up to the points where important state interests provide compelling justifications for intervention. Up to those points, the abortion decision in all its aspects is inherently, and primarily, a medical decision, and basic responsibility for it must rest with the physician. If an individual practitioner abuses the privilege of exercising proper medical judgment, the usual remedies, judicial and intra-professional, are available. . . .

Mr. Justice White, with whom Mr. Justice Rehnquist joins, dissenting.[2]

At the heart of the controversy in these cases are those recurring pregnancies that pose no danger whatsoever to the life or health of the mother but are, nevertheless, unwanted for any one or more of a variety of reasons—convenience, family planning, economics, dislike of children, the embarrassment of illegitimacy, etc. The common claim before us is that for any one of such reasons, or for no reason at all, and without asserting or claiming any threat to life or health, any woman is entitled to an abortion at her request if she is able to find a medical advisor willing to undertake the procedure.

The Court for the most part sustains this position: During the period prior to the time the fetus becomes viable, the Constitution of the United States values the convenience, whim, or caprice of the putative mother more than the life or potential life of the fetus; the Constitution, therefore, guarantees the right to an abortion as against any state law or policy seeking to protect the fetus from an abortion not prompted by more compelling reasons of the mother.

With all due respect, I dissent. I find nothing in the language or history of the Constitution to support the Court's judgment. The Court simply fashions and announces a new constitutional right for pregnant mothers and, with scarcely any reason or authority for its action, invests that right with sufficient substance to override most existing state abortion statutes. The upshot is that the people and the legislatures of the fifty States are constitutionally disentitled to weigh the relative importance of the continued existence and development of the fetus, on the one hand, against a spectrum of possible impacts on the mother, on the other hand. As an exercise of raw judicial power, the Court perhaps has authority to do what it does today; but in my view its judgment is an improvident and extravagant exercise of the power of judicial review that the Constitution extends to this Court.

The Court apparently values the convenience of the pregnant mother more than the continued existence and development of the life or potential life that she carries. Whether or not I might agree with that marshaling of values, I can in no event join the Court's judgment, because I find no constitutional warrant for imposing such an order of priorities on the people and legislatures of the States. In a sensitive area such as this, involving as it does issues over which reasonable men may easily and heatedly differ, I cannot accept the Court's exercise of its clear power of choice by interposing a constitutional barrier to state efforts to protect human life and by investing mothers and doctors with the constitutionally protected right to exterminate it. This issue, for the most part, should be left with the people and to the political processes the people have devised to govern their affairs.

It is my view, therefore, that the Texas statute is not constitutionally infirm because it denies abortions to those who seek to serve only their convenience rather than to protect their life or health. . . .

Notes

1. The name is a pseudonym.

2. This dissent was written in response to the Supreme Court's decision in *Doe* v. *Bolton*, but it was explicitly stated by the authors that the dissenting statement also applied to *Roe* v. *Wade*.

8

Webster v. Reproductive Health Services

In its decision of July 3, 1989, the United States Supreme Court reversed a decision of the United States Court of Appeals for the Eighth Circuit. The Court of Appeals had itself upheld the decision of a Federal District Court. The case involved a 1986 Missouri law regulating abortion. The preamble to the Missouri statute states that "the life of each human being begins at conception" and that "unborn children have protectable interests in life, health, and well-being." Key provisions of the law (1) prohibit the use of public employees and facilities to perform abortions not necessary to save the life of the mother and (2) specify that the physician, when having reason to believe that the woman is carrying a fetus of at least twenty weeks of gestational age, must adopt procedures necessary to determine the viability of the unborn child. This second provision is the highly controversial section 188.029 of the Missouri law. In the published opinions of the justices, this section is frequently referred to by number. The controversy over section 188.029 concerns the extent to which it mandates medical tests to determine viability of the fetus and the extent to which it modifies the Court's ruling in* Roe *v.* Wade *(1973).*

In the written opinions of the justices, when "court" is written with a lowercase "c, reference is to the District Court or the Eighth Circuit Court of Appeals. When "Court" is written with an uppercase "C, " reference is to the Supreme Court.—Eds.

Chief Justice Rehnquist announced the judgment of the Court and delivered the opinion of the Court. . . .

---

*What follows are excerpts of the plurality decision of the Court, in which Chief Justice Rehnquist delivered the judgment of the Court, joined in part by Justices White and Kennedy. Justices O'Connor and Scalia concurred with the judgment and concurred in part with the opinion, while Justices Blackmun, Brennan, Marshall, and Stevens dissented in part. (No. 88-605) Internal reference citations and footnotes have been deleted.—Eds.

This appeal concerns the constitutionality of a Missouri statute regulating the performance of abortions. The United States Court of Appeals for the Eighth Circuit struck down several provisions of the statute on the ground that they violated this Court's decision in *Roe* v. *Wade*. . . . We . . . now reverse [the decision of the Court of Appeals].

I

In June 1986, the Governor of Missouri signed into law [an act] . . . which amended existing state law concerning unborn children and abortions. The Act consisted of 20 provisions, 5 of which are now before the Court. The first provision, or preamble, contains "findings" by the state legislature that "[t]he life of each human being begins at conception," and that "unborn children have protectable interests in life, health, and well-being." The Act further requires that all Missouri laws be interpreted to provide unborn children with the same rights enjoyed by other persons, subject to the Federal Constitution and this Court's precedents. Among its other provisions, the Act requires that, prior to performing an abortion on any woman whom a physician has reason to believe is 20 or more weeks pregnant, the physician ascertain whether the fetus is viable by performing "such medical examinations and tests as are necessary to make a finding of the gestational age, weight, and lung maturity of the unborn child" (§ 188.029). The Act also prohibits the use of public employees and facilities to perform or assist abortions not necessary to save the mother's life, and it prohibits the use of public funds, employees, or facilities for the purpose of "encouraging or counseling" a woman to have an abortion not necessary to save her life (§§ 188.205, 188.210, 188.215).

In July 1986, five health professionals employed by the State and two nonprofit corporations brought this class action in the United States District Court for the Western District of Missouri to challenge the constitutionality of the Missouri statute. Plaintiffs, appellees in this Court,* sought declaratory and injunctive relief on the ground that certain statutory provisions violated the First, Fourth, Ninth, and Fourteenth Amendments to the Federal Constitution. They asserted violations of various rights, including the "privacy rights of pregnant women seeking abortions"; the "woman's right to an abortion"; the "righ[t] to privacy in the physician-patient relationship"; the physician's "righ[t] to practice medicine"; the pregnant woman's "right to life due to inherent risks involved in childbirth"; and the woman's right to "receive . . . adequate medical advice and treatment" concerning abortions.

Plaintiffs filed this suit "on their own behalf and on behalf of the entire class consisting of facilities and Missouri licensed physicians or other health

*Reproductive Health Services—Eds.

care professionals offering abortion services or pregnancy counseling and on behalf of the entire class of pregnant females seeking abortion services or pregnancy counseling within the State of Missouri." The two nonprofit corporations are Reproductive Health Services, which offers family planning and gynecological services to the public, including abortion services up to 22 weeks "gestational age," and Planned Parenthood of Kansas City, which provides abortion services up to 14 weeks gestational age. The individual plaintiffs are three physicians, one nurse, and a social worker. All are "public employees" at "public facilities" in Missouri, and they are paid for their services with "public funds." . . . The individual plaintiffs, within the scope of their public employment, encourage and counsel pregnant women to have nontherapeutic abortions. Two of the physicians perform abortions. . . . Following a 3-day trial in December 1986, the District Court declared seven provisions of the Act unconstitutional and enjoined their enforcement. . . . The Court of Appeals for the Eighth Circuit affirmed [the judgment of the District Court], with one exception not relevant to this appeal.

II

Decision of this case requires us to address four sections of the Missouri Act: (a) the preamble; (b) the prohibition on the use of public facilities or employees to perform abortions; (c) the prohibition on public funding of abortion counseling; and (d) the requirement that physicians conduct viability tests prior to performing abortions. We address these *seriatim*.

A

The Act's preamble, as noted, sets forth "findings" by the Missouri legislature that "[tlhe life of each human being begins at conception," and that "[u]nborn children have protectable interests in life, health, and well-being" (Missouri Revised Statute §§ 1.205.1[1], [2] [1986]). The Act then mandates that state laws be interpreted to provide unborn children with "all the rights, privileges, and immunities available to other persons, citizens, and residents of this state," subject to the Constitution and this Court's precedents (§ 1.205.2). . . .

The State contends that the preamble itself is precatory and imposes no substantive restrictions on abortions, and that appellees therefore do not have standing to challenge it. Appellees, on the other hand, insist that the preamble is an operative part of the Act intended to guide the interpretation of other provisions of the Act. They maintain, for example, that the preamble's definition of life may prevent physicians in public hospitals from dispensing certain forms of contraceptives, such as the intrauterine device.

In our view, . . . the preamble does not by its terms regulate abortion or any other aspect of appellees' medical practice. The Court has emphasized that *Roe* v. *Wade* "implies no limitation on the authority of a State to make a value judgment favoring childbirth over abortion."The preamble can be read simply to express that sort of value judgment.

We think the extent to which the preamble's language might be used to interpret other state statutes or regulations is something that only the courts of Missouri can definitively decide. . . . It will be time enough for federal courts to address the meaning of the preamble should it he applied to restrict the activities of appellees in some concrete way. Until then, this Court "is not empowered to decide . . . abstract propositions, or to declare, for the government of future cases, principles or rules of law which cannot affect the result as to the thing in issue in the case before it." We therefore need not pass on the constitutionality of the Act's preamble.

B

Section 188.210 provides that "[i]t shall be unlawful for any public employee within the scope of his employment to perform or assist an abortion, not necessary to save the life of the mother," while § 188.215 makes it "unlawful for any public facility to be used for the purpose of performing or assisting an abortion not necessary to save the life of the mother."The Court of Appeals held that these provisions contravened this Court's abortion decisions. We take the contrary view.

As we said earlier this Term in *DeShaney* v. *Winnebago County Dept. of Social Services*, "our cases have recognized that the Due Process Clauses generally confer no affirmative right to governmental aid, even where such aid may be necessary to secure life, liberty, or property interests of which the government itself may not deprive the individual." In *Maher* v. *Roe*, the Court upheld a Connecticut welfare regulation under which Medicaid recipients received payments for medical services related to childbirth, but not for nontherapeutic abortions. The Court rejected the claim that this unequal subsidization of childbirth and abortion was impermissible under *Roe* v. *Wade*. As the Court put it:

> The Connecticut regulation before us is different in kind from the laws invalidated in our previous abortion decisions. The Connecticut regulation places no obstacles—absolute or otherwise—in the pregnant woman's path to an abortion. An indigent woman who desires an abortion suffers no disadvantage as a consequence of Connecticut's decision to fund childbirth; she continues as before to dependent on private sources for the service she desires. The State may have made childbirth a more attractive alternative, thereby influencing the woman's decision, but it has imposed no

> restriction on access to abortions that was not already there. The indigency that may make it difficult—and in some cases, perhaps, impossible—for some women to have abortions is neither created nor in any way affected by the Connecticut regulation.

Relying on *Maher*, the Court in *Poelker* v. *Doe*, held that the city of St. Louis committed "no constitutional violation . . . in electing, as a policy choice, to provide publicly financed hospital services for childbirth without providing corresponding services for nontherapeutic abortions."

More recently, in *Harris* v. *McRae*, the Court upheld "the most restrictive version of the Hyde Amendment," which withheld from States federal funds under the Medicaid program to reimburse the costs of abortions, " 'except where the life of the mother would be endangered if the fetus were carried to term.' " . . .

Missouri's refusal to allow public employees to perform abortions in public hospitals leaves a pregnant woman with the same choices as if the State had chosen not to operate any public hospitals at all. The challenged provisions only restrict a woman's ability to obtain an abortion to the extent that she chooses to use a physician affiliated with a public hospital. This circumstance is more easily remedied, and thus considerably less burdensome, than indigency, which "may make it difficult—and in some cases, perhaps, impossible—for some women to have abortions" without public funding. Having held that the State's refusal to fund abortions does not violate *Roe* v. *Wade*, it strains logic to reach a contrary result for the use of public facilities and employees. If the State may "make a value judgment favoring childbirth over abortion and . . . implement that judgment by the allocation of public funds," surely it may do so through the allocation of other public resources, such as hospitals and medical staff.

. . . Nothing in the Constitution requires States to enter or remain in the business of performing abortions. Nor, as appellees suggest, do private physicians and their patients have some kind of constitutional right of access to public facilities for the performance of abortions. . . .

Thus we uphold the Act's restrictions on the use of public employees and facilities for the performance or assistance of nontherapeutic abortions.

C

The Missouri Act contains three provisions relating to "encouraging or counseling a woman to have an abortion not necessary to save her life." Section 188.205 states that no public funds can be used for this purpose; § 188.210 states that public employees cannot, within the scope of their employment, engage in such speech; and § 188.215 forbids such speech in public facilities. The Court of Appeals did not consider § 188.205 separately from

§§ 188.210 and 188.215. It held that all three of these provisions were unconstitutionally vague, and that "the ban on using public funds, employees, and facilities to encourage or counsel a woman to have an abortion is an unacceptable infringement of the woman's fourteenth amendment right to chose an abortion after receiving the medical information necessary to exercise the right knowingly and intelligently."

Missouri has chosen only to appeal the Court of Appeals' invalidation of the public funding provision, § 188.205. A threshold question is whether this provision reaches primary conduct, or whether it is simply an instruction to the State's fiscal officers not to allocate funds for abortion counseling. We accept, for purposes of decision, the State's claim that § 188.205 "is not directed at the conduct of any physician or health care provider, private or public," but "is directed solely at those persons responsible for expending public funds." . . .

D

Section 188.029 of the Missouri Act provides:

> Before a physician performs an abortion on a woman he has reason to believe is carrying an unborn child of twenty or more weeks gestational age, the physician shall first determine if the unborn child is viable by using and exercising that degree of care, skill, and proficiency commonly exercised by the ordinarily skillful, careful, and prudent physician engaged in similar practice under the same or similar conditions. In making this determination of viability, the physician shall perform or cause to be performed such medical examinations and tests as are necessary to make a finding of the gestational age, weight, and lung maturity of the unborn child and shall enter such findings and determination of viability in the medical record of the mother.

As with the preamble, the parties disagree over the meaning of this statutory provision. The State emphasizes the language of the first sentence, which speaks in terms of the physician's determination of viability being made by the standards of ordinary skill in the medical profession. Appellees stress the language of the second sentence, which prescribes such "tests as are necessary" to make a finding of gestational age, fetal weight, and lung maturity.

The Court of Appeals read § 188.029 as requiring that after 20 weeks "doctors *must* perform tests to find gestational age, fetal weight, and lung maturity."The court indicated that the tests needed to determine fetal weight at 20 weeks are "unreliable and inaccurate" and would add $125 to $250 to the cost of an abortion. It also stated that "amniocentesis, the only method available to determine lung maturity, is contrary to accepted medical practice until 28–30 weeks of gestation, expensive, and imposes significant health risks for both the pregnant woman and the fetus."

We must first determine the meaning of § 188.029 under Missouri law. Our usual practice is to defer to the lower court's construction of a state statute, but we believe the Court of Appeals has "fallen into plain error" in this case. . . .

We think the viability-testing provision makes sense only if the second sentence is read to require only those tests that are useful to making subsidiary findings as to viability. If we construe this provision to require a physician to perform those tests needed to make the three specified findings *in all circumstances*, including when the physician's reasonable professional judgment indicates that the tests would be irrelevant to determining viability or even dangerous to the mother and the fetus, the second sentence of § 188.029 would conflict with the first sentence's *requirement* that a physician apply his reasonable professional skill and judgment. It would also be incongruous to read this provision, especially the word "necessary," to require the performance of tests irrelevant to the expressed statutory purpose of determining viability. It thus seems clear to us that the Court of Appeals' construction of § 188.029 violates well-accepted canons of statutory interpretation used in the Missouri courts. . . .

The viability-testing provision of the Missouri Act is concerned with promoting the State's interest in potential human life rather than in maternal health. Section 188.029 creates what is essentially a presumption of viability at 20 weeks, which the physician must rebut with tests indicating that the fetus is not viable prior to performing an abortion. It also directs the physician's determination as to viability by specifying consideration, if feasible, of gestational age, fetal weight, and lung capacity. The District Court found that "the medical evidence is uncontradicted that a 20-week fetus is not viable," and that "23 1/2 to 24 weeks gestation is the earliest point in pregnancy where a reasonable possibility of viability exists." But it also found that there may be a 4-week error in estimating gestational age, which supports testing at 20 weeks.

In *Roe* v. *Wade*, the Court recognized that the State has "important and legitimate" interests in protecting maternal health and in the potentiality of human life. During the second trimester, the State "may, if it chooses, regulate the abortion procedure in ways that are reasonably related to maternal health." After viability, when the State's interest in potential human life was held to become compelling, the State "may, if it chooses, regulate, and even proscribe, abortion except where it is necessary, in appropriate medical judgment, for the preservation of the life or health of the mother."

. . . To the extent that § 188.029 regulates the method for determining viability, it undoubtedly does superimpose state regulation on the medical determination of whether a particular fetus is viable. The Court of Appeals and the District Court thought it unconstitutional for this reason. To the extent that the viability tests increase the cost of what are in fact second-trimester abortions, their validity may also be questioned under *Akron*, where the Court held that a requirement that second trimester abortions must be performed in hospitals was invalid because it substantially increased the expense of those procedures.

We think that the doubt cast upon the Missouri statute by these cases is not so much a flaw in the statute as it is a reflection of the fact that the rigid trimester analysis of the course of a pregnancy enunciated in *Roe* has resulted in subsequent cases like *Colautti* and *Akron* making constitutional law in this area a virtual Procrustean bed. . . .

*Stare decisis** is a cornerstone of our legal system, but it has less power in constitutional cases, where, save for constitutional amendments, this Court is the only body to make needed changes. We have not refrained from reconsideration of a prior construction of the Constitution that has proved "unsound in principle and unworkable in practice." We think the *Roe* trimester framework falls into this category.

In the first place, the rigid *Roe* framework is hardly consistent with the notion of a Constitution cast in general terms, as ours is, and usually speaking in general principles, as our does. The key elements of the *Roe* framework—trimesters and viability—are not found in the text of the Constitution or in any place else one would expect to find a constitutional principle. Since the bounds of the inquiry are essentially indeterminate, the result has been a web of legal rules that have become increasingly intricate, resembling a code of regulations rather than a body of constitutional doctrine. As Justice White has put it, the trimester framework has left this Court to serve as the country's "*ex officio* medical board with powers to approve or disapprove medical and operative practices and standards throughout the United States."

In the second place, we do not see why the State's interest in protecting potential human life should come into existence only at the point of viability, and that there should therefore be a rigid line allowing state regulation after viability but prohibiting it before viability. . . .

The tests that § 188.029 requires the physician to perform are designed to determine viability. The State here has chosen viability as the point at which its interest in potential human life must be safeguarded. See Missouri Revised Statute § 188.030 (1986) "No abortion of a viable unborn child shall be performed unless necessary to preserve the life or health of the woman." It is true that the tests in question increase the expense of abortion, and regulate the discretion of the physician in determining the viability of the fetus. Since the tests will undoubtedly show in many cases that the fetus is not viable, the tests will have been performed for what were in fact second-trimester abortions. But we are satisfied that the requirement of these tests permissibly furthers the State's interest in protecting potential human fife, and we therefore believe § 188.029 to be constitutional.

---

*Refers to the judicial principle that prior decisions of the Court should stand, i.e., not be overturned unless warranted on compelling constitutional grounds.—Eds.

. . . The Missouri testing requirement here is reasonably designed to ensure that abortions are not performed where the fetus is viable—an end which all concede is legitimate—and that is sufficient to sustain its constitutionality. . . .

III

Both appellants and the United States as *Amicus Curiae* have urged that we overrule our decision in *Roe* v. *Wade*. The facts of the present case, however, differ from those at issue in *Roe*. Here, Missouri has determined that viability is the point at which its interest in potential human life must be safeguarded. In *Roe*, on the other hand, the Texas statute criminalized the performance of *all* abortions, except when the mother's life was at stake. This case therefore affords us no occasion to revisit the holding of *Roe*, which was that the Texas statute unconstitutionally infringed the right to an abortion derived from the Due Process Clause. To the extent indicated in our opinion, we would modify and narrow *Roe* and succeeding cases.

Because none of the challenged provisions of the Missouri Act properly before us conflict with the Constitution, the judgment of the Court of Appeals is reversed.

Justice O'Connor, concurring in part and concurring in the judgment.

I concur in Parts I, II—A, II—B, and II—C of the Court's opinion.

I

Nothing in the record before us . . . indicates that . . . the preamble to Missouri's abortion regulation statute will affect a woman's decision to have an abortion. Justice Stevens . . . suggests that the preamble may also "interfere[] with contraceptive choices," because certain contraceptive devices act on a female ovum after it has been fertilized by a male sperm. The Missouri Act defines "conception" as "the fertilization of the ovum of a female by a sperm of a male," and invests "unborn children" with "protectable interests in life, health, and well-being," from "the moment of conception. . . ." . . . Similarly, certain *amici* suggest that the Missouri Act's preamble may prohibit the developing technology of *in vitro* fertilization, a technique used to aid couples otherwise unable to bear children in which a number of ova are removed from the woman and fertilized by male sperm. This process often produces excess fertilized ova ("unborn children" under the Missouri Act's definition) that are discarded rather than reinserted into the woman's uterus. It may be correct that the use of postfertilization contraceptive devices is constitutionally protected by *Griswold* and its progeny but, as with a woman's abortion decision, nothing in the record or the opinions below indicates that the preamble will affect a woman's decision to practice contraception. For that matter, nothing in appellees' original complaint . . . [indicates] that appellees sought to enjoin potential violations of *Griswold*. Neither is there any indication of the possibility that the preamble might be applied to prohibit the performance of *in vitro* fertilization. I agree with the Court, therefore, that all of these intimations of unconstitutionality are simply too hypothetical to support the use of declaratory judgment procedures and injunctive remedies in this case. . . .

II

In its interpretation of Missouri's "determination of viability" provision, . . . the plurality has proceeded in a manner unnecessary to deciding the question at hand. I agree with the plurality that it was plain error for the Court of Appeals to interpret the second sentence of Missouri Revised Statute § 188.029 as meaning that "doctors *must* perform tests to find gestational age, fetal weight, and lung maturity." . . .

Unlike the plurality, I do not understand these viability testing requirements to conflict with any of the Court's past decisions concerning state regulation of abortion. Therefore, there is no necessity to accept the State's invitation to reexamine the constitutional validity of *Roe* v. *Wade*. Where there is no need to decide a constitutional question, it is a venerable principle of this Court's adjudicatory processes not to do so for "[t]he Court will not 'anticipte a question of constitutional law in advance of the necessity of deciding it.' " Quite simply, "[i]t is not the habit of the court to decide questions of a constitutional nature unless absolutely necessary to a decision of the case." The Court today has accepted the State's every interpretation of its abortion statute and has upheld, under our existing precedents, every provision of that statute which is properly before us. Precisely for this reason reconsideration of *Roe* falls not into any "good-cause exception" to this "fundamental rule of judicial restraint. . . ." When the constitutional invalidity of a State's abortion statute actually turns on the constitutional validity of *Roe* v. *Wade*, there will be time enough to reexamine *Roe*. And to do so carefully. . . .

Justice Scalia, concurring in part and concurring in the judgment.

I join Parts I, II—A, II—B, and II—C of the opinion of the Chief Justice. As to Part II—D, I share Justice Blackmun's view, that it effectively would overrule *Roe* v. *Wade*. I think that should be done, but would do it more explicitly. Since today we contrive to avoid doing it, and indeed to avoid almost any decision of national import, I need to set forth my reasons, some of which have been well recited in dissents of my colleagues in other cases.

The outcome of today's case will doubtless be heralded as a triumph of judicial statesmanship. It is not that, unless it is statesmanlike needlessly to prolong this Court's self-awarded sovereignty over a field where it has little proper business since the answers to most of the cruel questions posed are political and not juridical—a sovereignty which therefore quite properly, but to the great damage of the Court, makes it the object of the sort of organized public pressure that political institutions in a democracy ought to receive.

Justice O'Connor's assertion that a "fundamental rule of judicial restraint" requires us to avoid reconsidering *Roe*, cannot be taken seriously. By finessing *Roe* we do not, as she suggests, adhere to the strict and venerable rule that we should avoid " 'decid[ing] questions of a constitutional nature.' " We have not disposed of this case on some statutory or procedural ground, but have decided, and could not avoid deciding, whether the Missouri statute meets the requirements of the United States Constitution. The only choice available is whether, in deciding that constitutional question, we should use *Roe* v. *Wade* as the benchmark, or something else. What is involved, therefore, is not the rule of avoiding constitutional issues where possible, but the quite separate principle that we will not " 'formulate a rule of constitutional law broader than is required by the precise facts to which it is to be applied.' " The latter is a sound general principle, but one often departed from when good reason exists. . . .

The Court has often spoken more broadly than needed in precisely the fashion at issue here, announcing a new rule of constitutional law. . . . It would be wrong, in any decision, to ignore the reality that our policy not to "formulate a rule of constitutional law broader than is required by the precise facts" has a frequently applied good-cause exception. But it seems particularly perverse to convert the policy into an absolute in the present case, in order to place beyond reach the inexpressibly "broader-than-was-required-by-theprecise-facts" structure established by *Roe* v. *Wade*.

The real question, then, is whether there are valid reasons to go beyond the most stingy possible holding today. It seems to me there are not only valid but compelling ones. Ordinarily, speaking no more broadly than is absolutely required avoids throwing settled law into confusion; doing so today preserves a chaos that is evident to anyone who can read and count. Alone sufficient to justify a broad holding is the fact that our retaining control through *Roe*, of what I believe to be, and many of our citizens recognize to be, a political issue, continuously distorts the public perception of the role of this Court. We can now look forward to at least another Term with carts full of mail from the public, and streets full of demonstrators, urging us—their unelected and life-tenured judges who have been awarded those extraordinary, undemocratic characteristics precisely in order that we might follow the law despite the popular will—to follow the popular will.

Indeed, I expect we can look forward to even more of that than before, given our indecisive decision today. . . .

It was an arguable question today whether § 188.029 of the Missouri law contravened this Court's understanding of *Roe* v. *Wade*, and I would have examined *Roe* rather than examining the contravention. Given the Court's newly contracted abstemiousness, what will it take, one must wonder, to permit us to reach that fundamental question? The result of our vote today is that we will not reconsider that prior opinion, even if most of the Justices think it is wrong, unless we have before us a statute that in fact contradicts it—and even then (under our newly discovered "no-broader-than-necessary" requirement) only minor problematical aspects of *Roe* will be reconsidered, unless one expects State legislatures to adopt provisions whose compliance with *Roe* cannot even be argued with a straight face. It thus appears that the mansion of constitutionalized abortion-law, constructed overnight in *Roe* v. *Wade*, must be disassembled door-jamb by door-jamb, and never entirely brought down, no matter how wrong it may be.

Of the four courses we might have chosen today—to reaffirm *Roe*, to overrule it explicitly, to overrule it *sub silentio*, or to avoid the question—the last is the least responsible. On the question of the constitutionality of § 188.029, I concur in the judgment of the Court and strongly dissent from the manner in which it has been reached.

Justice Blackmun, with whom Justice Brennan and Justice Marshall join, concurring in part and dissenting in part.

Today, *Roe* v. *Wade*, and the fundamental constitutional right of women to decide whether to terminate a pregnancy, survive but are not secure. Although the Court extricates itself from this case without making a single, even incremental, change in the law of abortion, the plurality and Justice Scalia would overrule *Roe* (the first silently, the other explicitly) and would return to the States virtually unfettered authority to control the quintessentially intimate, personal, and life-directing decision whether to carry a fetus to term. Although today, no less than yesterday, the Constitution and the decisions of this Court prohibit a State from enacting laws that inhibit women from the meaningful exercise of that right, a plurality of this Court implicitly invites every state legislature to enact more and more restrictive abortion regulations in order to provoke more and more test cases, in the hope that sometime down the line the Court will return the law of procreative freedom to the severe limitations that generally prevailed in this country before January 22, 1973. Never in my memory has a plurality announced a judgment of this Court that so foments disregard for the law and for our standing decisions.

Nor in my memory has a plurality gone about its business in such a deceptive fashion. At every level of its review, from its effort to read the real meaning out of the Missouri statute, to its intended evisceration of precedents and its deafening silence about the constitutional protections that it would jettison, the plurality obscures the portent of its analysis. With feigned restraint, the plurality announces that its analysis leaves *Roe* "undisturbed," albeit "modif[ied] and narrow[ed]." But this disclaimer is totally meaningless. The plurality opinion is filled with winks, and nods, and knowing glances to those who would do away with *Roe* explicitly, but turns a stone face to anyone in search of what the plurality conceives as the scope of a woman's right under the Due Process Clause to terminate a pregnancy free from the coercive and brooding influence of the State. The simple truth is that *Roe* would not survive the plurality's analysis, and that the plurality provides no substitute for *Roe*'s protective umbrella.

I fear for the future. I fear for the liberty and equality of the millions of women who have lived and come of age in the 16 years since *Roe* was decided. I fear for the integrity of, and public esteem for, this Court.

I dissent.

I

. . . Although I . . . am especially disturbed by its misapplication of our past decisions in upholding Missouri's ban on the performance of abortions at "public facilities," the plurality's discussion of these provisions is merely prologue to the consideration of the statute's viability-testing requirement, § 188.029—the only section of the Missouri statute that the plurality construes as implicating *Roe* itself. There, tucked away at the end of its opinion, the plurality suggests a radical reversal of the law of abortion; and there, primarily I direct my attention.

In the plurality's view, the viability-testing provision imposes a burden on second-trimester abortions as a way of furthering the State's interest in protecting the potential life of the fetus. Since under the *Roe* framework, the State may not fully regulate abortion in the interest of potential life (as opposed to maternal health) until the third trimester, the plurality finds it necessary, in order to save the Missouri testing provision, to throw out *Roe*'s trimester framework. In flat contradiction to *Roe*, the plurality concludes that the State's interest in potential life is compelling before viability, and upholds the testing provision because it "permissibly furthers" that state interest. . . .

Having set up the conflict between § 188.029 and the *Roe* trimester framework, the plurality summarily discards *Roe*'s analytic core as "unsound in principle and unworkable in practice.'" . . .

The plurality opinion is far more remarkable for the arguments that it does not advance than for those that it does. The plurality does not even mention, much less join, the true jurisprudential debate underlying this case: whether the Constitution includes an "unenumerated" general right to privacy as recognized in many of our decisions, most notably *Griswold* v. *Connecticut*, and *Roe*, and, more specifically, whether and to what extent such a right to privacy extends to matters of childbearing and family life, including abortion. . . .

But rather than arguing that the text of the Constitution makes no mention of the right to privacy, the plurality complains that the critical elements of the *Roe* framework—trimesters and viability—do not appear in the Constitution and are, therefore, somehow inconsistent with a Constitution cast in general terms. Were this a true concern, we would have to abandon most of our constitutional jurisprudence. As the plurality well knows, or should know, the "critical elements" of countless constitutional doctrines nowhere appear in the Constitution's text. . . .

With respect to the *Roe* framework, the general constitutional principle, indeed the fundamental constitutional right, for which it was developed is the right to privacy. . . . It is this general principle, the " 'moral fact that a person belongs to himself and not others nor to society as a whole,' " . . . that is found in the Constitution. The trimester framework simply defines and limits that right to privacy in the abortion context to accommodate, not destroy, a State's legitimate interest in protecting the health of pregnant women and in preserving potential human life. Fashioning such accommodations between individual rights and the legitimate interests of government, establishing benchmarks and standards with which to evaluate the competing claims of individuals and government, lies at the very heart of constitutional adjudication. To the extent that the trimester framework is useful in this enterprise, it is not only consistent with constitutional interpretation, but necessary to the wise and just exercise of this Court's paramount authority to define the scope of constitutional rights.

The plurality next alleges that the result of the trimester framework has "been a web of legal rules that have become increasingly intricate, resembling a code of regulations rather than a body of constitutional doctrine." Again, if this were a true and genuine concern, we would have to abandon vast areas of our constitutional jurisprudence. . . .

Finally, the plurality asserts that the trimester framework cannot stand because the State's interest in potential life is compelling throughout pregnancy, not merely after viability. The opinion contains not one word of rationale for its view of the State's interest. This "it-is-so-because-we-say-so"jurisprudence constitutes nothing other than an attempted exercise of brute force; reason, much less persuasion, has no place.

In answering the plurality's claim that the State's interest in the fetus is uniform and compelling throughout pregnancy, I cannot improve upon what Justice Stevens has written [in *Thornburgh*]:

> I should think it obvious that the State's interest in the protection of an embryo—even if that interest is defined as "protecting those who will be citizens" . . . —increases progressively and dramatically as the organism's capacity to feel pain, to experience pleasure, to survive, and to react to its surroundings increases day by day. The development of a fetus—and pregnancy itself—are not static conditions, and the assertion that the government's interest is static simply ignores this reality. . . . [U]nless the religious view that a fetus is a "person" is adopted . . . there is a fundamental and well-recognized difference between a fetus and a human being; indeed, if there is not such a difference, the permissibility of terminating the life of a fetus could scarcely be left to the will of the state legislatures. And if distinctions may be drawn between a fetus and a human being in terms of the state interest in their protection—even though the fetus represents one of "those who will be citizens"—it seems to me quite odd to argue that distinctions may not also be drawn between the state interest in protecting the freshly fertilized egg and the state interest in protecting the 9-month-gestated, fully sentient fetus on the eve of birth. Recognition of this distinction is supported not only by logic, but also by history and by our shared experiences.

For my own part, I remain convinced, as six other Members of this Court 16 years ago were convinced, that the *Roe* framework, and the viability standard in particular, fairly, sensibly, and effectively functions to safeguard the constitutional liberties of pregnant women while recognizing and accommodating the State's interest in potential human life. The viability line reflects the biological facts and truths of fetal development; it marks that threshold moment prior to which a fetus cannot survive separate from the woman and cannot reasonably and objectively be regarded as a subject of rights or interests distinct from, or paramount to, those of the pregnant woman. At the same time, the viability standard takes account of the undeniable fact that as the fetus evolves into its postnatal form, and as it loses its dependence on the uterine environment, the State's interest in the fetus' potential human life, and in fostering a regard for human life in general, becomes compelling. As a practical matter, because viability follows "quickening"—the point at which a woman feels movement in her womb—and because viability occurs no earlier than 23 weeks gestational age, it establishes an easily applicable standard for regulating abortion while providing a pregnant woman ample time to exercise her fundamental right with her responsible physician to terminate her pregnancy. Although I have stated previously for a majority of this Court that "[c]onstitutional rights do not always have easily ascertainable boundaries," to seek and establish those boundaries remains the special responsibility of this Court. In *Roe*, we discharged that responsibility as logic and science compelled. The plurality today advances not one reasonable argument as to why our judgment in that case was wrong and should he abandoned.

Having contrived an opportunity to reconsider the *Roe* framework, and then having discarded that framework, the plurality finds the testing provision unobjectionable because it "permissibly furthers the State's interest in protecting potential human life." . . .

The "permissibly furthers" standard completely disregards the irreducible minimum of *Roe*: the Court's recognition that a woman has a limited fundamental constitutional right to decide whether to terminate a pregnancy. That right receives no meaningful recognition in the plurality's written opinion. Since, in the plurality's view, the State's interest in potential life is compelling as of the moment of conception, and is therefore served only if abortion is abolished, every hindrance to a woman's ability to obtain an abortion must be "permissible." Indeed, the more severe the hindrance, the more effectively (and permissibly) the State's interest would be furthered. A tax on abortions or a criminal prohibition would both satisfy the plurality's standard. So, for that matter, would a requirement that a pregnant woman memorize and recite today's plurality opinion before seeking an abortion.

The plurality pretends that *Roe* survives, explaining that the facts of this case differ from those in Roe: here, Missouri has chosen to assert its interest in potential life only at the point of viability, whereas, in *Roe*, Texas had asserted that interest from the point of conception, criminalizing all abortions, except where the life of the mother was at stake. This, of course, is a distinction without a difference. The plurality repudiates every principle for which *Roe* stands; in good conscience, it cannot possibly believe that *Roe* lies "undisturbed" merely because this case does not call upon the Court to reconsider the Texas statute, or one like it. If the Constitution permits a State to enact any statute that reasonably furthers its interest in potential life, and if that interest arises as of conception, why would the Texas statute fail to pass muster? One suspects that the plurality agrees. It is impossible to read the plurality opinion and especially its final paragraph, without recognizing its implicit invitation to every State to enact more and more restrictive abortion laws, and to assert their interest in potential life as of the moment of conception. All these laws will satisfy the plurality's nonscrutiny, until sometime, a new regime of old dissenters and new appointees will declare what the plurality intends: that *Roe* is no longer good law.

Thus, "not with a bang, but a whimper," the plurality discards a landmark case of the last generation, and casts into darkness the hopes and visions of every woman in this country who had come to believe that the Constitution guaranteed her the right to exercise some control over her unique ability to bear children. The plurality does so either oblivious or insensitive to the fact that millions of women, and their families, have ordered their lives around the right to reproductive choice, and that this right has become vital to the full participation of women in the economic and political walks of American life. The plurality would clear the way once again for government to force upon women the physical labor and specific and direct medical and psychological harms that may accompany carrying a fetus to term. The plurality would clear the way again for the State to conscript a woman's body and to force upon her a "distressful life and future."

The result, as we know from experience, would be that every year hundreds of thousands of women, in desperation, would defy the law, and place their health and safety in the unclean and unsympathetic hands of back-alley abortionists, or they would attempt to perform abortions upon themselves, with disastrous results. Every year, many women, especially poor and minority women, would die or suffer debilitating physical trauma, all in the name of enforced morality or religious dictates or lack of compassion, as it may be.

Of the aspirations and settled understandings of American women, of the inevitable and brutal consequences of what it is doing, the tough-approach plurality utters not a word. This silence is callous. It is also profoundly destructive of the Court as an institution. To overturn a constitutional decision is a rare and grave undertaking. To overturn a constitutional decision that secured a fundamental personal liberty to millions of persons would be unprecedented in our 200 years of constitutional history. Although the doctrine of *stare decisis* applies with somewhat diminished force in constitutional cases generally, even in ordinary constitutional cases "any departure from *stare decisis* demands special justification."This requirement of justification applies with unique force where, as here, the Court's abrogation of precedent would destroy people's firm belief, based on past decisions of this Court, that they possess an unabridgeable right to undertake certain conduct.

As discussed at perhaps too great length above, the plurality makes no serious attempt to carry "the heavy burden of persuading . . . that changes in society or in the law dictate" the abandonment of *Roe* and its numerous progeny, much less the greater burden of explaining the abrogation of a fundamental personal freedom. Instead, the plurality pretends that it leaves *Roe* standing, and refuses even to discuss the real issue underlying this case: whether the Constitution includes an unenumerated right to privacy that encompasses a woman's right to decide whether to terminate a pregnancy. To the extent that the plurality does criticize the *Roe* framework, these criticisms are pure *ipse dixit.*

This comes at a cost. The doctrine of *stare decisis* "permits society to assume that bedrock principles are founded in the law rather than in the proclivities of individuals, and thereby contributes to the integrity of our constitutional system of government, both in appearance and in fact." Today's decision involves the most politically divisive domestic legal issue of our time. By refusing to explain or to justify its proposed revolutionary revision in the law of abortion, and by refusing to abide not only by our precedents, but also by our canons for reconsidering those precedents, the plurality invites charges of cowardice and illegitimacy to our door. I cannot say that these would be undeserved.

For today, at least, the law of abortion stands undisturbed. For today, the women of this Nation still retain the liberty to control their destinies. But the signs are evident and very ominous, and a chill wind blows.

I dissent.

Justice Stevens, concurring in part and dissenting in part.

Having joined Part II—C of the Court's opinion, I shall not comment on § 188.205 of the Missouri statute. With respect to the challenged portions of §§ 188.210 and 188.215, I agree with Justice Blackmun that the record identifies a sufficient number of unconstitutional applications to support the Court of Appeals' judgment invalidating those provisions. The reasons why I would also affirm that court's invalidation of § 188.029, the viability testing provision, and §§ 1.205.1(1)(2) of the preamble, require separate explanation.

It seems to me that in Part II—D of its opinion, the plurality strains to place a construction on § 188.029 that enables it to conclude, "[W]e would modify and narrow *Roe* and succeeding cases." . . . I agree with the Court of Appeals and the District Court that the meaning of the second sentence of § 188.029 is too plain to be ignored. The sentence twice uses the mandatory term "shall," and contains no qualifying language. If it is implicitly limited to tests that are useful in determining viability, it adds nothing to the requirement imposed by the preceding sentence.

My interpretation of the plain language is supported by the structure of the statute as a whole, particularly the preamble, which "finds" that life "begins at conception" and further commands that state laws shall be construed to provide the maximum protection to "the unborn child at every stage of development." I agree with the District Court that "[o]bviously, the purpose of this law is to protect the potential life of the fetus, rather than safeguard maternal health." A literal reading of the statute tends to accomplish that goal. Thus it is not "incongruous" to assume that the Missouri Legislature was trying to protect the potential human life of nonviable fetuses by making the abortion decision more costly. On the contrary, I am satisfied that the Court of Appeals, as well as the District Court, correctly concluded that the Missouri Legislature meant exactly what it said in the second sentence of § 188.029. I am also satisfied, for the reasons stated by Justice Blackmun, that the testing provision is manifestly unconstitutional under *Williams* v. *Lee Optical Co.*, "irrespective of the *Roe* framework." . . .

To the extent that the Missouri statute interferes with contraceptive choices, I have no doubt that it is unconstitutional under the Court's holdings in *Griswold* v. *Connecticut*, *Eisenstadt* v. *Baird*, and *Carey* v. *Population Services International*. . . .

Indeed, I am persuaded that the absence of any secular purpose for the legislative declarations that life begins at conception and that conception occurs at fertilization makes the relevant portion of the preamble invalid under the Establishment Clause of the First Amendment to the Federal Constitution. This conclusion does not, and could not, rest on the fact that the statement happens to coincide with the tenets of certain religions, or on the fact that the legislators who voted to enact it may have been motivated by religious considerations. Rather, it rests on the fact that the preamble, an unequivocal endorsement of a religious tenet of some but by no means all Christian faiths, serves no identifiable secular purpose. That fact alone compels a conclusion that the statute violates the Establishment Clause. . . .

. . . The preamble to the Missouri statute endorses the theological position that there is the same secular interest in preserving the life of a fetus during the first 40 or 80 days of pregnancy as there is after viability—indeed, after the time when the fetus has become a "person" with legal rights protected by the Constitution. To sustain that position as a matter of law, I believe Missouri has the burden of identifying the secular interests that differentiate the first 40 days of pregnancy from the period immediately before or after fertilization when, as *Griswold* and related cases establish, the Constitution allows the use of contraceptive procedures to prevent potential life from developing into full personhood. Focusing our attention on the first several weeks of pregnancy is especially appropriate because that is the period when the vast majority of abortions are actually performed.

As a secular matter, there is an obvious difference between the state interest in protecting the freshly fertilized egg and the state interest in protecting a 9-month-gestated, fully sentient fetus on the eve of birth. There can be no interest in protecting the newly fertilized egg from physical pain or mental anguish, because the capacity for such suffering does not yet exist; respecting a developed fetus, however, that interest is valid. . . .

The State's suggestion that the "finding" in the preamble to its abortion statute is , in effect, an amendment to its tort, property, and criminal law is not persuasive. The Court of Appeals concluded that the preamble "is simply an impermissible state adoption of a theory of when life begins to justify its abortion regulations." . . .

In my opinion the preamble to the Missouri statute is unconstitutional for two reasons. To the extent that it has substantive impact on the freedom to use contraceptive procedures, it is inconsistent with the central holding in *Griswold*. To the extent that it merely makes "legislative findings without operative effect," as the State argues, it violates the Establishment Clause of the First Amendment. . . .

9

Planned Parenthood of Southeastern Pennsylvania v. *Robert P. Casey*

Justice O'Connor, Justice Kennedy, and Justice Souter announced the judgment of the Court and delivered the opinion of the Court. . . .

I

Liberty finds no refuge in a jurisprudence of doubt. Yet nineteen years after our holding that the Constitution protects a woman's right to terminate her pregnancy in its early stages, *Roe* v. *Wade* (1973), that definition of liberty is still questioned. Joining the respondents as *amicus curiae*, the United States, as it has done in five other cases in the last decade, again asks us to overrule *Roe*. . . .

At issue in these cases are five provisions of the Pennsylvania Abortion Control Act of 1982 as amended in 1988 and 1989. . . . The act requires that a woman seeking an abortion give her informed consent prior to the abortion procedure, and specifies that she be provided with certain information at least twenty-four hours before the abortion is performed (§ 3205). For a minor to obtain an abortion, the act requires the informed consent of one of her parents, but provides for a judicial bypass option if the minor does not wish to or cannot obtain a parent's consent (§ 3206). Another provision of the act requires that, unless certain exceptions apply, a married woman seeking an abortion must sign a statement indicating that she has notified her husband of her intended abortion (§ 3209). The act exempts compliance with these three requirements in the event of a "medical emergency," which is

From *U.S. Supreme Court Reports* 112 S.C.T. 2791.

defined in § 3203 of the act. . . . In addition to the above provisions regulating the performance of abortions, the act imposes certain reporting requirements on facilities that provide abortion services [§§ 3207(b), 3214(a), 3214(f)].

Before any of these provisions took effect, the petitioners, who are five abortion clinics and one physician representing himself as well as a class of physicians who provide abortion services, brought this suit seeking declaratory and injunctive relief. Each provision was challenged as unconstitutional on its face. The District Court entered a preliminary injunction against the enforcement of the regulations, and, after a three-day bench trial, held all the provisions at issue here unconstitutional, entering a permanent injunction against Pennsylvania's enforcement of them. The Court of Appeals for the Third Circuit affirmed in part and reversed in part, upholding all of the regulations except for the husband notification requirement. We granted certiorari.

The Court of Appeals found it necessary to follow an elaborate course of reasoning even to identify the first premise to use to determine whether the statute enacted by Pennsylvania meets constitutional standards. And at oral argument in this Court, the attorney for the parties challenging the statute took the position that none of the enactments can be upheld without overruling *Roe* v. *Wade*. We disagree with that analysis; but we acknowledge that our decisions after *Roe* cast doubt upon the meaning and reach of its holding. Further, the Chief Justice admits that he would overrule the central holding of *Roe*. . . . State and federal courts as well as legislatures throughout the Union must have guidance as they seek to address this subject in conformance with the Constitution. Given these premises, we find it imperative to review once more the principles that define the rights of the woman and the legitimate authority of the State respecting the termination of pregnancies by abortion procedures.

After considering the fundamental constitutional questions resolved by *Roe*, principles of institutional integrity, and the rule of *stare decisis*, we are led to conclude this: the essential holding of *Roe* v. *Wade* should be retained and once again reaffirmed.

It must be stated at the outset and with clarity that *Roe*'s essential holding, the holding we reaffirm, has three parts. First is a recognition of the right of the woman to choose to have an abortion before viability and to obtain it without undue interference from the State. Before viability, the State's interests are not strong enough to support a prohibition of abortion or the imposition of a substantial obstacle to the woman's effective right to elect the procedure. Second is a confirmation of the State's power to restrict abortions after fetal viability, if the law contains exceptions for pregnancies which endanger a woman's life or health. And third is the principle that the State has legitimate interests from the outset of the pregnancy in protecting the health of the woman and the life of the fetus that may become a child. These principles do not contradict one another; and we adhere to each.

II

Constitutional protection of the woman's decision to terminate her pregnancy derives from the Due Process Clause of the Fourteenth Amendment. It declares that no State shall "deprive any person of life, liberty, or property, without due process of law." The controlling word in the case before us is "liberty." . . .

The most familiar of the substantive liberties protected by the Fourteenth Amendment are those recognized by the Bill of Rights. We have held that the Due Process Clause of the Fourteenth Amendment incorporates most of the Bill of Rights against the States. . . .

. . . It is a promise of the Constitution that there is a realm of personal liberty which the government may not enter. We have vindicated this principle before. Marriage is mentioned nowhere in the Bill of Rights and interracial marriage was illegal in most States in the nineteenth century, but the Court was no doubt correct in finding it to be an aspect of liberty protected against state interference by the substantive component of the Due Process Clause. . . .

Neither the Bill of Rights nor the specific practices of States at the time of the adoption of the Fourteenth Amendment marks the outer limits of the substantive sphere of liberty which the Fourteenth Amendment protects. . . . As the second Justice Harlan recognized:

> [T]he full scope of the liberty guaranteed by the Due Process Clause cannot be found in or limited by the precise terms of the specific guarantees elsewhere provided in the Constitution. This "liberty" is not a series of isolated points pricked out in terms of the taking of property; the freedom of speech, press, and religion; the right to keep and bear arms; the freedom from unreasonable searches and seizures; and so on. It is a rational continuum which, broadly speaking, includes a freedom from all substantial arbitrary impositions and purposeless restraints. . . .

In *Griswold*, we held that the Constitution does not permit a State to forbid a married couple to use contraceptives. That same freedom was later guaranteed, under the Equal Protection Clause, for unmarried couples. Constitutional protection was later extended to the sale and distribution of contraceptives. . . . It is settled now, as it was when the Court heard arguments in *Roe* v. *Wade*, that the Constitution places limits on a State's right to interfere with a person's most basic decisions about family and parenthood. . . .

The inescapable fact is that adjudication of substantive due process claims may call upon the Court in interpreting the Constitution to exercise that same capacity which by tradition courts always have exercised: reasoned judgment. Its boundaries are not susceptible of expression as a simple rule. That does not mean we are free to invalidate state policy choices with which we disagree; yet neither does it permit us to shrink from the duties of our office. As Justice Harlan observed:

> Due process has not been reduced to any formula; its content cannot be determined by reference to any code. The best that can be said is that through the course of this Court's decisions it has represented the balance which our Nation, built upon postulates of respect for the liberty of the individual, has struck between that liberty and the demands of organized society. If the supplying of content to this Constitutional concept has of necessity been a rational process, it certainly has not been one where judges have felt free to roam where unguided speculation might take them. The balance of which I speak is the balance struck by this country, having regard to what history teaches are the traditions from which it developed as well as the traditions from which it broke. That tradition is a living thing. A decision of this Court which radically departs from it could not long survive, while a decision which builds on what has survived is likely to be sound. No formula could serve as a substitute, in this area, for judgment and restraint.

Men and women of good conscience can disagree, and we suppose some always shall disagree, about the profound moral and spiritual implications of terminating a pregnancy, even in its earliest stage. Some of us as individuals find abortion offensive to our most basic principles of morality, but that cannot control our decision. Our obligation is to define the liberty of all, not to mandate our own moral code. The underlying constitutional issue is whether the State can resolve these philosophic questions in such a definitive way that a woman lacks all choice in the matter, except perhaps in those rare circumstances in which the pregnancy is itself a danger to her own life or health, or is the result of rape or incest.

It is conventional constitutional doctrine that where reasonable people disagree the government can adopt one position or the other. . . . That theorem, however, assumes a state of affairs in which the choice does not intrude upon a protected liberty. . . .

Our law affords constitutional protection to personal decisions relating to marriage, procreation, contraception, family relationships, child rearing, and education. . . . Our cases recognize "the right of the *individual*, married or single, to be free from unwarranted governmental intrusion into matters so fundamentally affecting a person as the decision whether to bear or beget a child." . . . Our precedents "have respected the private realm of family life which the state cannot enter." . . . These matters, involving the most intimate and personal choices a person may make in a lifetime, choices central to personal dignity and autonomy, are central to the liberty protected by the Fourteenth Amendment. At the heart of liberty is the right to define one's own concept of existence, of meaning, of the universe, and of the mystery of human life. Beliefs about these matters could not define the attributes of personhood were they formed under compulsion of the State.

These considerations begin our analysis of the woman's interest in terminating her pregnancy but cannot end it, for this reason: though the abortion decision may originate within the zone of conscience and belief, it is more than a philosophic exercise. Abortion is a unique act. It is an act fraught with consequences for others: for the woman who must live with the implications of her decision; for the persons who perform and assist in the procedure; for the spouse, family, and society which must confront the knowledge that these procedures exist, procedures some deem nothing short of an act of violence against innocent human life; and, depending on one's beliefs, for the life or potential life that is aborted. Though abortion is conduct, it does not follow that the State is entitled to proscribe it in all instances. That is because the liberty of the woman is at stake in a sense unique to the human condition and so unique to the law. The mother who carries a child to full term is subject to anxieties, to physical constraints, to pain that only she must bear. That these sacrifices have from the beginning of the human race been endured by woman with a pride that ennobles her in the eyes of others and gives to the infant a bond of love cannot alone be grounds for the State to insist she make the sacrifice. Her suffering is too intimate and personal for the State to insist, without more, upon its own vision of the woman's role, however dominant that vision has been in the course of our history and our culture. The destiny of the woman must be shaped to a large extent on her own conception of her spiritual imperatives and her place in society.

It should be recognized, moreover, that in some critical respects the abortion decision is of the same character as the decision to use contraception, to which *Griswold* v. *Connecticut*, *Eisenstadt* v. *Baird*, and *Carey* v. *Population Services International*, afford constitutional protection. We have no doubt as to the correctness of those decisions. They support the reasoning in *Roe* relating to the woman's liberty because they involve personal decisions concerning not only the meaning of procreation but also human responsibility and respect for it. As with abortion, reasonable people will have differences of opinion about these matters. One view is based on such reverence for the wonder of creation that any pregnancy ought to be welcomed and carried to full term no matter how difficult it will be to provide for the child and ensure its well-being. Another is that the inability to provide for the nurture and care of the infant is a cruelty to the child and an anguish to the parent. These are intimate views with infinite variations, and their deep, personal character underlay our decisions in *Griswold*, *Eisenstadt*, and *Carey*. The same concerns are present when the woman confronts the reality that, perhaps despite her attempts to avoid it, she has become pregnant.

It was this dimension of personal liberty that *Roe* sought to protect, and its holding invoked the reasoning and the tradition of the precedents we have discussed, granting protection to substantive liberties of the person. *Roe* was, of course, an extension of those cases and, as the decision itself indicated, the separate States could act in some degree to further their own legitimate interests in protecting prenatal life. The extent to which the legislatures of the States might act to outweigh the interests of the woman in choosing to terminate her pregnancy was a subject of debate both in *Roe* itself and in decisions following it.

While we appreciate the weight of the arguments made on behalf of the State in the case before us, arguments which in their ultimate formulation conclude that *Roe* should be overruled, the reservations any of us may have in reaffirming the central holding of *Roe* are outweighed by the explication of individual liberty we have given combined with the force of *stare decisis*. We turn now to that doctrine.

III

The obligation to follow precedent begins with necessity, and a contrary necessity marks its outer limit. With Cardozo, we recognize that no judicial system could do society's work if it eyed each issue afresh in every case that raised it. Indeed, the very concept of the rule of law underlying our own Constitution requires such continuity over time that a respect for precedent is, by definition, indispensable. At the other extreme, a different necessity would make itself felt if a prior judicial ruling should come to be seen so clearly as error that its enforcement was for that very reason doomed.

Even when the decision to overrule a prior case is not, as in the rare, latter instance, virtually foreordained, it is common wisdom that the rule of *stare decisis* is not an "inexorable command," and certainly it is not such in every constitutional case. Rather, when this Court reexamines a prior holding, its judgment is customarily informed by a series of prudential and pragmatic considerations designed to test the consistency of overruling a prior decision with the ideal of the rule of law, and to gauge the respective costs of reaffirming and overruling prior case. Thus, for example, we may ask whether the rule has proved to be intolerable simply in defying practical workability; whether the rule is subject to a kind of reliance that would lend a special hardship to the consequences of overruling and add inequity to the cost of repudiation; whether related principles of law have so far developed as to have left the old rule no more than a remnant of abandoned doctrine; or whether facts have so changed or come to be seen so differently, as to have robbed the old rule of significant application or justification.

So in this case we may inquire whether *Roe*'s central rule has been found unworkable; whether the rules limitation on state power could be removed without serious inequity to those who have relied upon it or significant damage to the stability of the society governed by the rule in question; whether the law's growth in the intervening years has left *Roe*'s central rule a doctrinal anachronism discounted by society; and whether *Roe*'s premises of fact have so far changed in the ensuing two decades as to render its central holding somehow irrelevant or unjustifiable in dealing with the issue it addressed.

1

Although *Roe* has engendered opposition, it has in no sense proven "unworkable," representing as it does a simple limitation beyond which a state law is unenforceable. While *Roe* has, of course, required judicial assessment of state laws affecting the exercise of the choice guaranteed against government infringement, and although the need for such review will remain as a consequence of today's decision, the required determinations fall within judicial competence.

2

The inquiry into reliance counts the cost of a rule's repudiation as it would fall on those who have relied reasonably on the rule's continued application. Since the classic case for weighing reliance heavily in favor of following the earlier rule occurs in the commercial context, where advance planning of great precision is most obviously a necessity, it is no cause for surprise that some would find no reliance worthy of consideration in support of *Roe*.

While neither respondents nor their *amici* in so many words deny that the abortion right invites some reliance prior to its actual exercise, one can readily imagine an argument stressing the dissimilarity of this case to one involving property or contract. Abortion is customarily chosen as an unplanned response to the consequence of unplanned activity or to the failure of conventional birth control, and except on the assumption that no intercourse would have occurred but for *Roe*'s holding, such behavior may appear to justify no reliance claim. Even if reliance could be claimed on that unrealistic assumption, the argument might run, any reliance interest would be *de minimis*. This argument would be premised on the hypothesis that reproductive planning could take virtually immediate account of any sudden restoration of state authority to ban abortions.

To eliminate the issue of reliance that easily, however, one would need to limit cognizable reliance to specific instances of sexual activity. But to do this would be simply to refuse to face the fact that for two decades of economic and social developments, people have organized intimate relationships and made choices that define their views of themselves and their places in society, in reliance on the availability of abortion in the event that contraception should fail. The ability of women to participate equally in the economic and social life of the nation has been facilitated by their ability to control their reproductive lives. The Constitution serves human values, and while the effect of reliance on *Roe* cannot be exactly measured, neither can the certain cost of overruling *Roe* for people who have ordered their thinking and living around that case be dismissed.

3

No evolution of legal principle has left *Roe*'s doctrinal footings weaker than they were in 1973. No development of constitutional law since the case was decided has implicitly or explicitly left *Roe* behind as a mere survivor of obsolete constitutional thinking.

It will be recognized, of course, that *Roe* stands at an intersection of two lines of decisions, but in whichever doctrinal category one reads the case, the result for present purposes will be the same. The *Roe* Court itself placed its holding in the succession of cases most prominently exemplified by *Griswold* v. *Connecticut*. . . . When it is so seen, *Roe* is clearly in no jeopardy, since subsequent constitutional developments have neither disturbed, nor do they threaten to diminish, the scope of recognized protection accorded to the liberty relating to intimate relationships, the family, and decisions about whether or not to beget or bear a child. . . .

Roe, however, may be seen not only as an exemplar of *Griswold* liberty but as a rule (whether or not mistaken) of personal autonomy and bodily integrity, with doctrinal affinity to cases recognizing limits on governmental power to mandate medical treatment or to bar its rejection. If so, our cases since *Roe* accord with *Roe*'s view that a State's interest in the protection of life falls short of justifying any plenary override of individual liberty claims. . . .

Finally, one could classify *Roe* as *sui generis*. If the case is so viewed, then there clearly has been no erosion of its central determination. The original holding resting on the concurrence of seven Members of the Court in 1973 was expressly affirmed by a majority of six in 1983 . . . and by a majority of five in 1986, . . . expressing adherence to the constitutional ruling despite legislative efforts in some States to test its limits. More recently, in *Webster* v. *Reproductive Health Services* (1989); . . . a majority of the Court either decided to reaffirm or declined to address the constitutional validity of the central holding of *Roe*. . . .

4

We have seen how time has overtaken some of *Roe*'s factual assumptions: advances in maternal health care allow for abortions safe to the mother later in pregnancy than was true in 1973, and advances in neonatal care have advanced viability to a point somewhat earlier. . . . But these facts go only to the scheme of time limits on the realization of competing interests, and the divergences from the factual premises of 1973 have no bearing on the validity of *Roe*'s central holding, that viability marks the earliest point at which the State's interest in fetal life is constitutionally adequate to justify a legislative ban on nontherapeutic abortions. The soundness or unsoundness of that constitutional judgment in no sense turns on whether viability occurs at approximately 28 weeks, as was usual at the time of *Roe*, at 23 to 24 weeks, as it sometimes does today, or at some moment even slightly earlier in pregnancy, as it may if fetal respiratory capacity can somehow be enhanced in the future. Whenever it may occur, the attainment of viability may continue to serve as the critical fact, just as it has done since *Roe* was decided; which is to say that no change in *Roe*'s factual underpinning has left its central holding obsolete, and none supports an argument for overruling it.

5

The sum of the precedential inquiry to this point shows *Roe*'s underpinnings unweakened in any way affecting its central holding. While it has engendered disapproval, it has not been unworkable. An entire generation has come of age free to assume *Roe*'s concept of liberty in defining the capacity of women to act in society, and to make reproductive decisions; no erosion of principle going to liberty or personal autonomy has left *Roe*'s central holding a doctrinal remnant; *Roe* portends no developments at odds with other precedent for the analysis of personal liberty; and no changes of fact have rendered viability more or less appropriate as the point at which the balance of interests tips. Within the bounds of normal *stare decisis* analysis, then, and subject to the considerations on which it customarily turns, the stronger argument is for affirming *Roe*'s central holding, with whatever degree of personal reluctance any of us may have, not for overruling it.

* * *

IV

From what we have said so far it follows that it is a constitutional liberty of the woman to have some freedom to terminate her pregnancy. We conclude that the basic decision in *Roe* was based on a constitutional analysis which we cannot now repudiate. The woman's liberty is not so unlimited, however, that from the outset the State cannot show its concern for the life of the unborn, and at a later point in fetal development the State's interest in life has sufficient force so that the right of the woman to terminate the pregnancy can be restricted.

That brings us, of course, to the point where much criticism has been directed at *Roe*, a criticism that always inheres when the Court draws a specific rule from what in the Constitution is but a general standard. We conclude, however, that the urgent claims of the woman to retain the ultimate control over her destiny and her body, claims implicit in the meaning of liberty, require us to perform that function. Liberty must not be extinguished for want of a line that is clear. And it falls to us to give some real substance to the woman's liberty to determine whether to carry her pregnancy to full term.

We conclude the line should be drawn at viability, so that before that time the woman has a right to choose to terminate her pregnancy. We adhere to this principle for two reasons. First, as we have said, is the doctrine of *stare decisis*. Any judicial act of line-drawing may seem somewhat arbitrary, but *Roe* was a reasoned statement, elaborated with great care. We have twice reaffirmed it in the face of great opposition. . . .

The second reason is that the concept of viability, as we noted in *Roe*, is the time at which there is a realistic possibility of maintaining and nourishing a life outside the womb, so that the independent existence of the second life can in reason and all fairness be the object of state protection that now overrides the rights of the woman. . . . Consistent with other constitutional norms, legislatures may draw lines which appear arbitrary without the necessity of offering a justification. But courts may not. We must justify the lines we draw. And there is no line other than viability which is more workable. To be sure, as we have said, there may be some medical developments that affect the precise point of viability, but this is an imprecision within tolerable limits given that the medical community and all those who must apply its discoveries will continue to explore the matter. The viability line also has, as a practical matter, an element of fairness. In some broad sense it might be said that a woman who fails to act before viability has consented to the State's intervention on behalf of the developing child.

The woman's right to terminate her pregnancy before viability is the most central principle of *Roe* v. *Wade*. It is a rule of law and a component of liberty we cannot renounce.

On the other side of the equation is the interest of the State in the protection of potential life. The *Roe* Court recognized the State's "important and legitimate interest in protecting the potentiality of human life." The weight to be given this state interest, not the strength of the woman's interest, was the difficult question faced in *Roe*. We do not need to say whether each of us, had we been Members of the Court when the valuation of the State interest came before it as an original matter, would have concluded, as the *Roe* Court did, that its weight is insufficient to justify a ban on abortions prior to viability even when it is subject to certain exceptions. The matter is not before us in the first instance, and coming as it does after nearly twenty years of litigation in *Roe*'s wake we are satisfied that the immediate question is not the soundness of *Roe*'s resolution of the issue, but the precedential force that must be accorded to its holding. And we have concluded that the essential holding of *Roe* should be reaffirmed.

Yet it must be remembered that *Roe* v. *Wade* speaks with clarity in establishing not only the woman's liberty but also the State's "important and legitimate interest in potential life." . . .

Roe established a trimester framework to govern abortion regulations. Under this elaborate but rigid construct, almost no regulation at all is permitted during the first trimester of pregnancy; regulations designed to protect the woman's health, but not to further the State's interest in potential life, are permitted during the second trimester; and during the third trimester, when the fetus is viable, prohibitions are permitted provided the life or health of the mother is not at stake. . . .

The trimester framework no doubt was erected to ensure that the woman's right to choose not become so subordinate to the State's interest in promoting fetal life that her choice exists in theory but not in fact. We do not agree, however, that the trimester approach is necessary to accomplish this objective. A framework of this rigidity was unnecessary and in its later interpretation sometimes contradicted the State's permissible exercise of its powers.

Though the woman has a right to choose to terminate or continue her pregnancy before viability, it does not at all follow that the State is prohibited from taking steps to ensure that this choice is thoughtful and informed. Even in the earliest stages of pregnancy, the State may enact rules and regulations designed to encourage her to know that there are philosophic and social arguments of great weight that can be brought to bear in favor of continuing the pregnancy to full term and that there are procedures and institutions to allow adoption of unwanted children as well as a certain degree of state assistance if the mother chooses to raise the child herself. " '[T]he Constitution does not forbid a State or city, pursuant to democratic processes, from expressing a preference for normal childbirth' " (*Webster* v. *Reproductive Health Services*). It follows that States are free to enact laws to provide a reasonable framework for a woman to make a decision that has such profound and lasting meaning. This, too, we find consistent with *Roe*'s central premises, and indeed the inevitable consequence of our holding that the State has an interest in protecting the life of the unborn.

We reject the trimester framework, which we do not consider to be part of the essential holding of *Roe*. Measures aimed at ensuring that a woman's choice contemplates the consequences for the fetus do not necessarily interfere with the right recognized in *Roe*, although those measures have been found to be inconsistent with the rigid trimester framework announced in that case. A logical reading of the central holding in *Roe* itself, and a necessary reconciliation of the liberty of the woman and the interest of the State in promoting prenatal life, require, in our view, that we abandon the trimester framework as a rigid prohibition on all previability regulation aimed at the protection of fetal life. The trimester framework suffers from these basic flaws: in its formulation it misconceives the nature of the pregnant woman's interest; and in practice it undervalues the State's interest in potential life, as recognized in *Roe*.

As our jurisprudence relating to all liberties save perhaps abortion has recognized, not every law which makes a right more difficult to exercise is, *ipso facto*, an infringement of that right. An example clarifies the point. We have held that not every ballot access limitation amounts to an infringement of the right to vote. Rather, the States are granted substantial flexibility in establishing the framework within which voters choose the candidates for whom they wish to vote.

The abortion right is similar. Numerous forms of state regulation might have the incidental effect of increasing the cost or decreasing the availability of medical care, whether for abortion or any other medical procedure. The fact that a law which serves a valid purpose, one not designed to strike at the right itself, has the incidental effect of making it more difficult or more expensive to procure an abortion cannot be enough to invalidate it. Only where state regulation imposes an undue burden on a woman's ability to make this decision does the power of the State reach into the heart of the liberty protected by the Due Process Clause.

For the most part, the Court's early abortion cases adhered to this view. In *Maher* v. *Roe* (1977), the Court explained: "*Roe* did not declare an unqualified 'constitutional right to an abortion,' as the District Court seemed to think. Rather, the right protects the woman from unduly burdensome interference with her freedom to decide whether to terminate her pregnancy." . . .

These considerations of the nature of the abortion right illustrate that it is an overstatement to describe it as a right to decide whether to have an abortion "without interference from the State." . . . All abortion regulations interfere to some degree with a woman's ability to decide whether to terminate her pregnancy. It is, as a consequence, not surprising that despite the protestations contained in the original *Roe* opinion to the effect that the Court was not recognizing an absolute right, . . . the Court's experience applying the trimester framework has led to the striking down of some abortion regulations which in no real sense deprived women of the ultimate decision. Those decisions went too far because the right recognized by *Roe* is a right "to be free from unwarranted governmental intrusion into matters so fundamentally affecting a person as the decision whether to bear or beget a child." Not all governmental intrusion is of necessity unwarranted; and that brings us to the other basic flaw in the trimester framework: even in *Roe*'s terms, in practice it undervalues the State's interest in the potential life within the woman.

Roe v. *Wade* was express in its recognition of the State's "important and legitimate interest[s] in preserving and protecting the health of the pregnant woman [and] in protecting the potentiality of human life." The trimester framework, however, does not fulfill *Roe*'s own promise that the State has an interest in protecting fetal life or potential life. *Roe* began the contradiction by using the trimester framework to forbid any regulation of abortion designed to advance that interest before viability. Before viability, *Roe* and subsequent cases treat all governmental attempts to influence a woman's decision on behalf of the potential life within her as unwarranted. This treatment is, in our judgment, incompatible with the recognition that there is a substantial state interest in potential life throughout pregnancy. . . .

The very notion that the State has a substantial interest in potential life leads to the conclusion that not all regulations must be deemed unwarranted. Not all burdens on the right to decide whether to terminate a pregnancy will be undue. In our view, the undue burden standard is the appropriate means of reconciling the State's interest with the woman's constitutionally protected liberty.

. . . Because we set forth a standard of general application to which we intend to adhere, it is important to clarify what is meant by an undue burden.

A finding of an undue burden is a shorthand for the conclusion that a state regulation has the purpose or effect of placing a substantial obstacle in the path of a woman seeking an abortion of a nonviable fetus. A statute with this purpose is invalid because the means chosen by the State to further the interest in potential life must be calculated to inform the woman's free choice, not hinder it. And a statute which, while furthering the interest in potential life or some other valid state interest, has the effect of placing a substantial obstacle in the path of a woman's choice cannot be considered a permissible means of serving its legitimate ends. To the extent that the opinions of the Court or of individual justices use the undue burden standard in a manner that is inconsistent with this analysis, we set out what in our view should be the controlling standard. . . . In our considered judgment, an undue burden is an unconstitutional burden. . . . Understood another way, we answer the question, left open in previous opinions discussing the undue burden formulation, whether a law designed to further the States's interest in fetal life which imposes an undue burden on the woman's decision before fetal viability could be constitutional. The answer is no.

Some guiding principles should emerge. What is at stake is the woman's right to make the ultimate decision, not a right to be insulated from all others in doing so. Regulations which do no more than create a structural mechanism by which the State, or the parent or guardian of a minor, may express profound respect for the life of the unborn are permitted, if they are not a substantial obstacle to the woman's exercise of the right to choose. . . . Unless it has that effect on her right of choice, a state measure designed to persuade her to choose childbirth over abortion will be upheld if reasonably related to that goal. Regulations designed to foster the health of a woman seeking an abortion are valid if they do not constitute an undue burden.

Even when jurists reason from shared premises, some disagreement is inevitable. . . . That is to be expected in the application of any legal standard which must accommodate life's complexity. We do not expect it to be otherwise with respect to the undue burden standard. We give this summary:

(a) To protect the central right recognized by *Roe* v. *Wade* while at the same time accommodating the State's profound interest in potential life, we will employ the undue burden analysis as explained in this opinion. An undue burden exists, and therefore a provision of law is invalid, if its purpose or effect is to place a substantial obstacle in the path of a woman seeking an abortion before the fetus attains viability.

(b) We reject the rigid trimester framework of *Roe* v. *Wade*. To promote the State's profound interest in potential life, throughout pregnancy the State may take measures to ensure that the woman's choice is informed, and measures designed to advance this interest will not be invalidated as long as their purpose is to persuade the woman to choose childbirth over abortion. These measures must not be an undue burden on the right.

(c) As with any medical procedure, the State may enact regulations to further the health or safety of a woman seeking an abortion. Unnecessary health regulations that have the purpose or effect of presenting a substantial obstacle to a woman seeking an abortion impose an undue burden on the right.

(d) Our adoption of the undue burden analysis does not disturb the central holding of *Roe* v. *Wade*, and we reaffirm that holding. Regardless of whether exceptions are made for particular circumstances, a State may not prohibit any woman from making the ultimate decision to terminate her pregnancy before viability.

(e) We also reaffirm *Roe*'s holding that "subsequent to viability, the State in promoting its interest in the potentiality of human life may, if it chooses, regulate, and even proscribe, abortion except where it is necessary, in appropriate medical judgment, for the preservation of the life or health of the mother."

These principles control our assessment of the Pennsylvania statute, and we now turn to the issue of the validity of its challenged provisions.

V

The Court of Appeals applied what it believed to be the undue burden standard and upheld each of the provisions except for the husband notification requirement. We agree generally with this conclusion but refine the undue burden analysis in accordance with the principles articulated above. We now consider the separate statutory sections at issue.

A

Because it is central to the operation of various other requirements, we begin with the statute's definition of medical emergency. Under the statute, a medical emergency is

> [t]hat condition which, on the basis of the physician's good faith clinical judgment, so complicates the medical condition of a pregnant woman as to necessitate the immediate abortion of her pregnancy to avert her death or for which a delay will create serious risk of substantial and irreversible impairment of a major bodily function.

Petitioners argue that the definition is too narrow, contending that it forecloses the possibility of an immediate abortion despite some significant health risks. If the contention were correct, we would be required to invalidate the restrictive operation of the provision, for the essential holding of *Roe* forbids a State from interfering with a woman's choice to undergo an abortion procedure if continuing her pregnancy would constitute a threat to her health.

The District Court found that there were three serious conditions which would not be covered by the statute: preeclampsia, inevitable abortion, and premature ruptured membrane. Yet, as the Court of Appeals observed, it is undisputed that under some circumstances each of these conditions could lead to an illness with substantial and irreversible consequences. While the definition could be interpreted in an unconstitutional manner, the Court of Appeals construed the phrase "serious risk" to include those circumstances. It stated: "we read the medical emergency exception as intended by the Pennsylvania legislature to assure that compliance with its abortion regulations would not in any way pose a significant threat to the life or health of a woman." . . . We . . . conclude that, as construed by the Court of Appeals, the medical emergency definition imposes no undue burden on a woman's abortion right.

B

We next consider the informed consent requirement. Except in a medical emergency, the statute requires that at least 24 hours before performing an abortion a physician inform the woman of the nature of the procedure, the health risks of the abortion and of childbirth, and the "probable gestational age of the unborn child." The physician or a qualified nonphysician must inform the woman of the availability of printed materials published by the State describing the fetus and providing information about medical assistance for childbirth, information about child support from the father, and a list of agencies which provide adoption and other services as alternatives to abortion. An abortion may not be performed unless the woman certifies in writing that she has been informed of the availability of these printed materials and has been provided them if she chooses to view them.

Our prior decisions establish that as with any medical procedure, the State may require a woman to give her written informed consent to an abortion. In this respect, the statute is unexceptional. Petitioners challenge the statute's definition of informed consent because it includes the provision of specific information by the doctor and the mandatory 24-hour waiting period. The conclusions reached by a majority of the justices in the separate opinions filed today and the undue burden standard adopted in this opinion require us to overrule in part some of the Court's past decisions, decisions driven by the trimester framework's prohibition of all previability regulations designed to further the State's interest in fetal fife.

In *Akron I* (1983), we invalidated an ordinance which required that a woman seeking an abortion be provided by her physician with specific information "designed to influence the woman's informed choice between abortion or childbirth." As we later described the *Akron I* holding in *Thornburgh* v. *American College of Obstetricians and Gynecologists*, there were two purported flaws in the Akron ordinance: the information was designed to dissuade the woman from having an abortion and the ordinance imposed "a rigid requirement that a specific body of information be given in all cases, irrespective of the particular needs of the patient. . . ."

To the extent *Akron I* and *Thornburgh* find a constitutional violation when the government requires, as it does here, the giving of truthful, nonmisleading information about the nature of the procedure, the attendant health risks and those of childbirth, and the "probable gestational age" of the fetus, those cases go too far, are inconsistent with *Roe*'s acknowledgment of an important interest in potential life, and are overruled. This is clear even on the very terms of *Akron I* and *Thornburgh*. Those decisions, along with *Danforth*, recognize a substantial government interest justifying a requirement that a woman be apprised of the health risks of abortion and childbirth. It cannot be questioned that psychological well-being is a facet of health. Nor can it be doubted that most women considering an abortion would deem the impact on the fetus relevant, if not dispositive, to the decision. In attempting to ensure that a woman apprehend the full consequences of her decision, the State furthers the legitimate purpose of reducing the risk that a woman may elect an abortion, only to discover later, with devastating psychological consequences, that her decision was not fully informed. If the information the State requires to be made available to the woman is truthful and not misleading, the requirement may be permissible.

We also see no reason why the State may not require doctors to inform a woman seeking an abortion of the availability of materials relating to the consequences to the fetus, even when those consequences have no direct relation to her health. An example illustrates the point. We would think it constitutional for the State to require that in order for there to be informed consent to a kidney transplant operation the recipient must be supplied with information about risks to the donor as well as risks to himself or herself. . . . [W]e depart from the holdings of *Akron I* and *Thornburgh* to the extent that we permit a State to further its legitimate goal of protecting the life of the unborn by enacting legislation aimed at ensuring a decision that is mature and informed, even when in so doing the State expresses a preference for childbirth over abortion. In short, requiring that the woman be informed of the availability of information relating to fetal development and the assistance available should she decide to carry the pregnancy to full term is a reasonable measure to insure an informed choice, one which might cause the woman to choose childbirth over abortion. This requirement cannot be considered a substantial obstacle to obtaining an abortion, and, it follows, there is no undue burden.

. . . Thus, a requirement that a doctor give a woman certain information as part of obtaining her consent to an abortion is, for constitutional purposes, no different from a requirement that a doctor give certain specific information about any medical procedure.

. . . Since there is no evidence on this record that requiring a doctor to give the information as provided by the statute would amount in practical terms to a substantial obstacle to a woman seeking an abortion, we conclude that it is not an undue burden. . . . Thus, we uphold the provision as a reasonable means to insure that the woman's consent is informed.

Our analysis of Pennsylvania's 24-hour waiting period between the provision of the information deemed necessary to informed consent and the performance of an abortion under the undue burden standard requires us to reconsider the premise behind the decision in *Akron I* invalidating a parallel requirement. In *Akron I* we said: "Nor are we convinced that the State's legitimate concern that the woman's decision be informed is reasonably served by requiring a 24-hour delay as a matter of course." We consider that conclusion to be wrong. The idea that important decisions will be more informed and deliberate if they follow some period of reflection does not strike us as unreasonable, particularly where the statute directs that important information become part of the background of the decision. The statute, as construed by the Court of Appeals, permits avoidance of the waiting period in the event of a medical emergency and the record evidence shows that in the vast majority of cases, a 24-hour delay does not create any appreciable health risk. In theory, at least, the waiting period is a reasonable measure to implement the State's interest in protecting the life of the unborn, a measure that does not amount to an undue burden.

Whether the mandatory 24-hour waiting period is nonetheless invalid because in practice it is a substantial obstacle to a woman's choice to terminate her pregnancy is a closer question. The findings of fact by the District Court indicate that because of the distances many women must travel to reach an abortion provider, the practical effect will often be a delay of much more than a day because the waiting period requires that a woman seeking an abortion make at least two visits to the doctor. The District Court also found that in many instances this will increase the exposure of women seeking abortions to "the harassment and hostility of anti-abortion protestors demonstrating outside a clinic." As a result, the District Court found that for those women who have the fewest financial resources, those who must travel long distances, and those who have difficulty explaining their whereabouts to husbands, employers, or others, the 24-hour waiting period will be "particularly burdensome."

These findings are troubling in some respects, but they do not demonstrate that the waiting period constitutes an undue burden. We do not doubt that, as the District Court held, the waiting period has the effect of "increasing the cost and risk of delay of abortions," but the District Court did not conclude that the increased costs and potential delays amount to substantial obstacles. Rather, applying the trimester framework's strict prohibition of all regulation designed to promote the State's interest in potential life before viability, the District Court concluded that the waiting period does not further the state "interest in maternal health" and "infringes the physician's discretion to exercise sound medical judgment." Yet, as we have stated, under the undue burden standard a State is permitted to enact persuasive measures which favor childbirth over abortion, even if those measures do not further a health interest. And while the waiting period does limit a physician's discretion, that is not, standing alone, a reason to invalidate it. In light of the construction given the statutes' definition of medical emergency by the Court of Appeals, and the District Court's findings, we cannot say that the waiting period imposes a real health risk.

We also disagree with the District Court's conclusion that the "particularly burdensome" effects of the waiting period on some women require its invalidation. A particular burden is not of necessity a substantial obstacle. Whether a burden falls on a particular group is a distinct inquiry from whether it is a substantial obstacle even as to the women in that group. And the District Court did not even conclude that the waiting period is such an obstacle even for the women who are most burdened by it. Hence, on the record before us, and in the context of this facial challenge, we are not convinced that the 24-hour waiting period constitutes an undue burden.

We are left with the argument that the various aspects of the informed consent requirement are unconstitutional because they place barriers in the way of abortion on demand. Even the broadest reading of *Roe*, however, has not suggested that there is a constitutional right to abortion on demand. Rather, the right protected by *Roe* is a right to decide to terminate a pregnancy free of undue interference by the State. Because the informed consent requirement facilitates the wise exercise of that right it cannot be classified as an interference with the right *Roe* protects. The informed consent requirement is not an undue burden on that right.

C

Section 3209 of Pennsylvania's abortion law provides, except in cases of medical emergency, that no physician shall perform an abortion on a married woman without receiving a signed statement from the woman that she has notified her spouse that she is about to undergo an abortion. The woman has the option of providing an alternative signed statement certifying that her husband is not the man who impregnated her; that her husband could not be located; that the pregnancy is the result of spousal sexual assault which she has reported; or that the woman believes that notifying her husband will cause him or someone else to inflict bodily injury upon her. A physician who performs an abortion on a married woman without receiving the appropriate signed statement will have his or her license revoked, and is liable to the husband for damages.

The District Court heard the testimony of numerous expert witnesses, and made detailed findings of fact regarding the effect of this statute. These included:

> "273. The vast majority of women consult their husbands prior to deciding to terminate their pregnancy. . . .
>
> "279. The 'bodily injury' exception could not be invoked by a married woman whose husband, if notified, would, in her reasonable belief, threaten to (a) publicize her intent to have an abortion to family, friends, or

acquaintances; (b) retaliate against her in future child custody or divorce proceedings; (c) inflict psychological intimidation or emotional harm upon her, her children, or other persons; (d) inflict bodily harm on other persons such as children, family members, or other loved ones; or (e) use his control over finances to deprive of necessary monies for herself or her children. . . .

"281. Studies reveal that family violence occurs in two million families in the United States. This figure, however, is a conservative one that substantially understates (because battering is usually not reported until it reaches life-threatening proportions) the actual number of families affected by domestic violence. In fact, researchers estimate that one of every two women will be battered at some time in their life. . . .

"282. A wife may not elect to notify her husband of her intention to have an abortion for a variety of reasons, including the husband's illness, concern about her own health, the imminent failure of the marriage, or the husband's absolute opposition to the abortion. . . .

"283. The required filing of the spousal consent form would require plaintiff-clinics to change their counseling procedures and force women to reveal their most intimate decision-making on pain of criminal sanctions. The confidentiality of these revelations could not be guaranteed, since the woman's records are not immune from subpoena. . . .

"284. Women of all class levels, educational backgrounds, and racial, ethnic and religious groups are battered. . . .

"285. Wife-battering or abuse can take on many physical and psychological forms. The nature and scope of the battering can cover a broad range of actions and be gruesome and torturous. . . .

"286. Married women, victims of battering, have been killed in Pennsylvania and throughout the United States. . . .

"287. Battering can often involve a substantial amount of sexual abuse, including marital rape and sexual mutilation. . . .

"288. In a domestic abuse situation, it is common for the battering husband to also abuse the children in an attempt to coerce the wife. . . .

"289. Mere notification of pregnancy is frequently a flashpoint for battering and violence within the family. The number of battering incidents is high during the pregnancy and often the worst abuse can be associated with pregnancy. . . . The battering husband may deny parentage and use the pregnancy as an excuse for abuse. . . .

"290. Secrecy typically shrouds abusive families. Family members are instructed not to tell anyone, especially police or doctors, about the abuse and violence. Battering husbands often threaten their wives or her children with further abuse if she tells an outsider of the violence and tells her that nobody will believe her. A battered woman, therefore, is highly unlikely to disclose the violence against her for fear of retaliation by the abuser. . . .

"291. Even when confronted directly by medical personnel or other helping professionals, battered women often will not admit to the battering because they have not admitted to themselves that they are battered. . . .

"294. A woman in a shelter or a safe house unknown to her husband is not 'reasonably likely' to have bodily harm inflicted upon her by her batterer, however her attempt to notify her husband pursuant to section 3209 could accidentally disclose her whereabouts to her husband. Her fear of future ramifications would be realistic under the circumstances.

"295. Marital rape is rarely discussed with others or reported to law enforcement authorities, and of those reported only few are prosecuted. . . .

"296. It is common for battered women to have sexual intercourse with their husbands to avoid being battered. While this type of coercive sexual activity would be spousal sexual assault as defined by the Act, many women may not consider it to be so and others would fear disbelief. . . .

"297. The marital rape exception to section 3209 cannot be claimed by women who are victims of coercive sexual behavior other than penetration. The 90-day reporting requirement of the spousal sexual assault statute, 18 Pa. Con. Stat. Ann. § 3218(c), further narrows the class of sexually abused wives who can claim the exception, since many of these women may be psychologically unable to discuss or report the rape for several years after the incident. . . .

"298. Because of the nature of the battering relationship, battered women are unlikely to avail themselves of the exceptions to section 3209 of the Act, regardless of whether the section applies to them."

These findings are supported by studies of domestic violence. The American Medical Association (AMA) has published a summary of the recent research in this field, which indicates that in an average 12-month period in this country, approximately two million women are the victims of severe assaults by their male partners. In a 1985 survey, women reported that nearly one of every eight husbands had assaulted their wives during the past year. The AMA views these figures as "marked underestimates," because the nature of these incidents discourages women from reporting them, and because surveys typically exclude the very poor, those who do not speak English well, and women who are homeless or in institutions or hospitals when the survey is conducted. According to the AMA, "[r]esearchers on family violence agree that the true incidence of partner violence is probably *double* the above estimates; or four million severely assaulted women per year. Studies suggest that from one-fifth to one-third of all women will be physically assaulted by a partner or ex-partner during their lifetime."Thus on an average day in the United States, nearly 11,000 women are severely assaulted by their male partners. Many of these incidents involve sexual assault. In families where wife-beating takes place, moreover, child abuse is often present as well.

Other studies fill in the rest of this troubling picture. Physical violence is only the most visible form of abuse. Psychological abuse, particularly forced social and economic isolation of women, is also common. Many victims of domestic violence remain with their abusers, perhaps because they perceive no superior alternative. Many abused women who find temporary refuge in shelters return to their husbands, in large part because they have no other source of income. Returning to one's abuser can be dangerous. Recent Federal Bureau of Investigation statistics disclose that 8.8 percent of all homicide victims in the United States are killed by their spouse. Thirty percent of female homicide victims are killed by their male partners.

The limited research that has been conducted with respect to notifying one's husband about an abortion, although involving samples too small to be representative, also supports the District Court's findings of fact. The vast majority of women notify their male partners of their decision to obtain an abortion. In many cases in which married women do not notify their husbands, the pregnancy is the result of an extramarital affair. Where the husband is the father, the primary reason women do not notify their husbands is that the husband and wife are experiencing marital difficulties, often accompanied by incidents of violence.

This information and the District Court's findings reinforce what common sense would suggest. In well-functioning marriages, spouses discuss important intimate decisions such as whether to bear a child. But there are minions of women in this country who are the victims of regular physical and psychological abuse at the hands of their husbands. Should these women become pregnant, they may have very good reasons for not wishing to inform their husbands of their decision to obtain an abortion. Many may have justifiable fears of physical abuse, but may be no less fearful of the consequences of reporting prior abuse to the Commonwealth of Pennsylvania. Many may have a reasonable fear that notifying their husbands will provoke further instances of child abuse; these women are not exempt from § 3209's notification requirement. Many may fear devastating forms of psychological abuse from their husbands, including verbal harassment, threats of future violence, the destruction of possessions, physical confinement to the home, the withdrawal of financial support, or the disclosure of the abortion to family and friends. These methods of psychological abuse may act as even more of a deterrent to notification than the possibility of physical violence, but women who are the victims of the abuse are not exempt from § 3209's notification requirement. And many women who are pregnant as a result of sexual assaults by their husbands will be unable to avail themselves of the exception for spousal sexual assault, because the exception requires that the woman have notified law enforcement authorities within 90 days of the assault, and her husband will be notified of her report once an investigation begins. If anything in this field is certain, it is that victims of spousal sexual assault are extremely reluctant to report the abuse to the government; hence, a great many spousal rape victims will not be exempt from the notification requirement imposed by § 3209.

The spousal notification requirement is thus likely to prevent a significant number of women from obtaining an abortion. It does not merely make abortions a little more difficult or expensive to obtain; for many women, it will impose a substantial obstacle. We must not blind ourselves to the fact that the significant number of women who fear for their safety and the safety of their children are likely to be deterred from procuring an abortion as surely as if the Commonwealth had outlawed abortion in all cases.

Respondents attempt to avoid the conclusion that § 3209 is invalid by pointing out that it imposes almost no burden at all for the vast majority of women seeking abortions. They begin by noting that only about 20 percent of the women who obtain abortions are married. They then note that of these women about 95 percent notify their husbands of their own volition. Thus, respondents argue, the effects of § 3209 are felt by only one percent of the women who obtain abortions. Respondents argue that since some of these women will be able to notify their husbands without adverse consequences or will qualify for one of the exceptions, the statute affects fewer than one percent of women seeking abortions. For this reason, it is asserted, the statute cannot be invalid on its face. We disagree with respondents' basic method of analysis.

The analysis does not end with the one percent of women upon whom the statute operates; it begins there. Legislation is measured for consistency with the Constitution by its impact on those whose conduct it affects. For example, we would not say that a law which requires a newspaper to print a candidate's reply to an unfavorable editorial is valid on its face because most newspapers would adopt the policy even absent the law. . . . The proper focus of constitutional inquiry is the group for whom the law is a restriction, not the group for whom the law is irrelevant.

Respondents' argument itself gives implicit recognition to this principle, at one of its critical points. Respondents speak of the one percent of women seeking abortions who are married and would choose not to notify their husbands of their plans. By selecting as the controlling class women who wish to obtain abortions, rather than all women or all pregnant women, respondents in effect concede that § 3209 must be judged by reference to those for whom it is an actual rather than irrelevant restriction. Of course, as we have said, § 3209's real target is narrower even than the class of women seeking abortions identified by the State: it is married women seeking abortions who do not wish to notify their husbands of their intentions and who do not qualify for one of the statutory exceptions to the notice requirement. The unfortunate yet persisting conditions we document above will mean that in a large fraction of the cases in which § 3209 is relevant, it will operate as a substantial obstacle to a woman's choice to undergo an abortion. It is an undue burden, and therefore invalid.

This conclusion is in no way inconsistent with our decisions upholding parental notification or consent requirements. Those enactments, and our judgment that they are constitutional, are based on the quite reasonable assumption that minors will benefit from consultation with their parents and that children will often not realize that their parents have their best interests at heart. We cannot adopt a parallel assumption about adult women.

We recognize that a husband has a "deep and proper concern and interest . . . in his wife's pregnancy and in the growth and development of the fetus she is carrying." With regard to the children he has fathered and raised, the Court has recognized his "cognizable and substantial" interest in their custody. If this case concerned a State's ability to require the mother to notify the father before taking some action with respect to a living child raised by both, therefore, it would be reasonable to conclude as a general matter that the father's interest in the welfare of the child and the mother's interest are equal.

Before birth, however, the issue takes on a very different cast. It is an inescapable biological fact that state regulation with respect to the child a woman is carrying will have a far greater impact on the mother's liberty than on the father's. The effect of state regulation on a woman's protected liberty is doubly deserving of scrutiny in such a case, as the State has touched not only upon the private sphere of the family but upon the very bodily integrity of the pregnant woman. The Court has held that "when the wife and the husband disagree on this decision, the view of only one of the two marriage partners can prevail. Inasmuch as it is the woman who physically bears the child and who is the more directly and immediately affected by the pregnancy, as between the two, the balance weighs in her favor." This conclusion rests upon the basic nature of marriage and the nature of our Constitution: "[T]he marital couple is not an independent entity with a mind and heart of its own, but an association of two individuals each with a separate intellectual and emotional makeup. If the right of privacy means anything, it is the right of the *individual*, married or single, to be free from unwarranted governmental intrusion into matters so fundamentally affecting a person as the decision whether to bear or beget a child." The Constitution protects individuals, men and women alike, from unjustified state interference, even when that interference is enacted into law for the benefit of their spouses.

There was a time, not so long ago, when a different understanding of the family and of the Constitution prevailed. In *Bradwell* v. *Illinois* (1873), three Members of the Court reaffirmed the common-law principle that "a woman had no legal existence separate from her husband, who was regarded as her head and representative in the social state; and, notwithstanding some recent modifications of this civil status, many of the special rules of law flowing from and dependent upon this cardinal principle still exist in full force in most States." Only one generation has passed since this Court observed that "woman is still regarded as the center of home and family life," with attendant "special responsibilities" that precluded full and independent legal status under the Constitution. These views, of course, are no longer consistent with our understanding of the family, the individual, or the Constitution.

In keeping with our rejection of the common-law understanding of a woman's role within the family, the Court held in *Danforth* that the Constitution does not permit a State to require a married woman to obtain her husband's consent before undergoing an abortion. The principles that guided the Court in Danforth should be our guides today. For the great many women who are victims of abuse inflicted by their husbands, or whose children are the victims of such abuse, a spousal notice requirement enables the husband to wield an effective veto over his wife's decision. Whether the prospect of notification itself deters such women from seeking abortions, or whether the husband, through physical force or psychological pressures or economic coercion, prevents his wife from obtaining an abortion until it is too late, the notice requirement will often be tantamount to the veto found unconstitutional in *Danforth*. The women most affected by this law—those who most reasonably fear the consequences of notifying their husbands that they are pregnant—are in the gravest danger.

The husband's interest in the life of the child his wife is carrying does not permit the State to empower him with this troubling degree of authority over his wife. . . .

Section 3209 embodies a view of marriage consonant with the common-law status of married women but repugnant to our present understanding of marriage and of the nature of the rights secured by the Constitution. Women do not lose their constitutionally protected liberty when they marry. The Constitution protects all individuals, male or female, married or unmarried, from the abuse of governmental power, even where that power is employed for the supposed benefit of a member of the individual's family. These considerations confirm our conclusion that § 3209 is invalid.

D

We next consider the parental consent provision. Except in a medical emergency, an unemancipated young woman under 18 may not obtain an abortion unless she and one of her parents (or guardian) provides informed consent as defined above. If neither a parent nor a guardian provides consent, a court may authorize the performance of an abortion upon a determination that the young woman is mature and capable of giving informed consent and has in fact given her informed consent, or that an abortion would be in her best interests.

We have been over most of this ground before. Our cases establish, and we reaffirm today, that a State may require a minor seeking an abortion to obtain the consent of a parent or guardian, provided that there is an adequate judicial bypass procedure. . . .

E

Under the recordkeeping and reporting requirements of the statute, every facility which performs abortions is required to file a report stating its name and address as well as the name and address of any related entity, such as a controlling or subsidiary organization. In the case of state-funded institutions, the information becomes public.

For each abortion performed, a report must be filed identifying: the physician (and the second physician where required); the facility; the referring physician or agency; the woman's age; the number of prior pregnancies and prior abortions she has had; gestational age; the type of abortion procedure; the date of the abortion; whether there were any pre-existing medical conditions which would complicate pregnancy; medical complications with the abortion; where applicable, the basis for the determination that the abortion was medically necessary; the weight of the aborted fetus; and whether the woman was married, and if so, whether notice was provided or the basis for the failure to give notice. Every abortion facility must also file quarterly reports showing the number of abortions performed broken down by trimester. In all events, the identity of each woman who has had an abortion remains confidential.

In *Danforth* we held that recordkeeping and reporting provisions "that are reasonably directed to the preservation of maternal health and that properly respect a patient's confidentiality and privacy are permissible." We think that under this standard, all the provisions at issue here except that relating to spousal notice are constitutional. Although they do not relate to the State's interest in informing the woman's choice, they do relate to health. The collection of information with respect to actual patients is a vital element of medical research, and so it cannot be said that the requirements serve no purpose other than to make abortions more difficult. Nor do we find that the requirements impose a substantial obstacle to a woman's choice. At most they might increase the cost of some abortions by a slight amount. While at some point increased cost could become a substantial obstacle, there is no such showing on the record before us.

Subsection (12) of the reporting provision requires the reporting of, among other things, a married woman's "reason for failure to provide notice" to her husband. This provision in effect requires women, as a condition of obtaining an abortion, to provide the Commonwealth with the precise information we have already recognized that many women have pressing reasons not to reveal. Like the spousal notice requirement itself, this provision places an undue burden on a woman's choice, and must be invalidated for that reason.

VI

Our Constitution is a covenant running from the first generation of Americans to us and then to future generations. It is a coherent succession. Each generation must learn anew that the Constitution's written terms embody ideas and aspirations that must survive more ages than one. We accept our responsibility not to retreat from interpreting the full meaning of the covenant in light of all of our precedents. We invoke it once again to define the freedom guaranteed by the Constitution's own promise, the promise of liberty.

10

DON STENBERG, ATTORNEY GENERAL OF NEBRASKA, ET AL., PETITIONERS V. *LEROY CARHART*

Justice Breyer delivered the opinion of the Court.

We again consider the right to an abortion. We understand the controversial nature of the problem. Millions of Americans believe that life begins at conception and consequently that an abortion is akin to causing the death of an innocent child; they recoil at the thought of a law that would permit it. Other millions fear that a law that forbids abortion would condemn many American women to lives that lack dignity, depriving them of equal liberty and leading those with least resources to undergo illegal abortions with the attendant risks of death and suffering. Taking account of these virtually irreconcilable points of view, aware that constitutional law must govern a society whose different members sincerely hold directly opposing views, and considering the matter in light of the Constitution's guarantees of fundamental individual liberty, this Court, in the course of a generation, has determined and then redetermined that the Constitution offers basic protection to the woman's right to choose. *Roe* v. *Wade* (1973); *Planned Parenthood of Southeastern Pennsylvania* v. *Casey* (1992). We shall not revisit those legal principles. Rather, we apply them to the circumstances of this case.

Three established principles determine the issue before us. We shall set them forth in the language of the joint opinion in *Casey.* First, before "viability . . . the woman has a right to choose to terminate her pregnancy."

Second, "a law designed to further the State's interest in fetal life which imposes an undue burden on the woman's decision before fetal viability" is unconstitutional. An "undue burden is . . . shorthand for the conclusion that a state regulation has the purpose or effect of placing a substantial obstacle in the path of a woman seeking an abortion of a nonviable fetus."

Third, "subsequent to viability, the State in promoting its interest in the potentiality of human life may, if it chooses, regulate, and even proscribe, abortion except where it is necessary, in appropriate medical judgment, for the preservation of the life or health of the mother."

We apply these principles to a Nebraska law banning "partial birth abortion." The statute reads as follows:

> No partial birth abortion shall be performed in this state, unless such procedure is necessary to save the life of the mother whose life is endangered by a physical disorder, physical illness, or physical injury, including a life-endangering physical condition caused by or arising from the pregnancy itself.

The statute defines "partial birth abortion" as

> an abortion procedure in which the person performing the abortion partially delivers vaginally a living unborn child before killing the unborn child and completing the delivery.

It further defines "partially delivers vaginally a living unborn child before killing the unborn child" to mean

> deliberately and intentionally delivering into the vagina a living unborn child, or a substantial portion thereof, for the purpose of performing a procedure that the person performing such procedure knows will kill the unborn child and does kill the unborn child.

The law classifies violation of the statute as a "Class III felony" carrying a prison term of up to 20 years, and a fine of up to $25,000. It also provides for the automatic revocation of a doctor's license to practice medicine in Nebraska.

We hold that this statute violates the Constitution.

I

A

Dr. Leroy Carhart is a Nebraska physician who performs abortions in a clinical setting. He brought this lawsuit in Federal District Court seeking a declaration that the Nebraska statute violates the Federal Constitution, and asking for an injunction forbidding its enforcement. After a trial on the merits, during which both sides presented several expert witnesses, the District Court held the statute unconstitutional. On appeal, the Eighth Circuit affirmed. We granted certiorari to consider the matter.

B

Because Nebraska law seeks to ban one method of aborting a pregnancy, we must describe and then discuss several different abortion procedures. Considering the fact that those procedures seek to terminate a potential human life, our discussion may seem clinically cold or callous to some, perhaps horrifying to others. There is no alternative way, however, to acquaint the reader with the technical distinctions among different abortion methods and related factual matters, upon which the outcome of this case depends. For that reason, drawing upon the findings of the trial court, underlying testimony, and related medical texts, we shall describe the relevant methods of performing abortions in technical detail.

The evidence before the trial court, as supported or supplemented in the literature, indicates the following:

(1) About 90% of all abortions performed in the United States take place during the first trimester of pregnancy, before 12 weeks of gestational age. During the first trimester, the predominant abortion method is "vacuum aspiration," which involves insertion of a vacuum tube (cannula) into the uterus to evacuate the contents. Such an abortion is typically performed on an outpatient basis under local anesthesia. Vacuum aspiration is considered particularly safe. The procedure's mortality rates for first trimester abortion are, for example, 5 to 10 times lower than those associated with carrying the fetus to term. Complication rates are also low. As the fetus grows in size, however, the vacuum aspiration method becomes increasingly difficult to use.

(2) Approximately 10% of all abortions are performed during the second trimester of pregnancy (12 to 24 weeks). In the early 1970s, inducing labor through the injection of saline into the uterus was the predominant method of second-trimester abortion. Today, however, the medical profession has switched from medical induction of labor to surgical procedures for most second trimester abortions. The most commonly used procedure is called "dilation and evacuation" (D). That procedure (together with a modified form of vacuum aspiration used in the early second trimester) accounts for about 95% of all abortions performed from 12 to 20 weeks of gestational age.

(3) D "refers generically to transcervical procedures performed at 13 weeks gestation or later." The AMA Report, adopted by the District Court, describes the process as follows.

Between 13 and 15 weeks of gestation,

> D is similar to vacuum aspiration except that the cervix must be dilated more widely because surgical instruments are used to remove larger pieces of tissue. Osmotic dilators are usually used. Intravenous fluids and an analgesic or sedative may be administered. A local anesthetic such as a parac-

ervical block may be administered, dilating agents, if used, are removed and instruments are inserted through the cervix into the uterus to removal fetal and placental tissue. Because fetal tissue is friable and easily broken, the fetus may not be removed intact. The walls of the uterus are scraped with a curette to ensure that no tissue remains.

After 15 weeks:

Because the fetus is larger at this stage of gestation (particularly the head), and because bones are more rigid, dismemberment or other destructive procedures are more likely to be required than at earlier gestational ages to remove fetal and placental tissue.

After 20 weeks:

Some physicians use intrafetal potassium chloride or digoxin to induce fetal demise prior to a late D (after 20 weeks), to facilitate evacuation.

There are variations in D operative strategy. However, the common points are that D involves (1) dilation of the cervix; (2) removal of at least some fetal tissue using nonvacuum instruments; and (3) (after the 15th week) the potential need for instrumental disarticulation or dismemberment of the fetus or the collapse of fetal parts to facilitate evacuation from the uterus.

(4) When instrumental disarticulation incident to D is necessary, it typically occurs as the doctor pulls a portion of the fetus through the cervix into the birth canal. Dr. Carhart testified at trial as follows:

Dr. Carhart: . . . The dismemberment occurs between the traction of . . . my instrument and the counter-traction of the internal os of the cervix. . . .

Counsel: So the dismemberment occurs after you pulled a part of the fetus through the cervix, is that correct?

Dr. Carhart: Exactly. Because you're using—The cervix has two strictures or two rings, the internal os and the external os . . . that's what's actually doing the dismembering. . . .

Counsel: When we talked before or talked before about a D, that is not—where there is not intention to do it intact, do you, in that situation, dismember the fetus in utero first, then remove portions?

Dr. Carhart: I don't think so. . . . I don't know of any way that one could go in and intentionally dismember the fetus in the uterus . . . It takes something that restricts the motion of the fetus against what you're doing before you're going to get dismemberment.

Dr. Carhart's specification of the location of fetal disarticulation is consistent with other sources.

(5) The D procedure carries certain risks. The use of instruments within the uterus creates a danger of accidental perforation and damage to neighboring organs. Sharp fetal bone fragments create similar dangers. And fetal tissue accidentally left behind can cause infection and various other complications. Nonetheless studies show that the risks of mortality and complication that accompany the D procedure between the 12th and 20th weeks of gestation are significantly lower than those accompanying induced labor procedures (the next safest midsecond trimester procedures.)

(6) At trial, Dr. Carhart and Dr. Stubblefield described a variation of the D procedure, which they referred to as an "intact D." Like other versions of the D technique, it begins with induced dilation of the cervix. The procedure then involves removing the fetus from the uterus through the cervix "intact," i.e., in one pass, rather than in several passes. It is used after 16 weeks at the earliest, as vacuum aspiration becomes ineffective and the fetal skull becomes too large to pass through the cervix. The intact D proceeds in one of two ways, depending on the presentation of the fetus. If the fetus presents head first (a vertex presentation), the doctor collapses the skull; and the doctor then extracts the entire fetus through the cervix. If the fetus presents feet first (a breech presentation), the doctor pulls the fetal body through the cervix, collapses the skull, and extracts the fetus through the cervix. The breech extraction version of the intact D is also known commonly as "dilation and extraction," or D. In the late second trimester, vertex, breech, and traverse/compound (sideways) presentations occur in roughly similar proportions.

(7) The intact D procedure can also be found described in certain obstetric and abortion clinical textbooks, where two variations are recognized. The first, as just described, calls for the physician to adapt his method for extracting the intact fetus depending on fetal presentation. This is the method used by Dr. Carhart. A slightly different version of the intact D procedure, associated with Dr. Martin Haskell, calls for conversion to a breech presentation in all cases.

(8) The American College of Obstetricians and Gynecologists describes the D procedure in a manner corresponding to a breech-conversion intact D, including the following steps:

> (1) deliberate dilatation of the cervix, usually over a sequence of days;
> (2) instrumental conversion of the fetus to a footling breech;
> (3) breech extraction of the body excepting the head; and
> (4) partial evacuation of the intracranial contents of a living fetus to effect vaginal delivery of a dead but otherwise intact fetus.

Despite the technical differences we have just described, intact D and D are sufficiently similar for us to use the terms interchangeably.

(9) Dr. Carhart testified he attempts to use the intact D procedure during weeks 16 to 20 because it (1) reduces the dangers from sharp bone fragments passing through the cervix, (2) minimizes the number of instrument passes needed for extraction and lessens the likelihood of uterine perforations caused by those instruments, (3) reduces the likelihood of leaving infection-causing fetal and placental tissue in the uterus, and (4) could help to prevent potentially fatal absorption of fetal tissue into the maternal circulation. The District Court made no findings about the D procedure's overall safety. The District Court concluded, however, that "the evidence is both clear and convincing that Carhart's D procedure is superior to, and safer than, the . . . other abortion procedures used during the relevant gestational period in the 10 to 20 cases a year that present to Dr. Carhart."

(10) The materials presented at trial referred to the potential benefits of the D procedure in circumstances involving nonviable fetuses, such as fetuses with abnormal fluid accumulation in the brain (hydrocephaly). Others have emphasized its potential for women with prior uterine scars, or for women for whom induction of labor would be particularly dangerous.

(11) There are no reliable data on the number of D abortions performed annually. Estimates have ranged between 640 and 5,000 per year.

II

The question before us is whether Nebraska's statute, making criminal the performance of a "partial birth abortion," violates the Federal Constitution, as interpreted in *Planned Parenthood of Southeastern Pa.* v. *Casey* (1992) and *Roe* v. *Wade*. We conclude that it does for at least two independent reasons. First, the law lacks any exception " 'for the preservation of the . . . health of the mother.' " Second, it "imposes an undue burden on a woman's ability" to choose a D abortion, thereby unduly burdening the right to choose abortion itself. We shall discuss each of these reasons in turn.

A

The *Casey* joint opinion reiterated what the Court held in *Roe*; that "subsequent to viability, the State in promoting its interest in the potentiality of human life may, if it chooses, regulate, and even proscribe, abortion *except where it is necessary, in appropriate medical judgment, for the preservation of the life or health of the mother*" (emphasis added).

The fact that Nebraska's law applies both pre- and postviability aggravates the constitutional problem presented. The State's interest in regulating abortion previability is considerably weaker than postviability. Since the law requires a health exception in order to validate even a postviability abortion regulation, it at a minimum requires the same in respect to previability regulation.

The quoted standard also depends on the state regulations "promoting [the State's] interest in the potentiality of human life." The Nebraska law, of course, does not directly further an interest "in the potentiality of human life" by saving the fetus in question from destruction, as it regulates only a *method* of performing abortion. Nebraska describes its interests differently. It says the law "show[s] concern for the life of the unborn," "prevent[s] cruelty to partially born children," and "preserve[s] the integrity of the medical profession." But we cannot see how the interest-related differences could make any difference to the question at hand, namely, the application of the "health" requirement.

Consequently, the governing standard requires an exception "where it is necessary, in appropriate medical judgment for the preservation of the life or health of the mother," for this Court has made clear that a State may promote but not endanger a woman's health when it regulates the methods of abortion.

Justice Thomas . . . limit[s] this principle to situations where the pregnancy itself creates a threat to health. He is wrong. *Casey* . . . recognize[s] that a State cannot subject women's health to significant risks both in that context, *and also* where state regulations force women to use riskier methods of abortion. Our cases have repeatedly invalidated statutes that in the process of regulating the *methods* of abortion, imposed significant health risks. They make clear that a risk to a women's health is the same whether it happens to arise from regulating a particular method of abortion, or from barring abortion entirely. . . .

1

Nebraska responds that the law does not require a health exception unless there is a need for such an exception. And here there is no such need, it says. It argues that "safe alternatives remain available" and "a ban on partial-birth abortion/D would create no risk to the health of women." The problem for Nebraska is that the parties strongly contested this factual question in the trial court below; and the findings and evidence support Dr. Carhart. The State fails to demonstrate that banning D without a health exception may not create significant health risks for women, because the record shows that significant medical authority supports the proposition that in some circumstances, D would be the safest procedure.

We shall reiterate in summary form the relevant findings and evidence. On the basis of medical testimony the District Court concluded that "Carhart's D procedure is . . . safer tha[n] the D and other abortion procedures used during the relevant gestational period in the 10 to 20 cases a year that present to Dr. Carhart." It found that the D procedure permits the fetus to pass through the cervix with a minimum of instrumentation. It thereby

> reduces operating time, blood loss and risk of infection; reduces complications from bony fragments; reduces instrument-inflicted damage to the uterus and cervix; prevents the most common causes of maternal mortality (DIC and amniotic fluid embolus); and eliminates the possibility of "horrible complications" arising from retained fetal parts."

The District Court also noted that a select panel of the American College of Obstetricians and Gynecologists concluded that D " 'may be the best or most appropriate procedure in a particular circumstance to save the life or preserve the health of a woman.' "

2

Nebraska, along with supporting *amici,* replies that these findings are irrelevant, wrong, or applicable only in a tiny number of instances. It says (1) that the D procedure is "little-used," (2) by only "a handful of doctors." It argues (3) that D and labor induction are at all times "safe alternative procedures." It refers to the testimony of petitioners' medical expert, who testified (4) that the ban would not increase a woman's risk of several rare abortion complications (disseminated intravascular coagulopathy and amniotic fluid embolus).

The Association of American Physicians and Surgeons et al., *amici* supporting Nebraska, argue (5) that elements of the D procedure may create special risks, including cervical incompetence caused by overdilitation, injury caused by conversion of the fetal presentation, and dangers arising from the "blind" use of instrumentation to pierce the fetal skull while lodged in the birth canal.

Nebraska further emphasizes (6) that there are no medical studies "establishing the safety of the partial-birth abortion/D procedure" and "no medical studies comparing the safety of partial-birth abortion/D to other abortion procedures." It points to (7) an American Medical Association policy statement that "there does not appear to be any identified situation in which intact D is the only appropriate procedure to induce abortion." And it points out (8) that the American College of Obstetricians and Gynecologists qualified its statement that D "may be the best or most appropriate procedure," by adding that the panel "could identify no circumstances under which [the D] procedure . . . would be the only option to save the life or preserve the health of the woman."

3

We find these eight arguments insufficient to demonstrate that Nebraska's law needs no health exception. For one thing, certain of the arguments are beside the point. The D procedure's relative rarity (argument [1]) is not highly relevant. The D is an infrequently used abortion procedure; but the health exception question is whether protecting women's health requires an exception for those infrequent occasions. A rarely used treatment might be necessary to treat a rarely occurring disease that could strike anyone—the State cannot prohibit a person from obtaining treatment simply by pointing out that most people do not need it. Nor can we know whether the fact that only a "handful" of doctors use the procedure (argument [2]) reflects the comparative rarity of late-second-term abortions, the procedure's recent development, the controversy surrounding it, or, as Nebraska suggests, the procedure's lack of utility.

For another thing, the record responds to Nebraska's (and *amici*'s) medically based arguments. In respect to argument (3), for example, the District Court agreed that alternatives, such as D and induced labor, are "safe" but found that the D method was significantly *safer* in certain circumstances. In respect to argument (4), the District Court simply relied on different expert testimony—testimony stating that "[a]nother advantage of the Intact D is that it eliminates the risk of embolism of cerebral tissue into the woman's blood stream."

In response to *amici*'s argument (5), the American College of Obstetricians and Gynecologists, in its own *amici* brief, denies that D generally poses risks greater than the alternatives. It says that the suggested alternative procedures involve similar or greater risks of cervical and uterine injury, for "D procedures, involve similar amounts of dilitation" and "of course childbirth involves even greater cervical dilitation." The College points out that Dr. Carhart does not reposition the fetus thereby avoiding any risks stemming from conversion to breech presentation, and that, as compared with D, D involves the same, if not greater, "blind" use of sharp instruments in the uterine cavity.

We do not quarrel with Nebraska's argument (6), for Nebraska is right. There are no general Medical studies documenting comparative safety. Neither do we deny the import of the American Medical Association's statement (argument [7])—even though the State does omit the remainder of that statement: "The AMA recommends that the procedure not be used *unless alternative procedures pose materially greater risk to the woman*" (emphasis added).

We cannot, however, read the American College of Obstetricians and Gynecologists panel's qualification (that it could not "identify" a circumstance where D was the "only" life- or health-preserving option) as if, according to

Nebraska's argument (8), it denied the potential health-related need for D. That is because the College writes the following in its *amici* brief:

> Depending on the physician's skill and experience, the D procedure can be the most appropriate abortion procedure for some women in some circumstances. D presents a variety of potential safety advantages over other abortion procedures used during the same gestational period. Compared to D involving dismemberment, D involves less risk of uterine perforation or cervical laceration because it requires the physician to make fewer passes into the uterus with sharp instruments and reduces the presence of sharp fetal bone fragments that can injure the uterus and cervix. There is also considerable evidence that D reduces the risk of retained fetal tissue, a serious abortion complication that can cause maternal death, and that D reduces the incidence of a "free floating" fetal head that can be difficult for a physician to grasp and remove and can thus cause maternal injury. That D procedures usually take less time than other abortion methods used at a comparable stage of pregnancy can also have health advantages. The shorter the procedure, the less blood loss, trauma, and exposure to anesthesia. The intuitive safety advantages of intact D are supported by clinical experience. Especially for women with particular health conditions, there is medical evidence that D may be safer than available alternatives.

4

The upshot is a District Court finding that D significantly obviates health risks in certain circumstances, a highly plausible record-based explanation of why that might be so, a division of opinion among some medical experts over whether D is generally safer, and an absence of controlled medical studies that would help answer these medical questions. Given these medically related evidentiary circumstances, we believe the law requires a health exception.

The word "necessary" in *Casey*'s phrase "necessary, in appropriate medical judgment, for the preservation of the life or health of the mother," cannot refer to an absolute necessity or to absolute proof. Medical treatments and procedures are often considered appropriate (or inappropriate) in light of estimated comparative health risks (and health benefits) in particular cases. Neither can that phrase require unanimity of medical opinion. Doctors often differ in their estimation of comparative health risks and appropriate treatment. And *Casey*'s words "appropriate medical judgment" must embody the judicial need to tolerate responsible differences of medical opinion—differences of a sort that the American Medical Association and American College of Obstetricians and Gynecologists' statements together indicate are present here.

For another thing, the division of medical opinion about the matter at most means uncertainty, a factor that signals the presence of risk, not its absence. That division here involves highly qualified knowledgeable experts on both sides of the issue. Where a significant body of medical opinion believes a procedure may bring with it greater safety for some patients and explains the medical reasons supporting that view, we cannot say that the presence of a different view by itself proves the contrary. Rather, the uncertainty means a significant likelihood that those who believe that D is a safer abortion method in certain circumstances may turn out to be right. If so, then the absence of a health exception will place women at an unnecessary risk of tragic health consequences. If they are wrong, the exception will simply turn out to have been unnecessary.

In sum, Nebraska has not convinced us that a health exception is "never necessary to preserve the health of women." Rather, a statute that altogether forbids D creates a significant health risk. The statute consequently must contain a health exception. This is not to say, as Justice Thomas and Justice Kennedy claim, that a State is prohibited from proscribing an abortion procedure whenever a particular physician deems the procedure preferable. By no means must a State grant physicians "unfettered discretion" in their selection of abortion methods. But where substantial medical authority supports the proposition that banning a particular abortion procedure could endanger women's health, *Casey* requires the statute to include a health exception when the procedure is "necessary, in appropriate medical judgment, for the preservation of the life or health of the mother." Requiring such an exception in this case is no departure from *Casey,* but simply a straightforward application of its holding.

B

The Eighth Circuit found the Nebraska statute unconstitutional because, in *Casey*'s words, it has the "effect of placing a substantial obstacle in the path of a woman seeking an abortion of a nonviable fetus." It thereby places an "undue burden" upon a woman's right to terminate her pregnancy before viability. Nebraska does not deny that the statute imposes an "undue burden" *if* it applies to the more commonly used D procedure as well as to D. And we agree with the Eighth Circuit that it does so apply.

Our earlier discussion of the D procedure, *supra,* at 5–7, shows that it falls within the statutory prohibition. The statute forbids "deliberately and intentionally delivering into the vagina a living unborn child, or a substantial portion thereof, for the purpose of performing a procedure that the person performing such procedure knows will kill the unborn child." We do not understand how one could distinguish, using this language, between D (where a foot or arm is drawn through the cervix) and D (where the body up to the head is drawn through the cervix). Evidence before the trial court makes clear that D will often involve a physician pulling a "substantial portion" of a still living fetus, say, an arm or leg, into the vagina prior to the death of the fetus. Indeed D involves dismemberment that commonly occurs only when the fetus meets resistance that restricts the motion of the fetus: "The dismemberment occurs between the traction of . . . [the] instrument and the counter-traction of the internal os of the cervix." And these events often do not occur until after a portion of a living fetus has been pulled into the vagina.

Even if the statute's basic aim is to ban D, its language makes clear that it also covers a much broader category of procedures. The language does not track the medical differences between D and D—though it would have been a simple matter, for example, to provide an exception for the performance of D and other abortion procedures. Nor does the statute anywhere suggest that its application turns on whether a portion of the fetus' body is drawn into the vagina as part of a process to extract an intact fetus after collapsing the head as opposed to a process that would dismember the fetus. Thus, the dissenters' argument that the law was generally intended to bar D can be both correct and irrelevant. The relevant question is *not* whether the legislature wanted to ban D, it is whether the law was intended to apply *only* to D. The plain language covers both procedures. A rereading of pages 5–10 of this opinion, as well as Justice Thomas's dissent at pages 5–7, will make clear why we can find no difference, in terms of *this* statute, between the D procedure as described and the D procedure as it might be performed. Both procedures can involve the introduction of a "substantial portion" of a still living fetus, through the cervix, into the vagina—the very feature of an abortion that leads Justice Thomas to characterize such a procedure as involving "partial birth."

The Nebraska State Attorney General argues that the statute does differentiate between the two procedures. He says that the statutory words "substantial portion" mean "the child up to the head." He consequently denies the statute's application where the physician introduces into the birth canal a fetal arm or leg or anything less than the entire fetal body. He argues further that we must defer to his views about the meaning of the state statute.

We cannot accept the Attorney General's narrowing interpretation of the Nebraska statute. This Court's case law makes clear that we are not to give the Attorney General's interpretative views controlling weight. It "rarely reviews a construction of state law agreed upon by the two lower federal courts." In this case, the two lower courts have both rejected the Attorney General's narrowing interpretation.

For another, our precedent warns against accepting as "authoritative" an Attorney General's interpretation of state law when "the Attorney General does not bind the state courts or local law enforcement authorities." Under Nebraska law, the Attorney General's interpretative views do not bind the state courts. (Attorney General's issued opinions, while entitled to "substantial weight" and "to be respectfully considered," are of "no controlling authority"). Nor apparently do they bind elected county attorneys, to whom Nebraska gives an independent authority to initiate criminal prosecutions. . . .

Regardless, even were we to grant the Attorney General's views "substantial weight," we still have to reject his interpretation, for it conflicts with the statutory language discussed above. The Attorney General, echoed by the dissents, tries to overcome that language by relying on other language in the statute; in particular, the words "partial birth abortion," a term ordinarily associated with the D procedure, and the words "partially delivers vaginally a living unborn child." But these words cannot help the Attorney General. They are subject to the statute's further *explicit statutory definition,* specifying that both terms include "delivering into the vagina a living unborn child, or a substantial portion thereof." When a statute includes an explicit definition, we must follow that definition, even if it varies from that term's ordinary meaning. That is to say, the statute, read "as a whole," leads the reader to a definition. That definition does not include the Attorney General's restriction—"the child up to the head." Its words, "substantial portion," indicate the contrary.

The Attorney General also points to the Nebraska Legislature's debates, where the term "partial birth abortion" appeared frequently. But those debates hurt his argument more than they help it. Nebraska's legislators focused directly upon the meaning of the word "substantial." One senator asked the bill's sponsor, "[Y]ou said that as small a portion of the fetus as a foot would constitute a substantial portion in your opinion. Is that correct?" The sponsoring senator replied, "Yes, I believe that's correct." ([S]ame senator explaining "substantial" would "indicate that more than a little bit has been delivered into the vagina," i.e., "[e]nough that would allow for the procedure to end up with the killing of the unborn child.") The legislature seems to have wanted to avoid more limiting language lest it become too easy to evade the statute's strictures. That goal, however, exacerbates the problem.

The Attorney General, again echoed by the dissents, further argues that the statute "distinguishes between the overall 'abortion procedure' itself and the separate 'procedure' used to kill the unborn child." Even assuming that the distinction would help the Attorney General make the D/D distinction he seeks, however, we cannot find any language in the statute that supports it. He wants us to read "procedure" in the statute's last sentence to mean "separate procedure," i.e., the killing of the fetus, as opposed to a whole procedure, i.e., a D or D abortion. But the critical word "separate" is missing. And the same word "procedure," in the same subsection and throughout the statute, is used to refer to an entire abortion procedure.

The dissenters add that the statutory words "partially delivers" can be read to exclude D. They say that introduction of, say, a limb or both limbs into the vagina does not involve "delivery." But obstetric textbooks and even dictionaries routinely use that term to describe any facilitated removal of tissue from the uterus, not only the removal of an intact fetus. In any event, the statute itself specifies that it applies *both* to delivering "an intact unborn child" or "a substantial portion thereof." The dissents cannot explain how introduction of a substantial portion of a fetus into the vagina pursuant to D is a "delivery," while introduction pursuant to D is not.

We are aware that adopting the Attorney General's interpretation might avoid the constitutional problem discussed in this section. But we are "without power to adopt a narrowing construction of a state statute unless such a construction is reasonable and readily apparent." For the reasons stated, it is not reasonable to replace the term "substantial portion" with the Attorney General's phrase "body up to the head."

In sum, using this law some present prosecutors and future Attorneys General may choose to pursue physicians who use D procedures, the most commonly used method for performing previability second trimester abortions. All those who perform abortion procedures using that method must fear prosecution, conviction, and imprisonment. The result is an undue burden upon a woman's right to make an abortion decision. We must consequently find the statute unconstitutional.

The judgment of the Court of Appeals is Affirmed.

Justice Scalia, dissenting.

I am optimistic enough to believe that, one day, *Stenberg* v. *Carhart* will be assigned its rightful place in the history of this Court's jurisprudence beside *Korematsu* and *Dred Scott.* The method of killing a human child—one cannot even accurately say an entirely unborn human child—proscribed by this statute is so horrible that the most clinical description of it evokes a shudder of revulsion. And the Court must know (as most state legislatures banning this procedure have concluded) that demanding a "health exception"—which requires the abortionist to assure himself that, in his expert medical judgment, this method is, in the case at hand, marginally safer than others (how can one prove the contrary beyond a reasonable doubt?)—is to give live-birth abortion free rein. The notion that the Constitution of the United States, designed, among other things, "to establish Justice, insure domestic Tranquility, . . . and secure the Blessings of Liberty to ourselves and our Posterity," prohibits the States from simply banning this visibly brutal means of eliminating our half-born posterity is quite simply absurd.

Even so, I had not intended to write separately here until the focus of the other separate writings (including the one I have joined) gave me cause to fear that this case might be taken to stand for an error different from the one that it actually exemplifies. Because of the Court's practice of publishing dissents in the order of the seniority of their authors, this writing will appear in the reports before those others, but the reader will not comprehend what follows unless he reads them first.*

* * *

The two lengthy dissents in this case have, appropriately enough, set out to establish that today's result does not follow from this Court's most recent pronouncement on the matter of abortion, *Planned Parenthood of Southeastern Pennsylvania* v. *Casey*. It would be unfortunate, however, if those who disagree with the result were induced to regard it as merely a regrettable misapplication of *Casey*. It is not that, but is *Casey's* logical and entirely predictable consequence. To be sure, the Court's construction of this statute so as to make it include procedures other than live-birth abortion involves not only a disregard of fair meaning, but an abandonment of the principle that even ambiguous statutes should be interpreted in such fashion as to render them valid rather than void. *Casey* does not permit *that* jurisprudential novelty—which must be chalked up to the Court's inclination to bend the rules when any effort to limit abortion, or even to speak in opposition to abortion, is at issue

But the Court gives a second and independent reason for invalidating this humane (not to say anti-barbarian) law: That it fails to allow an exception for the situation in which the abortionist believes that this live-birth method of destroying the child might be safer for the woman. (As pointed out by Justice Thomas, and elaborated upon by Justice Kennedy, there is no good reason to believe this is ever the case, but—who knows?—it sometime *might* be.)

I have joined Justice Thomas's dissent because I agree that today's decision is an "unprecedented expansio[n]" of our prior cases, "is not mandated" by *Casey*'s "undue burden" test, and can even be called (though this pushes me to the limit of my belief) "obviously irreconcilable with *Casey*'s explication of what its undue-burden standard requires." But I never put much stock in *Casey*'s explication of the inexplicable. In the last analysis, my judgment that *Casey* does not support today's tragic result can be traced to the fact that what I consider to be an "undue burden" is different from what the majority considers to be an "undue burden"—a conclusion that can not be demonstrated true or false by factual inquiry or legal reasoning. It is a value judgment, dependent upon how much one respects (or believes society ought to respect) the life of a partially delivered fetus, and how much one respects (or believes society ought to respect) the freedom of the woman who gave it life to kill it. Evidently, the five Justices in today's majority value the former less, or the latter more, (or both), than the four of us in dissent. Case closed. There

*The dissents of Justice Kennedy and Justice Thomas are not reprinted here. We recommend reading those dissents, especially by all who are concerned about the constitutional status of abortion rights as determined by the cases reprinted in this volume.

is no cause for anyone who believes in *Casey* to feel betrayed by this outcome. It has been arrived at by precisely the process *Casey* promised—a democratic vote by nine lawyers, not on the question whether the text of the Constitution has anything to say about this subject (it obviously does not); nor even on the question (also appropriate for lawyers) whether the legal traditions of the American people would have sustained such a limitation upon abortion (they obviously would); but upon the pure policy question whether this limitation upon abortion is "undue"—i.e., goes too far.

In my dissent in *Casey,* I wrote that the "undue burden" test made law by the joint opinion created a standard that was "as doubtful in application as it is unprincipled in origin," "hopelessly unworkable in practice," "ultimately standardless." Today's decision is the proof. As long as we are debating this issue of necessity for a health-of-the-mother exception on the basis of *Casey,* it is really quite impossible for us dissenters to contend that the majority is *wrong* on the law—any more than it could be said that one is *wrong in law* to support or oppose the death penalty, or to support or oppose mandatory minimum sentences. The most that we can honestly say is that we disagree with the majority on their policy-judgment-couched-as-law. And those who believe that a 5-to-4 vote on a policy matter by unelected lawyers should not overcome the judgment of 30 state legislatures have a problem, not with the *application* of *Casey,* but with its *existence. Casey* must be overruled.

While I am in an I-told-you-so mood, I must recall my bemusement, in *Casey,* at the joint opinion's expressed belief that *Roe* v. *Wade* had "call[ed] the contending sides of a national controversy to end their national division by accepting a common mandate rooted in the Constitution," and that the decision in *Casey* would ratify that happy truce. It seemed to me, quite to the contrary, that "*Roe* fanned into life an issue that has inflamed our national politics in general, and has obscured with its smoke the selection of Justices to this Court in particular, ever since"; and that, "by keeping us in the abortion-umpiring business, it is the perpetuation of that disruption, rather than of any *Pax Roeana,* that the Court's new majority decrees."Today's decision, that the Constitution of the United States prevents the prohibition of a horrible mode of abortion, will be greeted by a firestorm of criticism—as well it should. I cannot understand why those who *acknowledge* that, in the opening words of Justice O'Connor's concurrence, "[t]he issue of abortion is one of the most contentious and controversial in contemporary American society," persist in the belief that this Court, armed with neither constitutional text nor accepted tradition, can resolve that contention and controversy rather than be consumed by it. If only for the sake of its own preservation, the Court should return this matter to the people—where the Constitution, by its silence on the subject, left it—and let *them* decide, State by State, whether this practice should be allowed. *Casey* must be overruled.

11

Roe v. *Wade* at Twenty-Five

Still Illegitimate

Michael W. McConnell

Twenty-five years ago today, the U.S. Supreme Court handed down its decision legalizing abortion throughout the country. The day before *Roe* v. *Wade*, abortion was flatly illegal in almost all states, though a few had recently relaxed their laws. On the day after *Roe*, women suddenly had a constitutional right to get an abortion for any reason, a right that effectively applied at any time during the nine months of pregnancy. (In theory, states could still ban abortion in the last three months unless it was necessary for the health of the woman—but the court defined "health" so broadly as to make this limitation meaningless.) The number of abortions quickly soared to almost 1.5 million every year, roughly 30 percent of all pregnancies.

Roe v. *Wade* is the most enduringly controversial Court decision of the century, and rightly so. Rather than putting the issue to rest, the court converted it into the worst sort of political struggle—one involving angry demonstrators, nasty confirmation battles and confrontational sound bites. With ordinary politicians, who are masters of compromise, out of the picture, the issue became dominated by activists of passionate intensity on both extremes of the spectrum.

A Time for Controversy

Controversial decisions—even decisions that rend the body politic—are sometimes necessary. The Constitution stands for certain fundamental principles of free government, and there are times when the court must intervene to make sure they are not neglected. But when judges act on the basis of their own political predications, without regard to constitutional text or the decisions of representative institutions, the results are illegitimate.

The reasoning of *Roe* v. *Wade* is an embarrassment to those who take constitutional law seriously, even to many scholars who heartily support the outcome of the case. As John Hart Ely, former dean of Stanford Law School and a supporter of abortion rights, has written, *Roe* "is not constitutional law and gives almost no sense of an obligation to try to be."

The Court's reasoning proceeded in two steps. First, it found that a "right of privacy" exists under the Constitution, and that this right is "broad enough to encompass a woman's decision whether or not to terminate her pregnancy." Since this meant that the right to abortion is constitutionally protected, a state could interfere with the right only if it has a "compelling state interest" for doing so.

But the right of privacy is nowhere mentioned in the Constitution. Various judges, according to the Court, had found "at least the roots of that right" in the First Amendment, in the "penumbras of the Bill of Rights," in the Ninth Amendment, or in the "concept of liberty guaranteed by the first section of the Fourteenth Amendment." This vague statement is tantamount to confessing the Court did not much care where in the Constitution this supposed right might be found. All that mattered was it be "broad enough" to encompass abortion.

Even assuming a right of privacy can be excavated from somewhere, anywhere, in the Constitution, what does it mean? The Court avoided defining the term, except by giving examples from previous cases. The trouble is, counterexamples abound. The federal "right of privacy" has never been held to protect against laws banning drug use, assisted suicide, or even consensual sodomy—just to mention a few examples of crimes that are no less "private" than abortion. It is impossible to know what does and does not fall within this nebulous category.

Even assuming that there is a right of privacy, and that its contours can be discerned from the court's examples, surely it must be confined to activities that affect no one else. It would be an odd kind of privacy that confers the power to inflict injury on nonconsenting third parties. Yet the entire rationale for antiabortion laws is that an abortion *does* inflict injury on a nonconsenting third party, the fetus. It is not possible to describe abortion as a "privacy right" without first concluding that the fetus does not count as a third party with protectable interests.

That brings us to step two in the Court's argument. Far from resolving the thorny question of when a fetus is another person deserving of protection—surely the crux of the privacy right, if it exists—the justices determined that the issue is unresolvable. They noted that there has been a "wide divergence of thinking" regarding the "most sensitive and difficult question" of "when life begins." They stated that "[w]hen those trained in the respective disciplines of medicine, philosophy, and theology are unable to arrive at any consensus, the judiciary . . . is not in a position to speculate as to the answer."

According to the Court, the existence of this uncertainty meant that the state's asserted interest in protecting unborn life could not be deemed "compelling." But this leaves us with an entirely circular argument. The supposed lack of consensus about when life begins is important because when state interests are uncertain they cannot be "compelling"; and a compelling state interest is required before the state can limit a constitutional right. But the constitutional right in question ("privacy") only exists if the activity in question does not abridge the rights of a nonconsenting third party—the very question the Court says cannot be resolved. If it cannot be resolved, there is no way to determine whether abortion is a "right of privacy."

In any event, the Court's claim that it was not resolving the issue of "when life begins" was disingenuous. In our system, all people are entitled to protection from killing and other forms of private violence. The Court can deny such protection to fetuses only if it presupposes they are not persons.

One can make a pretty convincing argument, however, that fetuses *are* persons. They are alive; their species is *Homo sapiens.* They are not simply an appendage of the mother; they have a separate and unique chromosomal structure. Surely, before beings with all the biological characteristics of humans are stripped of their rights as "persons" under the law, we are entitled to an explanation of why they fall short. For the court to say it cannot "resolve the difficult question of when life begins" is not an explanation.

It is true, of course, that people honestly disagree about the question of when life begins. But divergence of opinion is not ordinarily a reason to take a decision away from the people and their elected representatives. One of the functions of democratic government is to provide a forum for debating and ultimately resolving controversial issues. Judges cannot properly strike down the acts of the political branches that do not clearly violate the Constitution. If no one knows when life begins, the courts have no basis for saying the legislature's answer is wrong. To be sure, abortion is an explosive issue, with noisy and self-righteous advocates on both sides. But the Supreme Court made it far more so by eliminating the possibility of reasoned legislative deliberation and prudent compromise.

It is often said that abortion is an issue that defies agreement or compromise. But if the polling data are correct, there has been a broad and surprisingly stable consensus among the American people for at least the past thirty years that rejects the uncompromising positions of both pro-choice and pro-life advocates. Large majorities (61 percent in a recent New York Times/CBS poll) believe that abortion should be legally available during the early months of pregnancy. There is also widespread support for legal abortions when the reasons are sufficiently weighty (rape, incest, probability of serious birth defect, serious danger to the mother's health).

But only 15 percent believe that abortion should generally be available after the first three months, when the fetus has developed a beating heart, fingers and toes, brain waves, and a full set of internal organs. Majorities oppose abortions for less weighty reasons, such as avoiding career interruptions. Even larger majorities (approaching 80 percent) favor modest regulations, like waiting periods and parental consent requirements, to guard against hasty and ill-informed decisions. (The Supreme Court has permitted some such regulations to stand in the years since *Roe*.) Most Americans would prohibit particularly grisly forms of the procedure, like partial-birth abortions.

Reject the Extremes

These opinions have persisted without significant change since the early 1970s, and are shared by women and men, young and old alike. On the question of abortion, Americans overwhelmingly reject the extremes. If the courts would get out of the business of regulating abortion, most legislatures would pass laws reflecting the moderate views of the great majority. This would provide more protection than the unborn have under current law, though probably much less than pro-life advocates would wish.

The Supreme Court brought great discredit on itself by overturning state laws regulating abortion without any persuasive basis in Constitutional text or logic. And to make matters worse, it committed these grave legal errors in the service of an extreme vision of abortion rights that the vast majority of Americans rightly consider unjust and immoral. *Roe* v. *Wade* is a useful reminder that government by the representatives of the people is often more wise, as well as more democratic, than rule by lawyers in robes.

12

On the Origins of Privacy

Melvin L. Wulf

Although *Roe* v. *Wade* still survives, its critics continue their unceasing attacks against the abortion-rights decision in the hope of persuading the conservative majority of the Supreme Court to over-turn it. The main target for conservative academics and lawyers is the right of privacy, which is the decision's constitutional foundation. Typical of their criticism was a *New York Times* Op-Ed article some months ago by Robert Bork, who accused the Court of having plucked the right of privacy out of thin air in the 1965 case *Griswold* v. *Connecticut*, and of creating a "new, free-floating, undefined right." This was "legislation from the bench," he wrote. *Griswold* held unconstitutional a Connecticut statute that prohibited couples from using contraceptives and also prohibited physicians from prescribing them.

As the lawyer who first submitted the notion of a modern constitutional right of privacy to the Supreme Court, I propose to show that, contrary to Bork's accusations, the process by which the Court adopted that right was intellectually and jurisprudentially scrupulous.

In 1960, I was the junior lawyer on the two-man legal staff of the American Civil Liberties Union. The Supreme Court had agreed to review a case named *Poe* v. *Ullman*, which challenged the constitutionality of the same Connecticut statute ultimately struck down in the *Griswold* decision. I nominated myself to write the ACLUs *amicus curiae* brief.

Poe v. *Ullman* was a case that had been organized and sponsored by Planned Parenthood. The four plaintiffs were a married couple, a married woman, and an obstetrician. The wife of the couple had had three consecutive pregnancies, all of which terminated in infants with multiple congen-

Originally titled "Constitutional Practice: On the Origins of Privacy." This article is reprinted with permission from *The Nation*.

ital abnormalities. The married woman had suffered from a variety of serious medical problems, and if she became pregnant her death was deemed inevitable. The Connecticut law was a serious invasion of the plaintiffs' right to enjoy sexual activity. Neither of the women wanted to run the risk of pregnancy, but at the same time they did not want to give up their sexual life. They could enjoy sex without the threat of pregnancy only if they could use contraceptives. The obstetrician, Dr. C. Lee Buxton, asserted that the anticontraceptive law interfered with his right to practice his profession.

The law's direct interference with the women's right to engage in safe sexual activity was a distinctive and profound invasion by the state into a decision that should belong to individuals alone. The Connecticut law directly interfered with that private decision.

Since both the plaintiffs' brief and Planned Parenthood's *amicus* brief concentrated on Dr. Buxton's right to practice his profession without arbitrary government interference, the privacy argument was an appropriate issue for the ACLU's *amicus* brief. Too often *amicus* briefs just agree with other briefs filed in a case and are useless to the Court. Here was an opportunity to say something different and useful. The question was how to transform my view of the case into constitutional doctrine.

The way of constitutional litigation, like all other litigation, is to tread a path already worn, insofar as that is possible. Judges dislike breaking entirely new ground. If they are considering adopting a novel principle, they prefer to rest their decision on earlier law if they can, and to show that the present case involves merely an incremental change, not a wholesale break with the past. Constitutional litigators are forever trying to persuade courts that the result they are seeking would be just a short step from some other case whose decision rests soundly on ancient precedent.

Since the issue of sexual privacy had not been raised in any earlier case, we employed the familiar technique of argument by analogy: If there is no exact counterpart to the particular case before the Court, there are others that resemble it in a general sort of way, and the principles applied in the similar cases should also be applied—perhaps even extended a little bit—to the new case.

In developing the argument, I first went to the Fourth Amendment of the Constitution: "The right of the people to be secure in their persons, houses, papers, and effects, against unreasonable searches and seizures, shall not be violated. . . ." Since the Fourth Amendment obviously protects privacy, we see right at the outset the falsity of Bork's argument that the modern Supreme Court invented that right. The men who drafted the Constitution considered protection of privacy important enough for a separate provision in the Bill of Rights. Arbitrary searches were one of the principal grievances that led to the Revolution. The importance of privacy as a principle protected by the Constitution was highlighted in a 1949 case, *Wolf* v. *Colorado*, in which the

Supreme Court said that it "is at the core of the Fourth Amendment—[and] is basic to a free society." Although the Fourth Amendment and the Court in *Wolf* refer specifically to police intrusions, the underlying privacy principle served our purpose as well.

Our brief opened with a reference to the *Wolf* decision. It then quoted a famous passage by Justice Louis Brandeis in a 1928 case, *Olmstead* v. *United States*, in which he proclaimed that the makers of the Constitution "conferred, as against the government, the right to be let alone," which he described as "the most comprehensive of rights and the right most valued by civilized men."

Having placed the notion of privacy in a settled historical and constitutional context, the brief announced that it was striking out into somewhat new territory, conceding that the Court "has not had the occasion to consider a case raising the question of the extent of the right to privacy in circumstances which touch the marrow of human behavior as presented in this case."

My instinct was to be cautious and conservative. Although ACLU lawyers in 1960 were thought to be slightly dangerous firebrands, I knew my place where the Supreme Court was concerned. The *Poe* case itself had deliberately been conceived as a conservative challenge on the part of married men and women asking only for the right to engage in licit conjugal sex. I emphasized the orthodoxy involved by referring to the plaintiffs' married status. I pointed out that the statute, by preventing "married couples" from using effective contraceptives, forced them to choose between sexual relations that would threaten the life and health of "the female spouse" and abstention from sex altogether. We included a footnote to a quotation by Justice Felix Frankfurter in commemorating Justice Learned Hand's fifty years on the bench. He said that Hand "has achieved the one thing in life that makes all the rest bearable—a happy marriage." It seemed a way to attract Frankfurter's interest and sympathy.

Having laid the conservative foundation, we argued that, apart from assuring minimum standards of child care and education, the government should not interfere in other aspects of marriage and family life, especially "sexual union, and the right to bear and raise a family." But the State of Connecticut, we said, "will tolerate sexual intercourse between spouses" only if the couples do not use contraceptives.

On the principle that it was necessary to tie the proposed expanded right of privacy to an established right, the brief drew on a 1952 Supreme Court case, *Rochin* v. *California*. That case arose when the police broke into the defendant's house, entered the bedroom, where Rochin was in bed with his wife, and tried unsuccessfully to extract some pills he had put into his mouth. Rochin was taken to a hospital, his stomach was pumped, and capsules containing morphine were retrieved. The Court held that the search was illegal, saying that it violated "decencies of civilized conduct."

The brief segued from the facts of *Rochin* to the facts of *Poe*, suggested their parallelism, raised the specter of police breaking into a couple's bedroom to secure evidence of contraceptive use, and asserted that, in this case, the plaintiffs "want legislators as well as policemen to stay out of their bedrooms." It seemed apt, even if obvious.

That analogy, however, was not going to be enough to establish an expanded right of privacy. It was necessary to establish an awareness of the Constitution's concern for family-oriented values. If we could show the Court that it had spoken previously to such values, we would enhance our privacy argument.

Two Supreme Court cases dealing with family-related subjects fit the bill. *Meyer* v. *Nebraska*, a 1923 case, involved a statute forbidding foreign languages from being taught in primary schools. *Pierce* v. *Society of Sisters*, a 1925 case, concerned a statute that required children between the ages of eight and sixteen to attend public schools only. The Supreme Court held both statutes unconstitutional. In *Meyer*, referring to the Fourteenth Amendment's due process clause, the Court said:

> Without doubt, it denotes not merely freedom from bodily restraint but also the right of the individual to contract, to engage in any of the common occupations of life, to acquire useful knowledge, to marry, establish a home and bring up children, to worship God according to the dictates of his own conscience, and generally, to enjoy those privileges long recognized at common law as essential to the orderly pursuit of happiness by free men.

In *Pierce* the Court said:

> We think it entirely plain that the Act of 1922 unreasonably interferes with the liberty of parents and guardians to direct the up-bringing and education of children under their control. . . . The child is not the mere creature of the state; those who nurture him and direct his destiny have the right, coupled with the high duty, to recognize and prepare him for additional obligations.

Those excerpts lent themselves to a generality about the Court's attitude toward the protection of family values inherent in the Constitution.

It is important to note that the *Meyer* and *Pierce* decisions were not framed in terms of privacy rights as such. Their constitutional foundation was the due process clause of the Fourteenth Amendment, which declares that no state may "deprive any person of life, liberty, or property without due process of law." The conservative Supreme Court of the late nineteenth and early twentieth centuries had invoked the "property" reference of the clause to strike down progressive social legislation. In the 1920s and 1930s, however, the Court increasingly employed the due process clause as a way to enforce the provisions of the Bill of Rights against the states, requiring them as well as the federal government to grant their citizens fundamental civil liberties.

However else the due process clause may have been interpreted up to 1960, it had not been used explicitly to articulate a protectable right of privacy. But the language from *Meyer* and *Pierce* certainly lent itself to supporting a right-to-privacy concept in a family context. I drew the two threads together by asserting that *Meyer* and *Pierce* "sustain the conclusion that the law, to a large extent, regards marriage and the family as the ultimate repository of personal freedom, and that the power vested in husband and wife to conduct the affairs of their family free of state intervention is virtually plenary."

We filed our brief in October 1960. The case was argued in March 1961 and decided in June. The decision was no decision. A five-man majority held that the anticontraception statute was never enforced and that contraceptives could in fact be freely purchased in Connecticut. In the language of constitutional litigation, the case was not "justiciable." Frankfurter wrote the opinion. He was not seduced by my invocation of his testimonial to Learned Hand.

But the right-of-privacy argument caught the particular attention of Justice John Harlan. Harlan was a gentleman from New York City with impeccable establishment credentials, a conservative who in his years on the Court did little that was unpredictable. But he dissented from the majority decision in *Poe* v. *Ullman* and articulated for the first time a coherent constitutional right of privacy, drawing directly upon the concepts and cases proposed in the ACLU brief.

Before specifically addressing the idea of a constitutional right of privacy, Harlan explained his understanding of the due process clause of the Fourteenth Amendment:

> Due process has not been reduced to any formula; its content cannot be determined by reference to any code. The best that can be said is that through the course of this Court's decisions it has represented the balance which our Nation, built upon the postulates of respect for the liberty of the individual, has struck between that liberty and the demands of organized society. . . . The balance of which I speak is the balance struck by this country, having regard to what history teaches are the traditions from which it developed as well as the traditions from which it broke. That tradition is a living thing. A decision of this Court which radically departs from it could not long survive, while a decision which builds on what has survived is likely to be sound.

That is as good a description of the life of the Constitution as there is in legal literature.

Having laid that jurisprudential foundation, Harlan then referred to both *Meyer* v. *Nebraska* and *Pierce* v. *Society of Sisters* to demonstrate that the

Court had earlier protected the sort of personal family interests claimed by the plaintiffs in the *Poe* case. He then turned his attention to the Connecticut anticontraceptive statute.

He first identified the conflict between the parties: The plaintiffs asserted that the statute deprived them "of a substantial measure of liberty in carrying on the most intimate of all personal relationships . . . without any rational, justifying purpose"; the state asserted that "the availability of contraceptive materials tends to minimize 'the disastrous consequence of dissolute action,' that is fornication and adultery."

The plaintiffs' lawyers, in addition to arguing that the state could not interfere with a physician's professional judgment, had also argued the general desirability of conceptive use by married couples. Harlan rejected that as a basis for his opinion, for he thought the principle was not completely free of dispute, thus paying his respects to the Catholic Church. Rejecting any argument based even inferentially on a moral principle that was not universally accepted, he chose instead to rest his decision on the constitutional principle that the state could not enforce its moral judgment "by intruding upon the most intimate details of the marital relation with the full power of the criminal law." It would require testimony "as to the mode and manner of the named couples' sexual relations." The Connecticut statute, he said, "allows the state to enquire into, prove and punish married people for the private use of their marital intimacy." That was the essence of Harlan's constitutional objection to the statute, what he called "the privacy of the home in its most basic sense."

Harlan acknowledged that the privacy invasion in *Poe* was different from the very tangible privacy protected by the Third and Fourth Amendments, which address actual physical intrusions into one's home. But, he said, the privacy interest involved in *Poe* could be unprotected "only if due process . . . is limited to what is explicitly provided in the Constitution, divorced from the rational purposes, historical roots, and subsequent developments of the relevant provisions."

Expanding on that notion of a living Constitution, Harlan asserted that "the Constitution protects the privacy of the home against all unreasonable intrusions of whatever character," that here "we have not an intrusion into the home so much as the life which characteristically has its place in the home," and that "if the physical curtilage of the home is protected, it is surely as a result of solicitude to protect the privacies of the life within."

In that way, Justice Harlan first articulated a right of privacy that went beyond the literal terms of the Constitution. His privacy concept was persuasively connected to the actual language of the Constitution, though he did not fear to offend the literal language employed by the draftsmen, which reflected only the concepts, interests, and concerns of their particular time and place. His opinion is in fact very limited, as emphasized by his remark that it was not be taken to "suggest that adultery, homosexuality, fornication, and incest are immune from criminal inquiry." Harlan was prepared to admit into his realm of sexual privacy only intercourse between husband and wife. Only Justice William O. Douglas agreed with Harlan in *Poe* v. *Ullman*.

Four years later, in *Griswold* v. *Connecticut*, the right of privacy was accepted as a constitutional principle by a seven-to-two majority, and Douglas wrote the majority opinion. He drew upon Harlan's opinion in *Poe*, as did Justices Arthur Goldberg and Byron White in separate opinions. Harlan joined the majority, of course, but wrote his own separate opinion in which he admonished the two dissenters, Hugo Black and Potter Stewart, for accusing the majority of failing to exercise judicial "self-restraint." That, of course, is the totemic phrase used by Robert Bork and his allies to condemn liberal jurists. Harlan's answer should be the standard reply to every accusation that the Supreme Court's abortion opinion, *Roe* v. *Wade*, and other opinions that the right wing despises, are the work of activist, liberal, legislating judges:

> Judicial self-restraint . . . will be achieved . . . only by continual insistence upon respect for the teachings of history, solid recognition of the basic values that underlie our society, and wise appreciation of the great roles that the doctrines of federalism and separation of powers have played in establishing and preserving American freedoms.

Bork has himself constructed a narrow theory of constitutionalism that is not a product of pure reason, as he would like us to believe, but only a reflection of his own political predilections. He has made it sufficiently clear in his published writings that he has a weak attachment to the idea of democracy and to civil liberties. Between Louis XIV and the citizens of France, he supports the king. His rejection by the Senate for a seat on the Supreme Court has not yet convinced him that his constitutional attitudes are unacceptable to the American people. He might perhaps learn the lesson better by reading Justice Harlan in *Poe* v. *Ullman* once more, if he has read it a first time.

13

Religious Liberty and Abortion Policy
Casey as Catch-22

Paul D. Simmons

Like the hapless Yossarian and his fellow GIs in the closing days of World War II, women facing abortion regulations face a frustrating and often humiliating Catch-22.[1] The movie version of the novel made the phrase an unforgettable and telling part of the American vocabulary. Joseph Heller movingly portrayed the trap of the permission/denial syndrome—what is given with one order is taken away with another—in a way that every woman facing an abortion can understand. Recent U.S. Supreme Court decisions regarding abortion have left women facing the classic dilemma captured so memorably by Heller's antiheroes. The dilemma goes to the heart of First Amendment concerns regarding abortion and public policy.

For years, two arguments about religious liberty have formed a significant part of the abortion debate. The first—that public policy should not be based upon narrowly construed sectarian perspectives—reflects the concern that First Amendment protections be safeguarded by policymakers. The second—that no group should seek to impose its own moral/theological beliefs upon others who hold differing beliefs regarded as equally personal and sacred—requests that religious communities and/or leaders be faithful to the social contract of tolerance.

The wisdom of this approach seems increasingly evident as the heat the abortion debate generates has intensified over the past three decades. The deep investment in the issue by various faith communities has led to acrimonious and divisive rhetoric and heavy-handed actions that threaten the cohesion of the social fabric, especially the civility that is necessary to maintain tolerance among and for all religious groups in a free and open society.

From *Journal of Church and State* 42, no. 1 (winter 2000). Reprinted with permission.

Recent Supreme Court decisions about abortion have raised substantive religious liberty issues without addressing them directly. The aim of this essay is not to deal with abortion as a *moral* problem, but to explore the meaning(s) of religious liberty and the implications of the *Casey* decision for interpreting the First Amendment. My thesis is that *Casey* amounts to a Catch-22 for women whose decision to undertake an abortion, based on their own personal understanding of morality, may be compromised by the activities of others who oppose abortion for moral or religious reasons. The dilemma cries out for attention from the Supreme Court, which thus far has refused to address the religious liberty issues at stake.

Defining the Religious Issue

Locating or defining the religious nature of the abortion debate is of central importance. Those who campaign to ban abortion contend that no religious issue is involved because it is simply the killing of innocent human life, something both believers and atheists can agree to oppose. Abortion is merely a legal issue to be settled by the politics of majority rule.[2]

Since the Supreme Court has not dealt with abortion in terms of the Free Exercise/No Establishment Clauses of the First Amendment, some have concluded that there are no such issues involved. *Roe* v. *Wade* evaded the question, even while recognizing the philosophical/religious conundrum in the notion of fetal personhood. Justice John Paul Stevens raised the establishment issue in *Webster*, and both he and Justice Harry A. Blackmun alluded to religious liberty concerns in *Casey.* Up to this point, however, decisions guaranteeing a right to an abortion have relied upon the "right to privacy" and "personal liberties" assured under the Fourteenth Amendment. Even so, First Amendment concerns have considerable importance and thus clarification of these issues with regard to the abortion debate is needed.

It has been established that there are certain matters which do not constitute violations of the First Amendment. First, *religious leaders may address issues of moral import in the public arena.* Freedom for religion means that religious people have every right to engage in the democratic process of shaping public opinion and policy.

Second, *a simple coincidence between religious doctrine and certain laws or regulations does not necessarily violate the First Amendment.* The charge that a sectarian *doctrine* lies behind public policy restricting access to abortion[3] fails to prove entanglement or favoritism amounting to religious establishment.[4]

Even so, I believe *both establishment and free exercise issues are at stake in the abortion debate.* These may be seen in efforts to establish protections for the pregnant woman, the attempt to attribute personhood to gestating life, the constraints imposed upon women seeking abortions, and the latitude permitted religious groups who seek legislative power through political processes. Of special concern are those proposals regarding fetal personhood that rest on abstract metaphysical opinion, and the actions of various religious groups whose determination to shape policy results in actions which infringe upon the religious liberties of others.

The issue for public policy, of course, is a definition of personhood that is appropriate in and for a pluralistic society. To be sure, any legal definition might resemble a religious opinion; the *question is whether the definition is reasonable, and whether it enhances or restricts protected personal liberties.* The first principle of religious liberty is that laws will not be based upon abstract metaphysical speculation, but will be fashioned through democratic processes in which every perspective is subject to critical analysis. Any proposal must be open either to revision or rejection.

Part of the genius of *Roe* v. *Wade* (now affirmed by *Casey*) was putting forward the standard of viability: that stage of development at which the fetus has sufficient neurological and physiological maturation to survive outside the womb. Prior to that, the fetus simply is not sufficiently developed to speak meaningfully of it as an independent being deserving and requiring the full protection of the law, i.e., a person. The notion of viability correlates biological maturation with personal identity in a way that can be recognized and accepted by reasonable people. It violates no group's religious teachings or any premise of logic to provide protections for a viable fetus. The same can hardly be said for those efforts to establish moral and legal parity between a zygote (fertilized ovum) and a woman, which create substantive First Amendment issues.

The first is the claim to special knowledge. The proposal to ban abortion legally is based on a claim that a pre-embryo is a person, *whether other people believe it or not.* As John Finnis put it "When philosophers discuss natural Law, they are talking about the fact that there is a reality which is what it is whether one personally likes it or not."[5] In other words, no matter what ordinary logic might indicate, the (philosophical) opinion of the theologian is really the truth. Those who disagree are either misguided, uninformed, or willfully ignorant.

A second feature of this approach is the contention that such moral premises are not sectarian or religious in nature. The Catholic dogma which holds that abortion is the taking of innocent human life is regarded as a principle of natural law.[6] Natural law is a construct employed by theologians which attempts to bridge the worlds of religion and reason, or of revelation and nature. It has roots in Greek philosophy but was wedded to Christian moral thought most systematically in the works of Thomas Aquinas. Basic to his approach was the notion that the laws of God permeate nature and may be discerned by human reason. No special disclosure by God is necessary since all people are endowed by reason, he argued. The divine logos permeates all of creation and provides a link between the Divine and human mind; the very structures of nature are available universally and embody the absolute moral law of God. It is thus held to be true for all people. Since it is available to and by reason, which all people have, and since it permeates nature, which everyone might observe, every person, whether believer or unbeliever, is obligated to obey the moral law.

Since neither nature nor reason is the special monopoly of the religious, secularists or atheists are also capable of discerning the divine mandate—it requires no special revelation. The only advantage of the church is that it is devoted to the God of the universe and has the special calling and divine appointment to carry God's authority to teach the truth by which all people are to live. The moral rule can thus claim both religious and nonreligious meanings and attempt to win the allegiance of both believers and nonbelievers. Such an argument allows the contention to be made that efforts to prohibit or severely limit abortion are not being made on the basis of religious or sectarian dogma and thus pose no First Amendment problems. The natural law construct makes that contention possible, but it is hardly persuasive.

The final step is from morality to law. When the truth of God is made obvious, the laws of the state should conform to it. Thus, the "strict moral" rule against abortion articulated by clergy should be implemented by civil law. The relation between the moral and the civil law is one that underscores the "duty of the public authority to insure that the civil law is regulated according to the fundamental norms of the moral law in matters concerning human rights, human life and the institution of the family."[7]

What seems obvious and convincing to the natural law theorist, however, often appears unconvincing if not ludicrous to the critic. To claim a monopoly on truth on both secular and religious ground is self—serving in the extreme. It fits well in the scheme of the sectarian claim to be the final arbiter of all truth and the embodiment of divine revelation, that is, to claim an absolute grounding for conclusions supposedly based on human reason. The ultimate outcome of that line of thought was found in "The Syllabus of Errors"[8] which claimed, among other things, that error has no rights. The Inquisition itself had been conducted on the fervent belief that the church was doing heretics a favor by saving them from the damnation to which their false beliefs would most certainly lead.

The absolutist attitude against abortion claimed by evangelicals of the new right makes similar arguments but appeals to the authority of Scripture instead of natural law theory. The fact that scholars equally committed to biblical authority do not agree with fundamentalist or evangelical interpretations does not deter them from the claim that the Bible teaches that zygotes are persons and that abortion is murder. They also claim a type of "special knowledge" though its roots are ostensibly in revelation, not reason. Their intolerance toward people with different opinions reflects assumptions about the special nature of their calling and the particularly offensive nature of elective abortion.

The fact that Inquisitions and heresy hunts are now more subtle than those of the pre-Reformation era often conceals the fact that the same structure of thought and authority is still at work. When religious authorities make absolute pronouncements as if they were patently true and obviously obligatory for all people whether acknowledged as a faith commitment or not, an authoritarian claim is laid bare that is inimical to democratic processes and undermines respect for differing religious beliefs. The clear message is that those who disagree are to be corrected or coerced to conform, since their opinions have no right to moral standing and thus are not to be respected in the court of conscience or, finally, even by civil Law.

The appeal to privileged knowledge that is available only to those within a special circle but is somehow mandatory for everyone is especially problematic. The assertions of religious authorities must finally be submitted to the critical scrutiny of common sense and reason in a secular or pluralist society.[9] Whether or not a zygote is a person is a question for reflective analysis by jurists, theologians, philosophers, sociologists, embryologists,[10] and a host of other people—most all of whom are interested in good public policy, solid morals, and family values.

Casey and Abortion Rights

Casey took a positive step in the direction of clarifying an important Establishment question at this point. It began by rightly affirming the "essential holding" of *Roe*[11] protecting the right of a woman to choose to have an abortion before viability.[12] It also affirmed the state's power to restrict abortions after viability as long as there are provisions to protect the woman's life and health. But the Court created a quagmire of logical and practical problems when it affirmed (without recognizing any contradiction) the legitimacy of state interests throughout the pregnancy in protecting the life of the fetus that may become a child.[13]

Rejecting Abstract Metaphysics As Law

The most significant finding of the Court from a religious liberty perspective is that the woman is *the* person whose constitutional rights are to be protected.[14] The Court found two important lines of precedent for affirming the right to an abortion. The first relates to procreative rights—a "recognized protection accorded to the liberty relating to intimate relationships, the family, and decisions about whether to beget or bear a child."[15] The second is the limits "on government power to mandate medical treatment or its rejection," as in the Cruzan ruling. *Roe,* said the Court, "may be seen not only as an exemplar of Griswold liberty but as a rule . . . of personal autonomy and bodily integrity. . . . "[16]

Antiabortion groups have attempted to overturn *Roe* and outlaw abortion based on the belief that a fetus is a person with constitutional protections.[17] Certain states had enacted legislation protecting the unborn from the moment of conception.[18] The preamble to the Missouri statute declares that "the life of each human being begins at conception" and that "unborn children have protectable interests in life, health, and well-being."[19]

Casey amounted to a strong affirmation of the woman as unquestionably *the person* whose rights are at stake in the abortion debate.[20] Whatever "rights" a fetus may have are subsidiary to those of the woman.[21] A fetus—at any stage of gestation—is not to be protected at the expense of the woman. The Court said emphatically that states may not outlaw abortion, in effect rejecting the underlying presupposition of fetal personhood as a basis for law.

The fact that many people believe strongly that a zygote is a person is by now well established. The First Amendment allows people to believe as they will as a matter of conscience or religious belief. That is a matter of freedom *of* religion. But as a definition of personhood for constitutional protections in a pluralistic society, the zygote-as-person rationale is untenable in the extreme.

As John Rawls put it, definitions for public policy "must be supported by ordinary observation and modes of thought . . . which are generally recognized as correct."[22] Abstract metaphysical speculation has its rightful place in theology; but it must finally be rejected as inappropriate to the logic necessary for democratic rule. The appropriate ground for abortion regulations, said *Casey*, is "reasoned judgment," the "boundaries [of which] are not susceptible of expression as a simple rule."[23] In a passage reminiscent of *Roe,* the majority questioned whether the state can resolve [the questions revolving around the profound moral and spiritual implications of terminating a pregnancy, even in its earliest stage] in such a definitive way that a woman lacks all choice in the matter, except perhaps in those rare circumstances in which the pregnancy is itself a danger to her own life or health, or is the result of rape or incest.[24]

Justice Blackmun put it strongly in saying that an abortion is not "the termination of life entitled to Fourteenth Amendment protection. Accordingly, a State's interest in protecting fetal life is not grounded in the Constitution. Nor, consistent with our Establishment Clause, can it be a theological or sectarian interest."[25]

A second prong of the metaphysical argument rejected by the Court concerned the nature and role of the woman as woman. The prohibition of abortion argument is typically a corollary of the notion that women are created to be child-bearers and nurturers; choosing abortion thus denies a woman's "essential being" and allowing abortion legally contradicts the nature of the good and just society. But, as *Casey* rightly held, to impose such abstract visions of woman-as-she-is-created-to-be upon all women through public policy is to violate constitutional rights. Considered phenomenologically, for instance, not all women consider themselves "created" or intended to be mothers. Their own sense of being is therefore contradicted and denigrated when a contrary notion is imposed through law.

Other religious liberty considerations stem from the fact that some religious traditions stress individualism and calling in a way that emphasizes voluntarism and variety in the response of faith. Forbidding the abortion option is thus to foreclose an alternative based in what some women regard as religious, moral, or spiritual mandates.

The Court therefore rejected the notion that public policy should define the woman's role. "The liberty of the woman is at stake in a sense unique to the human condition and so unique to the law," said *Casey.* "Her suffering is too intimate and personal for the State to insist, without more, upon its own vision of the woman's role, however dominant that vision has been in the course of our history and our culture." Her decision is to be based upon the "right to define one's own concept of existence, of meaning, of the universe, and of the mystery of human life." Her own destiny "must be shaped to a large extent on her own conception of her spiritual imperatives and her place in society."[26] The Court has said strongly that the decision about abortion belongs basically to that zone of conscience and belief unique to the woman as a person. It is her liberty that is uniquely at stake, limiting (though not absolutely) the ability of the state to impose its own views of the woman's role.[27]

By affirming the woman's rights, *Casey* went beyond *Roe* which had made abortion a matter of decision between the woman *and her physician. Roe* emphasized the right of the physician to practice medicine without interference from the law. But *Casey* focused on patient autonomy—the uniqueness of the decision *for the woman*: it is her "anxieties," "physical constraints," and "pain" that give prominence to her judgment.[28] The fact that women have been willing to make "sacrifices" to bear and nurture children, does not mean that the state can impose those roles upon them.

The concurring opinion by Justice Blackmun explicitly spoke to the issue of "gender equality."[29] By limiting abortion, he said, the state "conscripts women's bodies into its service, forcing women to continue their pregnancies, suffer the pains of childbirth, and in most instances provide years of maternal care," all of which goes uncompensated.[30] It is simply assumed to be a duty she owes the state. The Court rightly held that both good ethics and equal protection require that pregnancy and childbirth be voluntary and not coerced.

Abortion and Male Authority

Casey also struck down provisions requiring spousal notification,[31] which had the effect of maintaining male authority over the woman.[32] The physician was thus an agent of the state to enforce the paternal rule.

The Court held that such a statutory requirement would pose an "undue burden" on actions permitted under *Roe* and thus were invalid. "Women do not lose their constitutionally protected liberty when they marry," it said. "The Constitution protects all individuals, male or female, married or unmarried, from the abuse of governmental power, even where that power is employed for the supposed benefit of a member of the individual's family."[33]

Casey thus amounts to a further step in the realization of women's rights in America. The abortion debate has furthered the awareness that both the personhood of women and their exercise of procreative rights are uniquely at stake in pregnancy. While men typically share the burden of pregnancy and childbirth in certain ways, they do not know personally or experientially the threat and burden of an unwanted pregnancy. Thus, when consensus in the marriage breaks down, the woman is the final arbiter in the abortion decision.

RESCUERS AND *BRAY*

The strong affirmation of the woman's prerogatives and the uniqueness of her role in abortion decisions caused many to anticipate that the Court would support the use of the "Ku Klux Klan" law against antiabortion efforts to prevent access to abortion clinics.[34] The Reconstruction Era law bars conspiracies to deprive "any person or class of persons" of the equal protection of the law. Attorneys for women's groups had argued that demonstrations intended to shut down abortion clinics constituted a type of discrimination against women as a class, since only women have abortions. However, the Court held that federal judges could not apply the 1871 law to the disruptive tactics of Operation Rescue.[35] Justice Antonin Scalia, writing for the six-to-three majority, argued that both women and men can be found on both sides of the abortion debate, thus negating the "class" argument.[36] "Whatever one thinks of abortion," he said, "it cannot be denied that there are common and respectable reasons for opposing it, other than hatred of or condescension toward . . . women as a class."[37]

Both Justices Stevens and Sandra Day O'Connor took issue with Scalia. The test under the law, Stevens argued, is not hostility toward women, but whether it is "aimed at conduct that only members of the protected class have the capacity to perform."[38] The aim, he said, was "to deny every woman the opportunity to exercise a constitutional right that only women possess."[39] Pointing both to "massive defiance of the law" and "violent obstruction of the constitutional rights of their fellow citizens," Stevens argued that the protesters' strategy "represents a paradigm of the kind of conduct that the statute was intended to cover."[40]

In spite of the coherent and plausible arguments of both Stevens and O'Connor, those of Scalia prevailed. Scalia happens to embrace the notion that all issues in a democratic society should be settled by majority vote and thus has little patience for constitutional protections accorded minorities.[41] His religious commitments have also been shaped by a tradition that is profoundly and strongly opposed to the legal availability of abortion. The primary problem, however, is that there was no attention to the special category of people at issue in the clinic demonstrations. They were women who had reasons rooted in experience, moral perspectives, personal values, and religious commitments that supported their decision to terminate a pregnancy. As such, they deserved protection based on First Amendment considerations, none of which were raised.

The message from the Supreme Court regarding abortion is thus ambiguous, if not contradictory. *Casey* says strongly that women are the citizens at issue in the abortion dilemma. It is *the woman's* conscientious judgment that is to be protected. But in the *Bray* decision, the Court reverted to a paradigm that assumed abortion rights could be exercised only if the woman can win out in a pushing contest with those trying to prevent her from doing so. Scalia's comment that people differ about the morality or legal acceptability of the issue is simply to state the obvious. In no way does that characteristic of the political process alter the fact that only women (whose religious beliefs and moral framework allow abortion) are those whose rights are at stake. The *Bray* decision allows women to be subjected to the hostile opinion and actions of those who are strongly opposed to abortion, that is, to her moral and religious values. The "vote" includes the moral judgment of men, none of whom will ever be pregnant, and of women who are conscientiously opposed to abortion and thus feel no deprivation of *their* constitutional rights.

Several reasons seem to lie behind the reasoning of the Court majority. First is the *Court's deference to what it perceives as the ambivalence in American public opinion toward abortion.* Scalia believes strongly that public opinion, not the Court, should settle public policy toward abortion (as in *Webster*). Polls seem to show that Americans do not like abortion, but they want it legally available.[42] But how might that be translated into a finding to shape public policy?

At one level, such an opinion reflects a becoming reticence to deal with matters that are sensitive and often upsetting, much as polite company does not like to talk about the gory details of surgery or bodily functions. At another level, the perception is that good morals mandate compelling reasons to justify an abortion. Such reasons seem not to be present in a large number of elective abortions. That understandable and laudatory attitude on the part of thinking people shows the need for "disapproving" abortion, that is, not being simply indifferent toward what appears to be a callused attitude toward ending a problem pregnancy.

The other side of that ambivalence is that Americans want abortion to be legally available. That is the basic meaning of being "pro-choice." It is generally agreed that the majority of people are not "for" abortion if that means being enthusiastic about or indifferent toward pregnancy terminations. Most everyone, however, can think of circumstances under which good and moral women might reasonably and justifiably choose to terminate a pregnancy and be supported in doing so by the moral community. At a minimum, that means good morals require the legal availability of abortion, as *Casey* affirms.

Second, *the Court seems concerned to protect liberties associated with religious beliefs, free speech, and public assembly.* Thus it is reluctant to curtail the actions of even the most militant and aggressive antiabortion groups.[43] In *Schenck,* the Court rejected the notion that a "buffer zone" should protect women entering an abortion clinic to shield them from the harsh rhetoric and intimidating, often injurious handling by antiabortion protesters.[44] The decision followed its earlier comments in *Madsen* that a protective zone around a clinic "burdened more speech than necessary to serve a significant governmental interest."[45] The general principle, said the Court, is that "citizens must tolerate insulting, and even outrageous speech in order to provide adequate breathing space to the freedoms protected by the First Amendment."[46] The bottom line is that rights regarding free speech have greater protection than those regarding First Amendment rights regarding the free exercise of religion.

The most generous interpretation of the *Schenck* and *Madsen* decisions is that they tend to underscore the Court's commitment to protecting the freedoms of speech associated with religious and moral beliefs. That it is also protecting the most egregious forms of civil disturbances seems an irony requiring further attention. The strategies of brutal rhetoric and bodily assault employed by Rescuers seem to constitute harassment of those exercising legitimate constitutional protections, as Justice Kennedy's comments seem to admit.[47] Such actions might be construed either as violating the woman's bodily integrity, or as limiting a woman's free exercise of liberties premised on religious commitments. The abortion clinic becomes a battleground over religious liberties; but only one party is attempting to coerce the other. At what point is religious intolerance to be restrained?

LIMITING THE ABORTION OPTION

A final reason the Court may have had in mind was that protecting those who demonstrate against abortion providers is one way to *allow certain limitations to be imposed on the right to abortion.* That interpretation would be consistent with *Webster* that allowed states to provide incentives for childbirth (such as providing financial support), while instituting various impediments to securing an abortion. Thus states could ban abortion in hospitals receiving public funds, refuse to pay for the procedure, and forbid any public personnel from discussing abortion with a client.

Neither *Casey* nor *Bray* endorsed the heavy-handed measures of Rescuers as a way to discourage abortion. Even so, *Bray* gives strong encouragement to activists in the private sector. One way a state may now create hindrances to procuring an abortion is to be lenient toward disruptive demonstrations against women entering clinics.[48]

The consistency between *Webster* and *Casey* is certainly no virtue. It compromises both internal logic and basic constitutional rights. What is granted the woman with one hand is taken from her with the other; she is caught in a legal Catch-22. The rationale behind permitting limits, said *Casey*, is that the decision is "more than a philosophical exercise," which had been admitted as basic to the woman's choice. The Court went on to say:

> Abortion is a unique act. It is fraught with consequences for others, for the woman who must live with the implications of her decision; for the persons who perform and assist in the procedure; for the spouse, family and society which must confront the knowledge that these procedures exist, procedures some deem nothing short of an act of violence against innocent human life; and, depending on one's beliefs, for the life or potential life that is aborted.[49]

In short, it is an action about which others have strong feelings and vested interests that, in the mind of the Court, constitute grounds for limiting the woman's choice! The religious and moral sensibilities of the woman contemplating abortion may be submitted to the tribunal of people holding profoundly different religious opinions.

A Contest of Religious Conviction

The woman's situation is exacerbated by the fact that *Casey* also affirmed requirements for informed consent followed by a twenty-four-hour waiting period.[50] Abortion providers may be required to inform women contemplating abortion concerning gestational development, arguments against elective abortion, and alternatives to abortion such as adoption. The woman then must wait a day while further considering her choice.

The Pennsylvania statute was apparently accepted as a general corollary to the doctrine of informed consent which prevails in medical ethics.[51] However, there are types of "information" and styles of giving "information" that are more like insults, harassment, and intimidation than providing crucial data for responsible decision making. The Court admitted that the abortion decision belongs to "the zone of conscience and belief," but then allowed the conscientious convictions of another party to prevail in determining not only the information to be covered but the style in which it is delivered. Those familiar with the tactics of "pregnancy counseling centers" know only too well that women are harangued by antiabortion militants.[52] The badgering can take place even while insisting that abortion is still an option the woman may choose. The scenario conjured up is that of a Court-approved equivalent of the Grand Inquisitor in the medical context.

Limiting abortion by inducing shame is a major strategy of the antiabortion movement, as admitted by Gary Bauer, head of the ultraconservative Family Research Council. Domestic policy advisor to former President Reagan, Bauer noted that "legal or illegal, . . . abortion will be seen as a matter of shame and something to be avoided."[53] The aim is to institute "informed consent" procedures that deter women from choosing abortions; this is little more than a form of legalized abuse of a citizen attempting to exercise a constitutional right.

Even the choice of terminology when speaking of an abortion signals the posture of the speaker. Sympathetic counselors will likely use neutral or scientific terms like conceptus, zygote, embryo, or fetus when speaking of the entity in the uterus. And the procedure will likely be spoken of as removal, suctioning, or vacuuming. Loaded words like baby, unborn child, or infant will be used by those committed to deterring women from obtaining an abortion. And the procedure will be spoken of as killing, murder, dismembering, or destroying. Such freighted terminology is hardly "a scientifically impeccable choice of terms." It is an explicit but deniable attempt to manipulate the woman by inducing guilt and shame.[54]

The Court should be interested not only in informed consent, therefore, but also in the protection of the woman's religious and personal dignity. If she is treated with courtesy (as in Japan where women undergoing abortion are shown great deference),[55] whatever elements of remorse are present will be negligible or manageable. Bauer's comment points to the fact that the critical variable between the experience of women who wind up with profound guilt and those who see the experience more favorably may well be the type of informed consent process to which they have been subjected.

The Concern for Conscience

Casey's emphasis on conscientious belief as the grounds for personal liberty and bodily integrity is consistent with *Roe*'s concern for privacy as encompassing procreative decisions. Both notions somewhat capture the religious liberty concern for the respect due a person's moral commitments based upon ground-of-meaning beliefs. "Privacy" is not just a matter done in private; it is another name for conscience or the inferiority of compelling beliefs whether defined in religious or philosophical terms.[56] The concern for conscience is a corollary of the protections accorded under the First Amendment.

Casey thus dealt with important religious liberty concerns, without ever saying so.[57] Holding that the basic questions regarding abortion are rooted in "one's own concept of existence, of meaning, of the universe, and of the mystery of human life," the Court acknowledged the role of ground-of-meaning beliefs in defining fetal value and/or the moral acceptability of terminating an unwanted pregnancy. These, said the Court, are shaped by the woman's own "conception of her spiritual imperatives and her place in society."The question of abortion takes place in an arena in which the strong moral beliefs of the individual citizen *and not others* ought to prevail.

The Court thus seemed to settle an important Establishment question in the abortion debate. Declaring that states may not ban abortion, the Court in effect rejected the dogma of a zygote-as-person that would be a basic presupposition for a legal ban. States like Utah and Louisiana had tried to prohibit abortion based on the doctrine that one is a person "from the moment of conception."That many people believe that a zygote is a person does not alter the fact that the attribution of personhood to a zygote is based on metaphysical speculation, not scientific fact. Appeal must be made to "special metaphysical, e.g., religious premises," says Thomas Boles. The facts "provide no empirical basis for the thesis that the person of the child which the zygote will become is already present in the zygote."[58] In effect, to ban abortion is to base law on religious or sectarian opinion contrary to the guarantees against establishment of religion.[59]

The second part of the religious liberty issue, however, deals with "free exercise." In this area, *Casey* seems less sensitive to the protection of conscientious judgments. Allowing states to implement procedures to discourage the practice is to permit others to harass and cajole those women whose religious scruples and teachings (conscience) permit abortion as a moral option. Women whose conscience is formed *against* abortion are in no way required to terminate a pregnancy, of course, and thus never encounter the problem of harassment as a violation of conscientiously held convictions. Those who choose to abort may well encounter a hostile environment of opinion and action based on religious or moral viewpoints contrary to their own. They may well be humiliated and denigrated unless there are safeguards for the free and open exercise of their own profoundly held beliefs.

Abortion As Free Exercise

In sum, the establishment issue is focused in whether the fetus is a person protected, as are all citizens under the Constitution; the free exercise issue pertains to access to abortion services. The Supreme Court has approached abortion policy in precisely that sequence. We can confidently say that abortion *as such is* not a question of religious liberty on the grounds of free exercise.[60] Were it possible to establish that a fetus (from whatever stage of gestation) is a person, elective abortion would not be a legal option, certainly not on the basis of an appeal to the free exercise of religion. Just as religious belief cannot legalize human sacrifice or spousal abuse, if the Court was convinced the fetus is a person, abortion would be banned either as homicide or child abuse regardless of whatever a specific religious group may say about the rightness of the practice.

In all cases, the free exercise of religion is limited by the parameters established by the rights to life and liberty of other persons under the law. Thus, antichoice activists have worked feverishly to have embryos or fetuses (depending on the stage of gestation chosen) declared persons under the Constitution. If they are persons they are protected under constitutional guarantees.[61]

Privacy is one of those rights and it includes decisions regarding procreative choice from contraceptives (*Griswold*) to abortion (*Roe* and *Casey*). The appeal to the free exercise of one's religious beliefs and affections is thus quite simply to be able to make choices consistent with one's religious tradition regarding a constitutionally protected right. Elective abortion belongs to that arena of choice that has to do with the woman's pursuit of a meaningful life consistent with her own moral and personal values and religious beliefs, as *Casey* said so strongly and rightly.[62]

Free exercise also requires that such a choice must be without undue coercion. At one level, this standard requires that no woman is to be coerced to terminate a pregnancy. Those women who believe strongly that a fetus is an "unborn child" are protected from religious beliefs that run contrary to that opinion. Having a child is a basic freedom or entitlement in America, as one of those protected liberties that women may exercise without undue interference from others. The other side of the free exercise coin is that women who choose to terminate a pregnancy are doing so out of equally powerful ground-of-meaning beliefs that allow her to abort. She is exercising the religious convictions that help to shape her own sense of meaning about life and her sense of calling in life. Whether and/or when to become a mother is a decision fraught with responsibility and thus must be done only after due consideration of the consequences.

Those women whose conscience is formed against abortion for any reason have every right to appeal to the protection of the law against those who would injuriously cajole, criticize, or otherwise attempt to coerce her to abort. One could argue on eugenics grounds, for instance, that the common good should be protected against having children born who are known to have severe physical or neurological deficits. Such arguments, however, do not prevail against the prerogatives rooted in the religious and moral commitments of the pregnant woman. Her rights against coercion are protected.

Therefore, women who decide not to bring a pregnancy to term should have equal protection from harassment, injury, and coercion. Rabbi Shira Stern decided, along with her husband, Rabbi Donald Weber, to terminate a pregnancy in the fifth month of gestation. Tests showed that the fetus was affected by Tay-Sachs, a lethal genetic disease. Their decision to abort had the full support of their religious tradition and the community of which they were a part. But while she was lying on her hospital bed, a television program carried a strongly worded antiabortion message by then-President Ronald Reagan. He declared abortion to be "this nation's number one moral problem"; and stated that he would press for legislation to outlaw "the murder of unborn children."[63]

Had the "information" some states require to be given a woman prior to abortion been written or provided by a person with the moral or religious convictions of Mr. Reagan, Rabbi Stern would have been subjected to severe verbal abuse and personal humiliation. The conflict between speaker and hearer would have been at the ground-of-meaning level of foundational beliefs regarding fetal "personhood" and the moral acceptability of terminating a problem pregnancy. It would have been a clash of religious convictions. The one in a position of power and authority (information provider, health care professional) would have been able to harass and intimidate, to cajole and badger the one who was vulnerable and dependent—a pregnant woman who had decided to terminate a pregnancy.

The law now allows "informed consent" procedures that seem more humiliating than helpful, and it also allows abortion protesters to engage in egregious acts of rhetoric and efforts to impede the woman's decision to abort. Such actions are consistent with the Court's statements in *Webster,* which allowed "hindrances" or "impediments" to be placed in the path of women seeking abortions, and *Schenck,* which allowed verbal and emotional harassment.[64] The provision regarding informed consent is thus not as benign as it might otherwise appear. Under the rubric of a perfectly acceptable doctrine in medical ethics (i.e., informed consent), the Court is apparently willing to turn a blind eye and deaf ear to extensive infringements of one's "free exercise" of religious liberty.

At this level, the *Casey* decision has a glaring inconsistency. It speaks of conscience and moral beliefs as prevailing in decisions regarding abortion, but it allows a clash of opposite opinions to prevail in the clinic or delivery room. The reception or operating room should not become a forum for profoundly divisive and competing religious and moral visions. A vulnerable patient should not have to give account to a judgmental team of care providers.

The contradiction around which *Casey* was fashioned goes to the heart of First Amendment concerns. If, as Justice Blackmun noted in his dissent, "a State's interest in protecting fetal life is not grounded in the Constitution," then why might women be "discouraged" or hindered from exercising the option of abortion, certainly in the early stages of pregnancy? It hardly provides substantive reasons for allowing egregious hindrances. If she has already considered the data, examined the issues at stake, considered her circumstances, weighed her alternatives, and reached a conscientious decision, she may well discover the "informed consent process" to be a humiliating and degrading experience.

Casey thus perpetuated the Catch-22 allowed by *Webster.* Women seeking abortion are protected from the imposition of alien and odious opinions in one area; but they are subjected to injurious and abusive insults in another arena governed by contrary religious beliefs and practices.

CONCLUSION

Casey has therefore clarified important points *and* left a great deal to be desired and done in its response to the abortion debate, from the perspective of religious liberty concerns. Each state has enormous work to do in clarifying its approach to abortion within the permissible parameters allowed by *Casey.* While no state may ban abortion, hindrances to procure an abortion may be instituted in a variety of ways. The stage is set for a continuation of belligerent confrontations based on deeply held religious opinions regarding the morality of abortion.

The High Court would do well to examine abortion as an issue of religious liberty and First Amendment guarantees. It has done reasonably well in ferreting out what amounts to establishment issues; it would do well also to protect the free exercise of the woman's conscientious (i.e., religious) judgment.

NOTES

1. Joseph Heller, *Catch-22* (New York: Simon and Schuster, 1955).

2. D. J. Horan, et al., eds., *Abortion and the Constitution: Reversing Roe v. Wade Through the Courts* (Washington, D.C.: Georgetown University, 1987), p. xiv.

3. See, for instance, John Swomley, "Supreme Court's Abortion Decision Parallels Roman Catholic Bishop's Position," *Churchman's Human Quest* (September-October, 1989), pp. 16–17.

4. Both *Harris* v. *McRae,* 448 U.S. 297 (1980), and *Casey* at 2807 said the issue is not the coincidence between law and doctrine but whether a protected liberty is infringed.

5. See his comments in Horan, *Abortion and the Constitution*, p. 116.

6. There are other versions of natural law theory that are found among both Protestant and Roman Catholic theologians. The absolute ban on abortion among traditional Catholics typically appeals to the type here outlined For another approach, see Beverly W Harrison, *Our Right to Choose* (Boston, Mass.: Beacon Press, 1983).

7. Joseph Cardinal Ratzinger, *Instruction on Respect for Human Life in its Origin and on the Dignity of Procreation: Replies to Certain Questions of the Day.* Congregation for the Doctrine of the Faith (Rome: The Vatican, 1988), part 3.

8. Pope Pius IX, "Syllabus of Errors," 1864.

9. See Peter S. Wenz, *Abortion Rights as Religious Freedom* (Philadelphia, Pa.: Temple University Press, 1992), p. 112. Wenz contends *the question is* whether beliefs can be supported cogently with arguments or demonstrations whose premises include only secular beliefs." The issue, he says, is a matter of "epistemology," that is, the way in which knowledge is gained or claims are supported.

10. See Charles A. Gardner, "Is an Embryo a Person?" in *Abortion, Medicine and the Law*, 4th ed., eds. J. D. Butler and D. F. Walbert (New York: Facts on File, 1992), pp. 453–56.

11. See *Casey* at 2804 (I.5) and Stevens's dissent, 2844 (I.1).

12. *Casey* at 2804 (I.6[1][2][3]).

13. *Casey,* ibid. See also Rehnquist at 2867.

14. *Casey* 2812 at 5, and 2816 at [15].

15. Ibid., 2810 [II], and 2830 [37] citing *Eisenstadt* v. *Baird,* 405 U.S. at 453.

16. Ibid., 2810 [II, par. 3].

17. D. J. Horan and T. J. Balch, "*Roe* v. *Wade:* No Justification in History, Law or Logic," in *Abortion and the Constitution*, p. 76.

18. Guam, Utah, and Louisiana, for instance. See Rebunfeld, "On the Legal Status of the Proposition that 'Life Begins at Conception,'" *Stamford Law Review* 43 (1991): 599.

19. See *Webster* v. *Reproductive Health Services* 492 U.S. 490 (1989). Fetal personhood was not at issue in the Pennsylvania law that sought only to regulate the availability of abortion.

20. *Casey,* 2816 at [16].

21. *Casey,* 2818; see also Stevens's comments at 2839.

22. John A. Rawls, *A Theory of Justice* (Cambridge, Mass.: Harvard University Press, 1971), p. 213.

23. *Casey* at 2806.

24. Ibid.

25. Justice Stevens concurring in *Casey* at 2188, citing *Thornburgh* v. *American College of Obstetricians and Gynecologists,* 476 U.S. 747 (1986) at 778.

26. See *Casey,* II.[6], par. 6 (2807).

27. Ibid., [19].

28. Ibid. at 2807; see also Blackmun's comments.

29. Ibid., II.A.

30. Ibid.

31. Ibid., [35].

32. Pennsylvania barred a physician from performing an abortion for a married woman unless there was: (1) a signed statement from the woman that she had notified her spouse; (2) her certification that her husband was not the man who had impregnated her; or, (3) that her husband could not be located; or, (4) that the pregnancy resulted from spousal sexual assault which she had reported; or, (5) that the woman believed notifying her husband would result in serious bodily harm to herself.

33. Ibid. at 2831.

34. *Bray* v. *Alexandrian Women's Health Clinic, et. al.* 90-915, S.Ct. 13 January 1993.

35. See ibid., dissent by O'Connor, par. 1.

36. Ibid., opinion by Scalia, I.A.3.

37. Ibid., I.A.5.

38. Ibid., dissent by Stevens, V.6.

39. Ibid., V.7.

40. Ibid., V.8.

41. *Oregon* v. *Smith,* 494 U.S. 872 (1990); also see Wenz, *Abortion Rights*, pp. 246 ff.

42. "Whose Life is it?" *Time,* May 1, 1989, p. 21. The poll for CNN and *Time* by Yankelovich Clancy Shulman indicated that, while half of those questioned believe abortion is wrong, fully 67 percent believe the decision should be left to the woman in consultation with her doctor. *Roe* is supported by 54 percent and 62 percent of all respondents opposed any limits on abortion in the first three months of pregnancy.

43. See *Time*, May 4, 1992, pp. 27ff.

44. *Schenck* v. *Pro-Choice of Western New York*, 95-1065 (1997).

45. *Madsen* v. *Women's Health Center, Inc.*, 512 U.S. 753 (1994) at 774.

46. Citing *Boos* v. *Barry*, 485 U.S. 312 (1988) at 322.

47. See *Bray*, concurring opinion by Kennedy, as in par. 3.

48. Justice Kennedy's comments in his concurring opinion in *Bray* seem to admit as much. See "Abortion! the Future is Already Here," *Time*, May 4, 1992, pp. 27ff.

49. *Casey,* opinion by O'Connor, I.[6].3.

50. *Casey,* V.B.

51. Ibid., V.B. [34]. See T. L. Beauchamp and J. F. Childress, *Principles of Biomedical Ethics*, 3rd ed. (New York: Oxford University Press, 1989), p. 74, for a treatment of the importance and place of informed consent.

52. See "Crusading Against the Pro-Choice Movement," *Time*, October 21, 1991, p. 26.

53. Quoted in *Time*, May 4, 1992, p. 28.

54. B. J. George Jr., "State Legislatures Versus the Supreme Court: Abortion Legislation into the 1990s," in *Abortion, Medicine and the Law*, p. 4.

55. See Daniel Callahan, "Abortion; Some Ethical Issues," in *Abortion, Medicine and the Law*, p. 697; also see p. 8, n.19.

56. *U.S.* v. *Seeger,* 380 U.S. 163 (1965) at 165. *Seeger* clarified the question as

to whether one had to be a person committed to a distinctive community or tradition of belief in order to qualify for the Constitutional protections accorded the "religious." The answer was "no." All Americans may qualify as having profound beliefs which are the equivalent to what religious traditions and communities inculcate in their followers and which constitute ultimate concerns.

57. Justice Blackmun did refer to the Establishment provision of the First Amendment, but the Amendment was not itself the focus of the deliberation by the Court and did not figure in the decision of the majority. Cf. Blackmun in *Casey,* II.B.6 (2849).

58. Thomas Boles, "Zygotes, Souls, Substances and Persons," *Journal of Medicine and Philosophy* 15: 648.

59. Paul D. Simmons, "Religious Liberty and the Abortion Debate," *Journal of Church and State* 32 (summer 1990): 567–84.

60. *Harris* v. *McRae,* 448 U.S. 297 (1980), considered whether indigent women seeking an abortion had a right to public funding. The Court rejected the argument that government's refusal to pay for this medical procedure violated either the Establishment Clause of the First Amendment or the Equal Protection guarantees of the Fifth Amendment. Quite properly, no argument was advanced concerning the free exercise of religion. *United Slates Law Week* 48 (June 24, 1980): 50; Syllabus, 1(b) and 4, 48 LW 4942.

61. The argument frequently heard that the Supreme Court declared that African Americans were not persons in its infamous *Dred Scot* decision is hardly true. The Court did not deal with the issue of personhood, but questions of property. African Americans are persons when measured by any basic norms of human personhood. The same can hardly be said for an embryo or fetus. The fatal error in reasoning from racism to abortion can also be found in George McKenna's article, "On Abortion: A Lincolnian Position," *Atlantic Monthly* (September 1995): 51–68. McKenna dodges the issue of personhood by saying the question is a matter of "the stilling of heartbeats and brains" (68). His radical reductionism allows him to regard embryos as persons.

62. See *Casey* at II.[6], par. 6 (2807).

63. *New York Times*, May 22, 1985.

64. As in *Schenck* and *Madsen,* n. 48 and 49.

PART THREE

ABORTION

and Feminism

14

ABORTION AND THE SEXUAL AGENDA

Sidney Callahan

The abortion debate continues. In the latest and perhaps most crucial development, pro-life feminists are contesting pro-choice feminist claims that abortion rights are prerequisites for women's full development and social equality. The outcome of this debate may be decisive for the culture as a whole. Pro-life feminists, like myself, argue on good feminist principles that women can never achieve the fulfillment of feminist goals in a society permissive toward abortion.

These new arguments over abortion take place within liberal political circles. This round of intense intrafeminist conflict has spiraled beyond earlier Right-versus-Left abortion debates, which focused on "tragic choices," medical judgments, and legal compromises. Feminist theorists of the pro-choice position now put forth the demand for unrestricted abortion rights as a *moral imperative* and insist upon women's right to complete reproductive freedom. They morally justify the present situation and current abortion practices. Thus it is all the more important that pro-life feminists articulate their different feminist perspective. . . .

Pro-life feminists grant the good intentions of their pro-choice counterparts but protest that the pro-choice position is flawed, morally inadequate, and inconsistent with feminism's basic demands for justice. Pro-life feminists champion a more encompassing moral ideal. They recognize the claims of fetal life and offer a different perspective on what is good for women. The feminist vision is expanded and refocused.

From *Commonweal* (April 25, 1986): 232–38. Reprinted by permission of the publisher.

From the Moral Right to Control One's Own Body to a More Inclusive Ideal of Justice

The moral right to control one's own body does apply to cases of organ transplants, mastectomies, contraception, and sterilization; but it is not a conceptualization adequate for abortion. The abortion dilemma is caused by the fact that 266 days following a conception in one body, another body will emerge. One's own body no longer exists as a single unit but is engendering another organism's life. This dynamic passage from conception to birth is genetically ordered and universally found in the human species. Pregnancy is not like the growth of cancer or infestation by a biological parasite; it is the way every human being enters the world. Strained philosophical analogies fail to apply: having a baby is not like rescuing a drowning person, being hooked up to a famous violinist's artificial life-support system, donating organs for transplant—or anything else.

As embryology and fetology advance, it becomes clear that human development is a continuum. Just as astronomers are studying the first three minutes in the genesis of the universe, so the first moments, days, and weeks at the beginning of human life are the subject of increasing scientific attention. While neonatology pushes the definition of viability ever earlier, ultrasound and fetology expand the concept of the patient in utero. Within such a continuous growth process, it is hard to defend logically any demarcation point after conception as the point at which an immature form of human life is so different from the day before or the day after, that it can be morally or legally discounted as a nonperson. Even the moment of birth can hardly differentiate a nine-month fetus from a newborn. It is not surprising that those who countenance late abortions are logically led to endorse selective infanticide.

The same legal tradition which in our society guarantees the night to control one's own body firmly recognizes the wrongfulness of harming other bodies, however immature, dependent, different looking, or powerless. The handicapped, the retarded, and newborns are legally protected from deliberate harm. Pro-life feminists reject the suppositions that would except the unborn from this protection.

After all, debates similar to those about the fetus were once conducted about feminine personhood. Just as women, or blacks, were considered too different, too underdeveloped, too "biological," to have souls or to possess legal rights, so the fetus is now seen as "merely" biological life, subsidiary to a person. A woman was once viewed as incorporated into the "one flesh" of her husband's person; she too was a form of bodily property. In all patriarchal unjust systems, lesser orders of human life are granted rights only when wanted, chosen, or invested with value by the powerful.

Fortunately, in the course of civilization there has been a gradual realization that justice demands the powerless and dependent be protected against the uses of power wielded unilaterally. No human can be treated as a means to an end without consent. The fetus is an immature, dependent form of human life which only needs time and protection to develop. Surely, immaturity and dependence are not crimes.

In an effort to think about the essential requirements of a just society, philosophers like John Rawls recommend imagining yourself in an "original position," in which your position in the society to be created is hidden by a "veil of ignorance." You will have to weigh the possibility that any inequalities inherent in that society's practices may rebound upon you in the worst, as well as in the best, conceivable way. This thought experiment helps ensure justice for all.

Beverly Harrison argues that in such an envisioning of society everyone would institute abortion rights in order to guarantee that if one turned out to be a woman one would have reproductive freedom. But surely in the original position and behind the "veil of ignorance," you would have to contemplate the possibility of being the particular fetus to be aborted. Since everyone has passed through the fetal stage of development, it is false to refuse to imagine oneself in this state when thinking about a potential world in which justice would govern. Would it be just that an embryonic life—in half the cases, of course, a female life—be sacrificed to the right of a woman's control over her own body? A woman may be pregnant without consent and experience a great many penalties, but a fetus killed without consent pays the ultimate penalty.

It does not matter (*The Silent Scream* notwithstanding) whether the fetus being killed is fully conscious or feels pain. We do not sanction killing the innocent if it can be done painlessly or without the victim's awareness. Consciousness becomes important to the abortion debate because it is used as a criterion for "personhood" so often seen as the prerequisite for legal protection. Yet certain philosophers set the standard of personhood so high that half the human race could not meet the criteria during most of their waking hours (let alone their sleeping ones). Sentience, self-consciousness, rational decision-making, social participation? Surely no infant, or child under two, could qualify. Either our idea of person must be expanded or another criterion, such as human life itself, be employed to protect the weak in a just society. Pro-life feminists who defend the fetus empathetically identify with an immature state of growth passed through by themselves, their children, and everyone now alive.

It also seems a travesty of just procedures that a pregnant woman now, in effect, acts as sole judge of her own case, under the most stressful conditions. Yes, one can acknowledge that the pregnant woman will be subject to the potential burdens arising from a pregnancy, but it has never been thought right to have an interested party, especially the more powerful party, decide his or her own case when there may be a conflict of interest. If one considers the matter as a case of a powerful versus a powerless, silenced claimant, the pro-choice feminist argument can rightly be inverted; since hers is the body, hers the risk, and hers the greater burden, then how in fairness can a woman be the sole judge of the fetal right to life?

Human ambivalence, a bias toward self-interest, and emotional stress have always been recognized as endangering judgment. Freud declared that love and hate are so entwined that if instant thoughts could kill, we would all be dead in the bosom of our families. In the case of a woman's involuntary pregnancy, a complex, long-term solution requiring effort and energy has to compete with the immediate solution offered by a morning's visit to an abortion clinic. On the simple, perceptual plane, with imagination and thinking curtailed, the speed, ease, and privacy of abortion, combined with the small size of the embryo, tend to make early abortions seem less morally serious—even though speed, size, technical ease, and the private nature of an act have no moral standing.

As the most recent immigrants from nonpersonhood, feminists have traditionally fought for justice for themselves and the world. Women rally to feminism as a new and better way to live. Rejecting male aggression and destruction, feminists seek alternative, peaceful, ecologically sensitive means to resolve conflicts while respecting human potentiality. It is a chilling inconsistency to see pro-choice feminists demanding continued access to assembly-line, technological methods of fetal killing—the vacuum aspirator, prostaglandins, and dilation and evacuation. It is a betrayal of feminism, which has built the struggle for justice on the bedrock of women's empathy. After all, "maternal thinking" receives its name from a mother's unconditional acceptance and nurture of dependent, immature life. It is difficult to develop concern for women, children, the poor, and the dispossessed—and to care about peace—and at the same time ignore fetal life.

From the Necessity of Autonomy and Choice in Responsibility to an Expanded Sense of Responsibility

A distorted idea of morality overemphasizes individual autonomy and active choice. Morality has often been viewed too exclusively as a matter of human agency and decisive action. In moral behavior, persons must explicitly choose and aggressively exert their wills to intervene in the natural and social environments. The human will dominates the body, overcomes the given, breaks out of the material limits of nature. Thus if one does not choose to be pregnant or cannot rear a child, who must be given up for adoption, then better to abort the pregnancy. Willing, planning, choosing one's moral commitments through the contracting of one's individual resources becomes the premier model of moral responsibility.

But morality also consists of the good and worthy acceptance of the unexpected events that life presents. Responsiveness and response-ability to things unchosen are also instances of the highest human moral capacity. Morality is not confined to contracted agreements of isolated individuals. Yes, one is obligated by explicit contracts freely initiated, but human beings are also obligated by implicit compacts and involuntary relationships in which persons simply find themselves. To be embedded in a family, a neighborhood, a social system, brings moral obligations which were never entered into with informed consent.

Parent-child relationships are one instance of implicit moral obligations arising by virtue of our being part of the interdependent human community. A woman, involuntarily pregnant, has a moral obligation to the now-existing dependent fetus whether she explicitly consented to its existence or not. No pro-life feminist would dispute the forceful observations of pro-choice feminists about the extreme difficulties that bearing an unwanted child in our society can entail. But the stronger force of the fetal claim presses a woman to accept these burdens; the fetus possesses rights arising from its extreme need and the interdependency and unity of humankind. The woman's moral obligation arises both from her status as a human being embedded in the interdependent human community and her unique lifegiving female reproductive power. To follow the pro-choice feminist ideology of insistent individualistic autonomy and control is to betray a fundamental basis of the moral life.

From the Moral Claim of the Contingent Value of Fetal Life to the Moral Claim for the Intrinsic Value of Human Life

The feminist pro-choice position which claims that the value of the fetus is contingent upon the pregnant woman's bestowal—or willed, conscious "construction"—of humanhood is seriously flawed. The inadequacies of this position flow from the erroneous premises (1) that human value and rights can be granted by individual will; (2) that the individual woman's consciousness can exist and operate in an a priori isolated fashion; and (3) that "mere" biological, genetic human life has little meaning. Pro-life feminism takes a very different stance to life and nature.

Human life from the beginning to the end of development has intrinsic value, which does not depend on meeting the selective criteria or tests set up by powerful others. A fundamental humanist assumption is at stake here. Either we are going to value embodied human life and humanity as good things, or take some variant of the nihilist position that assumes human life is just one more random occurrence in the universe such that each instance of human life must explicitly be justified to prove itself worthy to continue. When faced with a new life, or an involuntary pregnancy, there is a world of difference in whether one first asks, "Why continue?" or "Why not?" Where is the burden of proof going to rest? The concept of "compulsory pregnancy" is as distorted as labeling life "compulsory aging."

In a sound moral tradition, human rights arise from human needs, and it is the very nature of a right, or valid claim upon another, that it cannot be denied, conditionally delayed, or rescinded by more powerful others at their behest. It seems fallacious to hold that in the case of the fetus it is the pregnant woman alone who gives or removes its right to life and human status solely through her subjective conscious investment or "humanization." Surely no pregnant woman (or any other individual member of the species) has created her own human nature by an individually willed act of consciousness, nor for that matter been able to guarantee her own human rights. An individual woman and the unique individual embryonic life within her can only exist because of their participation in the genetic inheritance of the human species as a whole. Biological life should never be discounted. Membership in the species, or collective human family, is the basis for human solidarity, equality, and natural human rights.

The Moral Right of Women to Full Social Equality from a Pro-Life Feminist Perspective

Pro-life feminists and pro-choice feminists are totally agreed on the moral right of women to the full social equality so far denied them. The disagreement between them concerns the definition of the desired goal and the best means to get there. Permissive abortion laws do not bring women reproductive freedom, social equality, sexual fulfillment, or full personal development.

Pragmatic failures of a pro-choice feminist position combined with a lack of moral vision are, in fact, causing disaffection among young women. Middle-aged pro-choice feminists blamed the "big chill" on the general conservative backlash. But they should look rather to their own elitist acceptance of male models of sex and to the sad picture they present of women's lives. Pitting women against their own offspring is not only morally offensive, it is psychologically and politically destructive. Women will never climb to equality and social empowerment over mounds of dead fetuses, numbering now in the millions. As long as most women choose to bear children, they stand to gain from the same constellation of attitudes and institutions that will also protect the fetus in the woman's womb—and they stand to lose from the cultural assumptions that support permissive abortion. Despite temporary conflicts of interest, feminine and fetal liberation are ultimately one and the same cause.

Women's rights and liberation are pragmatically linked to fetal rights because to obtain true equality, women need (1) more social support and changes in the structure of society, and (2) increased self-confidence, self-expectations, and self-esteem. Society in general, and men in particular, have to provide women more support in rearing the next generation, or our devastating feminization of poverty will continue. But if a woman claims the right to decide by herself whether the fetus becomes a child or not, what does this do to paternal and communal responsibility? Why should men share responsibility for child support or child rearing if they cannot share in what is asserted to he the woman's sole decision? Furthermore, if explicit intentions and consciously accepted contracts are necessary for moral obligations, why should men be held responsible for what *they* do not voluntarily choose to happen? By pro-choice reasoning, a man who does not want to have a child, or whose contraceptive fails, can be exempted from the responsibilities of fatherhood and child support. Traditionally, many men have been laggards in assuming parental responsibility and support for their children; ironically, ready abortion, often advocated as a response to male dereliction, legitimizes male irresponsibility and paves the way for even more male detachment and lack of commitment.

For that matter, why should the state provide a system of day care or child support, or require workplaces to accommodate women's maternity and the needs of child rearing? Permissive abortion, granted in the name of women's privacy and reproductive freedom, ratifies the view that pregnancies and children are a woman's private individual responsibility. More and more frequently, we hear some version of this old rationalization: if she refuses to get rid of it, it's her problem. A child becomes a product of the individual woman's freely chosen investment, a form of private property resulting from her own cost-benefit calculation. The larger community is relieved of moral responsibility.

With legal abortion freely available, a clear cultural message is given: conception and pregnancy are no longer serious moral matters. With abortion as an acceptable alternative, contraception is not as responsibly used; women take risks, often at the urging of male sexual partners. Repeat abortions increase, with all their psychological and medical repercussions. With more abortion there is more abortion. Behavior shapes thought as well as the other way round. One tends to justify morally what one has done; what becomes commonplace and institutionalized seems harmless. Habituation is a powerful psychological force. Psychologically it is also true that whatever is avoided becomes more threatening; in phobias it is the retreat from anxiety-producing events which reinforces future avoidance. Women begin to see themselves as too weak to cope with involuntary pregnancies. Finally, through the potency of social pressure and the force of inertia, it becomes more and more difficult, in fact almost unthinkable, *not* to use abortion to solve problem pregnancies. Abortion becomes no longer a choice but a "necessity."

But "necessity," beyond the organic failure and death of the body, is a dynamic social construction open to interpretation. The thrust of present feminist pro-choice arguments can only increase the justifiable indications for "necessary" abortion; every unwanted fetal handicap becomes more and more unacceptable. Repeatedly assured that in the name of reproductive freedom, women have a right to specify which pregnancies and which children they will accept, women justify sex selection, and abort unwanted females. Female infanticide, after all, is probably as old a custom as the human species possesses. Indeed, all kinds of selection of the fit and the favored for the good of the family and the tribe have always existed. Selective extinction is no new program.

There are far better goals for feminists to pursue. Pro-life feminists seek to expand and deepen the more communitarian, maternal elements of feminism—and move society from its male-dominated course. First and foremost women have to insist upon a different, woman-centered approach to sex and reproduction. While Margaret Mead stressed the "womb envy" of males in other societies, it has been more or less repressed in our own. In our male-dominated world, what men don't do doesn't count. Pregnancy, childbirth, and nursing have been characterized as passive, debilitating, animal-like. The disease model of pregnancy and birth has been entrenched. This female disease or impairment, with its attendant "female troubles," naturally handicaps women in the "real" world of hunting, war, and the corporate fast track. Many pro-choice feminists, deliberately childless, adopt the male perspective when they cite the "basic injustice that women have to bear the babies," instead of seeing the injustice in the fact that men cannot. Women's biologically unique capacity and privilege has been denied, despised, and suppressed under male domination; unfortunately, many women have fallen for the phallic fallacy.

Childbirth often appears in pro-choice literature as a painful, traumatic, life-threatening experience. Yet giving birth is accurately seen as an arduous but normal exercise of life-giving power, a violent and ecstatic peak experience, which men can never know. Ironically, some pro-choice men and women think and talk of pregnancy and childbirth with the same repugnance that ancient ascetics displayed toward orgasms and sexual intercourse. The similarity may not be accidental. The obstetrician Niles Newton, herself a mother, has written of the extended threefold sexuality of women, who can experience orgasm, birth, and nursing as passionate pleasure-giving experiences. All of these are involuntary processes of the female body. Only orgasm, which males share, has been glorified as an involuntary function that is nature's gift; the involuntary feminine processes of childbirth and nursing have been seen as bondage to biology.

Fully accepting our bodies as ourselves, what should women want? I think women will only flourish when there is a feminization of sexuality, very different from the current cultural trend toward masculinizing female sexuality. Women can never have the self-confidence and self-esteem they need to achieve feminist goals in society until a more holistic, feminine model of sexuality becomes the dominant cultural ethos. To say this affirms the view that men and women differ in the domain of sexual functioning, although they are more alike than different in other personality characteristics and competencies. For those of us committed to achieving sexual equality in the culture, it may be hard to accept the fact that sexual differences make it imperative to talk of distinct male and female models of sexuality. But if one wants to change sexual roles, one has to recognize preexisting conditions. A great deal of evidence is accumulating which points to biological pressures for different male and female sexual functioning.

Males always and everywhere have been more physically aggressive and more likely to fuse sexuality with aggression and dominance. Females may be more variable in their sexuality, but since Masters and Johnson, we know that women have a greater capacity than men for repeated orgasm and a more tenuous path to arousal and orgasmic release. Most obviously, women also have a far greater sociobiological investment in the act of human reproduction. On the whole, women as compared to men possess a sexuality which is more complex, more intense, more extended in time, involving higher investment, risks, and psychosocial involvement.

Considering the differences in sexual functioning, it is not surprising that men and women in the same culture have often constructed different sexual ideals. In Western culture, since the nineteenth century at least, most women have espoused a version of sexual functioning in which sex acts are embedded within deep emotional bonds and secure long-term commitments. Within these committed "pair bonds" males assume parental obligations. In the idealized Victorian version of the Christian sexual ethic, culturally endorsed and maintained by women, the double standard was not countenanced. Men and women did not need to marry to be whole persons, but if they did engage in sexual functioning, they were to be equally chaste, faithful, responsible, loving, and parentally concerned. Many of the most influential women in the nineteenth-century women's movement preached and lived this sexual ethic, often by the side of exemplary feminist men. While the ideal has never been universally obtained, a culturally dominant demand for monogamy, self-control, and emotionally bonded and committed sex works well for women in every stage of their sexual life cycles. When love, chastity, fidelity, and commitment for better or worse are the ascendant cultural prerequisites for sexual functioning, young girls and women expect protection from rape and seduction, adult women justifiably demand male support in child rearing, and older women are more protected from abandonment as their biological attractions wane.

Of course, these feminine sexual ideals always coexisted in competition with another view. A more male-oriented model of erotic or amative sexuality endorses sexual permissiveness without long-term commitment or reproductive focus. Erotic sexuality emphasizes pleasure, play, passion, individual self-expression, and romantic games of courtship and conquest. It is assumed that a variety of partners and sexual experiences are necessary to stimulate romantic passion. This erotic model of the sexual life has often worked satisfactorily for men, both heterosexual and gay, and for certain cultural elites. But for the average woman, it is quite destructive. Women can only play the erotic game successfully when, like the "*Cosmopolitan* women," they are young, physically attractive, economically powerful, and fulfilled enough in a career to be willing to sacrifice family life. Abortion is also required. As our society increasingly endorses this male-oriented, permissive view of sexuality, it is all too ready to give women abortion on demand. Abortion helps a woman's body be more like a man's. It has been observed that *Roe* v. *Wade* removed the last defense women possessed against male sexual demands.

Unfortunately, the modem feminist movement made a mistaken move at a critical juncture. Rightly rebelling against patriarchy, unequal education, restricted work opportunities, and women's downtrodden political status, feminists also rejected the nineteenth-century feminine sexual ethic. Amative erotic, permissive sexuality (along with abortion rights) became symbolically indentified with other struggles for social equality in education, work, and politics. This feminist mistake also turned off many potential recruits among women who could not deny the positive dimensions of their own traditional feminine roles, nor their allegiance to the older feminine sexual ethic of love and fidelity.

An ironic situation then arose in which many pro-choice feminists preach their own double standard. In the world of work and career, women are urged to grow up, to display mature self-discipline and self-control; they are told to persevere in long-term commitments, to cope with unexpected obstacles by learning to tough out the inevitable sufferings and setbacks entailed in life and work. But this mature ethic of commitment and self-discipline, recommended as the only way to progress in the world of work and personal achievement, is discounted in the domain of sexuality.

In pro-choice feminism, a permissive, erotic view of sexuality is assumed to be the only option. Sexual intercourse with a variety of partners is seen as "inevitable" from a young age and as a positive growth experience to be managed by access to contraception and abortion. Unfortunately, the pervasive cultural conviction that adolescents, or their elders, cannot exercise sexual self-control, undermines the responsible use of contraception. When a pregnancy occurs, the first abortion is viewed in some pro-choice circles as a *rite de passage*. Responsibly choosing an abortion supposedly ensures that a young woman will take charge of her own life, make her own decisions, and carefully practice contraception. But the social dynamics of a permissive, erotic model of sexuality, coupled with permissive laws, work toward repeat abortions. Instead of being empowered by their abortion choices, young women having abortions are confronting the debilitating reality of *not* bringing a baby into the world; *not* being able to count on a committed male partner; *not* accounting oneself strong enough, or the master of enough resources, to avoid killing the fetus. Young women are hardly going to develop the self-esteem, self-discipline, and self-confidence necessary to confront a male-dominated society through abortion.

The male-oriented sexual orientation has been harmful to women and children. It has helped bring us epidemics of venereal disease, infertility, pornography, sexual abuse, adolescent pregnancy, divorce, displaced older women, and abortion. Will these signals of something amiss stimulate pro-choice feminists to rethink what kind of sex ideal really serves women's best interests? While the erotic model cannot encompass commitment, the committed model can—happily—encompass and encourage romance, passion, and playfulness. In fact, within the security of long-term commitments, women may he more likely to experience sexual pleasure and fulfillment.

The pro-life feminist position is not a return to the old feminine mystique. That espousal of "the eternal feminine" erred by viewing sexuality as so sacred that it cannot be humanly shaped at all. Woman's *whole* nature was supposed to be opposite to man's, necessitating complementary and radically different social roles. Followed to its logical conclusion, such a view presumes that reproductive and sexual experience is necessary for human fulfillment. But as the early feminists insisted, no woman has to marry or engage in sexual intercourse to be fulfilled, nor does a woman have to give birth and raise children to be complete, nor must she stay home and function as an earth mother. But female sexuality does need to be deeply respected as a unique potential and trust. Since most contraceptives and sterilization procedures really do involve only the woman's body rather than destroying new life, they can be an acceptable and responsible moral option.

With sterilization available to accelerate the inevitable natural ending of fertility and childbearing, a woman confronts only a limited number of years in which she exercises her reproductive trust and may have to respond to an unplanned pregnancy. Responsible use of contraception can lower the probabilities even more. Yet abortion is not decreasing. The reason is the current permissive attitude embodied in the law, not the "hard cases" which constitute 3 percent of today's abortions. Since attitudes, the law, and behavior interact, pro-life feminists conclude that unless there is an enforced limitation of abortion, which currently confirms the sexual and social status quo, alternatives will never be developed. For women to get what they need in order to combine childbearing, education, and careers, society has to recognize that female bodies come with wombs. Women and their reproductive power, and the children women have, must be supported in new ways. Another and different round of feminist consciousness raising is needed in which all of women's potential is accorded respect. This time, instead of humbly buying entrée by conforming to male lifestyles, women will demand that society accommodate to them.

New feminist efforts to rethink the meaning of sexuality, femininity, and reproduction are all the more vital as new techniques for artificial reproduction, surrogate motherhood, and the like present a whole new set of dilemmas. In the long run, the very long run, the abortion debate may be merely the opening round in a series of far-reaching struggles over the role of human sexuality and the ethics of reproduction. Significant changes in the culture, both positive and negative in outcome, may begin as local storms of controversy. We may be at one of those vaguely realized thresholds when we had best come to full attention. What kind of people are we going to be? Pro-life feminists pursue a vision for their sisters, daughters, and granddaughters. Will their great-granddaughters be grateful?

15

Our Bodies, Our Souls

Naomi Wolf

> I had an abortion when I was a single mother and my daughter was two years old. I would do it again. But you know how in the Greek myths when you kill a relative you are pursued by furies? For months, it was as if baby furies were pursuing me.

These are not the words of a benighted, superstition ridden teenager lost in America's cultural backwaters. They are the words of a Cornell-educated, urban-dwelling, Democratic-voting forty-year-old cardiologist—I'll call her Clare. Clare is exactly the kind of person for whom being pro-choice is an unshakeable conviction. If there were a core constituent of the movement to secure abortion rights, Clare would be it. And yet: her words are exactly the words to which the pro-choice movement is not listening.

At its best, feminism defends its moral high ground by being simply faithful to the truth: to women's real-life experiences. But, to its own ethical and political detriment, the pro-choice movement has relinquished the moral frame around the issue of abortion. It has ceded the language of right and wrong to abortion foes. The movement's abandonment of what Americans have always, and rightly, demanded of their movements—an ethical core—and its reliance instead on a political rhetoric in which the fetus means nothing are proving fatal.

The effects of this abandonment can be measured in two ways. First of all, such a position causes us to lose political ground. By refusing to look at abortion within a moral framework, we lose the millions of Americans who want to support abortion as a legal right but still need to condemn it as a moral iniquity. Their ethical allegiances are then addressed by the pro-life movement, which is willing to speak about good and evil.

But we are also in danger of losing something more important than votes; we stand in jeopardy of losing what can only be called our souls. Clinging to a rhetoric about abortion in which there is no life and no death, we entangle our beliefs in a series of self-delusions, fibs and evasions. And we risk becoming precisely what our critics charge us with being: callous, selfish, and casually destructive men and women who share a cheapened view of human life.

In the following pages, I will argue for a radical shift in the pro-choice movement's rhetoric and consciousness about abortion: I will maintain that we need to contextualize the fight to defend abortion rights within a moral framework that admits that the death of a fetus is a real death; that there are degrees of culpability, judgment, and responsibility involved in the decision to abort a pregnancy; that the best understanding of feminism involves holding women as well as men to the responsibilities that are inseparable from their rights; and that we need to be strong enough to acknowledge that this country's high rate of abortion—which ends more than a quarter of all pregnancies—can only be rightly understood as what Dr. Henry Foster was brave enough to call it: "a failure."

Any doubt that our current pro-choice rhetoric leads to disaster should be dispelled by the famous recent defection of the woman who had been Jane Roe. What happened to Norma McCorvey? To judge by her characterization in the elite media and by some prominent pro-choice feminists, nothing very important. Her change of heart about abortion was relentlessly "explained away" as having everything to do with the girlish motivations of insecurity, fickleness, and the need for attention, and little to do with any actual moral agency.

This dismissive (and, not incidentally, sexist and classist) interpretation was so highly colored by subjective impressions offered up by the very institutions that define objectivity that it bore all the hallmarks of an exculpatory cultural myth: poor Norma—she just needed stroking. She was never very stable, the old dear—first she was a chess piece for the pro-choice movement ("just some anonymous person who suddenly emerges," in the words of one NOW member) and then a codependent of the Bible-thumpers. Low self-esteem, a history of substance abuse, ignorance—these and other personal weaknesses explained her turnaround.

To me, the first commandment of real feminism is: when in doubt, listen to women. What if we were to truly, respectfully listen to this woman who began her political life as, in her words, just "some little old Texas girl who got in trouble"? We would have to hear this: perhaps Norma McCorvey actually had a revelation that she could no longer live as the symbol of a belief system she increasingly repudiated.

Norma McCorvey should be seen as an object lesson for the pro-choice movement—a call to us to search our souls and take another, humbler look at how we go about what we are doing. For McCorvey is in fact an American Everywoman: She is the lost middle of the abortion debate, the woman whose allegiance we forfeit by our refusal to use a darker and sterner and more honest moral rhetoric.

McCorvey is more astute than her critics; she seems to understand better than the pro-choice activists she worked with just what the woman-in-the-middle believes: "I believe in the woman's right to choose. I'm like a lot of people. I'm in the mushy middle," she said. McCorvey still supports abortion rights through the first trimester—but is horrified by the brutality of abortion as it manifests more obviously further into a pregnancy. She does not respect the black-and-white ideology on either side and insists on referring instead, as I understand her explanation, to her conscience. What McCorvey and other Americans want and deserve is an abortion-rights movement willing publicly to mourn the evil—necessary evil though it may be—that is abortion. We must have a movement that acts with moral accountability and without euphemism.

With the pro-choice rhetoric we use now, we incur three destructive consequences—two ethical, one strategic: hardness of heart, lying, and political failure.

Because of the implications of a Constitution that defines rights according to the legal idea of "a person," the abortion debate has tended to focus on the question of "personhood" of the fetus. Many pro-choice advocates developed a language to assert that the fetus isn't a person, and this, over the years, has developed into a lexicon of dehumanization. Laura Kaplan's *The Story of Jane*, an important forthcoming account of a pre-Roe underground abortion service, inadvertently sheds light on the origins of some of this rhetoric: service staffers referred to the fetus—well into the fourth month—as "material" (as in "the amount of material that had to be removed . . ."). The activists felt exhilaration at learning to perform abortions themselves instead of relying on male doctors: "When a staffer removed the speculum and said, 'There, all done,' the room exploded in excitement." In an era when women were dying of illegal abortions, this was the understandable exhilaration of an underground resistance movement.

Unfortunately, though, this cool and congratulatory rhetoric lingers into a very different present. In one woman's account of her chemical abortion, in the January/February 1994 issue of *Mother Jones*, for example, the doctor says, "By Sunday you won't see on the monitor what we call the heartbeat." The author of the article, D. Redman, explains that one of the drugs the doctor administered would "end the growth of the fetal tissue." And we all remember Dr. Joycelyn Elder's remark, hailed by some as refreshingly frank and pro-woman, but which I found remarkably brutal: that "We really need to get over this love affair with the fetus. . . . "

How did we arrive at this point? In the early 1970s, Second Wave feminism adopted this rhetoric in response to the reigning ideology in which motherhood was invoked as an excuse to deny women legal and social equality. In a climate in which women risked being defined as mere vessels while their fetuses were given "personhood" at their expense, it made sense that women's advocates would fight back by depersonalizing the fetus.

The feminist complaint about the pro-life movement's dehumanization of the pregnant woman in relation to the humanized fetus is familiar and often quite valid: pro-choice commentators note that the pro-life film *The Silent Scream* portrayed the woman as "a vessel"; Ellen Frankfort's *Vaginal Politics*, the influential feminist text, complained that the fetus is treated like an astronaut in a spaceship.

But, say what you will, pregnancy confounds Western philosophy's idea of the autonomous self: the pregnant woman is in fact both a person in her body and a vessel. Rather than seeing both beings as alive and interdependent—seeing life within life—and acknowledging that sometimes, nonetheless, the woman must choose her life over the fetus's, Second Wave feminists reacted to the dehumanization of women by dehumanizing the creatures within them. In the death struggle to wrest what Simone de Beauvoir called transcendence out of biological immanence, some feminists developed a rhetoric that defined the unwanted fetus as at best valueless; at worst an adversary, a "mass of dependent protoplasm."

Yet that has left us with a bitter legacy. For when we defend abortion rights by emptying the act of moral gravity we find ourselves cultivating a hardness of heart. Having become pregnant through her partner's and her own failure to use a condom, Redman remarks that her friend Judith, who has been trying to find a child to adopt, begs her to carry the pregnancy to term. Judith offers Redman almost every condition a birth-mother could want "Let me have the baby," she quotes her friend pleading. "You could visit her anytime, and if you ever wanted her back, I promise I would let her go." Redman does not mention considering this possibility. Thinking, rather, about the difficulty of keeping the child—"My time consumed by the tedious, daily activities that I've always done my best to avoid. Three meals a day. Unwashed laundry . . . "—she schedules her chemical abortion.

The procedure is experimental and the author feels "almost heroic," thinking of how she is blazing a trail for other women. After the abortion process is underway, the story reaches its perverse epiphany: Redman is on a Women's Day march when the blood from the abortion first appears. She exults at this: "Our bodies, our lives, our right to decide. . . . My life feels luxuriant with possibility. For one precious moment, I believe that we have the power to dismantle this system. I finish the march, borne along by the women. . . . "As for the pleading Judith, with everything she was ready to offer a child, and the phantom baby? They are both off-stage, silent in this chilling drama of "feminist" triumphalism.

And why should we expect otherwise? In this essay, the fetus (as the author writes, "the now-inert material from my womb") is little more than a form of speech: a vehicle to assert the author's identity and autonomy.

The pro-life warning about the potential of widespread abortion to degrade reverence for life does have a nugget of truth: a free-market rhetoric about abortion can, indeed, contribute to the eerie situation we are now facing, wherein the culture seems increasingly to see babies not as creatures to whom parents devote their lives but as accoutrements to enhance parental quality of life. Day by day, babies seem to have less value in themselves, in a matrix of the sacred, than they do as products with a value dictated by a market economy.

Stories surface regularly about "worthless" babies left naked on gratings or casually dropped out of windows, while "valuable," genetically correct babies are created at vast expense and with intricate medical assistance for infertile couples. If we fail to treat abortion with grief and reverence, we risk forgetting that, when it comes to the children we choose to bear, we are here to serve them whomever they are; they are not here to serve us.

Too often our rhetoric leads us to tell untruths. What Norma McCorvey wants, it seems, is for abortion-rights advocates to face, really face, what we are doing: "Have you ever seen a second-trimester abortion?" she asks. "It's a baby. It's got a face and a body, and they put him in a freezer and a little container."

Well, so it does; and so they do.

The pro-choice movement often treats with contempt the pro-lifers' practice of holding up to our faces their disturbing graphics. We revile their placards showing an enlarged scene of the aftermath of a D & C abortion; we are disgusted by their lapel pins with the little feet, crafted in gold, of a ten-week-old fetus; we mock the sensationalism of *The Silent Scream*. We look with pity and horror at someone who would brandish a fetus in formaldehyde—and we are quick to say that they are lying: "Those are stillbirths, anyway," we tell ourselves.

To many pro-choice advocates, the imagery is revolting propaganda. There is a sense among us, let us be frank, that the gruesomeness of the imagery belongs to the pro-lifers; that it emerges from the dark, frightening minds of fanatics; that it represents the violence of imaginations that would, given half a chance, turn our world into a scary, repressive place. "People like us" see such material as the pornography of the pro-life movement.

But feminism at its best is based on what is simply true. While pro-lifers have not been beyond dishonesty, distortion, and the doctoring of images (preferring, for example, to highlight the results of very late, very rare abortions), many of those photographs are in fact photographs of actual D & Cs; those footprints are in fact the footprints of a ten-week-old fetus; the pro-life slogan, "Abortion stops a beating heart," is incontrovertibly true. While images of violent fetal death work magnificently for pro-lifers as political polemic, the pictures are not polemical in themselves: they are biological facts. We know this. Since abortion became legal nearly a quarter century ago, the fields of embryology and perinatology have been revolutionized—but the pro-choice view of the contested fetus has remained static. This has led to a bizarre bifurcation in the way we who are pro-choice tend to think about wanted as opposed to unwanted fetuses; the unwanted ones are still seen in schematic black-and-white drawings while the wanted ones have metamorphosed into vivid and moving color. Even while Elders spoke of our need to "get over" our love affair with the unwelcome fetus, an entire growth industry—Mozart for your belly; framed sonogram photos; home fetal-heart-beat stethoscopes—is devoted to sparking fetal love affairs in other circumstances, and aimed especially at the hearts of overscheduled yuppies. If we avidly cultivate love for the ones we bring to term, and "get over" our love for the ones we don't do we not risk developing a hydroponic view of babies—and turn them into a product we can cull for our convenience?

Any happy couple with a wanted pregnancy and a copy of *What to Expect When You're Expecting* can see the cute, detailed drawings of the fetus whom the book's owner presumably is not going to abort, and can read the excited descriptions of what that fetus can do and feel, month by month. Anyone who has had a sonogram during pregnancy knows perfectly well that the four-month-old fetus responds to outside stimulus—"Let's get him to look this way," the technician will say, poking gently at the belly of a delighted mother-to-be. *The Well Baby Book*, the kind of whole-grain, holistic guide to pregnancy and childbirth that would find its audience among the very demographic that is most solidly pro-choice reminds us that: "Increasing knowledge is increasing the awe and respect we have for the unborn baby and is causing us to regard the unborn baby as a real person long before birth. . . . "

So, what will it be: Wanted fetuses are charming, complex, REM-dreaming little beings whose profile on the sonogram looks just like Daddy, but unwanted ones are mere "uterine material"? How can we charge that it is vile and repulsive for pro-lifers to brandish vile and repulsive images if the images are real? To insist that the truth is in poor taste is the very height of hypocrisy. Besides, if these images are often the facts of the matter, and if we then claim that it is offensive for pro-choice women to be confronted by them, then we are making the judgment that women are too inherently weak to face a truth about which they have to make a grave decision. This view of women is unworthy of feminism. Free women must be strong women, too; and strong women, presumably, do not seek to cloak their most important decisions in euphemism.

Other lies are not lies to others, but to ourselves. An abortion-clinic doctor, Elizabeth Karlin, who wrote a recent "Hers" column in the *New York Times*, declared that "there is only one reason I've ever heard for having an abortion: the desire to be a good mother."

While that may well be true for many poor and working-class women—and indeed research shows that poor women are three times more likely to have abortions than are better-off women—the elite, who are the most vociferous in their morally unambiguous pro-choice language, should know perfectly well how untrue that statement often is in their own lives. All abortions occupy a spectrum, from full lack of alternatives to full moral accountability. Karlin and many other pro-choice activists try to situate all women equally at the extreme endpoint of that spectrum, and it just isn't so. Many women, including middle-class women, do have abortions because, as one such woman put it, "They have a notion of what a good mother is and don't feel they can be that kind of mother at this phase of their lives." In many cases, that is still a morally defensible place on the spectrum; but it is not the place of absolute absolution that Dr. Karlin claims it to be. It is, rather, a place of moral struggle, of self-interest mixed with selflessness, of wished-for good intermingled with necessary evil.

Other abortions occupy places on the spectrum that are far more culpable. Of the abortions I know of, these were some of the reasons: to find out if the woman could get pregnant; to force a boy or man to take a relationship more seriously; and, again and again, to enact a rite of passage for affluent teenage girls. In my high school, the abortion drama was used to test a boyfriend's character. Seeing if he would accompany the girl to the operation or, better yet, come up with the money for the abortion could almost have been the 1970s Bay Area equivalent of the 1950s fraternity pin.

The affluent teenage couples who conceive because they can and then erase the consequences—and the affluent men and women who choose abortion because they were careless or in a hurry or didn't like the feel of latex—are not the moral equivalent of the impoverished mother who responsibly, even selflessly, acknowledges she already has too many mouths to feed. Feminist rights include feminist responsibilities; the right to obtain an abortion brings with it the responsibility to contracept. Fifty-seven percent of unintended pregnancies come about because the parents used no contraception at all. Those millions certainly include women and men too poor to buy contraception, girls and boys too young and ill-informed to know where to get it, and countless instances of marital rape, coerced sex, incest, and couplings in which the man refused to let the woman use protection.

But they also include millions of college students, professional men and women, and middle- and upper-middle-class people (11 percent of abortions are obtained by people in households with incomes of higher than $50,000) who have no excuse whatsoever for their carelessness. "There is only one reason I've ever heard for having an abortion: the desire to be a good mother"—this is a falsehood that condescends to women struggling to be true agents of their own souls, even as it dishonors through hypocrisy the terminations that are the writer's subject.

Not to judge other men and women without judging myself, I know this assertion to be false from my own experience. Once, I made the choice to take a morning-after pill. The heavily pregnant doctor looked at me, as she dispensed it, as if I were the scum of the earth.

If what was going on in my mind had been mostly about the well-being of the possible baby, that pill would never have been swallowed. For that potential baby, brought to term, would have had two sets of loving middle-income grandparents, an adult mother with an education, and even, as I discovered later, the beginning of diaper money for its first two years of life (the graduate fellowship I was on forbade marriage but, frozen in time before women were its beneficiaries, said nothing about unwed motherhood). Because of the baby's skin color, even if I chose not to rear the child, a roster of eager adoptive parents awaited him or her. If I had been thinking only or even primarily about the baby's life, I would have had to decide to bring the pregnancy, had there been one, to term.

No: there were two columns in my mind—Me" and "Baby"—and the first won out. And what was in it looked something like this: unwelcome intensity in the relationship with the father; desire to continue to "develop as a person" before "real" parenthood; wish to encounter my eventual life partner without the off-putting encumbrance of a child; resistance to curtailing the nature of the time remaining to me in Europe. Essentially, this column came down to: I am not done being responsive only to myself yet.

At even the possibility that the cosmos was calling my name, I cowered and stepped aside. I was not so unlike those young louts who father children and run from the specter of responsibility. Except that my refusal to be involved with this potential creature was as definitive as a refusal can be.

Stepping aside in this way is analogous to draft evasion; there are good and altruistic reasons to evade the draft, and then there are self-preserving reasons. In that moment, feminism came to one of its logical if less-than-inspiring moments of fruition: I chose to sidestep biology; I acted—and was free to act—as if I were in control of my destiny, the way men more often than women have let themselves act. I chose myself on my own terms over a possible someone else, for self-absorbed reasons. But "to be a better mother"? "Dulce et decorum est . . . "? Nonsense.

Now, freedom means that women must be free to choose self or to choose selfishly. Certainly for a woman with fewer economic and social choices than I had—for instance, a woman struggling to finish her higher education, without which she would have little hope of a life worthy of her talents—there can indeed be an obligation to choose self. And the defense of some level of abortion rights as fundamental to women's integrity and equality has been made fully by others, including, quite effectively, Ruth Bader Ginsberg. There is no easy way to deny the powerful argument that a woman's equality in society must give her some irreducible rights unique to her biology, including the right to take the life within her life.

But we don't have to lie to ourselves about what we are doing at such a moment. Let us at least look with clarity at what that means and not whitewash self-interest with the language of self-sacrifice. The landscape of many such decisions looks more like Marin County than Verdun. Let us certainly not be fools enough to present such spiritually limited moments to the world with a flourish of pride, pretending that we are somehow pioneers and heroines and even martyrs to have snatched the self, with its aims and pleasures, from the pressure of biology.

That decision was not my finest moment. The least I can do, in honor of the being that might have been, is simply to know that.

Using amoral rhetoric, we weaken ourselves politically because we lose the center. To draw an inexact parallel, many people support the choice to limit the medical prolongation of life. But, if a movement arose that spoke of our "getting over our love affair" with the terminally ill, those same people would recoil into a vociferous interventionist position as a way to assert their moral values. We would be impoverished by a rhetoric about the end of life that speaks of the ill and the dying as if they were meaningless and of doing away with them as if it were a bracing demonstration of our personal independence.

Similarly, many people support necessary acts of warfare (Catholics for a Free Choice makes the analogy between abortion rights and such warfare). There are legal mechanisms that allow us to bring into the world the evil of war. But imagine how quickly public opinion would turn against a president who waged war while asserting that our sons and daughters were nothing but cannon fodder. Grief and respect are the proper tones for all discussions about choosing to endanger or destroy a manifestation of life.

War is legal; it is sometimes even necessary. Letting the dying die in peace is often legal and sometimes even necessary. Abortion should be legal; it is sometimes even necessary. Sometimes the mother must be able to decide that the fetus, in its full humanity, must die. But it is never right or necessary to minimize the value of the lives involved or the sacrifice incurred in letting them go. Only if we uphold abortion rights within a matrix of individual conscience, atonement and responsibility can we both correct the logical and ethical absurdity in our position—and consolidate the support of the center.

Many others, of course, have wrestled with this issue: Camille Paglia, who has criticized the "convoluted casuistry" of some pro-choice language; Roger Rosenblatt, who has urged us to permit but discourage abortion; Laurence Tribe, who has noted that we place the fetus in shadow in order to advance the pro-choice argument. But we have yet to make room for this conversation at the table of mainstream feminism.

And we can't wait much longer. Historical changes—from the imminent availability of cheap chemical abortifacients to the ascendancy of the religious right to Norma McCorvey's defection—make the need for a new abortion-rights language all the more pressing.

In a time of retrenchment, how can I be so sure that a more honest and moral rhetoric about abortion will consolidate rather than scuttle abortion rights? Look at what Americans themselves say. When a recent *Newsweek* poll asked about support for abortion using the rare phrasing, "It's a matter between a woman, her doctor, her family, her conscience and her God," a remarkable 72 percent of the respondents called that formulation "about right." This represents a gain of thirty points over the abortion-rights support registered in the latest Gallup poll, which asked about abortion without using the words "God" or "conscience." When participants in the Gallup poll were asked if they supported abortion "under any circumstances" only 32 percent agreed; only 9 percent more supported it under "most" circumstances. Clearly, abortion rights are safest when we are willing to submit them to a morality beyond just our bodies and our selves.

But how, one might ask, can I square a recognition of the humanity of the fetus, and the moral gravity of destroying it, with a pro-choice position? The answer can only be found in the context of a paradigm abandoned by the left and misused by the right: the paradigm of sin and redemption.

It was when I was four months pregnant, sick as a dog, and in the middle of an argument, that I realized I could no longer tolerate the fetus-is-nothing paradigm of the pro-choice movement. I was being interrogated by a conservative, and the subject of abortion rights came up. "You're four months pregnant," he said. "Are you going to tell me that's not a baby you're carrying?"

The accepted pro-choice response at such a moment in the conversation is to evade: to move as swiftly as possible to a discussion of "privacy" and "difficult personal decisions" and "choice." Had I not been so nauseated and so cranky and so weighed down with the physical gravity of what was going on inside me, I might not have told what is the truth for me. "Of course it's a baby," I snapped. And went rashly on: "And if I found myself in circumstances in which I had to make the terrible decision to end this life, then that would be between myself and God."

Startlingly to me, two things happened: the conservative was quiet; I had said something that actually made sense to him. And I felt the great relief that is the grace of long-delayed honesty.

Now, the G-word is certainly a problematic element to introduce into the debate. And yet "God" or "soul"—or, if you are secular and prefer it, " conscience"—is precisely what is missing from pro-choice discourse. There is a crucial difference between "myself and my God" or "my conscience"—terms that imply moral accountability—and "myself and my doctor," the phrasing that Justice Harry Blackmun's wording in *Roe* ("inherently, and primarily, a medical decision") has tended to promote in the pro-choice movement. And that's not even to mention "between myself and myself" (Elders: "It's not anybody's business if I went for an abortion"), which implies just the relativistic relationship to abortion that our critics accuse us of sustaining.

The language we use to make our case limits the way we let ourselves think about abortion. As a result of the precedents in *Roe* (including *Griswold* v. *Connecticut* and *Eisenstadt* v. *Baird*), which based a woman's right to an abortion on the Ninth and Fourteenth Amendments' implied right to personal privacy, other unhelpful terms are also current in our discourse. Pro-choice advocates tend to cast an abortion as "an intensely personal decision."To which we can say, No: one's choice of carpeting is an intensely personal decision. One's struggles with a life-and-death issue must be understood as a matter of personal conscience. There is a world of difference between the two, and it's the difference a moral frame makes.

Stephen L. Carter has pointed out that spiritual discussion has been robbed of a place in American public life. As a consequence we tend—often disastrously—to use legislation to work out right and wrong. That puts many in the position of having to advocate against abortion rights in order to proclaim their conviction that our high rate of avoidable abortion (one of the highest in developed countries, five times that of the Netherlands, for example) is a social evil; and, conversely, many must pretend that abortion is not a transgression of any kind if we wish to champion abortion rights. We have no ground on which to say that abortion is a necessary evil that should be faced and opposed in the realm of conscience and action and even soul; yet remain legal.

But American society is struggling to find its way forward to a discourse of right and wrong that binds together a common ethic for the secular and the religious. When we do that, we create a moral discourse that can exist in its own right independent of legislation, and we can find ground to stand upon.

Norma McCorvey explained what happened to her in terms of good and evil: she woke in the middle of the night and felt a presence pushing violently down on her. "I denounce you, Satan," she announced. This way of talking about evil is one of the chief class divisions in America: working-class people talk about Satan, and those whom Paul Fussell calls "the X group"—those who run the country—talk instead about neurotic guilt. While the elite scoff at research that shows that most Americans maintain a belief in the embodiment of evil—"the devil"—they miss something profound about the human need to make moral order out of chaos. After all, the only real difference between the experience described by Clare, the Cornell-educated pro-choicer, and McCorvey, the uneducated ex-alcoholic, is a classical allusion.

There is a hunger for a moral framework that we pro-choicers must reckon with. In the Karlin "Hers" column, the author announced proudly that pregnant women are asked by the counselor in the office, "So, how long have you been pro-choice?" Dr. Karlin writes that "Laughter and the answer, 'About ten minutes,' is the healthiest response. 'I still don't believe in abortion,' some women say, unaware that refusal to take responsibility for the decision means that I won't do the procedure."

How is this "feminist" ideological coercion any different from the worst of pro-life shaming and coercion? The women who come to a clinic that is truly feminist—that respects women—are entitled not only to their abortions but also to their sense of sin.

To use the term "sin" in this context does not necessarily mean, as Dr. Karlin believes, that a woman thinks she must go to hell because she is having an abortion. It may mean that she thinks she must face the realization that she has fallen short of who she should be; and that she needs to ask forgiveness for that, and atone for it. As I understand such a woman's response, she is trying to take responsibility for the decision.

We on the Left tend to twitch with discomfort at that word "sin." Too often we have become religiously illiterate, and so we deeply misunderstand the word. But in all of the great religious traditions, our recognition of sin, and then our atonement for it, brings on God's compassion and our redemption. In many faiths, justice is linked, as it is in medieval Judaism and in Buddhism, to compassion. From Yom Kippur and the Ash Wednesday-to-Easter cycle to the Hindu idea of karma, the individual's confrontation with her or his own culpability is the first step toward ways to create and receive more light.

How could one live with a conscious view that abortion is an evil and still be pro-choice? Through acts of redemption, or what the Jewish mystical tradition calls tikkun; or "mending." Laurence Tribe, in *Abortion: The Clash of Absolutes*, notes that "memorial services for the souls of aborted fetuses are fairly common in contemporary Japan," where abortions are both legal and readily available. Shinto doctrine holds that women should make offerings to the fetus to help it rest in peace; Buddhists once erected statues of the spirit guardian of children to honor aborted fetuses (called "water children" or "unseeing children"). If one believes that abortion is killing and yet is still pro-choice, one could try to use contraception for every single sex act; if one had to undergo an abortion, one could then work to provide contraception, or jobs, or other choices to young girls; one could give money to programs that provide prenatal care to poor women; if one is a mother or father, one can remember the abandoned child every time one is tempted to be less than loving—and give renewed love to the living child. And so on: tikkun.

But when you insist, as the "Hers" column writer did, on stripping people of their sense of sin, they react with a wholesale backing-away into a rigid morality that reimposes order: hence, the ascendancy of the Religious Right.

Just look at the ill-fated nomination of Dr. Henry Foster for Surgeon General. The Republicans said "abortion," and the discussion was over. The Democrats, had they worked out a moral framework for progressivism, could have responded: "Yes: our abortion rate is a terrible social evil. Here is a man who can help put a moral framework around the chaos of a million and a half abortions a year. He can bring that rate of evil down. And whichever senator among you has ever prevented an unplanned pregnancy—and Dr. Foster has—let him ask the first question."

Who gets blamed for our abortion rate? The ancient Hebrews had a ritual of sending a "scapegoat" into the desert with the community's sins projected upon it. Abortion doctors are our contemporary scapegoats. The prolifers obviously scapegoat them in one way: if pro-lifers did to women what they do to abortion doctors—harassed and targeted them in their homes and workplaces—public opinion would rapidly turn against them; for the movement would soon find itself harassing the teachers and waitresses, housewives and younger sisters of their own communities. The pro-life movement would have to address the often all-too-pressing good reasons that lead good people to abort. That would be intolerable, a tactical defeat for the pro-life movement, and as sure to lose it "the mushy middle" as the pro-choice movement's tendency toward rhetorical coldness loses it the same constituency.

But pro-choicers, too, scapegoat the doctors and clinic workers. By resisting a moral framework in which to view abortion we who are pro-abortion rights leave the doctors in the front lines, with blood on their hands: the blood of the repeat abortions—at least 43 percent of the total; the suburban summer country club rite-of-passage abortions; the "I don't know what came over me, it was such good Chardonnay" abortions; as well as the blood of the desperate and the unpreventable and accidental and the medically necessary and the violently conceived abortions. This is blood that the doctors and clinic workers often see clearly, and that they heroically rinse and cause to flow and rinse again. And they take all our sins, the pro-choice as well as the pro-life among us, upon themselves.

And we who are pro-choice compound their isolation by declaring that that blood is not there.

As the world changes and women, however incrementally, become more free and more powerful, the language in which we phrase the goals of feminism must change as well. As a result of the bad old days before the Second Wave of feminism, we tend to understand abortion as a desperately needed exit from near-total male control of our reproductive lives. This scenario posits an unambiguous chain of power and powerlessness in which men control women and women, in order to survive, must have unquestioned control over fetuses. It is this worldview, all too real in its initial conceptualization, that has led to the dread among many pro-choice women of departing from a model of woman-equals-human-life, fetus-equals-not-much.

This model of reality may have been necessary in an unrelenting patriarchy. But today, in what should be, as women continue to consolidate political power, a patriarchy crumbling in spite of itself, it can become obsolete.

Now: try to imagine real gender equality. Actually, try to imagine an America that is female-dominated, since a true working democracy in this country would reflect our fifty-four to forty-six voting advantage.

Now imagine such a democracy, in which women would be valued so very highly, as a world that is accepting and responsible about human sexuality; in which there is no coerced sex without serious jail time; in which there are affordable, safe contraceptives available for the taking in every public health building; in which there is economic parity for women—and basic economic subsistence for every baby born; and in which every young American woman knows about and understands her natural desire as a treasure to cherish, and responsibly, when the time is right, on her own terms, to share.

In such a world, in which the idea of gender as a barrier has become a dusty artifact, we would probably use a very different language about what would be—then—the rare and doubtless traumatic event of abortion. That language would probably call upon respect and responsibility, grief and mourning. In that world we might well describe the unborn and the never-to-be-born with the honest words of life.

And in that world, passionate feminists might well hold candlelight vigils at abortion clinics, standing shoulder to shoulder with the doctors who work there, commemorating and saying goodbye to the dead.

PART FOUR

ABORTION
and Christianity

16

WE MUST RESCUE THEM

Gary Leber

Operation Rescue is a pro-life activist organization founded for the purpose of saving *in utero* babies who are about to be killed by an abortionist. We are dedicated to saving the lives of preborn children and to preventing exploitation of their mothers by those in the medical community who have decided that it is permissible to kill a fellow human being for profit. We have seated ourselves nonviolently in front of the doors of abortion mills all across this country on days when babies are scheduled to die. We call these actions *rescues*, or *rescue missions*, rather than demonstrations, sit-ins, or protests, because they actually result in the saving of human lives. We intervene nonviolently, primarily because of a spiritual commitment to absorb some of the violence already being waged against helpless children.

When Jesus died on the cross, he absorbed the violence of our sin, the violence that was meant for us. Also, the scriptures teach: "But if you do what is right and suffer for it you patiently endure it, this finds favor with God" (1 Pet. 2:20b, New American Standard Bible). Even though many in the movement would not be viewed as pacifists, being willing to use force to save their own children from an attacker, this does not make them a violent people. Rescue missions have successfully saved lives, and world history teaches us that nonviolent direct action to effect social change *works*.

These points, as well as our spiritual commitment, affirm our pledge to remain peaceful. As a direct result of 502 rescue missions in the United States, Canada, and Europe since November 1987, in which women changed their minds and didn't go through with their planned abortion, there have been at least 421 children saved from abortion on the day they were scheduled to die.

Hastings Center Reports 19, no. 6 (November/December 1989): 26–27.

We are convinced by medical evidence as well as by religious and ethical convictions that a woman has no right to have her own child killed. She is carrying within her a separate and totally unique human being. Thanks to the actions of over 49,000 rescuers to date who have risked arrest and jailing, these 421 children (as well as probably hundreds of others) who would otherwise have been disposed of in a medical garbage can, are *alive today*.

I am part of a growing group that believes *all* human life is sacred from the moment of conception until natural death. This includes Down syndrome children and unwanted, unloved children whom over one million adoptive parents in this country are waiting to receive and love. It includes those children who were not given a chance to live subsequent to amniocentesis. It even includes the relatively small number of children who are the products of rape and incest, who should not have to pay for the sins of their fathers by being aborted. It also includes the elderly in nursing homes and those in the final stages of Parkinson's disease. Life may be hard, but we should let God be God and cease meddling with His creation.

Ethical thinking on these matters has become distorted because, in an affluent society, we tend to worship at the altar of convenience and prosperity. Sad to say, the medical profession has not been unaffected by this trend. Many, including medical professionals, ask: "How will this affect society?" "How will this affect *my* fife?" "How much will it cost *me*?" "Can *I* get a tax deduction?" "If I allow my unwanted child to be killed (via abortion), will I be able to finish school?"

Such questions reveal that we as a society have lost our way. We don't think or act as if there are any *unchanging* reference points for life-and-death matters. We make our "ethical" decisions based upon the changing "needs" of society. But is this because there aren't any unchanging reference points or because we have forgotten them in the name of "progress"?

The reference points that I speak of are decreed by our Creator and found in His book that helped birth this nation—the Bible. Allow me to introduce a few of God's reference points from His book:

"You shall not murder" (Exod. 20.13).

It is *never* right to kill an innocent person. Some might maintain that the Supreme Court has determined that *fetuses are not persons*. But the Court also once said that blacks were not persons. Consider, by contrast, how before birth you and I are viewed by God.

> For thou didst form my inward parts; Thou didst weave me in my mother's womb. I will give thanks to thee, for I am fearfully and wonderfully made; Wonderful are Thy works, and my soul knows it very well. My frame was not hidden from Thee, when I was made in secret, and skillfully wrought in the depths of the earth. Thine eyes have seen my unformed substance; and in Thy book they were all written, the days that were ordained for me, when as yet there was not one of them. (Ps. 139:13–16)

"Thine eyes have seen *my unformed* substance"—much earlier than virtually any child is killed by an abortionist. Innocent blood is shed every time an abortion is committed. I believe that one day those who kill children in the womb will be brought to justice, for "Whoever shed man's blood, by man his blood shall be shed, for in the image of God, He made man" (Gen. 9:6).

With my pro-life companions, I ask that we as a nation return to God's reference points. According to the truth of Psalm 139, fetuses, embryos, and unwanted pregnancies all fall into the same category—human beings who are precious and highly valued in the sight of God. Instead, we've treated our nation's future as so much therapeutic meat. We've taken our children and our children's children and thrown them to the medical garbage piles of America. Twenty-five million Americans have been "legally" killed since 1973.

Some now maintain that we might use the "tissue" from abortions to help treat Parkinson's and other diseases.[1] This may sound very appealing at first, but such thinking has already opened the door to barbaric practices that are making their appearance slowly and discretely as they did in Nazi Germany. The wolf is already loose in the manger.

It will not do to complain that there is worldwide consensus that something like Nazi Germany must not happen again or that we are too civilized to let it happen. In this country alone, we've already destroyed *four times* the number of people that Hitler did.

God's truths have been either willfully ignored or distorted by all of us at one time or another. As a result much unethical behavior can be rationalized into existence. Like a boat without an anchor, so is our thinking without the guidance of God's truth. There was a time in this country when it was *unthinkable* for those in the medical profession to commit abortion. The profession was and is meant for *healing*, not killing. And since we as a society have allowed many lawmakers and justices to shift to this type of thinking apart from the foundation upon which this nation was built, we have suffered terribly. This country is set up to be run by "consent of the governed," but we have consented to our own sexual promiscuity, our own progressively worse violence against each other and our children, our own drug culture and deadly epidemics.

This raises a key aspect of the Rescue movement, *repentance*. Those of us involved in rescues are being called to repentance for *not* acting on behalf of these helpless children and their mothers. We are also calling upon our country to repent of its condoning of this holocaust. Godly repentance is healthy, not shameful. It shows that we are acknowledging God's way of seeking a return to a right relationship with Him.

To those in the medical ethics community and fellow readers of this *Report*, I ask that we acknowledge God's reference points for life. Let's receive back His simple yet unchanging standards of ethics and morals as found in *His* report, the Bible. None of us have the right to play God.

Meanwhile, my family and I are committed to do what is ethical and to "rescue those being taken away to death" (Prov. 24:11, The Living Bible). We ask those of you in the medical community to assist us however you can.

Sad to say, children are continuing to die. Jesus said that whatever we did to the least of His brethren, we were doing to Him. That is a principal motivation for Operation Rescue: To serve our Lord by serving the least and most innocent of His brethren. This is why we don't view our actions primarily as "civil disobedience," but rather *biblical obedience*. Our goal is to save lives, not break the law.

We will continue to place our bodies peacefully in front of the doors of abortuaries all across this nation until we see legalized child-killing and exploitation of women vanquished from our land. We don't consent anymore. It's that simple.

NOTE

1. See John A. Robertson, "Rights, Symbolism, and Public Policy in Fetal Tissue Transplants," and Kathleen Nolan, "*Genug ist Genug*: A Fetus is Not a Kidney," *Hastings Center Report* 18, no. 6 (December 1988): 5-19.

17

A Catholic Theologian at an Abortion Clinic

Daniel C. Maguire

I should not have been nervous the first day I drove to the abortion clinic. After all, I wasn't pregnant. There would be no abortions done this day. I would see no patients and no picketers. And yet tremors from a Catholic boyhood wrenched my usually imperturbable stomach. I was filled with dread and foreboding.

What was it that brought this Philadelphia Irish-Catholic male moral theologian to the clinic door? Abortion has not been my academic obsession. My wife and I have had no personal experience with abortion, although it once loomed as a possible choice in our lives. Our first son, Danny, was diagnosed as terminally ill with Hunter's syndrome when Margie was three months pregnant with our second child. However, amniocentesis revealed that the fetus, now Tommy, was normal.

The stimulus for my visit was the woman who agonized with Margie and me over the decision she had rather conclusively made, and asked us, as ethicists, to ponder with her all the pros and cons. She was almost six weeks pregnant. Her life situation was seriously incompatible with parenting and she could not bear the thought of adoption. After her abortion, she told us she had made the right decision, but she paid the price in tears and trauma.

More generally, I was drawn to this uneasy experience by women. I have often discussed abortion with women in recent years, been struck by how differently they viewed it. I experienced their resentment at the treatment of the subject by the male club of moral theologians. One woman, an author and professor at a Chicago seminary, wrote me after reading my first

Originally published in *The National Catholic Reports*. Reprinted by permission of Daniel C. Maguire, professor of moral theology, Marquette University.

article on abortion ("Abortion: A Question of Catholic Honesty," *The Christian Century*, September 14–21, 1983) thanking me and surprising me. She said she found it difficult to use the American bishops' pastoral letter on nuclear war because these *men* could agonize so long over the problems of *men* who might decide to end the world, but had not a sympathetic minute for the moral concerns of a woman who judges that she cannot bring her pregnancy to term.

I knew that my visit would not give me a woman's understanding of the abortion decision, but I hoped it might assist me, in the phrase of French novelist Jean Sulivan, to "lie less" when I write about this subject and to offend less those women who come this way in pain.

Those who write on liberation theology go to Latin America to learn; those who write on abortion stay at their desks. Until recently, all churchly writing on abortion has been done by deskbound celibate males. If experience is the plasma of theory, the experience obtained in a clinic three blocks from Marquette, where I teach and have done research on abortion, could only enhance my theological ministry.

Meeting the Clinic Staff

One day last May, I called the Milwaukee Women's Health Organization and spoke to its director, Elinor Yeo, an ordained minister of the United Church of Christ. I was afraid she would find my request to spend time at her clinic unseemly and out of order. She said she would call back when she finished an interview with a patient and spoke to her staff. She called later to tell me that the staff was enthusiastic about my prospective visits, adding the ironic note that the patient she was interviewing when I first called was a Marquette University undergraduate.

The clinic door still had traces of red paint from a recent attack. The door was buzzed open only after I was identified. A sign inside read: PLEASE HELP OUR GUARD. WE MAY NEED WITNESSES IF THE PICKETS GET OUT OF CONTROL. YOU CAN HELP BY OBSERVING AND LETTING HIM/HER KNOW IF YOU SEE TROUBLE. I realized that these people live and work in fear of "pro-life" violence. In the first half of this year there have been fifty-eight reported incidents of criminal violence at clinics, including bombing, arson, shootings, and vandalism.

Elinor Yeo sat with me for more than an hour describing the clinic's activities. Half of its patients are teenagers; half, Catholics; and 20 percent, black. Of the fourteen patients seen on a single day the previous week, one was thirteen years old; one, fourteen; and one, fifteen. Nationally, most abortions are performed within eight weeks of conception, at which point the *conceptus* is still properly called an embryo; 91 percent are within twelve weeks. At this clinic, too, most abortions are performed in the first two months. Most of the patients are poor; the clinic is busiest at the time when welfare checks come in. The normal cost for an abortion here is $185. For those on public assistance, it is $100.

I asked Elinor about the right-to-lifers' claim that most women who have abortions are rich. She replied: "The typical age of an abortion patient at this clinic is nineteen years." In what sense is a nineteen-year-old woman with an unwanted pregnancy rich?

I asked about the charge that doing abortions makes doctors rich. She assured me that, given their budget, all the doctors who work for them would make more if they remained in their offices. These doctors are also sometimes subject to harassment and picketing at their homes. Their care of patients is excellent, and they often end up delivering babies for these same women at some later date.

Each patient is given private counseling. About half want their male partners with them for these sessions. If there is any indication that the man is more anxious for the abortion than the woman, private counseling is carefully arranged. Every interested woman is offered the opportunity to study charts on embryonic and fetal development, and all women are informed of alternatives to abortion. The consent form, to be signed at the end of the interview and counseling sessions, includes the words: "I have been informed of agencies and services available to assist me to carry my pregnancy to term should I desire. . . . The nature and purposes of an abortion, the alternatives to pregnancy termination, the risks involved, and the possibility of complications have been fully explained to me."

All counselors stress reproductive responsibility. Two of the counselors have worked with Elinor for fourteen years. One is the mother of five children; the other, of three. Free follow-up advice on contraception is made available. It is the explicit goal of the counselors not to have the woman return for another abortion. According to Yeo, those most likely to have repeat abortions are women who reject contraceptive information and say they will never have sex again until they are married. It became ironically clear to me that the women working in this abortion clinic prevent more abortions than the zealous pickets demonstrating outside.

Yeo says that only 5 percent of the patients have ever seriously considered adoption as an alternative. *Abortion* or *keeping* are the two options considered by these young women. (Ninety-five percent of teenagers who deliver babies keep them, according to Elinor Yeo.)

Adoption is, of course, the facile recommendation of the bumper-sticker level of this debate. One patient I spoke to at a subsequent visit to the clinic told me how unbearable the prospect was of going to term and then giving up the born baby. For impressive reasons she found herself in no condition to have a baby. Yet she had begun to take vitamins to nourish the embryo in case she changed her mind. "If I continued this nurture for nine months, how could I hand over to someone else what would then be my baby?" It struck me forcefully how aloof and misogynist it is not to see that the adoption path is full of pain. Here is one more instance of male moralists prescribing the heroic for women as though it were simply moral and mandatory.

The surgery lasts some five to fifteen minutes. General anesthesia is not needed in these early abortions. Most women are in and out of the clinic in two and one-half hours. They return in two weeks for a checkup. These early abortions are done by suction. I was shown the suction tube that is used and was surprised to find that it is only about twice the width of a drinking straw. This is early empirical information for me as to *what* it is that is aborted at this stage.

All patients are warned about pregnancy aftermath groups that advertise and offer support but actually attempt to play on guilt and recruit these women in their campaign to outlaw all abortions, even those performed for reasons of health. One fundamentalist Protestant group in Milwaukee advertises free pregnancy testing. When the woman arrives, they subject her to grisly slides on abortions of well-developed fetuses. They take the woman's address and phone number and tell her they will contact her in two weeks at home. The effects of this are intimidating and violative of privacy and often lead to delayed abortions of more-developed fetuses.

Meeting the Women

My second visit was on a Saturday when the clinic was busy. I arrived at 8:30 in the morning. The picketers were already there, all men, except for one woman with a boy of ten. A patient was in the waiting room, alone. We greeted each other, and I sat down and busied myself with some papers, wondering what was going on in her mind. I was later to learn that she was five to six weeks pregnant. I was told that she was under psychiatric care for manic-depression, and receiving high doses of lithium to keep her mood swings under control. However, lithium in high doses may be injurious to the formation of the heart in embryos and early fetuses.

Pro-life? Pro-choice? How vacuous the slogans seemed in the face of this living dilemma. What life options were open to this woman? Only at the expense of her emotional well-being could a reasonably formed fetus come to term. This woman had driven alone a long distance that morning to get to the clinic and she would have to return home alone afterward. She had to walk to the door past demonstrators showing her pictures of fully formed fetuses and begging her: "Don't kill your baby! Don't do it." However well-intentioned they may be, in what meaningful moral sense were those picketers in this instance pro-life?

As I watched this woman I thought of one of my colleagues who had recently made a confident assertion that there could be no plausible reason for abortion except to save the physical life of the woman or if the fetus was anencephalic. This woman's physical life was not at risk and the embryo would develop a brain. But saving *life* involves more than cardiopulmonary continuity. How is it that in speaking of women we so easily reduce human life to physical life? What certitudes persuade theologians that there are only two marginal reasons to justify abortion? Why is the Vatican comparably sure that while there may be *just* wars with incredible slaughter, there can be no *just* abortions? Both need to listen to the woman on lithium as she testifies that life does not always confine itself within the ridges of our theories.

With permission I sat in on some of the initial interviews with patients. The first two were poor teenagers, each with one infant at home, and each trying to finish high school. One was out of work. Elinor Yeo let her know that they were now hiring at Wendy's. I was impressed that the full human plight of the patients was of constant concern to the staff. The other young woman had just gotten a job after two years and would lose it through pregnancy. One woman counted out her $100 and said: "I hate to give this up; I need it so much."

The staff told me about the various causes of unwanted pregnancies. One staff member said that it would seem that most young men have "scorn for condoms." "Making love" does not describe those sexual invasions. For these hostile inseminators nothing is allowed to interfere with their pleasure. Often there is contraceptive failure. One recent case involved a failed vasectomy. Sometimes conception is admittedly alcohol- and drug-related. A few women concede that they were "testing the relationship." Often it is a case of a broken relationship where the woman, suddenly alone, feels unable to bring up a child. Economic causes were most common. Lack of job, lack of insurance, a desire to stay in school and break out of poverty.

I wondered how many "pro-lifers" voted for Ronald Reagan because of his antiabortion noises, even though Reaganomics decreased the income of the lowest fifth of society's families by 8 percent while increasing the income of the rich. More of this could only be more poverty, more ruin, more social chaos, more unwanted pregnancies, and more women at clinic doors.

Meeting the Picketers

The picketers are a scary lot. Because of them a guard has to be on duty to escort the patients from their cars. Before the clinic leased the adjacent parking lot—making it their private property—some picketers used to attack the cars of the women, screaming and shaking the car. The guard told me he was once knocked down by a picketer. Without the guard, some of the demonstrators surround an unescorted woman and force her to see and hear their message. Other picketers simply carry placards and pray. One day, twenty boys from Libertyville, Illinois, were bused in to picket. They were not passive. They had been taught to shout at the women as they arrived. One staff member commented: "Statistically, one-quarter to one-third of these boys will face abortion situations in their lives. I wonder how this experience will serve them then."

A reporter from the Milwaukee *Journal* arrived, and I followed her when she went out to interview the picketers. Two picketers recognized me. Since I have been quoted in the press in ways that did not please, I am a persona non grata to this group. I had a chance to feel what the women patients endure. "You're in the right place, Maguire. In there, where they murder the babies." I decided they were not ripe for dialogue, so I remained silent and listened in on the interview.

I learned that some of these men had been coming to demonstrate every Saturday for nine years. Their language was filled with allusions to the Nazi Holocaust. Clearly, they imagine themselves at the ovens of Auschwitz, standing in noble protest as innocent *persons* are led to their death. There could hardly be any higher drama in their lives. They seem not to know that the Nazis were antiabortion too—for Aryans. They miss the anti-Semitism and insult in this use of Holocaust imagery. The 6 million murdered Jews and more than 3 million Poles, Gypsies, and homosexuals were actual, not potential, persons who were killed. Comparing their human dignity to that of prepersonal embryos is no tribute to the Holocaust dead.

Sexism, too, is in bold relief among the picketers. Their references to "these women" coming here to "kill their babies" are dripping with hatred. It struck me that for all their avowed commitment to life, these are the successors of the witch-hunters.

Meeting the Embryos

On my third visit to the clinic, I made bold to ask to see the products of some abortions. I asked in such a way as to make refusal easy, but my request was granted. The aborted matter is placed in small cloth bags and put in jars awaiting disposal. I asked to see the contents of one of the bags of a typical abortion—a six- to nine-week pregnancy—and it was opened and placed in a small metal cup for examination. I held the cup in my hands and saw a small amount of unidentifiable fleshy matter in the bottom of the cup. The quantity was so little that I could have hidden it if I had taken it into my hand and made a fist.

It was impressive to realize that I was holding in the cup what many people think to be the legal and moral peer of a woman, if not, indeed, her superior. I thought, too, of the Human Life Amendment that would describe what I was seeing as a citizen of the United States with rights of preservation that would countermand the good of the woman bearer. I have held babies in my hands and now I held this embryo. I know the difference.

CONCLUSIONS

- My visits to the clinic made me more anxious to maintain the legality of abortions for women who judge they need them. There are no moral grounds for political consensus against this freedom on an issue where good experts and good people disagree. It also made me anxious to work to reduce the need for abortion by fighting the causes of unwanted pregnancies: *sexism* enforced by the institutions of church, synagogue, and state that diminishes a woman's sense of autonomy; *poverty* induced by skewed budgets; *antisexual* bias that leads to eruptive sex; and the other *macro* causes of these micro tragedies.
- I came to understand that abortion can be the *least* violent option facing a woman. It is brutally insensitive to pretend that for women who resort to abortion, death is the only extremity they face.
- I came away from the clinic with a new longing for a moratorium on self-righteousness and sanctimonious utterances from Catholic bishops on the subject of abortion. An adequate Catholic theology of abortion has not yet been written. But the bishops sally forth as though this complex topic were sealed in a simple negative. Bishops like New York's John O'Connor, who use tradition as though it were an oracle instead of an unfinished challenge, are not helping at all. A position like O'Connor's has two yields: (a) it insults the Catholic intellectual tradition by making it look simplistic, and (b) it makes the bishops the allies of a right wing that has been using its newfound love of embryos as an ideological hideaway for many who resist the bishops' call for peace and social justice.
- Finally, I come from the abortion clinic with an appeal to my colleagues in Catholic moral theology. Many theologians (especially clerics) avoid this issue or behave weirdly or skittishly when they touch it. How do Catholic theologians justify their grand silence when they are allowing physicalism, crude historical distortions, and fundamentalistic notions of "church teaching" to parade as "the Catholic position"? Why are ethical errors that are thoroughly lambasted in the birth-control debate tolerated when the topic is abortion? Geraldine Ferraro and Governor Mario Cuomo of New York are taking the heat and trying to do the theology on this subject. Their debts to American Catholic theologians are minuscule. What service

> do we church teachers give when errors, already corrected in theology, are allowed to roam unchallenged in the pastoral and political spheres? Why are nonexperts, church hierarchy or not, allowed to set the *theological* terms of this debate? What service is it to ecumenism to refuse serious dialogue not only with women but with mainline Jewish and Protestant theologians on this issue? Vatican II said that "ecumenical dialogue could start with discussions concerning the application of the gospel to moral questions." That dialogue has not happened on abortion, and our brothers and sisters from other communions are waiting for it.

I realize, as do my colleagues in Catholic ethics, that abortion is not a pleasant topic. At its best, abortion is a negative value, unlike the positive values of feeding the poor and working for civil rights. On top of that it has become the litmus test of orthodoxy, and that spells danger in the Catholic academe. But, beyond all this, we in the Catholic family have been conditioned against an objective and empathic understanding of abortion. We are more sensitized to embryos than to the women who bear them. I claim no infallibility on this subject, but I do insist that until we open our affections to enlightenment here, we will none of us be wise.

18

Personhood, the Bible, and Abortion

Paul D. Simmons

The primary theological issue posed by the abortion debate centers on the personhood of the fetus. Evangelical Christians who are working for a constitutional "human life" amendment to ban abortion argue that the Bible teaches: (1) that the fetus is a person, and (2) that abortion is murder. Harold Brown states the position strongly: "The Bible prohibits the taking of innocent human life. If the developing fetus is shown to be a human being . . . (or) if human life has begun, then abortion is homicide and not permissible."[1] Though the starting point is ostensibly different, Brown's statement is in essential agreement with that of Pope Piux XII: "Innocent human life, in whatever condition it is found, is withdrawn, from the very first moment of its existence, from any direct deliberate attack."

Francis Schaeffer is another influential evangelical calling for a ban on abortion and claiming the Bible as his authority. Along with C. Everett Koop, U.S. Surgeon General and former surgeon-in-chief of the children's hospital in Philadelphia, Schaeffer produced a five-episode color motion picture series entitled *Whatever Happened to the Human Race?* based on their book by that title. Interestingly, Schaeffer and Koop rely more upon rational and "scientific" arguments to support their notion of the personhood of the fetus. Schaeffer is greatly influenced by Scholasticism in spite of all he has to say against "secular humanism." They do appeal to the biblical principles of the uniqueness of person and the worth of personal life which is rooted in the image of God.

The religious notion of the image of God has no biological counterpart. Even so, Schaeffer and Koop identify "image" with genotype. Thus, the

From "Personhood, the Bible, and the Abortion Debate," pp. 3–26. Reprinted by permission of the author. Portions of this material are from his book, *Birth and Death* (Westminster Press, 1983).

unborn should be regarded as persons from the time of conception: "No additional factor is necessary for a later time," say Schaeffer and Koop. "All that makes up the adult is present as the ovum and the sperm are united—the whole genetic code!"[2]

However, there are logical, moral, and biblical-theological reasons for not accepting the easy equation of conceptus with person. Logically, for instance, no one can deny the continuum with fertilization to maturity and adulthood. That does not mean, however, that every step on the continuum has the same value or constitutes the same entity. The best analogy of that is a fertilized hen egg. Given the proper incubation environment, the egg becomes a chicken and the chicken grows to become a hen or rooster. However, few of us are confused about the entity we are eating when we have eggs for breakfast. An egg—even a fertilized egg—is still an egg and not a chicken.

The genetic definition of personhood confuses potentialities with actualities. Potentialities are certainly important but they do not have the same value as actualities. "An embryo is not a person but the possibility or the probability of there being a person many months or even years in the future," Charles Hartshorne has argued. "Obviously possibilities are important, but to blur the distinction between them and actualities is to darken counsel."[3] The same point is made by John Stott in saying that the decision to abort for reasons of maternal health is "a choice between an actual human being and a potential human being."[4]

The fallacy of this definition of person is also seen when the argument is reduced *ad absurdum*. Every body cell of a person contains one's DNA, or genetic code. This is why, theoretically at least, persons may be cloned or duplicated. If one uses the genetic definition of person one would have to regard every body cell as a human being since each cell has the potentiality for becoming another person through cloning. Think also of the implications of this definition for surgery or the excision of cancer cells from the body!

The fatal weakness of this argument is its radical reductionism. The easy equation of "person" with "fertilized ovum" (zygote) moves from a terribly complex entity to an irreducible minimum. A zygote is a cluster of cells but hardly complex or developed enough to qualify as "person." A person or human being has capacities of reflective choice, rational response, social experience, moral perception, and self-awareness. Both the person and the zygote have "life" and both are "human" since they belong to *Homo sapiens*. But a zygote or blastocyst do not fully embody the qualities that pertain to personhood. A great deal more complex development and growth are necessary before the attributes of "person" are acquired.

Morally speaking, the claim that a conceptus is a human being is to introduce what Sissela Bok has called "a premature ultimate."[5] People have an absolute value in Western morality but fetuses do not. They have value but they are not of equal moral value with actual persons, in particular, the pregnant woman.

The Bible and the Fetus

This distinction seems basic to the Biblical story in Exod. 21:22-25—an important passage for the abortion debate. Here is an account of a pregnant woman who becomes involved in a brawl between two men and has a miscarriage. A distinction is then made between the penalty that is to be exacted for the loss of the fetus and any injury to the woman. For the fetus, a fine is paid as determined by the husband and the judges (verse 22). However, if the woman is injured or dies, *lex talionus* is applied: "thou shalt give life for life, eye for eye, tooth for tooth, hand for hand, foot for foot, burning for burning, wound for wound, stripe for stripe" (verses 23-25).

The story has only limited application to the current abortion debate since it deals with accidental, not willful, pregnancy termination. Even so, the distinction made between the protection accorded the woman and that accorded the fetus under covenant law is important. The woman has full standing as a person under the covenant, the fetus has only a relative standing, certainly inferior to that of the woman. This passage gives no support to the parity argument that gives equal religious and moral worth to woman and fetus.

Cottrell challenges this view, saying that parity is actually assumed by the passage. His argument is that verse 22 refers to the early birth of an otherwise healthy child (no harm), and that *lex talionus* applies to both fetus and mother in case of injury. "What is contrasted," he says, "is a situation in which harm comes to neither mother nor child, and a situation in which either one or the other is harmed."[6]

However, Cottrell's interpretation is problematic. Three things should be noted. First, he stands virtually alone among scholarly translators and interpreters of this text. The novelty of his interpretation seems dictated more by necessity than the text. Second, the Talmud sees verse 21 as a miscarriage, equivalent to a property loss by the father. While tradition does not establish truth, one would think that ancient interpretation would be helpful in dealing with awkward textual materials.

Third, Cottrell forces the implication from his treatment of this passage that "God considers the unborn child fully human." One can hardly derive a theology or even a statement of personhood from this passage. The biblical writer was not dealing with such a complex question—he is treating only those regulations that pertain to the covenant community. This is not a statement about their personhood (as, for instance, with slaves, oxen, etc.) but about punishment for accidents or injury. The most that can be said is that a distinction in value is made—both fetus and woman had value, but not equal value and thus not equal protection.

Fourth, there are other fundamentalist scholars who disagree with Cottrell. Waltke notes that Lev. 24:17 required the death penalty for anyone who "kills any human life," and says this plainly is not the case in Exodus 21 for killing a fetus. He concluded that the fetus was not reckoned as a soul in the Old Testament.[7]

The Biblical View of Person

The biblical portrait of person does not begin with an explanation of conception but with a portrayal of the creation of Adam and Eve. God created man as male and female. Three texts are of critical importance. The first is Gen. 2:7, which declares: "Then the Lord God formed man of dust from the ground, and breathed into his nostrils the breath of life; and man became a living soul." The biological aspects of personhood are metaphorically portrayed in terms of "dust" or "clay." God as the origin and giver of life is captured by his breathing life into the clay he has fashioned. The declaration "became a living soul" designated the persons as animated flesh. As the person is breathed into, so they breathe.

The second text distinguishes persons from the animal creation. Gen. 1:26–28 declares that "God made man in his own image, in the image of God he created him." The biblical portrait of person centers in the notion of *the image of God*, which is not a physical likeness but a similarity of powers or abilities. These capacities or powers are spiritual, personal, relational, moral, and intellectual. Of all the creatures fashioned by God, only people are able to relate to the Creator in obedience or rebellion. Only they experience those godlike powers of self-transcendence and self-awareness. This creature, like God, may be introspective, retrospective, and pro-spective. This one may reflect on the past, anticipate the future and discern the activity of God in his/her personal life and history.

The third text portrays the person as a moral decision maker. In Gen. 3:22 God says: "behold, mankind is become as one of us, to know good and evil. . . ." To be a person is to be a choice maker, reflecting God's own ability to distinguish good from evil, right from wrong. This does not mean people have perfect knowledge of right and wrong as some intrinsic gift from birth. Decisions must be made on the basis of one's understanding of God's will. The fact that they "ate of the tree of knowledge of good and evil" means that people are given the burden and responsibility of making decisions that reflect their unique place in God's creation.

The biblical portrait of person, therefore, is that of a complex, many-sided creature with godlike abilities and the moral responsibility to make choices. The fetus hardly meets those characteristics. At best, it begins to attain those biological basics necessary to show such capacities with the formation of a neocortex or no earlier than the second half of gestation.

The one who unquestionably fits this portrayal is the woman or mother in question. Because the pregnancy is hers, so the decision is uniquely hers. Certainly, the entire circle of those most intimately involved with the abortion question are persons—reflecting on the meaning of this moment, considering the data, weighing the facts of the past, anticipating the future, and making some decision. The abortion question focuses on the personhood of the woman, who in turn considers the potential personhood of the fetus in terms of the multiple dimensions of her own history and the future.

This is a godlike decision. Like the Creator, she reflects upon what is good for the creation of which she is agent. As steward of those powers, she uses them for good and not ill—both for herself, the fetus, and the future of humankind itself. She is aware that God wills health and happiness for herself, for those she may bring into the world, and the future of the human race. Thus, she is engaged in reflecting on her own well-being, the genetic health of the fetus, and the survival of the human race.

Searching the Scriptures

Two principles of biblical interpretation must be kept in mind when using the Bible to provide warrants or supports for a particular teaching. The first is that the text must be thoroughly examined for its specific meaning. The historical and textual context, the nature of the material, the meanings of terms, and other factors will all need to be assessed in coming to a clear understanding of the meaning of the passage. The second principle of interpretation/application is that a text or passage cannot be used to settle a technical question that is not specifically dealt with in the text. Literary devices such as metaphor and symbol cannot be pressed into the quest for scientific data, for instance, nor can a passage cast in a celebrative, doxological mood be used as if it were a descriptive, systematic, and thus definitive explanation of a more technical problem. In short, a text must not be used to draw conclusions that are not germane to the text itself.

These principles are important to bear in mind when searching the Scripture for teaching regarding the personhood of the fetus. Antiabortion evangelicals are fond of citing over one hundred biblical passages which they regard as teaching that the fetus is a person. An examination of some of the more important passages reveals the problems involved in such applications.

Ps. 139:13–15 is an oft-quoted text that bears examination:

> For thou didst form my inward parts [kidneys[, thou didst knit [weave] me together in my mother's womb . . . My frame [bones] was not hidden from thee when I was being made in secret, intricately wrought in the depth of the earth.

Antiabortion evangelicals take this passage as teaching that the fetus is a person. They further argue that the Psalmist is saying that God caused the pregnancy and knew him during gestation.

Numerous problems are posed by this interpretation, not the least of which is the fact that the Psalmist was not dealing with the question of abortion. He is free to use poetry and metaphor without trying to be precise or definitive about the point in gestation at which one is regarded as a person. In short, a nontechnical, poetic passage is used as if it were a careful, technical, and systematic declaration regarding personhood. The Hebrews did not think in abstract terms or deal with the stages or processes of gestational development.

Further problems emerge if the passage is taken for its literal meaning. If it is truly a factual or technical statement, scientific understandings of gestation are challenged. The Psalmist's reference to being "wrought in the depths of the earth" reflects the notion that the fetus (or the self) was developed "in the earth" and then introduced into the woman's womb. Plato's *Republic* (III, 414, C–E) recorded the Phoenician myth about people being formed and fed in the womb of the earth, which provides an interesting comparison to, if not parallel to, the Psalmist's statement.

It is also possible that the passage reflects the Aristotelian idea that the male sperm is the complete seed from which the offspring comes. The male sperm, it was believed, was like the acorn or maple seed. All that is required is a proper incubation environment. The woman is only the incubator for the genetic material provided by the man.

The text is a poetic way of celebrating God's love for people. The Psalmist declares that God's love surrounds the person in every comer or dimension of existence. He captures the exhilaration and thrill of religious wonder as he reflects upon the marvel of one's being in and before God. The person is the creation of the power of God and is doubly blessed when one's being is enraptured by knowing that we are not the power of our own existence and that we can know the Creator who has brought us into being. The 139th Psalm is understandably important in the worship and liturgy of Judaism and Christianity. It enables the believer better to celebrate one's being and relates it to God's caring love.

Those who treat this passage as a definitive, scientific teaching confuse poetry with prose and a mood of celebration with the need for explanation. The purpose of the passage is to capture the celebrative mood of joy and wonder in being for those who can reflect upon their origins and contemplate what it means to be before God. There is absolutely no intention or purpose in the text to deal with the question of elective abortion or whether the fetus is a person. The speaker reflects the awareness that we all begin prior to birth and that the entire creative process is a source of mystery and awe. All that is rooted in the creative and mysterious ways of God who brings us into being. It is another declaration of the truth that "it is God who has made us and not we ourselves" (Ps. 100:3).

The passage thus reflects the foundational awareness for the Judaeo-Christian doctrine of God as Creator. God is the source of all that is. He is the power that has transformed organic life from simplicity to complexity through a process of patient sovereignty. The most complex expression of life is found in personal existence—in the self-awareness and reflective self-transcendence of human beings. Knowing anything, however, is to know that life is not self-generating. Only God can bring something into being out of nothing. The distinctive question for religion is not *how* God has accomplished that miracle—that question belongs to the domain of scientific investigation. The biblical faith affirms that it is *God* who has made us.

A second passage often cited by antiabortionists is Jer. 1:5, where the prophet declares, speaking for God:

> Before I formed you in the belly I knew you; and before you came forth out of the womb, I sanctified you, and I ordained you a prophet unto the nations.

Shoemaker says this passage ascribes personhood to all unborn fetuses.[8] The text will not bear the weight of such an application, however. The passage deals with Jeremiah's calling as a prophet. He is establishing his credentials as one who has been called and appointed by God. His emphatic declaration is that God brought him into being for this very purpose (cf. Isa. 49:1-5). Thus, the passage is highly personal and specific. It is not a rational discourse on how God creates people or whether every fetus should be counted as a person. Jeremiah declared that God *knew* him, *formed* him, and *consecrated* him. He is making no similar claim for everyone. All this supports his central claim that God is the reason for his existence and the source of his authority to preach as a prophet. Shoemaker's claim that this passage teaches that God causes every pregnancy is a bogus application for it perverts and distorts the central meaning of the text, which deals with calling not conception.

A similar problem is posed by the antiabortion interpretation of Luke 1:41-42 which deals with the meeting between Mary and Elizabeth, both of whom are pregnant. Elizabeth, now six months pregnant with the one destined to be the forerunner of Jesus, John the Baptist, heard the voice of Mary, who has just discovered that she is pregnant. Luke says:

> And when Elizabeth heard the greeting of Mary, the babe leaped in her womb; and Elizabeth was filled with the Holy Spirit and she exclaimed with a loud cry, "Blessed are you among women, and blessed is the fruit of your womb!"

Again, antiabortion evangelicals take this as a passage teaching that fetuses are people, focusing as they do on "the babe leaped. . . ."

Problems abound with such an interpretation. The passage makes it clear, for instance, that it is Elizabeth who responds to God's revelation. She did the speaking, declaring the special blessedness of Mary and her child-to-be. The central point of the passage is theological and practical. It deals with the special role and authority of Jesus. The relation of John to Jesus was a source of considerable confusion during their ministries. The Gospel writers took pains to spell out the fact that John was a forerunner to Jesus, the Messiah, the Son of God. This crucial theological point should not be missed. John was a special servant of God, but was subservient to Jesus, a point emphasized at Jesus' baptism (Matt. 3:13–17; John 1:29–34) and elsewhere (cf. Mark 1:4–11; Matt. 11:2–6; Luke 7:18–23).

It is faulty biblical interpretation to generalize from this passage to the personhood of (every) fetus. Such an approach confuses the intention and meaning of the text with a contemporary debate entirely foreign to the mind of the writer. One might more reasonably use the passage to argue that "quickening" or viability at about the sixth month of pregnancy should be the stage of development at which the fetus might be regarded as a person. Even this application is an inference, however, and should not be regarded as a clear teaching of the text in question.

Anticipatory Parenthood

Some light might also be shed on the abortion debate by distinguishing between actual personhood and anticipatory or attributed personhood.[9] To put it another way, there is both an objective and a subjective side to regarding the fetus as person. Objectively, for instance, the fetus is not a person for it has not acquired the capacities or characteristics that define an entity as a person. Subjectively, however, the pregnant woman or the couple in question may regard the conceptus as a person and provide it with all the respect and protection a person should be accorded.

Couples who want a child and plan a family may and should regard the conceptus as a person. The pregnant woman may joyfully welcome the news that she has a baby on the way. By talking to the fetus, stroking the bulging womb, and celebrating the pregnancy, the child is brought into the circle of the human family. It is not yet a person, but it is already regarded as—it is named and accepted as—a person.

The essential difference is the value of the fetus to those involved in the pregnancy. It is not *vitality* but the acceptance, affirmation, recognition, and love of the fetus that grants personhood and assures that it will become a person. The experience of the fetus as person—as an entity of personal worth is the basis for symbiotic bonding between mother and child. A woman who wants a child and values her pregnancy will be convinced that she is carrying a baby, a person. No other designation conveys the reality of this experience of one who is "other" than the mother. She recognizes it as another self; it is not a "thing" nor simply a part of her body.

This important human phenomenon of attributed personhood is often overlooked by those who support the legal availability of abortion and believe certain reasons for elective abortion are morally justifiable. The search for objective criteria often seems cold and calculating to those who have only experienced the joyous, celebrative side of pregnancy. It is inconceivable to them that any woman would choose to terminate a pregnancy. They often react with fear, horror, and anger at people they believe to be unappreciative of the values of gestating life.

The mistake made at that point is to confuse anticipatory with *actual* personhood. To experience a fetus as person is not the same as discovering the personhood of the fetus. The fetus is not a person by any objective criteria, but may most certainly be ascribed personhood on highly subjective grounds.

Not every pregnancy results in a personal relationship between woman and fetus. Pregnancy is not always a happy occasion—it may be a destructive experience fraught with horror and threat to the woman. Far from being regarded as a person to be protected and loved, a conceptus may be experienced as a threat to personal well-being or a reminder of sexual abuse or the dangers attending the processes of conception and gestation.

Extreme caution is necessary when moving from positive experiences that cause people to sing the praises of God (as in Pss. 8, 139; Jer. 1:5; et al.), to conclusions that every similar occasion should be equally celebrated. The human experience of pregnancy is tremendously varied and reactions to or understandings of God's activity is understandably different. This problem focuses the issue of divine providence in the human experience of pregnancy under adverse circumstances. If God is to be praised and his glory celebrated when people experience the joys of pregnancy and childbirth, is the experience of pregnancy always to be regarded as the action of divine providence?

Personhood and Providence

What is at issue is the way God is related to the entire process of conception and birth or the processes of nature as such. Fundamentalists often portray God as the cause and power of all that is and argue that God is governing all natural processes.

Believing that the workings of nature are virtually the actions of God is important for the absolutism of their stance against abortion. Not only is the conceptus regarded as of equal value and personhood with the woman, conception is an act of God. The pregnancy would have to be a direct threat to the life of the mother for termination to be justifiable as an act of self-defense. All other pregnancies are to be accepted, regardless of extenuating circumstances as in rape, incest, or fetal deformity.

Shoemaker argues that abortion is forbidden in cases of rape. He begins with a non sequitur about not executing the rapist for the crime and asks rhetorically if we then are to mete out capital punishment upon the innocent unborn? He then sets forth the clinching argument, by saying: "God forbid that we should regard any situation as so tragic that God could not have prevented it if he so chose."[10] He proceeds to apply the same logic to cases of incest and fetal deformity. For him, God makes no mistakes!

In effect, Shoemaker is arguing that God is responsible for the pregnancy by rape. God wills the pregnancy since "he could have prevented it." Logically, Shoemaker would also have to argue that God is responsible for the rape since the rape "could have been prevented" and since the rape was necessary for the impregnation.

What is at stake in the fundamentalist posture is a Calvinistic stress on the sovereignty of God. It combines theological beliefs about the power and activity of God with a type of "law of nature." As Waltke says, "the causal connection between sexual intercourse and conception . . . is simply the means whereby God, the first cause of all things, gives his blessing."[11] In other words, however it happens in nature is the way God does it. No moral significance is made of the fact that between 25 and 50 percent of all pregnancies end without implantation and thus pass through the monthly menses of the woman. Spontaneous abortion is not morally questionable since God causes such things.

This line of reasoning extends to the problem of radical fetal deformity. Shoemaker assures believers in such cases that "God makes no mistakes!" U.S. Surgeon General C. Everett Koop argues that God creates genetic handicaps! He cites God's speech to Moses in Exodus 4:11: "Who has made man's mouth? Who makes him dumb, or deaf, or seeing, or blind? Is it not I, the Lord?"[12]

Explaining why God would do such things may take one of two forms. Either (1) it is a punishment for sin, or (2) it is an opportunity for Christian growth in spirituality. Shoemaker comforts the woman raped and impregnated by assuring her that "no testings will overtake one except those God has permitted men [*sic!*] to experience."

Such views of divine providence pose profound problems regarding the use of Scripture and a Christian understanding of the problem of evil. Using God's statement to Moses to explain genetic deformity betrays careless exegesis. The context was Moses' reluctance to become God's spokesman, fearing he would not be persuasive. "Dumb," "deaf," and "blind" are metaphors of speaking and understanding God's truth. This passage has nothing whatever to do with genetic handicaps.

Of greater significance is the question of the moral nature of God. Jesus emphatically rejected the notion that God causes evil things to happen to people either as punishment for sin or as a test of faith (Matt. 12:22-26; Luke 11:14-23). The Christian belief is that God is love (1 John 4:8) and that his actions are good (Matt. 19:17). Arguing that God either causes or permits rape or incest and consequent pregnancy, or that God causes every hideous anomaly is to say blasphemous and heretical things about God. Central to the teaching of Jesus was the idea that God is love and goodness. He emphatically denounced and refused the traditional theology that God caused evil things to happen. He drew a very simple test for deciding: "If you who are evil know how to give good gifts to your children, how much more shall your heavenly Father give good things to those who ask him?" (Matt. 7:11).

For some people, it is more acceptable to portray God as cruel than to suggest he may not be in total control. However, to blame evil on God is to risk confusing the work of Beelzebub with that of the Holy Spirit (Matt. 12:22-36; Luke 11:14-23). Jesus made it plain that an accounting would be made of those who attribute evil to God.

A second problem posed by a fundamentalist notion of providence involves the role of persons as stewards in the processes of nature and medical science. People are portrayed as the passive victims of whatever may befall. God only gives strength to bear tragedy; he gives no permission to interrupt a pregnancy regardless of fetal condition, circumstance of impregnation, or threat to the wellbeing of the woman. It is unthinkable, therefore, to believe that people—made in the image of God—may have to make some godlike decisions regarding their stewardship of procreative powers as in abortion. This is "forbidden territory" for human intervention.

However, the fundamentalist argument is contradictory. Though it is argued that nature's way is God's way, it is also argued that doctors should intervene to keep nature from terminating a deformed fetus by miscarriage or spontaneous abortion. They cannot have it both ways. To adopt the passive, noninterventionist posture is to undermine religious support for all of medical science.

Is it not more consistent to follow the clues given in a doctrine of Christian stewardship? As stewards, people work with God for the good of the entire created world—people, nature, and world alike. Human knowledge of the processes that hinder or help gives a divine mandate for people to make choices for human good and against those evils sure to afflict the human family. Therapeutic abortions may well be seen as morally responsible actions in the face of tragedy or evils that contradict the will of God. No woman who is impregnated by rape or incest is obligated to bear the further burden of completed pregnancy and childbearing. God coerces no one to become a parent and certainly is no party to the evil and violence of rape or incest. Terminating such a pregnancy is to act with God to prevent further threat to the health and well-being of the woman.

Aborting a fetus that is radically deformed may well be a morally responsible action to prevent the greater evil of a child's being born dying with an incurable illness (as in Tay-Sachs) or totally incapacitating anomalies, as with anencephaly. People cannot be indifferent to the anguish and burden of genetic deformities and illnesses. Nor can they be passive in the face of increasing genetic knowledge. Mistakes—often horrible and non-correctable mistakes—are made in nature. Genetic codes can be terribly confused. Being stewards with God requires making decisions about the genetic health of our children. Choice not chance is the divine mandate.

The third problem with the fundamentalist view of providence concerns its limited and inadequate view of grace. Shoemaker declares that God gives "sustaining grace" to those afflicted with pregnancy by rape or incest or those bearing fetuses which are radically deformed. That God does provide sustaining grace in such situations we do not doubt. But does grace not also give permission to act in spite of ambiguity and with boldness lay hold of the promise of forgiveness?

Karl Barth understood the paradox in the command of God with regard to abortion. He set the subject in the context of "The Protection of Life" and explained "the great summons to halt issued by the command" forbidding the willful taking of human life.[13] Barth thundered God's "no!" to any such action.

However, there is another side to God's command, said Barth. After hearing the "no!" we must be prepared "to stand by the truth that at some time or other, perhaps on the far frontier of all other possibilities, it may have to happen in obedience to the commandment that men must be killed by men."[14] Certainly, the life of the unborn is not an absolute. It cannot claim to be preserved in all circumstances. God may command the active participation of others in the killing of germinating life.[15] When he does it does not constitute murder.[16]

It is noteworthy that, while Barth is quoted by antiabortionists to support their stand, they never mention the fact that he also supported abortion. Barth saw a paradox at the heart of the biblical message concerning human stewardship in the protection of germinating life. The freedom to abort is a necessary part of the meaning of the grace of God in the tragic circumstances of life.

Personhood and Religious Liberty

The uniqueness of personhood is also at stake in the concern with religious liberty. The special relationship of the individual to God, the capacities for spiritual and moral decision making and the sanctity of religious belief are all brought together in what is meant by soul competence and liberty of conscience. The biblical emphasis on individual responsibility to and before God is expressed in terms of the priesthood of all believers (1 Pet. 2:9) which sharpens the notion of *imago dei* and moral knowledge. The truth cuts two ways: (1) the person has direct access to God and has both the ability and the moral responsibility to know and do his will, and (2) no other person or group has the right to stand between the believer and God. Religious imperialism and moralistic authoritarianism contradict this biblical truth. The arrogance of judgmentalism—of pronouncing judgment upon or impeding another's exercise of conscientious belief—is the biblical meaning of "playing God," as the story of Joseph shows (Gen. 45).

Conscience is the name given the governing principles of life to which a person is ultimately committed. The totality of the self and thus the integrity of personhood is involved in the moral dictates of conscience. This is the primary arena of the spirit's struggle with the moral claims made by the will of God. It is here that one obeys or disobeys God. One's relationship to God is premised upon one's obedience to conscience. The depths of one's own being, therefore, and the ground of meaning of one's own existence are expressed in the struggles of conscience.

The violation of conscience is therefore of ultimate concern on religious ground. To override or disobey conscience is to do violence to the transcendent dimensions of human existence. To the one whose conscience is captive to God and open to his leadership, decisions relating to moral issues come with the full force of the Divine Command.

The liberty of conscience thus establishes an important constraint on public policy. The claims of conscience establish the outer limits of state authority and the intrusion or imposition of any other coercive force such as other religious authorities. The individual cannot surrender the claims of conscience to the state any more than the state can claim to be able to set the limits to which conscience must be obeyed. This is the basis for restricting the powers of Congress to prohibit the free exercise of religion and/or to impose alien and odious doctrines upon people who do not share particular dogmatic formulation. Belief is not to be prescribed nor is acting upon one's religious convictions to be subject to punishment by the state.

The First Amendment says quite simply that: "Congress shall make no law respecting an establishment of religion nor prohibiting the free exercise thereof." The two critical portions deal with what have been called the "establishment" and the "free exercise" clauses. Congress is constrained and limited in its lawmaking capacities in these two vital areas of life. This simple but profoundly important amendment was intended to guarantee that:

- Congress would not make any religious group or church the established or favored or official church of the nation;

- Congress would not interfere in doctrinal disputes settling by law theological controversies that had not gained consensus among various bodies; no one group's doctrine would be made law for everyone;
- Dissent on religious opinion could not become the basis of criminal prosecution nor would acting on grounds of religious belief be the basis for ostracism or discrimination under the law;
- Government would not interfere with religious exercises; it would occupy itself with maintaining domestic tranquility (including assuring that religious groups could not harass or persecute other religious groups) and defending the country against enemies both domestic and foreign; and
- Religion was to be entirely voluntary; the people were to be free to be religious or not religious; the mind was not to be coerced in matters of religious opinion.

In sum, a careful delineation of spheres of influence was articulated and intended that established important constraints around the types of activity that were appropriate to and to be permitted by both church and state. Each was to be free from undue coercion or influence by the other. Religions were to be free to promulgate doctrines and participate in political activity but politics could not be used to coerce unbelievers to conform in belief or practice. Congress is not a doctrine-making or orthodoxy-assuring body, unlike the ancient councils called by kings and emperors at the behest of religious leaders to settle theological controversies. Further, no favoritism or partiality among the various religious groups is to be shown in public policy. Government policies toward religious groups is to be even-handed or neutral. Laws reflecting moral opinions based upon a narrow construal of religious doctrine are forbidden in a land founded upon the principle of a free church in a free state. The framers of the Constitution knowingly and explicitly rejected the church-over-state, the state-over-church, and the theocratic patterns.

Unfortunately, the Reagan administration has little appreciation for and little understanding of the First Amendment guarantees of religious liberty. It has consistently supported a Human Life Amendment to ban abortion and has openly linked public policy to the most traditional and conservative Roman Catholic theory on human fertility control. The linkage between these two attitudes is well established in Roman Catholic history. That they should now become the controlling theological perspectives for domestic and foreign policy governing questions about human fertility control is cause for both grief and alarm—grief because of the misery to which it is contributing and alarm because of the violations of the First Amendment. The Reagan administration has done more to fuel the fires of ancient religious antagonisms and to encourage assaults on the separation of church and state than any other administration in American history.

The abortion issue is a case in point. That the permissibility or lack thereof for elective abortion is rooted in profoundly held religious and moral beliefs can and has been documented. The American commitment to pluralism in religious conviction is also solidly rooted in constitutional guarantees. The question that has emerged, however, is whether the intolerance of the minority and an administration committed to do battle with the First Amendment will permit room for differences of opinion and practice. Shall religious liberty be protected or violated in the name of dogmatic and political imperialism? Even William F. Buckley Jr. acknowledges this as the core of the question:

> I respect those . . . (who) believe that the right to abort is an exercise in the implications of pluralism and that under the circumstances the anti-abortion sanction is to be resisted as an effort to impose a single cultural authority over the whole of society.[17]

In the absence of consensus among religious groups as to fetal personhood and as to the value of fetal life or its claims upon the pregnant woman and the community, no law can be decreed based upon the most narrow and rigid proposal without doing damage to and being in violation of the First Amendment.

At stake in the abortion debate is the role of religious liberty as a constraint in the politics of dogmatic belief. The quest for political power by various religious groups is often little more than a smokescreen for religious bigotry and intolerance. Beneath the types of actions undertaken and the types of proposals supported are profound assumptions regarding the relation of morality to public policy and the relations of church to state.

The establishment clause is violated by the intent of all those efforts to pass a "human life amendment" or to define the fetus from the moment of conception as a person and citizen under the Constitution. This is an effort to enact one group's dogma as everyone's law. Such notions of personhood are understandable and supportable only as religious understandings, not as public policy. Nor is the dogma of fetal personhood widely held as a religious belief. Those who reject it do so out of equally powerful theological and biblical understandings. Differences of opinion on religious grounds is precisely what the Constitution is designed to protect.

The free exercise clause is violated by efforts to coerce conscience or punish those who act on grounds of conscientious belief to terminate an unwanted pregnancy. This may well be the single most important consideration in the public policy dimensions of the abortion debate. The question of whether we are to respect and protect honest differences of opinion or whether we seek to violate the integrity of belief of those who disagree with us.

CONCLUSION

The biblical understanding of personhood explains the profound silence of the Bible on the matter of elective abortion. That there are no prohibitions is rather amazing if, as some contend, the Bible is so clear in its teaching against the practice. Certainly we know there were harsh penalties for abortion found among surrounding mid-Eastern cultures. The Assyrian code (ca. 1500 B.C.) declared that "any woman who causes to fall what her womb holds . . . shall be tried, convicted and impaled upon a stake and shall not be buried." The Hebrews knew of such codes which tacitly acknowledge that abortion was practiced.

The absence of specific prohibitions in Scripture could mean either: (1) no Hebrew or Christian ever terminated a problem pregnancy, or (2) abortion was a private, personal, and religious matter, not subject to civil regulation. The latter seems the most plausible explanation. Hebrew law gave considerable status to women in contrast to the harsh and repressive attitudes toward women found in surrounding cultures. Women were equal bearers of God's image and equal sharers in the tasks of stewardship (Gen. 1:28–30). The emphases fell upon the woman as one with the godlike ability and responsibility to make choices. As a person before God and others she bears the unique burden of the decision. The abortion question focuses the personhood of the woman who reflects on the meaning of her pregnancy, considers the data, examines her motives and moral commitments, and anticipates the future. The decision is uniquely hers for the pregnancy is highly personal. It was not socially regulated except as specified in Exodus 21.

The same pattern prevailed in the New Testament era. Even Paul, the great apostle who gave directions for moral living to Christians in pagan society, made no mention of abortion. For all his practical guidance, not once does the subject appear in his lists of vices or prohibited actions. Apparently, he regarded abortion as a matter to be dealt with on the basis of faith, grace, and Christian freedom. In this matter, the believer is to "work out your own salvation in fear and trembling . . . " (Phil. 2:12).

The absence of prohibitions against abortion does not mean either that abortion was widely practiced or that there was a cavalier attitude about pregnancy termination. Then, as now, elective abortion posed substantive issues with which a woman or couple must come to terms. Respect for germinating life, one's own beliefs and life plan will all enter the deliberation. Certainly reasons beyond mere convenience will be needed to offset the gravity of terminating germinal existence. Abortion is never to be encouraged but it is not a forbidden option.

Contemporary Christians will do well to follow the biblical pattern in treating the subject of elective abortion. The claim that the Bible teaches that the fetus is a person from the moment of conception is problematic at best. Such a judgment rests on subjective and personal factors, not explicit biblical teachings. The Bible's portrait of person centers on the woman and the man who unquestionably bear the image of God and five in responsible relation to him. Further, the absence of civil prohibition—even in a theocratic society!—is a worthy model to follow. The biblical writers' silence reveals a becoming reticence to judge too quickly concerning the morality of another person's choice. It is eloquent testimony to the sacredness of this choice for women and their families and the privacy in which it is to be considered. God's grace is extended to those who accept the responsibilities of parenthood and to those who must make difficult choices in the midst of the moral ambiguity of tragic and perplexing circumstances.

Notes

1. Harold O. J. Brown, *Death Before Birth* (Nashville: Thomas Nelson, 1977), p. 119.

2. Francis A. Schaeffer and C. Everett Koop, *Whatever Happened to the Human Race?* (Old Tappan, N.J.: Fleming N. Revell, 1979), p. 41.

3. Charles Hartshorne, "Ethics and the Process of Living," Conference on Refigion, Ethics and the Life Process, Institute of Religion and Human Development, Texas Medical Center, March 18–19, 1974.

4. John Stott, "Reverence for Human Life," *Christianity Today*, June 9, 1972, p. 12.

5. Sissela Bok, "Who Shall Count as a Human Being?" in *Abortion: Pro and Con*, ed. Robert L. Perkins (Cambridge, Mass.: Schenkman, 1964).

6. Jack W. Cottrell, "Abortion and the Mosaic Law," *Christianity Today*, March 16, 1973, p. 8.

7. Bruce K. Waltke, "The Old Testament and Birth Control," *Christianity Today*, November 8, 1978.

8. Donald Shoemaker, *Abortion, the Bible and the Christian* (Cincinnati: Hayes, 1976), p. 37.

9. See Paul D. Simmons, *Birth and Death: Bioethical Decision Making*, pp. 171ff., where the importance of this distinction is applied to considerations regarding biochemical parenting.

10. Shoemaker, *Abortion, the Bible, and the Christian*, p. 30.

11. Bruce K. Waltke, "Reflections from the Old Testament on Abortion," Address to the Evangelical Theological Society, December 29, 1975, p. 11.

12. See C. Everett Koop, "Deception on Demand," *Moody Monthly* (May 1980): 27.

13. Karl Barth, *Church Dogmatics* III/4 (Edinburgh: T. T. Clark, 1961), p. 416.

14. Ibid.

15. Ibid., p. 420.

16. Ibid., p. 421.

17. William F. Buckley Jr., *Firing Line*, October 5, 1977, New York City; PBS, November 4, 1977.

19

CHRISTIANS AND ABORTION

Richard Schoenig

Christians have been in the forefront of opposition to induced abortions. The Catholic Church and conservative Protestant groups, such as Operation Rescue, have opposed abortion and have campaigned legally and politically to outlaw the practice. The heart of their objection to abortion is their belief that at the moment of conception God provides an immortal soul to each fertilized human egg, thereby entitling it to full moral protection. Given this belief, every preborn individual, even at the undifferentiated fertilized egg stage, has the same right to life as any adult human; consequently, any abortion is murder.

In what follows I bring into focus three major ways in which Christians' belief that abortion is morally wrong is not fully coherent with other central Christian beliefs. I suggest that Christian abortion opponents should think more carefully about their belief that abortion is morally wrong, especially in light of other beliefs central to their own religious tradition.

ABORTION AND SALVATION

Eternal life for humans, in heaven or hell, is part of conservative Christian tradition; this doctrine appears in Christianity's three ancient and still widely accepted creeds: the Apostles' Creed, the Nicene Creed, and the Athanasian Creed. According to this tradition and the creeds, God provides happiness in heaven for the saved and suffering in hell for the damned. For most conservative Christians, the most important goal of earthly life is to earn eternal salvation and to avoid eternal damnation. Different Christian views about how God metes out salvation or damnation need not concern us here.

What does concern us here, however, is the fate of aborted humans. If they are not saved, then this fact seems to undermine God's goodness. According to St. Paul, for example, "For this is good and acceptable in the sight of God our Savior, Who will have all men to be saved, and to come unto the knowledge of the truth." (1 Timothy 2:3-4) St. Paul's suggestion is evidently that God prefers all to attain salvation. In addition, aborted humans are innocent, and thus cannot have done anything to offend God. Finally, these aborted humans are not responsible for their being aborted and hence are not responsible for their inability to satisfy God's criteria for salvation.

Southern Baptists, for example, hold that "up to the point of accountability. . . Christ's atonement covers the [human] race, and all who die before reaching this stage of development are saved." In addition, the synoptic Gospels pointedly show Jesus' concern for infants and young children: "And they brought unto him also infants, that he would touch them: but when his disciples saw it, they rebuked them. But Jesus called them unto him, and said, 'Suffer little children to come unto me, and forbid them not: for of such is the kingdom of God.'" (Luke 19:15-16. See also Matt. 18:1-6; Mark 9:36-39, 10:13-16.) There is no reason to think God would have less concern for aborted humans.

Given the foregoing considerations, it appears that abortion actually confers on preborn humans an advantage over most other human beings by guaranteeing them eternal happiness. Although preborn humans may be deprived of the opportunity to live full earthly lives, what do they importantly lose from the perspective of conservative Christianity? As the Gospels say, "For what shall it profit a man, if he shall gain the whole world, and lose his own soul?" (Mark 8:36; Matt. 16:26). In addition, more than a few humans are born and have earthly lives that are—to borrow a phrase from Thomas Hobbes—"solitary, poor, nasty, brutish, and short." To put the point more flippantly, "being born ain't always all it's cracked up to be." To die in innocence, according to this conservative Christian view, is to die in the state of salvation.

If this reasoning seems mere rationalization, consider the following thought experiment. Assume the Christian doctrine of salvation is true, including the divine judgment leading to heaven or hell, along with the idea embedded in the biblical passage, "For what shall it profit a man, if he shall gain the whole world, and lose his own soul." Assume also that you are a pre-born human and that you are asked to choose between these two alternatives: (1) be aborted and directly receive eternal happiness, or (2) be born, attain the age of accountability, and take the chance that you may—or may not—satisfy God's requirements for salvation.

Would not rational conservative Christians choose the first alternative? The first alternative seems especially preferable if one remembers that many conservative Christians, those influenced by John Calvin for example, believe that salvation is not the lot of most people. Even Jesus himself suggested that many will not be saved. "Then said one unto him, 'Lord, are there few that be saved?' And he said unto them, 'Strive to enter in at the strait gate: for many, I say unto you, will seek to enter in, and shall not be able.'" (Luke 13:23–24; see also Matt. 7:13–14) The Christian doctrine of salvation seems to guarantee aborted preborn humans eternal happiness, apparently undermining the religious rationale for opposition to abortion.

Christian abortion opponents may respond that abortion is nevertheless wrong because it may bring legal, psychological, or religious harm to the parents. However, such harm to the parents, according to the view adopted here, they should be willing to endure in order to guarantee the eternal salvation of their offspring. From the parents' point of view, their own harm should be a small price to pay for the infinite gain achieved for their aborted child.

Christian abortion opponents might still claim that abortion's harmful effects on the church and society make it wrong. One may respond from a Christian perspective that the church and society have exactly the point of enabling people to achieve their greatest good, the salvation of heaven; and such salvation is "automatic" for innocent, aborted, preborn humans. In short, if one accepts the Christian doctrine of salvation, then the practice of abortion seems not to undermine the function of church or society.

Finally, and perhaps most importantly, Christians may argue that abortion is wrong because it contravenes God's plan for the conceptus. However, assuming God does not overrule people's free choices, any plan he may have involving creatures with free will would have to be provisional because it would always be subject to the free choices of free creatures. Still, no human choice could harm God since, as the most perfect being, he is quite beyond harm. In fact, as mentioned above, abortion positively contributes to an end that God does desire, namely, that all people be saved.

I conclude that, given commonly accepted views about Christian salvation, abortion causes no significant harm to God, the aborted human, the church, or society. If immorality is in some way a function of harm to the innocent, then one is hard pressed to explain why, given standard Christian views about salvation, abortion should be regarded as immoral.

In summary, there is at least serious tension, if not outright inconsistency, among the following beliefs of Christian abortion opponents: (1) helping others to their salvation is not only not immoral, but is good; (2) abortion guarantees preborn humans salvation; (3) abortion is immoral.

Abortion Prevention and Violence

More than 1.5 million abortions are performed in the United States every year. If all preborn humans are morally equivalent to adult humans, and abortion therefore is murder, then we are truly in the midst of a holocaust of innocents of immense proportions that would make Herod blush and Hitler envious. Yet, though extensive nonviolent efforts to end abortion have failed, the vast majority of Christian abortion opponents and their organizations still condemn violent actions aimed at stopping abortions, including such actions as bombing clinics and executing abortion providers.

I suggest that the belief that violent action aimed at stopping abortions is immoral is inconsistent with the idea that all preborn humans are morally equivalent to adults, and also inconsistent with a belief—one Christians share with most other people—that it is not immoral to protect the innocent by force if necessary. In the case of abortion, the threat of death for the preborn is imminent and serious. Moreover, recent history confirms that extensive democratic and electoral campaigns by many Christians to change laws permitting abortion have proven fruitless. Other nonviolent protest tactics have also been futile. Unless abortion opponents and their organizations are utterly committed to passivity, fatal force is the last resort to stop a massive slaughter of the preborn. Not only is fatal force morally justified; it may even be required.

Imagine that you come upon an intruder in your house who is about to stab your newborn baby. Few morally sensitive people would condemn you for killing the intruder, if that were the only way to prevent the imminent stabbing. How can Christians congruously disavow, for example, the actions of John Salvi in killing abortion providers in order to prevent them from performing abortions? It certainly will not do to reply that Salvi's actions were against the law. Christians have never held that proper moral behavior is fully consistent with statute law.

Furthermore, no major Christian group has held that the use of fatal force against those engaged in the slaughter of innocents during the Nazi era was morally wrong. To the contrary, Christians solemnly honor the memory of millions of dutiful men and women who sacrificed their lives during World War II to stop the Nazi Holocaust. If in our country today there were organizations killing more than a million and a half innocents each year with legal immunity, as there were in Nazi Germany in the forties, morally sensitive persons would be unlikely to condemn violent resistance to such slaughter. More likely, they would consider it positively heroic and perhaps even morally obligatory for some in certain circumstances, as it was in their thought about the Nazi killing machine.

Christian abortion opponents might reject the claim of inconsistency for their denunciation of antiabortion violence by citing a strand of Christian thinking (Augustine, Luther, etc.) which holds that the legitimate use of violence is restricted to public authority except in cases of self-defense. However, there are two formidable obstacles for this response. First, from a John Salvi-like perspective the problem in the United States today, as it was in Nazi Germany, is the absence of legitimate public authority to stop the carnage.

Therefore, men and women of good conscience must, in effect, become that legitimate authority.

Second, if this strand of Christian thinking restricting the use of violence to public authority except in the case of self defense were accepted, then violent defense of an innocent third party, like the defense of the aforementioned baby from a homicidal intruder, would have to be condemned since it would not be an instance of self-defense not carried out by a public authority. This conclusion would certainly be difficult for most Christians (as well as others) to accept.

In summary, I have argued that there are serious inconsistencies among beliefs of Christian abortion opponents, the following in particular: (1) abortion is the wrongful killing of the innocent; (2) defending the lives of the morally innocent permits or requires the use of force, including fatal force, if alternatives do not work; (3) the use of violence to stop abortion when alternatives do not work is properly condemned.

Abortion and the Fate of Frozen Fertilized Human Eggs

About 2 million American couples per year seek treatment for infertility at U.S. in vitro fertilization clinics. In the most common procedures eight eggs are harvested from the prospective mother and all are fertilized at one time. Then four of the fertilized eggs are used for the procedure and four others frozen for future use. Most of the frozen fertilized eggs are in a very early (two- to-four-cell) stage of undifferentiated development. Although exact figures are hard to come by, there are probably tens of thousands of frozen fertilized human eggs (zygotes) throughout the world in which the creating parties have no apparent further interest. Institutions warehousing these unclaimed frozen zygotes have begun to inquire about the legal ramifications of disposing of them. At present in most jurisdictions the legal question of the zygotes remains unsettled.

The most commonly cited Old Testament reference to the status of the fetus is Exod. 21:22–23, where causing the death of a pregnant woman was a capital crime, whereas causing the death of her fetus was punishable by a fine. This passage has suggested to many Jewish scholars that the fetus should not be considered morally a human. Later the Septuagint (Greek) version of the Hebrew bible presented Exod. 21:22 somewhat differently as holding that if the fetus was "formed" the penalty was capital punishment, but if "unformed" it was again a fine. The earliest Christian view on abortion was that it was a grave sin at any stage of development. However, by the third and fourth centuries Latin church fathers such as Jerome and Augustine held that abortion is not homicide until the "scattered elements" are formed into a body. In the twelfth century, according to the codification of canon law by Gratian, the soul is not infused into the body until the fetus is formed, where formed meant various things, usually a specific time (forty days) or quickening (Aquinas). The most commonly accepted conservative Christian view of the status of the fetus today is that God infuses a soul from the moment of conception.

The ethical question relevant here is what is the morally correct way to deal with unclaimed frozen zygotes? For Christian abortion opponents who believe that conception defines the moral humanity of the fetus the answer seems clear. The zygotes must be rescued and set on a path to complete their human development. To do nothing would signal complicity in the death of innocent persons, along with a moral guilt comparable to that of accomplices in murder. Thus, given the standard conservative Christian position, one is morally required to see to it that all frozen zygotes find uteruses to nurture them to birth.

For those who accept the conservative Christian position, the plight of a frozen zygote is not unlike that of a young child drowning in a shallow pond. In both situations rescue is a moral necessity. It is not optional or supererogatory. Yet, while abortion opponent groups have registered strong moral disapproval of the in vitro fertilization which produces frozen zygotes, they have not insisted that capable females provide their reproductive faculties to bring these zygotes to birth. The Vatican, for instance, while decrying the destruction of frozen zygotes as a "prenatal massacre," has only urged, not required, Catholic couples to adopt the frozen zygotes in order eventually to bring them to birth. In light of the strict moral implications of the conservative Christian view, the Vatican's response is discordantly permissive. Just as morality is not satisfied by urging the rescue of a drowning child, morality is also not satisfied by urging the rescue of frozen zygotes. Yet neither the Vatican nor any other abortion opposition group has taken the more rigorous position.

Christian abortion opponents may respond that the analogy of the plight of the frozen zygote to that of the drowning child is weak; rescuing the child requires only a few minutes of effort, while rescuing frozen zygotes takes at least nine months of serious effort. Moreover, no financial liability accompanies the rescue of a drowning child, while some financial burden is involved in bringing the zygote to term.

This sort of pro-choice reasoning is unacceptable to abortion opponents because of their belief that when innocent lives are at stake, incommodity or economic burden is irrelevant. If frozen fertilized eggs truly are morally protected humans in danger of being destroyed apart from someone's rescue of them, then consistency requires Christian female abortion opponents to use their own reproductive abilities to bring the unwanted zygotes to term. Like the child drowning in the pond, the frozen zygotes require rescue by morally decent people.

In summary, I find a serious inconsistency in affirming the human moral stature of zygotes while not insisting on bringing to implantation and birth all unclaimed frozen fertilized eggs.

Conclusion

I do not claim to have shown that abortion is absolutely morally permissible. I have shown that there are serious tensions, and perhaps inconsistencies, in the beliefs of conservative Christian abortion opponents. If abortion is the grave moral offense they claim, then they should make some adjustments in other central, traditional, Christian beliefs that seem otherwise to have conflicting implications about the issue of abortion.

20

Life in the Tragic Dimension
A Sermon on Abortion

Roger A. Paynter

An old adage says: "There is no fool like an old fool, unless it's a young fool." Being two weeks shy of thirty-seven, I'm not quite ready to say that I am old, but the aches and pains I have after a game of touch football convince me that I am no longer young, either. So, being neither an "old fool" nor a "young fool," I guess I am just foolish—or at least a couple of you have suggested as much to me this week because of my sermon topic this morning. Oh, you haven't actually come out and called me foolish, but you have said, "Why ask for trouble? This is such a volatile issue; there is no way you can win." But, of course, "winning" isn't the issue when you bear the responsibility of standing behind this pulpit, or any pulpit, for that matter. The issue is to try to bring to bear the mercy and love and wisdom of the Gospel on the difficult realities of life. Other reasons also have motivated me to under-take such a difficult task. We have recently, for instance, experienced the anniversary of the Supreme Court's 1973 *Roe* v. *Wade* decision, which gave women a right to choose with regard to abortion. In addition, the Southern Baptist Christian Life Commission has designated this as "Sanctity of Human Life" Sunday and asked Southern Baptist ministers to address the issue. Those are my reasons for choosing this particular Sunday to address the issue, but I have known, and I mean that in the sense of a conviction, I have *known* that the Gospel of Grace to which I am committed would not allow me forever to avoid this issue in a sermon.

No issue is more emotionally turbulent at this time than the abortion issue. The sheer amount of published material confirms that. Consequently, no one sermon, no series of sermons for that matter, could begin to take

---

Delivered to the Lake Shore Baptist Church in Waco, Texas, on January 18, 1987. Reprinted by permission of the author.

into consideration every dimension of this issue. We could spend weeks dealing only with the Roman Catholic position, or the issue as it relates to poverty, or the difference between a moral and a medical decision, or the relationship of the rights of women to other human rights. If I have learned anything in these last few weeks of preparation, it is that there is simply "too much." There is so much to say, in fact, that I have a very, very hard time imagining how someone can investigate this issue and maintain even the slightest shred of arrogance about the "correctness" of his or her position. Yet people do maintain that, on both sides of the issue.

I have a hard time understanding an attitude of complete confidence because abortion is just about the most extraordinarily complex medical, legal, philosophical, social, and moral issue I have investigated. I want to try to address some of the moral dimensions from a pastoral perspective, and to try to avoid becoming moralistic in the process. In making that effort, I follow this bit of advice from William Sloane Coffin in his sermon on abortion: "Think thoughts that are as clear as possible, but no clearer; say things as simply as possible, but no simpler."[1]

Let me begin with some personal statements. First, I have been in support of the *Roe* v. *Wade* decision. At one point in my life, I took a very liberal stance toward that decision, almost viewing abortion as simply another means of birth control. I hate to cast this in terms of liberal versus conservative, but if one has to, I guess you could say that I have grown more conservative, though I would prefer to say that I have come to a position of understanding the issue from a perspective of more complexity than before. Two things have deeply influenced me in this direction. What little counseling I have done with women and men surrounding the abortion issue has made me aware of its tragic dimension. Second, next Sunday is the fourth birthday of my adopted son, whom I love more than I can possibly say. His birth mother, a seventeen-year-old high school student, faced, I feel sure, the hard issue of whether to abort, and I thank God daily that she did not. Yet, as deeply as I feel about my son, strange as it may sound, I'm glad the young mother had the ability to make a choice—for her sake. So, I am in support of *Roe* v. *Wade*.

My second personal statement is this: I have come to grieve deeply at the proliferation of abortions—over a million during each of the last few years—because it suggests to me that procreation and abortion decisions are not taken with enough moral seriousness.

The third personal statement I would make is that I find myself incapable of being any kind of absolute moral judge over a woman who makes the painful decision to abort. Yes, men are a part of this issue as well. They do participate in the origin of the fetus, and they also grieve over the difficulty of the decision. But it is essentially an issue confronting the woman, for she is the one who lives intimately with the consequences of her decision. She is the one who has to submit to the medical procedure of abortion. She is the one who, if young, might have to drop out of school, stress her body, and if she so decides, grow up too soon with a baby at her hip. Above all, regardless of age, she is the one who has to make a very complex, morally sensitive decision in a relatively short period of time. With that in mind, I recognize that it may be very difficult for you who are women to hear a man address the issue. (Believe me, I'm probably more in favor of women pastors right now than ever before.)

Now, let me paint the issue in its most extreme ideological perspectives and then muddy the water a bit. These are the expressions that most often get media coverage.

On one extreme is the position that sees the fetus as a piece of human tissue, no more, and the abortion decision as no more a moral choice than removing any other item of mere tissue. This position would say that a woman's right to abortion is absolute. I have read expressions of this position a couple of times, and I have seen it posed in television debates, but I have never known anyone to claim it as *their* position. Each writer or speaker qualifies his or her position in some manner.

The other extreme, the "Right to Life" position, says that from conception the life begun is a human person and to abort a fetus is murder. The fetus's right to life is *absolute*.

Now let me begin to "muddy the waters" by saying that an absolute right—that is, *one* right taken out of the framework of *all other rights*—is often what gets us into trouble. As Abraham Heschel said, "The opposite of a profound truth is another profound truth and the opposite of a human right is another human right."[2]

The first point I would make is that the worlds of medicine, philosophy, and the law have been unable to determine a "magic moment" when personhood begins. Life begins at conception, but when does human personhood begin? A variety of positions have been taken:

(1) *conception*, the point at which the new genotype is set.
(2) *implantation*, when the conceptus implants in the mother's womb (fourteen days). (By the way, the IUD contraceptive device comes into consideration here, for it works not by preventing conception, but by keeping implantation from occurring.)
(3) *eight weeks*, when the cerebral cortex begins to form and all internal organs are formed. Both Aristotle and Augustine believed that a male fetus obtained its soul at forty days and a female fetus was ensouled at eighty to ninety days. Augustine called this homonization—the point at which a developing embryo experiences "ensoulment." Before this point (eight weeks), Augustine allowed for the possibility of abortion. Arguing about the possible resurrec-

tion of aborted fetuses, "which are fully formed," he says about those not fully formed: "Who is not disposed to think that unformed fetuses perish like seeds which have been fructified." There is a whole history of important positions that the early church fathers held with respect to this issue, a history that the Roman Church would rather not admit into consideration.[3]

(4) *quickening*, (sixteen to eighteen weeks) when the mother feels the fetus move.

(5) *viability*, when the unborn child can survive outside the mother's body (around twenty-six weeks). This is the point when the Supreme Court protects the life of the unborn. A woman can have an abortion in the last "trimester" only if her life is at stake.

(6) *birth*, when the baby draws its first breath.

Thousands of years of debate are represented in these positions, and still there is no consensus about when human life becomes a human person. Despite the efforts of movies like *The Silent Scream*, no scientific information can yet determine when unborn life becomes a human person. Just as medical science has never absolutely, clearly, and without an ounce of reservation been able to determine when a dying person loses personhood, science cannot tell us with absolute clarity when personhood begins.

But neither has the church formed a consensus on the question, "When does personhood begin?" One of the reasons for this lack of consensus is that the Bible has no clear word. In the absence of such a clear mandate, a number of interpretations have arisen. Let me share some with you. I repeat, there is no place in the Bible where it is said: "Thou shalt not have an abortion."

The primary Jewish position is that human personhood begins when the baby is born and draws breath. Gen. 2:7 declares that "God breathed into his nostrils the breath of life and man became a living soul." Elsewhere, there is a place in Old Testament law (Exod. 21:22–25) that makes a value distinction between the life of the mother and the life of the unborn:

> When men strive together and hurt a woman with child, so that this is miscarriage, and yet no harm follows, the one who hurt her shall be fined, according as the woman's husband shall lay upon him . . . if any harm follows then you shall give life for life, eye for eye, tooth for tooth, hand for hand. . . .

That is, if the being in utero is harmed, a fine is imposed; if the mother dies, then the life of the injurer is demanded. While this is not the noblest form of jurisprudence, it is the only passage in the Bible directly applicable to the abortion issue. The New Testament, by the way, is completely and strangely silent.[4]

Now, the "Right to Life" people have, as you well know, a number of biblical passages at their disposal—the prominent ones being from Jeremiah, Job, and the Psalmist:

> Before I formed you in the womb, I knew you. (Jer. 1:4–5)
>
> Your own hands shaped me, molded me. (Job 10:8)
>
> For thou didst form my inward parts—Thou didst knit me together in my mother's womb. (Ps. 139:13)

These passages are all poetic expressions of the truth that God is the Creator and the source of all creative processes. They should instill in us a reverence toward all life, unborn as well as born. However, I do not think we should use them as proof of when, in the complex physical, spiritual process of creation, fetal life becomes human personhood. Poetry and "legal or scientific" arguments do not mix well. When a man says he has a broken heart, the physician does not do "open-heart" surgery. So I object in principle to the poetry of Gen. 2:7 (God "breathing" into us his breath and making us living souls) being used as a prooftext to defend abortion. And I object to Psalm 139 (God "knitting" us in our mother's womb) being used as a prooftext to condemn abortion.[5] The poetic language of the Bible is designed to inspire us to respect all life, but it is not designed to determine when fetal life becomes human personality. We are therefore left before the mystery of life with a question mark in our hearts. That leads me to the Scripture that expresses my *knowing* and *unknowing*: "As you do not know how the Spirit comes to the bones in the womb of the mother with child, so you do not know the work of God who makes everything" (Eccles.11:5).

The Bible does not prohibit abortion, but it always encourages a respect for life. Left with this ambiguity, believers have through the years taken very different positions. The Jewish community, for the most part, has valued the life and health of the mother above that of the unborn.[6] The Roman Catholic Church has held its very clear position only since 1869 and Pope Pius IX. It has always been against the abortion of a human being—don't get me wrong—but thinkers in the Catholic Church have held diverse opinions about when the fetus becomes an ensouled being. A diversity of opinions is still held, but no longer formally. The issue is now covered by the legislative function of the church. Abortions can get you excommunicated. You cannot have an abortion, even to save the life of the mother. You may try to save the mother's life and *indirectly* end the life of the fetus. This is to be contrasted, in Catholic reasoning, from directly aborting the fetus.[7] By the way, the legislative function of the Catholic Church is different from the teaching office, the Magisterium. The pope is infallible only in the teaching, not in the legislative area. Therefore, the prohibition of abortion is not governed by papal infallibility.[8]

Protestant groups have taken a whole range of positions. Southern Baptists have repeatedly gone on record as opposing abortion, except in the case of rape, incest, severe fetal deformity, or danger to the mother's health.[9] Thus, we must invoke the Protestant principle which says that in cases where Scripture is not clear, final interpretation should be left to each individual person, given guidance within his or her community of faith. The Roman Catholic position, of course, is that the church interprets Scripture for all its people on all issues.

Where do we go? Here are some suggestions for your consideration. This may or may not be a word from the Lord; you will have to decide. I offer it to you with fear and trembling, so great is the mystery of life and death at any point on the human spectrum.

(1) Conception is the beginning of life. The Bible teaches respect for all life, so unborn life deserves our deep respect.
(2) We cannot know when a fetus develops human personhood, so I cannot take either extreme position dogmatically. I cannot say that the fetus is just another mass of cells; neither can I say that it is a human person whose life, when we end it, makes us murderers.
(3) Every abortion represents a critical decision and should never be taken as casual birth control.
(4) We must be very careful in even mentioning God's will. We cannot glibly claim God's will is involved in every conception. I cannot ascribe to God's will conception by rape or by incest or by a couple in no position to marry and parent a child. These are all occurrences in a tragic and sinful world. Thus, abortion is not the automatic breaking of God's will. Neither can we glibly say that it is God's will that we perform abortion. In general, we should say that God is against the ending of all life, but that in some tragic circumstances, he understands—even allows—and certainly forgives the choices we have to make.[10]
(5) Making choices about abortion teaches us how to journey through the tragic dimension of life. This dimension includes violence and poverty, genetic defects, and pregnancy outside marriage. It includes unwise choices that result in severe and stressful consequences. It includes tragedy that comes when we have done nothing wrong. The tragic dimension of life is when there are no good choices left and everyone loses; when the choices left are not between good and evil, but between the lesser of two evils; or when we painfully, prayerfully, consider what is least bad.[11]

All of us find ourselves in places where no good solution is left. We can only measure the losses and compare the hurt. In such cases, we find ourselves cast out of the innocence of Eden, making choices we hate to make but have to make—with fear and trembling—amid confession and tears.[12]

And the church's role? It is to guide in the decision-making process by doing what I'm doing: safeguarding the woman's freedom of religion to make the choice; to affirm her in her willingness to bear a child under difficult circumstances if that is her choice; and if she decides instead to have an abortion, not to tell her what she should be feeling. Instead:

if she feels guilt—to offer and act out the Grace of God;

if she feels grief—to offer and act out the Comfort of God;

if she feels remorse—to offer and act out the Peace of God;

if she feels fear—to offer and act out the Love of God.

Many, if not most, of us are disturbed by this issue and by the number of abortions. Maybe we can help people make wiser, more educated choices. We have that responsibility. But, life being what it is, abortion decisions will always have to be made—at least until further technology comes along that may preclude it. Since there is no moral consensus or biblical mandate, we should accord women the legal, moral, and religious freedom to choose. And since abortion is a serious moral crisis, we should be around to guide her beforehand and to support and love her through whatever decision she, under God, makes.[13]

This sermon is an interim report, influenced by the thinking of others, and struggled with at a personal level by one who does not have all the answers. It is the best I can do, for now. I say it with apprehension and some sadness. It is as clear as I can think, but no clearer—it is as simple as I can speak, but no simpler. May God have grace and understanding for women who must make such decisions—and for preachers who talk about it.

NOTES

1. William Sloane Coffin, *The Courage to Love* (New York: Harper and Row, 1984), p. 49.

2. Abraham Joshua Heschel, from the original version of his sermon on abortion.

3. Jane Hurst, *The History of Abortion in the Catholic Church: The Untold Story* (Washington, D.C.: Catholics for a Free Choice, 1981), p. 7.

4. H. Stephen Shoemaker, "The Moral Crisis of Abortion," unpublished sermon.

5. Ibid.

6. Rabbi David Feldman as quoted by Paul Simmons, *Birth and Death: Bioethical Decisionmaking* (Philadelphia: Westminster Press, 1983), p. 94.

7. Hurst, *The History of Abortion in the Catholic Church*, p. 17.

8. Ibid., p. 2.

9. Southern Baptist Christian Life Commission pamphlet on abortion, p. 1.

10. Shoemaker, "The Moral Crisis of Abortion."

11. Ibid.

12. William Willimon, *Sighing for Eden* (Nashville: Abingdon Press, 1985), p. 24.

13. Coffin, *The Courage to Love*.

PART FIVE

ABORTION
and Moral Philosophy

21

A Defense of Abortion

Judith Jarvis Thomson

Most opposition to abortion relies on the premise that the fetus is a human being, a person, from the moment of conception. The premise is argued for, but, as I think, not well. Take, for example, the most common argument. We are asked to notice that the development of a human being from conception through birth into childhood is continuous; then it is said that to draw a line, to choose a point in this development and say "before this point the thing is not a person, after this point it is a person" is to make an arbitrary choice, a choice for which in the nature of things no good reason can be given. It is concluded that the fetus is, or anyway that we had better say it is, a person from the moment of conception. But this conclusion does not follow. Similar things might be said about the development of an acorn into an oak tree, and it does not follow that acorns are oak trees, or that we had better say they are. Arguments of this form are sometimes called "slippery slope arguments"—the phrase is perhaps self-explanatory—and it is dismaying that opponents of abortion rely on them so heavily and uncritically.

I am inclined to agree, however, that the prospects for "drawing a line" in the development of the fetus look dim. I am inclined to think also that we shall probably have to agree that the fetus has already become a human person well before birth. Indeed, it comes as a surprise when one first learns how early in its life it begins to acquire human characteristics. By the tenth week, for example, it already has a face, arms and legs, fingers and toes; it has internal organs, and brain activity is detectable.[1] On the other hand, I think that the premise is false, that the fetus is not a person from the moment of conception. A newly fertilized ovum, a newly implanted clump of cells, is no more a person

---

than an acorn is an oak tree. But I shall not discuss any of this. For it seems to me to be of great interest to ask what happens if, for the sake of argument, we allow the premise. How, precisely, are we supposed to get from there to the conclusion that abortion is morally impermissible? Opponents of abortion commonly spend most of their time establishing that the fetus is a person, and hardly any time explaining the step from there to the impermissibility of abortion. Perhaps they think the step too simple and obvious to require much comment. Or perhaps instead they are simply being economical in argument. Many of those who defend abortion rely on the premise that the fetus is not a person, but only a bit of tissue that will become a person at birth; and why pay out more arguments than you have to? Whatever the explanation, I suggest that the step they take is neither easy nor obvious, that it calls for closer examination than it is commonly given, and that when we do give it this closer examination we shall feel inclined to reject it.

I propose, then, that we grant that the fetus is a person from the moment of conception. How does the argument go from here? Something like this, I take it. Every person has a right to life. So the fetus has a right to life. No doubt the mother has a right to decide what shall happen in and to her body; everyone would grant that. But surely a person's right to life is stronger and more stringent than the mother's right to decide what happens in and to her body, and so outweighs it. So the fetus may not be killed; an abortion may not be performed.

It sounds plausible. But now let me ask you to imagine this. You wake up in the morning and find yourself back to back in bed with an unconscious violinist. A famous unconscious violinist. He has been found to have a fatal kidney ailment, and the Society of Music Lovers has canvassed all the available medical records and found that you alone have the right blood type to help. They have therefore kidnapped you, and last night the violinist's circulatory system was plugged into yours, so that your kidneys can be used to extract poisons from his blood as well as your own. The director of the hospital now tells you, "Look, we're sorry the Society of Music Lovers did this to you—we would never have permitted it if we had known. But still, they did it, and the violinist now is plugged into you. To unplug you would be to kill him. But never mind, it's only for nine months. By then he will have recovered from his ailment, and can safely be unplugged from you." Is it morally incumbent on you to accede to this situation? No doubt it would be very nice of you if you did, a great kindness. But do you *have* to accede to it? What if it were not nine months, but nine years? Or longer still? What if the director of the hospital says, "Tough luck, I agree, but you've now got to stay in bed, with the violinist plugged into you, for the rest of your life. Because remember this. All persons have a right to life, and violinists are persons. Granted you have a right to decide what happens in and to your body, but a person's right to life outweighs your right to decide what happens in and to your body. So you cannot ever be unplugged from him." I imagine you would regard this as outrageous, which suggests that something really is wrong with that plausible-sounding argument I mentioned a moment ago.

In this case, of course, you were kidnapped; you didn't volunteer for the operation that plugged the violinist into your kidneys. Can those who oppose abortion on the ground I mentioned make an exception for a pregnancy due to rape? Certainly. They can say that persons have a right to life only if they didn't come into existence because of rape; or they can say that all persons have a right to life, but that some have less of a right to life than others, in particular, that those who came into existence because of rape have less. But these statements have a rather unpleasant sound. Surely the question of whether you have a right to life at all, or how much of it you have, shouldn't turn on the question of whether or not you are the product of a rape. And in fact the people who oppose abortion on the ground I mentioned do not make this distinction, and hence do not make an exception in case of rape.

Nor do they make an exception for a case in which the mother has to spend the nine months of her pregnancy in bed. They would agree that would be a great pity, and hard on the mother; but all the same, all persons have a right to life, the fetus is a person, and so on. I suspect, in fact, that they would not make an exception for a case in which, miraculously enough, the pregnancy went on for nine years, or even the rest of the mother's life.

Some won't even make an exception for a case in which continuation of the pregnancy is likely to shorten the mother's life; they regard abortion as impermissible even to save the mother's life. Such cases are nowadays very rare, and many opponents of abortion do not accept this extreme view. All the same, it is a good place to begin: a number of points of interest come out in respect to it.

(1) Let us call the view that abortion is impermissible even to save the mother's life "the extreme view." I want to suggest first that it does not issue from the argument I mentioned earlier without the addition of some fairly powerful premises. Suppose a woman has become pregnant, and now learns that she has a cardiac condition such that she will die if she carries the baby to term. What may be done for her? The fetus, being a person, has a right to life, but as the mother is a person too, so has she a right to life. Presumably they have an equal right to life. How is it supposed to come out that an abortion may not be performed? If mother and child have an equal right to life, shouldn't we perhaps flip a coin? Or should we add to the mother's right to life her right to decide what happens in and to her body, which everybody seems to be ready to grant—the sum of her rights now outweighing the fetus's right to life?

The most familiar argument here is the following: We are told that performing the abortion would be directly killing[2] the child, whereas doing nothing would not be killing the mother, but only letting her die. Moreover, in killing the child, one would be killing an innocent person, for the child has committed no crime, and is not aiming at his mother's death. And then there are a variety of ways in which this might be continued. (1) But as directly killing an innocent person is always and absolutely impermissible, an abortion may not be performed. Or, (2) as directly killing an innocent person is murder, and murder is always and absolutely impermissible, an abortion may not be performed. Or, (3) as one's duty to refrain from directly killing an innocent person is more stringent than one's duty to keep a person from dying, an abortion may not be performed. Or, (4) if one's only options are directly killing an innocent person or letting a person die, one must prefer letting the person die, and thus an abortion may not be performed.[3]

Some people seem to have thought that these are not further premises which must be added if the conclusion is to be reached, but that they follow from the very fact that an innocent person has a right to life. But this seems to me to be a mistake, and perhaps the simplest way to show this is to bring out that while we must certainly grant that innocent persons have a right to life, the theses in (1) through (4) are all false. Take (2), for example. If directly killing an innocent person is murder, and thus impermissible, then the mother's directly killing the innocent person inside her is murder, and thus is impermissible. But it cannot seriously be thought to be murder if the mother performs an abortion on herself to save her life. It cannot seriously be said that she *must* refrain, that she *must* sit passively by and wait for her death. Let us look again at the case of you and the violinist. There you are, in bed with the violinist, and the director of the hospital says to you, "It's all most distressing, and I deeply sympathize, but you see this is putting an additional strain on your kidneys, and you'll be dead within the month. But you *have* to stay where you are all the same. Because unplugging you would be directly killing an innocent violinist, and that's murder, and that's impermissible." If anything in the world is true, it is that you do not commit murder, you do not do what is impermissible, if you reach around to your back and unplug yourself from that violinist to save your life.

The main focus of attention in writings on abortion has been on what a third party may or may not do in answer to a request from a woman for an abortion. This is in a way understandable. Things being as they are, there isn't much a woman can safely do to abort herself. So the question asked is what a third party may do, and what the mother may do, if it is mentioned at all, is deduced, almost as an afterthought, from what it is concluded that third parties may do. But it seems to me that to treat the matter in this way is to refuse to grant to the mother that very status of person which is so firmly insisted on for the fetus. For we cannot simply read off what a person may do from what a third party may do. Suppose you find yourself trapped in a tiny house with a growing child. I mean a very tiny house, and a rapidly growing child—you are already up against the wall of the house and in a few minutes you'll be crushed to death. The child on the other hand won't be crushed to death; if nothing is done to stop him from growing he'll be hurt, but in the end he'll simply burst open the house and walk out a free man. Now I could well understand it if a bystander were to say, "There's nothing we can do for you. We cannot choose between your life and his, we cannot be the ones to decide who is to live, we cannot intervene." But it cannot be concluded that you, too, can do nothing, that you cannot attack it to save your life. However innocent the child may be, you do not have to wait passively while it crushes you to death. Perhaps a pregnant woman is vaguely felt to have the status of house, to which we don't allow the right of self-defense. But if the woman houses the child, it should be remembered that she is a person who houses it.

I should perhaps stop to say explicitly that I am not claiming that people have a right to do anything whatever to save their lives. I think, rather, that there are drastic limits to the right of self-defense. If someone threatens you with death unless you torture someone else to death, I think you have not the right, even to save your life, to do so. But the case under consideration here is very different. In our case there are only two people involved, one whose life is threatened, and one who threatens it. Both are innocent: the one who is threatened is not threatened because of any fault, the one who threatens does not threaten because of any fault. For this reason we may feel that we bystanders cannot intervene. But the person threatened can.

In sum, a woman surely can defend her life against the threat to it posed by the unborn child, even if doing so involves its death. And this shows not merely that the theses in (1) through (4) are false; it shows also that the extreme view of abortion is false, and so we need not canvass any other possible ways of arriving at it from the argument I mentioned at the outset.

(2) The extreme view could of course be weakened to say that while abortion is permissible to save the mother's life, it may not be performed by a third party, but only by the mother herself. But this cannot be right either. For what we have to keep in mind is that the mother and the unborn child are not like two tenants in a small house which has, by an unfortunate mistake, been rented to both: the mother *owns* the house. The fact that she does adds to the offensiveness of deducing that the mother can do nothing from the supposition that third parties can do nothing. But it does more than this: it casts a bright light on the supposition that third parties can do nothing. Certainly it lets us see that a third party who says "I cannot choose between you" is fooling himself if he thinks this is impartiality. If Jones has found and fastened on a certain coat, which he needs to keep him from freezing, but which Smith also needs to keep him from freezing, then it is not impartiality that says "I cannot choose between you" when Smith owns the coat. Women have said again and again "This body is *my* body!" and they have reason to feel angry,

reason to feel that it has been like shouting into the wind. Smith, after all, is hardly likely to bless us if we say to him, "Of course it's your coat, anybody would grant that it is. But no one may choose between you and Jones who is to have it."

We should really ask what it is that says "no one may choose" in the face of the fact that the body that houses the child is the mother's body. It may be simply a failure to appreciate this fact. But it may be something more interesting, namely the sense that one has a right to refuse to lay hands on people, even where it would be just and fair to do so, even where justice seems to require that somebody do so. Thus justice might call for somebody to get Smith's coat back from Jones, and yet you have a right to refuse to be the one to lay hands on Jones, a right to refuse to do physical violence to him. This, I think, must be granted. But then what should be said is not "no one may choose," but only "*I* cannot choose," and indeed not even this, but "*I* will not *act*," leaving it open that somebody else can or should, and in particular that anyone in a position of authority, with the job of securing people's rights, both can and should. So this is no difficulty. I have not been arguing that any given third party must accede to the mother's request that he perform an abortion to save her life, but only that he may.

I suppose that in some views of human life the mother's body is only on loan to her, the loan not being one which gives her any prior claim to it. One who held this view might well think it impartiality to say "I cannot choose." But I shall simply ignore this possibility. My own view is that if a human being has any just, prior claim to anything at all, he has a just, prior claim to his own body. And perhaps this needn't be argued for here anyway, since, as I mentioned, the arguments against abortion we are looking at do grant that the woman has a right to decide what happens in and to her body.

But although they do grant it, I have tried to show that they do not take seriously what is done in granting it. I suggest the same thing will reappear even more clearly when we turn away from cases in which the mother's life is at stake, and attend, as I propose we now do, to the vastly more common cases in which a woman wants an abortion for some less weighty reason than preserving her own life.

(3) Where the mother's life is not at stake, the argument I mentioned at the outset seems to have a much stronger pull. "Everyone has a right to life, so the unborn person has a right to life." And isn't the child's right to life weightier than anything other than the mother's own right to life, which she might put forward as ground for an abortion?

This argument treats the right to life as if it were unproblematic. It is not, and this seems to me to be precisely the source of the mistake.

For we should now, at long last, ask what it comes to, to have a right to life. In some views having a right to life includes having a right to be given at least the bare minimum one needs for continued life. But suppose that what in fact *is* the bare minimum a man needs for continued life is something he has no right at all to be given? If I am sick unto death, and the only thing that will save my life is the touch of Henry Fonda's cool hand on my fevered brow, then all the same, I have no right to be given the touch of Henry Fonda's cool hand on my fevered brow. It would be frightfully nice of him to fly in from the West Coast to provide it. It would be less nice, though no doubt well meant, if my friends flew out to the West Coast and carried Henry Fonda back with them. But I have no right at all against anybody that he should do this for me. Or again, to return to the story I told earlier, the fact that for continued life that violinist needs the continued use of your kidneys does not establish that he has a right to be given the continued use of your kidneys. He certainly has no right against you that *you* should give him continued use of your kidneys. For nobody has any right to use your kidneys unless you give him such a right; and nobody has the right against you that you shall give him this right—if you do allow him to go on using your kidneys, this is a kindness on your part, and not something he can claim from you as his due. Nor has he any right against anybody else that *they* should give him continued use of your kidneys. Certainly he had no right against the Society of Music Lovers that they should plug him into you in the first place. And if you now start to unplug yourself, having learned that you will otherwise have to spend nine years in bed with him, there is nobody in the world who must try to prevent you, in order to see to it that he is given something he has a right to be given.

Some people are rather stricter about the right to life. In their view, it does not include the right to be given anything, but amounts to, and only to, the right not to be killed by anybody. But here a related difficulty arises. If everybody is to refrain from killing that violinist, then everybody must refrain from doing a great many different sorts of things. Everybody must refrain from slitting his throat, everybody must refrain from shooting him—and everybody must refrain from unplugging you from him. But does he have a right against everybody that they shall refrain from unplugging you from him? To refrain from doing this is to allow him to continue to use your kidneys. It could be argued that he has a right against us that we should allow him to continue to use your kidneys. That is, while he had no right against us that we should give him the use of your kidneys, it might be argued that he anyway has a right against us that we shall not now intervene and deprive him of the use of your kidneys. I shall come back to third-party interventions later. But certainly the violinist has no right against you that you shall allow him to continue to use your kidneys. As I said, if you do allow him to use them, it is a kindness on your part, and not something you owe him.

The difficulty I point to here is not peculiar to the right to life. It reappears in connection with all the other natural rights; and it is something which an adequate account of rights must deal with. For present purposes it is enough just to draw attention to it. But I would stress that I am not arguing that people do not have a right to life—quite to the contrary, it seems to me that the primary control we must place on the acceptability of an account of rights is that it should turn out in that account to be a truth that all persons have a right to life. I am arguing only that having a right to life does not guarantee having either a right to be given the use of or a right to be allowed continued use of another person's body—even if one needs it for life itself. So the right to life will not serve the opponents of abortion in the very simple and clear way in which they seem to have thought it would.

(4) There is another way to bring out the difficulty. In the most ordinary sort of case, to deprive someone of what he has a right to is to treat him unjustly. Suppose a boy and his small brother are jointly given a box of chocolates for Christmas. If the older boy takes the box and refuses to give his brother any of the chocolates, he is unjust to him, for the brother has been given a right to half of them. But suppose that, having learned that otherwise it means nine years in bed with that violinist, you unplug yourself from him. You surely are not being unjust to him, for you gave him no right to use your kidneys, and no one else can have given him any such right. But we have to notice that in unplugging yourself, you are killing him; and violinists, like everybody else, have a right to life, and thus in the view we were considering just now, the right not to be killed. So here you do what he supposedly has a right you shall not do, but you do not act unjustly to him in doing it.

The emendation which may be made at this point is this: the right to life consists not in the right not to be killed, but rather in the right not to be killed unjustly. This runs a risk of circularity, but never mind: it would enable us to square the fact that the violinist has a right to life with the fact that you do not act unjustly toward him in unplugging yourself, thereby killing him. For if you do not kill him unjustly, you do not violate his right to life, and so it is no wonder you do him no injustice.

But if this emendation is accepted, the gap in the argument against abortion stares us plainly in the face: it is by no means enough to show that the fetus is a person, and to remind us that all persons have a right to life—we need to be shown also that killing the fetus violates its right to life, i.e., that abortion is unjust killing. And is it?

I suppose we may take it as a datum that in a case of pregnancy due to rape the mother has not given the unborn person a right to the use of her body for food and shelter. Indeed, in what pregnancy could it be supposed that the mother has given the unborn person such a right? It is not as if there were unborn persons drifting about the world, to whom a woman who wants a child says "I invite you in."

But it might be argued that there are other ways one can have acquired a right to the use of another person's body than by having been invited to use it by that person. Suppose a woman voluntarily indulges in intercourse, knowing of the chance it will issue in pregnancy, and then she does become pregnant; is she not in part responsible for the presence, in fact the very existence, of the unborn person inside her? No doubt she did not invite it in. But doesn't her partial responsibility for its being there itself give it a right to the use of her body? If so, then her aborting it would be more like the boy's taking away the chocolates, and less like your unplugging yourself from the violinist—doing so would be depriving it of what it does have a right to, and thus would be doing it an injustice.

And then, too, it might be asked whether or not she can kill it even to save her own life: If she voluntarily called it into existence, how can she now kill it, even in self-defense?

The first thing to be said about this is that it is something new. Opponents of abortion have been so concerned to make out the independence of the fetus, in order to establish that it has a right to life, just as its mother does, that they have tended to overlook the possible support they might gain from making out that the fetus is *dependent* on the mother, in order to establish that she has a special kind of responsibility for it, a responsibility that gives it rights against her which are not possessed by any independent person—such as an ailing violinist who is a stranger to her.

On the other hand, this argument would give the unborn person a right to its mother's body only if her pregnancy resulted from a voluntary act, undertaken in full knowledge of the chance a pregnancy might result from it. It would leave out entirely the unborn person whose existence is due to rape. Pending the availability of some further argument, then, we would be left with the conclusion that unborn persons whose existence is due to rape have no right to the use of their mothers' bodies, and thus that aborting them is not depriving them of anything they have a right to and hence is not unjust killing.

And we should also notice that it is not at all plain that this argument really does go even as far as it purports to. For there are cases and cases, and the details make a difference. If the room is stuffy, and I therefore open a window to air it, and a burglar climbs in, it would be absurd to say, "Ah, now he can stay, she's given him a right to the use of her house—for she is partially responsible for his presence there, having voluntarily done what enabled him to get in, in full knowledge that there are such things as burglars, and that burglars burgle." It would be still more absurd to say this if I had had bars installed outside my windows, precisely to prevent burglars from getting in, and a burglar got in only because of a defect in the bars. It remains equally absurd if we imagine it is not a burglar who climbs in, but an innocent person who blunders or falls in. Again, suppose it were like this: people-seeds drift about in the air like pollen, and if you open your windows, one may drift in and take root in your carpets or upholstery. You don't want children, so you fix up your windows with fine mesh screens, the very best you can buy. As can happen, however, and on very, very rare occasions does happen, one of the screens is defective; and a seed drifts in and takes root. Does the person-plant who now develops have a right to the use of your house? Surely not—despite the fact that you voluntarily opened your windows, you knowingly kept carpets and upholstered furniture, and you knew that screens were sometimes defective. Someone may argue that you are responsible for its rooting, that it does have a right to your house, because after all you *could* have lived out your life with bare floors and furniture, or with sealed windows and doors. But this won't do—for by the same token anyone can avoid a pregnancy due to rape by having a hysterectomy, or anyway by never leaving home without a (reliable!) army.

It seems to me that the argument we are looking at can establish at most that there are *some* cases in which the unborn person has a right to the use of its mother's body, and therefore *some* cases in which abortion is unjust killing. There is room for much discussion and argument as to precisely which, if any. But I think we should sidestep this issue and leave it open, for at any rate the argument certainly does not establish that all abortion is unjust killing.

(5) There is room for yet another argument here, however. We surely must all grant that there may be cases in which it would be morally indecent to detach a person from your body at the cost of his life. Suppose you learn that what the violinist needs is not nine years of your life, but only one hour: all you need to do to save his life is to spend one hour in that bed with him. Suppose also that letting him use your kidneys for that one hour would not affect your health in the slightest. Admittedly you were kidnapped. Admittedly you did not give anyone permission to plug him into you. Nevertheless it seems to me plain you ought to allow him to use your kidneys for that hour—it would be indecent to refuse.

Again, suppose pregnancy lasted only an hour, and constituted no threat to life or health. And suppose that a woman becomes pregnant as a result of rape. Admittedly she did not voluntarily do anything to bring about the existence of a child. Admittedly she did nothing at all which would give the unborn person a right to the use of her body. All the same it might well be said, as in the newly emended violinist story, that she *ought* to allow it to remain for that hour that it would be indecent in her to refuse.

Now some people are inclined to use the term "right" in such a way that it follows from the fact that you ought to allow a person to use your body for the hour he needs, that he has a right to use your body for the hour he needs, even though he has not been given that right by any person or act. They may say that it follows also that if you refuse, you act unjustly toward him. This use of the term is perhaps so common that it cannot be called wrong; nevertheless it seems to me to be an unfortunate loosening of what we would do better to keep a tight rein on. Suppose that box of chocolates

I mentioned earlier had not been given to both boys jointly, but was given only to the older boy. There he sits, stolidly eating his way through the box, his small brother watching enviously. Here we are likely to say "You ought not to be so mean. You ought to give your brother some of those chocolates." My own view is that it just does not follow from the truth of this that the brother has any right to any of the chocolates. If the boy refuses to give his brother any, he is greedy, stingy, callous—but not unjust. I suppose that the people I have in mind will say it does follow that the brother has a right to some of the chocolates, and thus that the boy does act unjustly if he refuses to give his brother any. But the effect of saying this is to obscure what we should keep distinct, namely the difference between the boy's refusal in this case and the boy's refusal in the earlier case, in which the box was given to both boys jointly, and in which the small brother thus had what was from any point of view clear title to half.

A further objection to so using the term "right" that from the fact that A ought to do a thing for B, it follows that B has a fight against A that A do it for him, is that it is going to make the question of whether or not a man has a right to a thing turn on how easy it is to provide him with it; and this seems not merely unfortunate, but morally unacceptable. Take the case of Henry Fonda again. I said earlier that I had no right to the touch of his cool hand on my fevered brow, even though I needed it to save my life. I said it would be frightfully nice of him to fly in from the West Coast to provide me with it, but that I had no right against him that he should do so. But suppose he isn't on the West Coast. Suppose he has only to walk across the room, place a hand briefly on my brow—and lo, my life is saved. Then surely he ought to do it, it would be indecent to refuse. Is it to be said "Ah, well, it follows that in this case she has a right to the touch of his hand on her brow, and so it would be an injustice in him to refuse"? So that I have a right to it when it is easy for him to provide it, though no right when it's hard? It's rather a shocking idea that anyone's rights should fade away and disappear as it gets harder and harder to accord them to him.

So my own view is that even though you ought to let the violinist use your kidneys for the one hour he needs, we should not conclude that he has a right to do so—we should say that if you refuse, you are, like the boy who owns all the chocolates and will give none away, self-centered and callous, indecent in fact, but not unjust. And similarly, that even supposing a case in which a woman pregnant due to rape ought to allow the unborn person to use her body for the hour he needs, we should not conclude that he has a right to do so; we should conclude that she is self-centered, callous, indecent, but not unjust, if she refuses. The complaints are no less grave; they are just different. However, there is no need to insist on this point. If anyone does wish to deduce "he has a right" from "you ought," then all the same he must surely grant that there are cases in which it is not morally required of you that you allow that violinist to use your kidneys, and in which he does not have a right to use them, and in which you do not do him an injustice if you refuse. And so also for mother and unborn child. Except in such cases as the unborn person has a right to demand it—and we were leaving open the possibility that there may be such cases—nobody is morally *required* to make large sacrifices, of health, of all other interests and concerns, of all other duties and commitments, for nine years, or even for nine months, in order to keep another person alive.

(6) We have in fact to distinguish between two kinds of Samaritan: the Good Samaritan and what we might call the Minimally Decent Samaritan. The story of the Good Samaritan, you will remember, goes like this:

> A certain man went down from Jerusalem to Jericho, and fell among thieves, which stripped him of his raiment, and wounded him, and departed, leaving him half dead.
>
> And by chance there came down a certain priest that way; and when he saw him, he passed by on the other side.
>
> And likewise a Levite, when he was at the place, came and looked on him, and passed by on the other side.
>
> But a certain Samaritan, as he journeyed, came where he was; and when he saw him he had compassion on him.
>
> And went to him, and bound up his wounds, pouring in oil and wine, and set him on his own beast, and brought him to an inn, and took care of him.
>
> And on the morrow, when he departed, he took out two pence, and gave them to the host, and said unto him, "Take care of him; and whatsoever thou spendest more, when I come again, I will repay thee." (Luke 10:30-35)

The Good Samaritan went out of his way, at some cost to himself, to help one in need of it. We are not told what the options were, that is, whether or not the priest and the Levite could have helped by doing less than the Good Samaritan did, but assuming they could have, then the fact they did nothing at all shows they were not even Minimally Decent Samaritans, not because they were not Samaritans, but because they were not even minimally decent.

These things are a matter of degree, of course, but there is a difference, and it comes out perhaps most clearly in the story of Kitty Genovese, who, as you will remember, was murdered while thirty-eight people watched or listened, and did nothing at all to help her. A Good Samaritan would have rushed out to give direct assistance against the murderer. Or perhaps we had better allow that it would have been a Splendid Samaritan who did this, on the ground that it would have involved a risk of death for himself. But the thirty-eight not only did not do this, they did not even trouble to pick up a phone to call the police. Minimally Decent Samaritanism would call for doing at least that, and their not having done it was monstrous.

After telling the story of the Good Samaritan, Jesus said, "Go, and do thou likewise." Perhaps he meant that we are morally required to act as the Good Samaritan did. Perhaps he was urging people to do more than is morally required of them. At all events it seems plain that it was not morally required of any of the thirty-eight that he rush out to give direct assistance at the risk of his own life, and that it is not morally required of anyone that he give long stretches of his life—nine years or nine months—to sustaining the life of a person who has no special right (we were leaving open the possibility of this) to demand it.

Indeed, with one rather striking class of exceptions, no one in any country in the world is *legally* required to do anywhere near as much as this for anyone else. The class of exceptions is obvious. My main concern here is not the state of the law in respect to abortion, but it is worth drawing attention to the fact that in no state in this country is any man compelled by law to be even a Minimally Decent Samaritan to any person; there is no law under which charges could be brought against the thirty-eight who stood by while Kitty Genovese died. By contrast, in most states in this country women are compelled by law to be not merely Minimally Decent Samaritans, but Good Samaritans to unborn persons inside them.* This doesn't by itself settle anything one way or the other, because it may well be argued that there should be laws in this country—as there are in many European countries—compelling at least Minimally Decent Samaritanism. But it does show that there is a gross injustice in the existing state of the law. And it shows also that the groups currently working against liberalization of abortion laws, in fact working toward having it declared unconstitutional for a state to permit abortion, had better start working for the adoption of Good Samaritan laws generally, or earn the charge that they are acting in bad faith.

I should think, myself, that Minimally Decent Samaritan laws would be one thing, Good Samaritan laws quite another, and in fact highly improper. But we are not here concerned with the law. What we should ask is not whether anybody should be compelled by law to be a Good Samaritan, but whether we must accede to a situation in which somebody is being compelled—by nature, perhaps—to be a Good Samaritan. We have, in other words, to look now at third-party interventions. I have been arguing that no person is morally required to make large sacrifices to sustain the life of another who has no right to demand them, and this even where the sacrifices do not include life itself; we are not morally required to be Good Samaritans or anyway Very Good Samaritans to one another. But what if a man cannot extricate himself from such a situation? What if he appeals to us to extricate him? It seems to me plain that there are cases in which we can,

---

*The reader is reminded that this article was published before the U.S. Supreme Court rendered its decison in *Roe* v. *Wade*.—Eds.

cases in which a Good Samaritan would extricate him. There you are, you were kidnapped, and nine years in bed with that violinist lie ahead of you. You have your own life to lead. You are sorry, but you simply cannot see giving up so much of your life to the sustaining of his. You cannot extricate yourself, and ask us to do so. I should have thought that—in light of his having no right to the use of your body—it was obvious that we do not have to accede to your being forced to give up so much. We can do what you ask. There is no injustice to the violinist in our doing so.

(7) Following the lead of the opponents of abortion, I have throughout been speaking of the fetus merely as a person, and what I have been asking is whether or not the argument we began with, which proceeds only from the fetus's being a person, really does establish its conclusion. I have argued that it does not.

But of course there are arguments and arguments, and it may be said that I have simply fastened on the wrong one. It may be said that what is important is not merely the fact that the fetus is a person, but that it is a person for whom the woman has a special kind of responsibility issuing from the fact that she is its mother. And it might be argued that all my analogies are therefore irrelevant—for you do not have that special kind of responsibility for that violinist, Henry Fonda does not have that special kind of responsibility for me. And our attention might be drawn to the fact that men and women both are compelled by law to provide support for their children.

I have in effect dealt (briefly) with this argument in section 4 above; but a (still briefer) recapitulation now may be in order. Surely we do not have any such "special responsibility" for a person unless we have assumed it, explicitly or implicitly. If a set of parents do not try to prevent pregnancy, do not obtain an abortion, and then at the time of birth of the child do not put it out for adoption, but rather take it home with them, then they have assumed responsibility for it, they have given it rights, and they cannot now withdraw support from it at the cost of its life because they now find it difficult to go on providing for it. But if they have taken all reasonable precautions against having a child, they do not simply by virtue of their biological relationship to the child who comes into existence have a special responsibility for it. They may wish to assume responsibility for it, or they may not wish to. And I am suggesting that if assuming responsibility for it would require large sacrifices, then they may refuse. A Good Samaritan would not refuse—or anyway, a Splendid Samaritan, if the sacrifices that had to be made were enormous. But then so would a Good Samaritan assume responsibility for that violinist; so would Henry Fonda, if he is a Good Samaritan, fly in from the West Coast and assume responsibility for me.

(8) My argument will be found unsatisfactory on two counts by many of those who want to regard abortion as morally permissible. First, while I do argue that abortion is not impermissible, I do not argue that it is always

permissible. There may well be cases in which carrying the child to term requires only Minimally Decent Samaritanism of the mother, and this is a standard we must not fall below. I am inclined to think it a merit of my account precisely that it does not give a general yes or a general no. It allows for and supports our sense that, for example, a sick and desperately frightened fourteen-year-old schoolgirl, pregnant due to rape, may *of course* choose abortion, and that any law which rules this out is an insane law. And it also allows for and supports our sense that in other cases resort to abortion is even positively indecent. It would be indecent in the woman to request an abortion, and indecent in a doctor to perform it , if she is in her seventh month, and wants the abortion just to avoid the nuisance of postponing a trip abroad. The very fact that the arguments I have been drawing attention to treat all cases of abortion, or even all cases of abortion in which the mother's life is not at stake, as morally on a par ought to have made them suspect at the outset.

Secondly, while I am arguing for the permissibility of abortion in some cases, I am not arguing for the right to secure the death of the unborn child. It is easy to confuse these two things in that up to a certain point in the life of the fetus it is not able to survive outside the mother's body; hence removing it from her body guarantees its death. But they are importantly different. I have argued that you are not morally required to spend nine months in bed, sustaining the life of that violinist; but to say this is by no means to say that if, when you unplug yourself, there is a miracle and he survives, you then have a right to turn around and slit his throat. You may detach yourself even if this costs him his life; you have no right to be guaranteed his death, by some other means, if unplugging yourself does not kill him. There are some people who win feel dissatisfied by this feature of my argument. A woman may be utterly devastated by the thought of a child, a bit of herself, put out for adoption and never seen or heard of again, She may therefore want not merely that the child be detached from her, but more, that it die. Some opponents of abortion are inclined to regard this as beneath contempt—thereby showing insensitivity to what is surely a powerful source of despair. All the same, I agree that the desire for the child's death is not one which anybody may gratify, should it turn out to be possible to detach the child alive.

At this place, however, it should be remembered that we have only been pretending throughout that the fetus is a human being from the moment of conception. A very early abortion is surely not the killing of a person, and so is not dealt with by anything I have said here.

Notes

1. Daniel Callahan, *Abortion: Law, Choice and Morality* (New York: Macmillan, 1970), p. 373. This book gives a fascinating survey of the available information on abortion. The Jewish tradition is surveyed in David M. Feldman, *Birth Control in Jewish Law* (New York: New York University Press, 1968), part 5, the Catholic tradition in John T. Noonan Jr., "An Almost Absolute Value in History," in *The Morality of Abortion*, ed. John T. Noonan Jr. (Cambridge, Mass.: Harvard University Press, 1970).

2. The term "direct" in the arguments I refer to is a technical one. Roughly, what is meant by "direct killing" is either killing as an end in itself, or killing as a means to some end, for example, the end of saving someone else's life.

3. The thesis in (4) is in an interesting way weaker than those in (1), (2), and (3): they rule out abortion even in cases in which both mother and child will die if the abortion is not performed. By contrast, one who held the view expressed in (4) could consistently say that one needn't prefer letting two persons die to killing one.

22

Nature As Demonic in Thomson's Defense of Abortion

John T. Wilcox

"A Defense of Abortion,"[1] by Judith Jarvis Thomson, is now "the most widely reprinted essay in all of contemporary philosophy."[2] It must be important. Nevertheless, though references to it are common, and though many writers appraise it briefly, one does not find in the literature much *detailed* criticism of it or speculation on its significance. In my judgment, the arguments in it are extremely unpersuasive. But that claim raises its own difficulty: Why would an essay which lacks cogency have become so widely read and so widely praised? If it lacks argumentative force, as I claim and argue here, what does it have, instead? Of course Thomson writes with a surreal lucidity; that explains some of her appeal. Indeed, her essays can achieve the paradoxical beauty that one sees in some of the famous pre-Socratic and Sophistic arguments. Who knows? Maybe we could spend a century vying for the best refutation of them, the way the West has spent two and a half millennia refuting Zeno. I argue here that an important source of her failure and of her success lies in the covert mythology underlying much of her thought. Her arguments contain crucial logical difficulties unless we presuppose a certain kind of mythical understanding of reality. The myth in question is most implausible; but I think that it expresses important aspects of women's lives in this half of the twentieth century.

What Thomson argues is that even if the fetus is a person, and so even if it has a right to life, nevertheless it does not have a right to the use of the mother's body, and so the mother may abort it—unless completing her pregnancy would be so easy that even a "Minimally Decent Samaritan" would be obligated to carry it to term. For Thomson, the fetus has no rights to its

From *New Scholasticism* 63, no. 4 (autumn 1989): 463-84.

mother's body unless she *gives* it such rights, unless she voluntarily assumes responsibility for it. Any obligation the mother owes the fetus, apart from her consent, are not matters of rights, or of justice, but of charity; and the requirements of charity for Thomson are not very stringent. Consequently, most abortions are morally permissible—even, to repeat, even if the fetus is a person, with a right to life.[3]

Thomson argues mainly by telling her memorable story of a violinist who will die without the use of your kidneys. In her story, you wake up one morning to discover that you have been kidnapped and surgically connected to a violinist to save his life. She eventually discusses variations on this story, but in its initial version you will need to remain hooked up for nine months; disconnecting before the end of that time will kill him. The situation, she notes, has many of the features of pregnancy—even on the "pro-life" view: the violinist is a person, as the conservatives say the fetus is; in consequence, he has a right to life, as they say the fetus has; he is innocent—he himself had no active role in the kidnapping, or [I guess] in any other wrongdoing—just as the fetus is innocent; and the only way he can be saved is through the use of your body, just as the fetus normally needs its mother's body. So the situations are in many ways parallel, even if we grant some of the controversial assumptions which the conservatives argue for. But it seems obvious to Thomson, and to many of her readers, that the violinist has no *right* to your kidneys, and so that if you let him use them for nine months it is a ***kindness*** on your part, not a matter of respecting his rights. So she concludes that the same is true of pregnancy: the fetus has no rights to its mother's body; if the mother allows it to remain, and so to live, it is a matter of her kindness toward it, not a matter of its rights. Furthermore, Thomson says, kindness obligations do not really require that you save the violinist at such cost to yourself, you should be kind to your fellow man in little ways—say by telephoning when a phone call could save his life—but you have no obligation to make heroic or saintly sacrifices for your neighbor. You should be a Minimally Decent Samaritan, but you do not have to be a Good, much less a Splendid, Samaritan. So if you decide to help the violinist for nine months, you have acted above and beyond the call of strict duty, even on grounds of chanty or kindness. By analogy, then, the mother who makes serious sacrifices for the fetus in her womb is doing more than charity requires. So if she decides to abort it—unless the burden of carrying it would he minimal—she has done no wrong.

Thomson presents an analogous argument about Henry Fonda, but I will ignore it here since it raises no additional issues. In fact, it may be simpler: Henry Fonda lets you die without violating your rights, whereas you actually kill[4] the violinist without violating his rights, in Thomson's analysis. In both arguments, Thomson says the question is whether a person's right to life (and his mortal need of help) gives him the right to another person's lifesaving services, or gives another person an obligation to save his life. Thomson says no. Put another way, the issue is the nature and extent of one's obligations to other persons, granted that they have the right to life. However, sometimes Thomson also introduces considerations of the rights of the possible helper—of the mother, in the abortion case. I will ignore here Thomson's claim that the mother *owns* her body, and so has proprietor's rights over it; I think that is false,[5] but I cannot discuss everything. Later I will discuss her claim that the mother has self-defense rights which may be exercised in abortion. I think that claim is directly related to much of what bothers me about her essay.

One might criticize Thomson either at a general level, in terms of the ethical theory implicit in her arguments, or at a more concrete level, in terms of her analysis of pregnancy and abortion. If one were to take the more general approach, as some do, clearly one would have to question her claim that we have no obligation to be *Good* Samaritans. Perhaps it is a sign of our times that she thought she could reject a central teaching of Jesus with so little fuss. Americans live now in an age of rather narrow individualism,[6] in which Thomson and many of her readers think that *of course* we have only minimal duties to our fellow men. One certainly could question that. Perhaps Jesus, and the Jewish tradition behind him, were more sensible than Thomson is. But arguing that is a large task, one I am not competent to undertake. I only note the problem, and note also that this may be one reason some religious people are so upset about abortion. I will give some other reasons later.

Again, if one were to criticize Thomson at a general level, one would have to ask whether it is true that the only obligations we have to others are of the three sorts Thomson discusses: to respect their rights as persons; to be charitable; and to respect the special rights we have voluntarily granted them. I doubt if this view is correct. I think, for example, that I had obligations to my parents, when they were alive, which did not fall into any of these three categories. Again we see the rather narrow individualism in Thomson's view, and another way in which it underplays "traditional family values." But I do not want to argue the case against it at this general level. Instead, I want to look carefully at what Thomson says about pregnancy. I believe that when we do, we can see there the implausibility of her argument—and also make some suggestions about the subterranean source of her great success.

Her argument is basically an argument by analogy: pregnancy is supposed to be analogous to being hooked up to an unconscious violinist. And so what is true (given her general principles) in one case is supposed to be true in the other. The force of the argument clearly depends upon the strength of the analogy. But it is clear that there are great disanalogies between the two cases. Indeed, some wags have said that only someone at MIT could have come up with such an implausible analogy. Let us explore some of the problems.

First: the violinist example is *weird*. (This is a technical term.)[7] No one in the history of mankind has ever been kidnapped for the purpose Thomson explains. It is not clear, medically, that anyone could be in the situation described—such that only that person's kidneys could save the violinist. But pregnancy is the opposite of weird. Granted, it can be wittily described so as to sound unusual—e.g., "walking around with another person inside you"—but actually few things, except death, are as usual as pregnancy. We all, every man Jack of us, and every woman Jill, too, begin in our mother's body.[8] If there is a key to human life, surely it is pregnancy. So in Thomson's essay we have something as universal and necessary as pregnancy compared to something so rare it has never happened and perhaps never could happen.

I think that is significant. Some people try to look at this matter very abstractly, and say that right is right, whether it happens one time or billions of times;[9] but in a serious sense, something that happens all the time and is necessary *is different*, by virtue of that fact, from what is rare or impossible. So it will be plausible to regard them differently from an ethical point of view. It is at least arguable, and many theorists believe, that the moralities we have represent some ways of dealing with the realities and regularities of human life; and they may not fit well the irregularities or impossibilities. Our teaching methods, when they work, fit the kinds of students we ordinarily have; they might not be suitable for Martians or Venusians. And vice versa. Similarly for our moral principles. So what is appropriate for kidnapped kidney bearers and their violinist parasites might not be appropriate for mothers and the babes in their wombs.[10]

A second difference between pregnancy and the violinist scenario is that the woman and her fetus are of one flesh and blood,[11] the child is *her* child; she is its mother; but that violinist is a total "stranger" (Thomson's own word)—not your family member, not your cousin, not even your club member or business partner or fellow parishioner or even your countryman—at least as far as Thomson tells us. What you and he have in common is that you are a person and he is a person. Thomson does not believe, and many of her readers do not believe, that a total stranger has a right to your kidneys for nine months or that you do him an injustice if you deny him their use. The relationship between you and that stranger *is* the relationship in the New Testament story between "a certain man" and "a certain Samaritan"—it is merely that you are both human beings. And so your obligations to him have to be understood in terms of universal human rights or in terms of general charity—just as she says. Her concept of how demanding charity is may be a good deal lower than Jesus', but she is right for the violinist case, to see these as the only relevant issues. But your own child is not just "a certain man" to you, a "stranger"; and you are not just "a certain Samaritan" to your own child. I really think that I have obligations to my children, and to my natural brother, as I had obligations to my parents when they were alive (and maybe still), that are not merely human-rights or Good Samaritan obligations. Jesus' story of the Good Samaritan, after all, was in response to a question about the "neighbor"—who is my neighbor, in the commandment to love my neighbor as myself? In that story, the answer implicit is probably that the neighbor is the fellow human being who is in need of my aid.[12] The thrust of the story is expansive, against the human, all-too-human temptation to think that we have obligations only to a few. But I see nothing in that story, or in common sense, to suggest that our relationship to our own children should be construed merely as a relationship to other human beings, "neighbors," strangers.[13] (Consider Thomson's Henry Fonda story. I'll grant that Henry Fonda had little or no obligation to save Judith Thomson. But if *Jane Fonda* had been the one Henry could have saved, with a touch on her fevered brow, surely it would have been monstrous to refuse.)

There is a third problem that I see—a double problem—and it is the problem that many undergraduates see right off. In the violinist scenario, you do nothing to get yourself into the mess; you wake up one morning and simply "find yourself" hooked up to the violinist. Worse, you are in the predicament only because you have been kidnapped—which means that your rights have been violated, you have been done an injustice. So we have injustice and a total lack of voluntariness; perhaps it is because the kidnappers have not obtained your consent that they *are* kidnappers and unjust—and that is *why* I treat this as one problem, though in a sense it is a double problem. But in the normal case of pregnancy, one has voluntarily engaged in the sexual relations which led to conception; and therefore in the normal case one is not pregnant only through some injustice, some violation of one's rights.[14] So it is not at all clear that one's obligations in the violinist case really parallel a woman's obligations in a normal pregnancy—that is, a pregnancy not due to rape.

Now Thomson is aware that the involuntariness (she does not mention the injustice) of the violinist case presents a difficulty for her argument; and her own theory of special rights is that they are all voluntarily granted; so she needs to discuss, and does discuss, the question of whether the mother has *given* her child a right to use her body. Her discussion is quite interesting, but, I think, unsatisfactory.

Several times in the essay she mentions rape, which of course involves involuntariness, though she never dwells on the subject for long. "I suppose we may take it as a datum that in a case of pregnancy due to rape the mother has not given the unborn person a right to the use of her body. . . ." Now if we take her aim in this essay to be *very* modest, perhaps this would be all she needs to say. After all, we might take her to be arguing only the very thin thesis that the personhood of the fetus, or its right to life, would not by itself give it a right to the mother's body; for in the rape pregnancy we have—assuming her ethical theory—a case of a fetus who, even if a person with the right to life, does not have the right to its mother's body—because the mother has not voluntarily granted it such a right. That alone would show that abortion would not *always* violate the rights of the fetus. But that would not apply to many cases; I would guess that the pregnancies due to rape are a one-digit percentage of the total.[15] And, though Thomson does at points suggest that she is defending only the very thin claim that *some* abortion is permissible, the general thrust of the essay is that the mother is largely free to do as she pleases, not that the mother in rape cases is free. And the title of the essay is "A Defense of Abortion," not "A Defense of Abortion in Rape Cases."[16]

However, I think that one of the merits of Thomson's approach is that—if worked out rightly, instead of her way—it offers promise of understanding how rape could be a legitimate excuse or maybe justification for abortion. If we take a purely right-to-life approach, then it seems, as she sees, that we have to have first-class and second-class moral citizens; we have to give persons conceived in rape fewer rights or less serious rights than other persons. That has, as she says, "a rather unpleasant sound." But if we have an approach growing out of Thomson's, then the issue is not the natural rights of the fetus, but its special rights, its granted rights, or the assumed responsibilities of the parents. Thomson's approach makes this promising shift of focus.

Or rather, it starts to make this shift. It sees that a woman who has been raped "has not *given* the unborn person a right to the use of her body" (my emphasis). Next Thomson should consider the usual, nonrape case. Instead, she begins to move her discussion back to fantasy: "Indeed," she asks archly, "in what pregnancy could it be supposed that the mother has given the unborn person such a right? It is not as if there were unborn persons drifting about the world, to whom a woman who wants a child says 'I invite you in.' " So no woman is voluntarily pregnant, no woman has given the unborn person rights to her body, *in that bad-metaphysical sense*. But what about the ordinary sense of voluntariness and acquisition of responsibility? A woman voluntarily engages in sexual intercourse, knowing full well what the consequences may be. Might we say sensibly that in the ordinary case she *has* given the fetus special rights to her body, that she has voluntarily given herself some responsibility for the fetus, and so that she does then do it an injustice if she aborts it?"[17]

Now this is a thesis that I would want to see incorporated into a fully worked-out view of abortion. So I am very much interested in Thomson's arguments against it; and I think that they are all quite weak. I think that they show a strange notion of responsibility, and a strange notion of nature, both of which are related to a strange notion of "self-defense" which operates in this essay (and in many other essays in support of abortion rights). Thomson argues that the voluntariness of normal sexuality does *not* give the fetus any rights. To try to make this view plausible, she presents a series of new (and also memorable) scenarios.

(a) "If the room is stuffy, and I therefore open a window to air it, and a burglar climbs in, it would be absurd to say, 'Ah, now he can stay, she's given him a right to the use of her house—for she is partially responsible for his presence there, having voluntarily'" and so forth.

(b) "It would be still more absurd to say this if I had had bars installed outside my windows, precisely to prevent burglars from getting in, and a burglar got in only because of a defect in the bars." So the woman who has sex carelessly, and the woman who has sex carefully but is unlucky, are, Thomson thinks, in the same situation; neither invited the guest in, and so neither gave the guest any rights to the use of her body. *But in both of these stories there is a burglar*. A burglar of course has no right to be in Thomson's house. Whether she leaves the door unlocked or double locks it, he has no right to be there. No burglar could successfully plead that he had a right to be there in either case. He does her a wrong in entering. But surely it is misguided to think that the fetus does you a wrong in being conceived, that he violates your rights by being conceived. "My rights have been violated!—I've become pregnant!" Can we really imagine a sensible woman saying that? The burglar is guilty; his being there is his guilt; the fetus is innocent; he is innocent in being there. Thomson's rights have been violated, she has been done an injustice, when the burglar enters her house; but her rights have not been violated, she has not been done an injustice, if she gets pregnant after voluntarily having intercourse. In ordinary pregnancy, you and your partners are the only ones responsible; you and he have done voluntarily what got you pregnant. There is no burglar, no rights-violator, on the scene—unless we imagine that *nature* is the violator. "Here we were, minding our own business, having intercourse—when nature got me pregnant." As there you were, minding your business, airing out your room—when the burglar violated your rights to your house. To fill out this story of Thomson's, to make the typical pregnancy analogous to burglary, *we have to introduce some unjust force* analogous to the burglar: nature, perhaps—nature as demonic, out to get you, violating your rights as you innocently go about your business.

(c) Thomson thinks it absurd to say the burglar has rights to your house just because your efforts to keep him out were not 100 percent effective—as of course it is. Then: "It remains equally absurd if we imagine it is not a burglar who climbs in, but an innocent person who blunders or falls in." Now this is a littler harder to deal with. People rarely blunder and fall into other people's houses, but I'm sure it could happen. I saw a colleague innocently trying to start my car one day; my car looks like his, and in his absent-mindedness he assumed that it was his. Something similar might happen with houses, I guess; or you might live in a basement apartment and someone could fall against your window and fall into your apartment. In that case he is innocent—unless he was culpably negligent (as the fetus never is). He has no right to stay, and probably he will apologize for being there and then depart. If you thought he was a dangerous burglar you might defend yourself, perhaps even with deadly force; if you realized from the start that he was innocent, you would not injure him (further), but would ask him to leave, or would help him to leave if he needed help. Is any of this parallel to pregnancy? Not closely. We do not have unconceived fetuses wandering about, stumbling and failing into wombs. When a fetus is conceived "accidentally," that is, without the parents intending a pregnancy, it is the parents who have "blundered" or had bad luck, not the fetus. One would never have good reason to suspect that the fetus was there either by its intention or by its blunder. Nevertheless we might ask whether it was where it had no right to be, just because you had not "invited it in" in the sense of intending a conception. The only sense I can make of this suggestion is that you have some sort of right not to be pregnant; I think this must be what this argument of Thomson's assumes. *Do* you have such a right? Against whom? It is very odd to think that the fetus, either unintentionally or intentionally, has violated a right of anyone in being conceived, which is not an action on its part; so who or what has violated the alleged right not to be pregnant? Nature? Chance? Is it not more plausible to say that when you voluntarily engaged in intercourse—and you knew or should have known what that could entail—then you did, by that act, give the fetus rights to your body, that you did by that act acquire responsibility for whatever fetus might be conceived as a result of that act? This would be like driving and then being responsible for the automobile accident you caused, even if there were (as there always is) an element of luck in the situation. Of course, the accident may have been caused by another driver. But who else could be the responsible party in a normal conception, except one or both of the two who engaged in intercourse? Do we really want to imagine that nature or chance is a third party, acting on them so as to violate their rights?

(d) Then Thomson gives us a science-fiction scenario:

> Again, suppose it were like this: people-seeds drift about in the air like pollen, and if you open your windows, one may drift in and take root in your carpets or upholstery. You don't want children, so you fix up your windows with fine mesh screens, the very best you can buy. As can happen, however, and on very, very rare occasions does happen, one of the screens is defective; and a seed drifts in and takes root. Does the person-plant who develops have a right to the use of your house? Surely not—despite the fact that you voluntarily opened your windows. . . .

Now I am very much mistrustful of the use of science-fiction arguments in ethics. I have already expressed doubts about comparing pregnancy, the most usual and essential thing in our lives, to being hooked up to a violinist, a most unlikely predicament. But now Thomson goes further; she transports us to a whole 'nother world, where the birds and the bees have no place, and babies (not *your* babies, just babies) come from people-seeds that drift about like pollen. Then she relies upon our intuition—*her* intuition—that in such a world the person-plants which sprout in your house have no fight to be there. But what would such a world really be like? If people-seeds are like pollen, would putting up screens help at all? Would not you, the house resident, be giving off seeds yourself, and so trapping your own pollen-seeds in your house? Or rather: since pollen is not the right metaphor, after all: would you not have to keep people who gave off pollen out of your house, because their pollen might fertilize your flowers, and then you would give off seeds (like dandelion seeds, say, not like pollen) which might be trapped in your house? And you would like your fertilized seed to be cared for by someone else rather than yourself? Or what? We really are not told enough to know what such a world would be like, and hence what kinds of obligations for their seed-children we might think parents would have. My own guess is that in such a world such vegetative organisms would not be enough like people to have rights to life or to deserve charity, and that their parents would not be rational enough to understand a concept of obligation. But how would one know, from what Thomson tells us? This sort of problem is found in almost all science-fiction arguments. Our ethical intuitions are shaped by this world and would be clumsy in a real other world; but when we are not really transported to another world, but only asked to imagine a little bit of another one, our intuitions fail us entirely.

(e) Thomson, however, imagines that we are not at sea here but are arguing vigorously pro and con. She thinks someone would argue against her that you *would* be responsible for the people-seeds that got through your screens: "because after all you *could* have lived out your life with bare floors and furniture, or with sealed windows and doors." Thomson replies: "this won't do—for by the same token anyone can avoid a pregnancy due to rape by having a hysterectomy, or anyway by never leaving home without a (reliable!) army." Notice that again she argues by imagining that there is a rights-violator, a would-be rapist this time, in the picture. She knows that rape is a violation of your rights, no matter what precautions you have taken; so she is thinking that having people-seeds growing against your wishes, or having a fetus growing in you when you did not want to be pregnant, is a violation of your rights.[18] But is it? Who or what plays the role of the rapist, in the ordinary pregnancy? Is it, again, nature? You took all ordinary precautions; and yet you are pregnant. This is supposed to be analogous to being raped, in spite of the fact that you took precautions against being raped. But surely it is not analogous, for there is no analogue to the rapist—unless, of course, nature, or chance, is the rapist, the aggressor, the rights-violator. Again, to fill out the analogy, we need something like a demonic nature in the background, taking advantage of our innocence, violating our rights against it while we go about our innocent business, maliciously outwitting our cleverest devices for protecting ourselves.

The same odd strain of a demonic nature may have been present in the original story of the violinist. You were kidnapped, after all; you woke up to find that you had been kidnapped, etc., by the Society of Music Lovers, which wished to save the violinist, and treated you so unjustly out of a misguided concern for music. But what, in ordinary pregnancy, is analogous to the Society of Music Lovers? Is it nature? Is the assumption that nature, in her desire to see that the species is propagated, violates our rights by getting innocent women pregnant? Does Thomson presuppose a sort of bitch goddess, a demonic, that is, a malevolent, nature? Or a well-wishing but misguided and unjust nature? Surely just such a presupposition is what we need to make the story complete, to make the analogy complete.

And this same demonic strain is present—must be present to make sense of—Thomson's analysis of abortion rights as self-defense rights. Whom is one defending oneself against, when one has an abortion? Thomson speaks briefly of self-defense in what I take to be the standard way. She speaks of someone "who threatens you with death unless you" do what he wants you to do; in such a case, we obviously have someone making clear that he will do you harm unless you do for him what you would not ordinarily or voluntarily do, of your own free will. He "threatens" you "with death"; that means that he announces, or otherwise makes clear, that he will inflict this upon you if you do not obey him. But the fetus does not "threaten" you in that sense; it does not announce or make clear its intention to do you harm unless you obey it. The fetus sometimes presents a threat, or sometimes there is a threat posed by the fetus, but this is not the same sense of a threat. And consequently we do not have self-defense, or not in the same (standard) sense. If my colleague Anthony Preus announces he will kill me if I do not stay away from my classes, he is threatening me in the standard sense, the sense that justifies self-defense;[19] but if he gives such fine lectures in medical ethics that no one wants to take my courses, and so poses a threat to my continued well-being, I cannot successfully plead self-defense if I shoot him to end this threat to my interests. (As he said when I mentioned this argument to him, "That's the Ferdinand Marcos sense of 'self-defense.'"

Liquidating your rivals is not what "self-defense" implies, nor is it justified, however much their legitimate activities may threaten your interests. But if the fetus is just going about its business in your body, not violating any of your rights, then you cannot plead "self-defense" in killing it, however much it may pose a threat to your interests.[20] The case involves the wrong sense of a "threat" to you, and therefore the wrong sense of "self-defense."[21]

Thomson first brings in the notion of "self-defense" in elaboration of her tiny-house scenario, where you are trapped—"you find yourself trapped"—

in the tiny-house with the child whose growth will crush you unless you kill it first. But how did you get "trapped" in such a tiny house? Did you walk in and give the child a growing potion, though you knew that this potion would cause such growth as to "threaten" your life? If so, you would not be justified in subsequently killing the child and pleading self-defense; you got yourself into the predicament, you did not just "find" yourself there. Or is it that the child himself, knowing he would grow in that way, locked the door and swallowed the key? Then it is self-defense when you kill him, for he has evil intentions and it is he who trapped you there. But pregnancy is not like *that*. Who is it who traps you, in ordinary pregnancy? Perhaps the idea behind this is that you are going about your business, having intercourse sometimes though you know that it can lead to pregnancy, and then nature, or chance, throws you a curve—makes you pregnant, though other women, having intercourse, as often perhaps, do not get pregnant. Or makes you pregnant, though men, also having intercourse, never get pregnant. Unfair! There is an unjust force at work, and one has to defend oneself against its workings.[22]

But of course all this is mythology and implausible mythology. There is no good reason to regard nature (or chance) as a sort of agent, a she, or a he, a personlike being, acting upon our lives, making some women pregnant; much less is there reason to apply moral categories to such an "agent's" "actions," so that we can claim sometimes that what nature "does" to us is unjust or a violation of our rights. A person can violate your rights; but do we really want to think of nature as a person, and as a person who violates rights we have against it? I think not. The two assumptions in the view are most implausible.

Now there is an old belief in our culture that there is a divine Person "behind" nature—or even that nature *is* such a Person—and so that when nature "acts" there really is a personal act, and act of a divine Person. And people have believed that these acts are somehow good, right, proper, holy, worthy of our reverence. Beliefs like this are central to the biblical heritage of the West and to some of the Greek and Roman sources of our culture. Many of us still live in terms of such beliefs, though the consensus today surely is that they go beyond the evidence and are a matter of faith, not of rational justification; and that the articulation of that faith must be analogical or metaphorical or symbolic somehow—surely God or nature is not *just* like a person, and his "acts," or its "acts," are not quite like paradigmatic acts; and that whatever terms of evaluation we give in expressing our reverence for them must likewise be not literally appropriate.[23] Many of us today are trying to live without this kind of mythical understanding of life. Perhaps we should; that is a complex issue. But the pro-choice philosophers like Thomson seem to presuppose a reverse mythology, a mythology of a personal nature which is malevolent and which violates our rights. They seem to presuppose that nature is personlike, and that moral categories apply to it; and that it turns out to be like a rapist or burglar or kidnapper in its dealings with us. If one wants to adopt such a mythology, surely one should say so openly and then argue for it, responding to the many theoretical and practical difficulties it presents. Thomson and writers like her[24] do not. They simply presuppose it without even seeing that they do. *Why?*

Is it just that they want to reach the conclusions they believe in, want to so badly that they miss the mistake in their arguments? Or is it that the implicitly demonic (or paranoid?) view of reality appeals to something important in their psychical reality? Is it that they, like many women, do feel trapped in a tiny place, do feel as if a hostile, larger-than-human force is at work against them, do feel as if suddenly they find themselves the victims of a great injustice? Perhaps they do; that would indeed be my guess. But surely *nature* is not such a force; if there is a larger-than-individual force at work here, surely it consists of the social forces and structures which continue to oppress women. But talking in ways which presuppose a mythology about an oppressive nature helps but little, for it diverts attention from the real oppression.

I conclude with one last point about the difference between being pregnant and being hooked up to Thomson's violinist: there is no analogue *of the father of the child* in the violinist scenario. (The Society of Music Lovers loves music, not you; it kidnaps you, it does not make love to you.) Thomson misses that. Indeed, a striking aspect of her essay is that fathers are virtually absent from her analysis. I think that she knows where babies really come from, but she never mentions the father of the fetus, and so she never asks what kinds of obligations for it *he* might have. The only reference to a male parent in her whole essay is in a brief story of a couple who "do not obtain an abortion" but "take [their baby] home with them" (from the hospital, I assume)—and so "assume" responsibility for the child and thereby "give" it rights in relation to them. Implicitly, in her thought, men are liberated already from all responsibility for their children, unless they decide to assume it; her view is not very different from that of the handsome young man on the PBS study of illegitimacy: when asked whether it bothered him that his girlfriend might get pregnant, he replied, "That's on her, man." Implicitly this is Thomson's view, too. Fathers have no duties. So naturally she wonders whether mothers have any. One might advance here an equity argument: if fathers have no responsibilities, neither do mothers. And I think that part of women's rage about abortion restrictions can be traced to their awareness of how greatly, in our society, men *have been* liberated from responsibility; the shotgun wedding is no more, and mothers and welfare agencies have thought that it was pointless to ask unwed fathers to pay child support. Given that climate, of course women want to be "free," too. But none of this is discussed in Thomson's essay; she just assumes that the whole burden is on the mother and then asks how great the burden should be. But there is an outrage behind the assumption, and she seems unaware of it. Thomson is more right than she knows—there *is* an injustice in the background of much pregnancy. But the injustice is not that women are pregnant—nature does not kidnap, rape, or burglarize women or make them pregnant. Nor does nature require that men abandon their children. We, contemporary men and women, have let ourselves drift into this predicament. And it is unjust: though normal sex requires the willing participation of two parties, women are being left with most of the responsibility for the children thus conceived. If we are looking for real injustices behind the plight of pregnant women, nonmythical analogues to the Society of Music Lovers, here is one place which must be examined.[25]

NOTES

1. Originally published in *Philosophy and Public Affairs* 1 (1971).

2. So says her editor, William Parent, in Judith Jarvis Thomson, *Rights, Restitution, and Risk* (Cambridge, Mass.: Harvard University Press, 1986), p. vii.

3. This seems to me by far the most plausible interpretation of her view; but here I simply assume it, I do not argue for it.

4. Thomson speaks of killing, though some of those who have responded to her essay think that the violinist example and/or abortion involve only letting die. I should note here an important *other* difference in the Henry Fonda argument; you did not—at least as far as Thomson tells us—acquire the strange illness which Fonda could cure through any action of your own, unlike the normal pregnancy case, or through any unwelcome and unjust action of others, unlike the violinist case. So the Fonda example evades one of my more important lines of argument below. But I am not arguing that everything Thomson writes is informed by the demonic conception of nature; I am only claiming that a great deal of it is.

5. Contrary to what she says, the alternative is not that a person's body is on loan to that person. Literally, my body is not property at all, and so is neither owned nor on loan. After I die it may become the property of a medical institute, if I or my executors take the appropriate actions; in that case, the institute could assert property rights over against burglars who might try to steal it. (I knew a student who stole a human head from a medical school.) But right now my body is not anyone's property, I think. Nor do I think a coherent theology could be worked out in which my body would turn out to be *literally* God's property or on loan from him to me. But these are large claims, and my main interests and Thomson's are elsewhere.

6. I am indebted here to Philip Abbott, "Philosophers and the Abortion Question," *Political Theory* 6 (1978): 313–35. Abbott's sense of many of the issues is similar to mine. He speaks of "greedy individuals." He worries about argument from "bizarre situations."

7. The context should make clear what I mean. I do not intend to deny any obvious facts about pregnancy.

8. Do I need to apologize for not recognizing in vitro fertilization as presenting exceptions?

9. Thomson's standard mode of argument, throughout her career, has relied upon the "bizarre" or "fantasy" (Abbott's terms—see above, n. 6), upon the "fanciful" (Paul Ramsey's term in "Abortion: A Review Article," *The Thomist* 37 [1973]: 314–22).

10. The weirdness in the violinist argument is also found in Thomson's Henry Fonda argument. She speculates on her right to the touch of his cool hand on her fevered brow, in case she is sick in such a peculiar way that his touch is the only thing that can save her. She imagines that a similar relationship holds between a fetus and the woman who can save it. But is it really sensible to think that pregnancy, the secret of all our lives, is analogous in moral ways to a fairy-tale illness and a fairy-tale cure, complete with a knight in a shining jetliner? One can at least wonder—assuming that a reasonable morality is called for in some sense by the things of this world, not by the stuff of fantasy.

11. Again I overlook a bit of modern technology, which allows a woman to carry a fetus from another's ovum. My argumentative style is the polar opposite of Thomson's.

12. There are other elements in Jesus' story which are probably not relevant here. The questioner asked who was *x*'s (his own) neighbor, but Jesus asked who was neighbor to *y* (the man in need); and the story pointedly has a Samaritan, not a Jew, as the one who fulfills the law in this case.

13. Though I would not emphasize the ad hominem argument, at one point Thomson herself speaks in an idiom which shows that, even at MIT, down deep she knows that the relationships are not the same. She says that her argument concludes that a woman ordinarily has the right to defend herself against the threat that the fetus poses, but not a right to kill the fetus after an abortion, if by chance it survives the procedure. She says she wants to make this clear even though she is sympathetic with a woman who "may be utterly devastated by the thought of a child, *a bit of herself*, put out for adoption and never seen or heard of again"(my italics). She says that this "is surely a powerful source of despair" for some women. But why should that be, if the fetus is just a stranger, another human being? (There are a lot of human beings one never sees or hears from.) Those women sense, and Thomson does too with part of her mind, that analysis of family relationships in terms of relations among strangers is implausible. (Of course, "a bit of herself" is exaggeration. Thomson lurches from underplaying the relationship to sentimentally over-playing it. There is a lesson here, too.)

14. Of course, one can say that there is widespread background injustice against women and that this injustice somehow colors their sexual relations, and so that in some attenuated sense they become pregnant, even in the ordinary case, only through some injustice; and, similarly, only through some coercion. I do not deny that there is some sense in this kind of talk, but I do not think it will carry us very far on this issue, unless it takes us to a denial of responsibility in all areas of women's lives. And anyway, Thomson means that being pregnant is analogous to being hooked up to the violinist. The injustice there, and the lack of voluntariness, are not of any of these attenuated varieties, but are of the ordinary, garden-variety sort: you were kidnapped. Only after rape do we have pregnancy involving injustice and involuntariness closely analogous to the violinist scenario.

15. Where I teach, in a recent year the school infirmary counseled thirty-three students with unwanted pregnancies; only one of those cases involved rape.

16. Much could be written about the conflicting signals Thomson gives concerning her intentions. But that would mean another essay. I think it best in this one to simply state what I think the dominant lines of her thought are.

17. I do not say that sexual intercourse should be regarded as committing the participants to die for any offspring produced. The view I suggest here holds that we have very serious obligations to our children, not that we owe them our lives, or anything else considerably above what the normal care for children requires in our society. If we are going to protect the unborn, we should protect them as we protect our other children; not in any exaggerated manner.

18. If she is *not* assuming this, then the argument collapses immediately.

19. Of course, it would not normally justify *killing* him.

20. An abortion might be justified anyway in some cases, if the position in n. 17 above is correct; but the issue is not self-defense rights.

21. *Many* defenders of abortion speak of "self-defense" in Thomson's way; see for example the essay by Jane English, "Abortion and the Concept of a Person," *Canadian Journal of Philosophy* 5 (1975). In English's essay, you defend yourself by killing the innocent; but they are directed by a mad scientist who hypnotizes them and makes them attack you. Like Thomson, English presupposes a demonic nature. But some opponents of abortion also speak of self-defense rights; see John T. Noonan, "An Almost Absolute Value in History," in *The Morality of Abortion*, ed. John T. Noonan (Cambridge, Mass.: Harvard University Press, 1970), pp. 51–59.

22. By killing others, the innocent. (See English's essay mentioned above in n. 21. Many of Thomson's later essays look for weird situations in which this might be legitimate.)

23. Unless some of these terms ("holy"?) are used paradigm atically in this way. See Rudolph Otto's reflections.

24. English's essay—see n. 21 above—comes to mind.

25. Earlier drafts of this paper were read at the Creighton Club and to the Philosophy Departments of the State University of New York at Binghamton and the University of South Carolina; comments on all three occasions have been helpful. Robert Hallborg's advice was especially useful.

23

On the Moral and Legal Status of Abortion

Mary Anne Warren

We will be concerned with both the moral status of abortion, which for our purposes we may define as the act which a woman performs in voluntarily terminating, or allowing another person to terminate, her pregnancy, and the legal status which is appropriate for this act. I will argue that, while it is not possible to produce a satisfactory defense of a woman's right to obtain an abortion without showing that a fetus is not a human being, in the morally relevant sense of that term, we ought not to conclude that the difficulties involved in determining whether or not a fetus is human make it impossible to produce any satisfactory solution to the problem of the moral status of abortion. For it is possible to show that, on the basis of intuitions which we may expect even the opponents of abortion to share, a fetus is not a person, and hence not the sort of entity to which it is proper to ascribe full moral rights.

* * *

The question which we must answer in order to produce a satisfactory solution to the problem of the moral status of abortion is this: How are we to define the moral community, the set of beings with full and equal moral rights, such that we can decide whether a human fetus is a member of this community or not? What sort of entity, exactly, has the inalienable rights to life, liberty, and the pursuit of happiness? Jefferson attributed these rights to all *men*, and it may or may not be fair to suggest that he intended to attribute them *only* to men. Perhaps he ought to have attributed them to all human beings. If so, then we arrive, first at [John] Noonan's problem of defining what makes a being human, and, second, at the equally vital ques-

From the *Monist* 57 (January 1973): 43–61. Reprinted by permission of the publisher.

tion which Noonan does not consider, namely: What reason is there for identifying the moral community with the set of all human beings, in whatever way we have chosen to define that term?

1. On the Definition of "Human"

One reason why this vital second question is so frequently overlooked in the debate over the moral status of abortion is that the term "human" has two distinct, but not often distinguished, senses. This fact results in a slide of meaning, which serves to conceal the fallaciousness of the traditional argument that since (1) it is wrong to kill innocent human beings, and (2) fetuses are innocent human beings, then (3) it is wrong to kill fetuses. For if "human" is used in the same sense in both (1) and (2) then, whichever of the two senses is meant, one of these premises is question-begging. And if it is used in two different senses then of course the conclusion doesn't follow.

Thus, (1) is a self-evident moral truth,[1] and avoids begging the question about abortion, only if "human being" is used to mean something like "a fun-fledged member of the moral community." (It may or may not also be meant to refer exclusively to members of the species *Homo sapiens*.) We may call this the *moral* sense of "human." It is not to be confused with what we will call the *genetic* sense, i.e., the sense in which any member of the species is a human being, and no member of any other species could be. If (1) is acceptable only if the moral sense is intended, (2) is non-question-begging only if what is intended is the genetic sense.

In "Deciding Who is Human," Noonan argues for the classification of fetuses with human beings by pointing to the presence of the full genetic code, and the potential capacity for rational thought (p. 135). It is clear that what he needs to show, for his version of the traditional argument to be valid, is that fetuses are human in the moral sense, the sense in which it is analytically true that all human beings have full moral rights. But, in the absence of any argument showing that whatever is genetically human is also morally human, and he gives none, nothing more than genetic humanity can be demonstrated by the presence of the human genetic code. And, as we will see, the *potential* capacity for rational thought can at most show that an entity has the potential for *becoming* human in the moral sense.

2. Defining the Moral Community

Can it be established that genetic humanity is sufficient for moral humanity? I think that there are very good reasons for not defining the moral community in this way. I would like to suggest an alter-native way of defining the moral community, which I will argue for only to the extent of explaining why it is, or should be, self-evident. The suggestion is simply that the moral community consists of all and only *people*, rather than all and only human beings;[2] and probably the best way of demonstrating its self-evidence is by considering the concept of personhood, to see what sorts of entity are and are not persons, and what the decision that a being is or is not a person implies about its moral rights.

What characteristics entitle an entity to be considered a person? This is obviously not the place to attempt a complete analysis of the concept of personhood, but we do not need such a fully adequate analysis just to determine whether and why a fetus is or isn't a person. All we need is a rough and approximate list of the most basic criteria of personhood, and some idea of which, or how many, of these an entity must satisfy in order to properly be considered a person.

In searching for such criteria, it is useful to look beyond the set of people with whom we are acquainted, and ask how we would decide whether a totally alien being was a person or not. (For we have no right to assume that genetic humanity is necessary for personhood.) Imagine a space traveler who lands on an unknown planet and encounters a race of beings utterly unlike any he has ever seen or heard of. If he wants to be sure of behaving morally toward these beings, he has to somehow decide whether they are people, and hence have full moral rights, or whether they are the sort of thing which he need not feel guilty about treating as, for example, a source of food.

How should he go about making this decision? If he has some anthropological background, he might look for such things as religion, art, and the manufacturing of tools, weapons, or shelters, since these factors have been used to distinguish our human from our prehuman ancestors, in what seems to be closer to the moral than the genetic sense of "human." And no doubt he would be right to consider the presence of such factors as good evidence that the alien beings were people, and morally human. It would, however, be overly anthropocentric of him to take the absence of these things as adequate evidence that they were not, since we can imagine people who have progressed beyond, or evolved without ever developing, these cultural characteristics.

I suggest that the traits which are most central to the concept of personhood, or humanity in the moral sense, are, very roughly, the following:

(1) consciousness (of objects and events external and/or internal to the being), and in particular the capacity to feel pain;
(2) reasoning (the *developed* capacity to solve new and relatively complex problems);
(3) self-motivated activity (activity which is relatively independent of either genetic or direct external control);
(4) the capacity to communicate, by whatever means, messages of an

indefinite variety of types, that is, not just with an indefinite number of possible contents, but on indefinitely many possible topics;

(5) the presence of self-concepts, and self-awareness, either individual or racial, or both.

Admittedly, there are apt to be a great many problems involved in formulating precise definitions of these criteria, let alone in developing universally valid behavioral criteria for deciding when they apply. But I will assume that both we and our explorer know approximately what (1)-(5) mean, and that he is also able to determine whether or not they apply. How, then, should he use his findings to decide whether or not the alien beings are people? We needn't suppose that an entity must have *all* of these attributes to be properly considered a person; (1) and (2) alone may well be sufficient for personhood, and quite probably (1)-(3) are sufficient. Neither do we need to insist that any one of these criteria is *necessary* for personhood, although once again (1) and (2) look like fairly good candidates for necessary conditions, as does (3), if "activity" is construed so as to include the activity of reasoning.

All we need to claim, to demonstrate that a fetus is not a person is that any being which satisfies *none* of (1)-(5) is certainly not a person. I consider this claim to be so obvious that I think anyone who denied it, and claimed that a being which satisfied none of (1)-(5) was a person all the same, would thereby demonstrate that he had no notion at all of what a person is—perhaps because he had confused the concept of a person with that of genetic humanity. If the opponents of abortion were to deny the appropriateness of these five criteria, I do not know what further arguments would convince them. We would probably have to admit that our conceptual schemes were indeed irreconcilably different, and that our dispute could not be settled objectively.

I do not expect this to happen, however, since I think that the concept of a person is one which is very nearly universal (to people), and that it is common to both pro-abortionists and antiabortionists, even though neither group has fully realized the relevance of this concept to the resolution of their dispute. Furthermore, I think that on reflection even the antiabortionists ought to agree not only that (1)-(5) are central to the concept of personhood, but also that it is a part of this concept that all and only people have full moral rights. The concept of a person is in part a moral concept; once we have admitted that *x* is a person we have recognized, even if we have not agreed to respect, *x*'s right to be treated as a member of the moral community. It is true that the claim that *x* is a *human being* is more commonly voiced as part of an appeal to treat *x* decently than is the claim that *x* is a person, but this is either because "human being" is here used in the sense which implies personhood, or because the genetic and moral senses of "human" have been confused.

Now if (1)-(5) are indeed the primary criteria of personhood, then it is clear that genetic humanity is neither necessary nor sufficient for establishing that an entity is a person. Some human beings are not people, and there may well be people who are not human beings. A man or woman whose consciousness has been permanently obliterated but who remains alive is a human being which is no longer a person; defective human beings with no appreciable mental capacity, are not and presumably never will be people; and a fetus is a human being which is not yet a person, and which therefore cannot coherently be said to have full moral rights. Citizens of the next century should be prepared to recognize highly advanced, self-aware robots or computers, should be such developed, and intelligent inhabitants of other worlds, should such be found, as people in the fullest sense, and to respect their moral rights. But to ascribe full moral rights to an entity which is not a person is as absurd as to ascribe moral obligations and responsibilities to such an entity.

3. Fetal Development and the Right to Life

Two problems arise in the application of these suggestions for the definition of the moral community to the determination of the precise moral status of a human fetus. Given that the paradigm example of a person is a normal adult human being, then (1) How like this paradigm, in particular how far advanced since conception, does a human being need to be before it begins to have a right to life by virtue, not of being fully a person as of yet, but of being *like* a person? and (2) To what extent, if any, does the fact that a fetus has the *potential* for becoming a person endow it with some of the same rights? Each of these questions requires some comment.

In answering the first question, we need not attempt a detailed consideration of the moral rights of organisms which are not developed enough, aware enough, intelligent enough, etc., to be considered people, but which resemble people in some respects. It does seem reasonable to suggest that the more like a person, in the relevant respects, a being is, the stronger is the case for regarding it as having a right to life, and indeed the stronger its right to life is. Thus we ought to take seriously the suggestion that, insofar as "the human individual develops biologically in a continuous fashion . . . the rights of a human person might develop in the same way."[3] But we must keep in mind that the attributes which are relevant in determining whether or not an entity is enough like a person to be regarded as having some of the same moral rights are no different from those which are relevant to determining whether or not it is fully a person—i.e., are no different from (1)-(5)—and that being genetically human, or having recognizably human facial and other physical features, or detectable brain activity, or the capacity to survive outside the uterus, are simply not among these relevant attributes.

Thus it is clear that though a seven- or eight-month fetus has features which make it apt to arouse in us almost the same powerful protective instinct as is commonly aroused by a small infant, nevertheless it is not significantly more personlike than is a very small embryo. It is *somewhat* more personlike; it can apparently feel and respond to pain, and it may even have a rudimentary form of consciousness, insofar as its brain is quite active. Nevertheless, it seems safe to say that it is not fully conscious, in the way that an infant of a few months is, and that it cannot reason, or communicate messages of indefinitely many sorts, does not engage in self-motivated activity, and has no self-awareness. Thus, in the *relevant* respects, a fetus, even a fully developed one, is considerably less personlike than is the average mature mammal, indeed the average fish. And I think that a rational person must conclude that if the right to life of a fetus is to be based upon its resemblance to a person, then it cannot be said to have any more right to life than, let us say, a newborn guppy (which also seems to be capable of feeling pain), and that a right of that magnitude could never override a woman's right to obtain an abortion, at any stage of her pregnancy.

There may, of course, be other arguments in favor of placing legal limits upon the stage of pregnancy in which an abortion may be performed. Given the relative safety of the new techniques of artifically inducing labor during the third trimester, the danger to the woman's life or health is no longer such an argument. Neither is the fact that people tend to respond to the thought of abortion in the later stages of pregnancy with emotional repulsion, since mere emotional responses cannot take the place of moral reasoning in determining what ought to be permitted. Nor, finally, is the frequently heard argument that legalizing abortion, especially late in the pregnancy, may erode the level of respect for human life, leading, perhaps, to an increase in unjustified euthanasia and other crimes. For this threat, if it is a threat, can be better met by educating people to the kinds of moral distinctions which we are making here than by limiting access to abortion (which limitation may, in its disregard for the rights of women, be just as damaging to the level of respect for human rights).

Thus, since the fact that even a fully developed fetus is not personlike enough to have any significant right to life on the basis of its personlikeness shows that no legal restrictions upon the stage of pregnancy in which an abortion may be performed can be justified on the grounds that we should protect the rights of the older fetus; and since there is no other apparent justification for such restrictions, we may conclude that they are entirely unjustified. Whether or not it would be *indecent* (whatever that means) for a woman in her seventh month to obtain an abortion just to avoid having to postpone a trip to Europe, it would not, in itself, be *immoral*, and therefore it ought to be permitted.

4. Potential Personhood and the Right to Life

We have seen that a fetus does not resemble a person in any way which can support the claim that it has even some of the same rights. But what about its *potential*, the fact that if nurtured and allowed to develop naturally it will very probably become a person? Doesn't that alone give it at least some right to life? It is hard to deny that the fact that an entity is a potential person is a strong prima facie reason for not destroying it; but we need not conclude from this that a potential person has a right to life by virtue of that potential. It may be that our feeling that it is better, other things being equal, not to destroy a potential person is better explained by the fact that potential people are still (felt to be) an invaluable resource, not to be lightly squandered. Surely, if every speck of dust were a potential person, we would be much less apt to conclude that every potential person has a right to become actual.

Still, we do not need to insist that a potential person has no right to life whatever. There may well be something immoral, and not just imprudent, about wantonly destroying potential people, when doing so isn't necessary to protect anyone's rights. But even if a potential person does have some prima facie right to life, such a right could not possibly outweigh the right of a woman to obtain an abortion, since the rights of any actual person invariably outweigh those of any potential person, whenever the two conflict. Since this may not be immediately obvious in the case of a human fetus, let us look at another case.

Suppose that our space explorer falls into the hands of an alien culture, whose scientists decide to create a few hundred thousand or more human beings, by breaking his body into its component cells, and using these to create fully developed human beings, with, of course, his genetic code. We may imagine that each of these newly created men will have all of the original man's abilities, skills, knowledge, and so on, and also have an individual self-concept, in short that each of them will be a bona fide (though hardly unique) person. Imagine that the whole project will take only seconds, and that its chances of success are extremely high, and that our explorer knows all of this, and also knows that these people will be treated fairly. I maintain that in such a situation he would have every right to escape if he could, and thus to deprive all of these potential people of their potential lives; for his right to life outweighs all of theirs together, in spite of the fact that they are all genetically human, all innocent, and all have a very high probability of becoming people very soon, if only he refrains from acting.

Indeed, I think he would have a right to escape even if it were not his life which the alien scientists planned to take, but only a year of his freedom, or, indeed, only a day. Nor would he be obligated to stay if he had gotten captured (thus bringing all these people-potentials into existence) because of his own carelessness, or even if he had done so deliberately, knowing the consequences. Regardless of how he got captured, he is not morally obligated to remain in captivity for *any* period of time for the sake of permitting any number of potential people to come into actuality, so great is the margin by which one actual person's right to liberty outweighs whatever right to life even a hundred thousand potential people have. And it seems reasonable to conclude that the rights of a woman will outweigh by a similar margin whatever right to life a fetus may have by virtue of its potential personhood.

Thus, neither a fetus's resemblance to a person, nor its potential for becoming a person provides any basis whatever for the claim that it has any significant right to life. Consequently, a woman's right to protect her health, happiness, freedom, and even her life, by terminating an unwanted pregnancy, will always override whatever right to life it may be appropriate to ascribe to a fetus, even a fully developed one. And thus, in the absence of any overwhelming social need for every possible child, the laws which restrict the right to obtain an abortion, or limit the period of pregnancy during which an abortion may be performed, are a wholly unjustified violation of a woman's most basic moral and constitutional rights.

NOTES

1. Of course, the principle that it is (always) wrong to kill innocent human beings is in need of many other modifications, e.g., that it may be permissible to do so to save a greater number of other innocent human beings, but we may safely ignore these complications here.

2. From here on, we will use "human" to mean genetically human, since the moral sense seems closely connected to, and perhaps derived from, the assumption that genetic humanity is sufficient for membership in the moral community.

3. Thomas L. Hayes, "A Biological View," *Commonweal* 85 (March 17, 1967): 677–78; quoted by Daniel Callahan in *Abortion, Law, Choice, and Morality* (London: Macmillan & Co., 1970).

24

An Appeal for Consistency

Harry J. Gensler

If you asked ten years ago for my view on the morality of abortion, I would have said "I don't have a view—the issue confuses me." But now I think that abortion is wrong and that certain Kantian consistency requirements more or less force us into thinking this. Part III will present my reasoning. But first, in Parts I and II, I will show why various traditional and recent arguments on abortion do not work.

I. A Traditional Antiabortion Argument

One common traditional argument goes this way:

> The killing of innocent human life is wrong.
>
> The fetus is innocent human life.
>
> Therefore, the killing of the fetus is wrong.

This seemingly simple argument raises some difficult questions:

> Is it "always wrong" or "normally wrong"? And if the latter, how do we decide the difficult cases?
>
> Is the fetus "innocent" if it is attacking the life or health or social well-being of the woman?

From "A Kantian Argument against Abortion," *Philosophical Studies* 49 (1986): 83-98. Reprinted by permission of Kluwer Academic Publishers.

Is there a clear and morally weighty distinction between "killing" and "letting die"—or between "direct killing" and "indirect killing"?

I will not discuss these important questions; a short essay on abortion must leave many questions unanswered. But I will discuss this one: "What does the term 'human life' in the abortion argument mean?" People sometimes presume that the meaning of the term is clear and that the major problem is the factual one of whether the fetus is "human life" (in some clear sense). But I think that the term in this context is fuzzy and could be used in different senses.

Suppose we found a Martian who could discuss philosophy; would he be "human"? We need to make distinctions: the Martian would be "human" in the sense of "animal capable of reasoning" ("rational animal") but not in the sense of "member of the species *Homo sapiens*"—so the Martian is "human" in one sense but not in another. Which of these senses should be used in the abortion argument? The fetus is not yet an "animal capable of reasoning." Is it a "member of the species *Homo sapiens*"? That depends on whether the unborn are to be counted as "members" of a species—ordinary language can use the term either way. In the biology lab we all (regardless of our views on abortion) distinguish between "human" fetuses and "mouse" fetuses—so in this sense (the "genetic sense") the fetus is human. But in counting the number of mice or humans in the city of Chicago we all (regardless of our views on abortion) count only the born—so in this sense ("the population-study sense") the fetus is not a human. So is the fetus a "human"? In two senses of this term that we have distinguished the answer would be NO while in a third sense the answer would be YES; whether the fetus is "human" depends on what is meant by "human."

Human life has been claimed to begin at various points:

(1) at conception.
(2) when individuality is assured (and the zygote cannot split or fuse with another).
(3) when the fetus exhibits brain waves.
(4) when the fetus could live apart.
(5) at birth.
(6) when the being becomes self-conscious and rational.

Here we do not have a factual disagreement over when there emerges, in the same clear sense of the term, a "human"; rather we have six ways to use the term. Answer (1) is correct for the "genetic sense," (5) for the "population-study sense," and (6) for the "rational animal sense"; answers (2) to (4) reflect other (possibly idiosyncratic) senses. And there are likely other senses of "human" besides these six. Which of these are we to use in the first premise ("The killing of innocent *human* life is wrong")? We get different principles depending on which sense of the term "human" we use.

Can we decide which sense to use by appealing to scientific data? No, we cannot. Scientific data can help us judge whether a specific individual is "human" in some specified sense (e.g., sense [3] or sense [4]) but it cannot tell us which sense of "human" to use in our principle.

Can we decide by "intuition"—by following the principle that *seems* most correct? Note that moral intuitions depend greatly on upbringing and social milieu. Most Catholics were brought up to have intuitions in line with sense (1) (the "genetic sense"). Many ancient Romans and Greeks were trained to have sense (6) intuitions (allowing abortion *and* infanticide). And many Americans today are being brought up to have sense (5) intuitions (allowing abortion but not infanticide). Is there any way to resolve this clash—other than simply praising our own intuitions and insulting contrary ones? Can we carry on the argument further? I think we can and that the Kantian appeal to consistency provides a way to resolve the issue rationally.

II. Some Recent Pro-Abortion Arguments

Before getting to the Kantian approach, let us consider three arguments in defense of abortion. A common utilitarian argument goes this way:

> Anything having a balance of good results (considering everyone) is morally permissible.
>
> Abortion often has a balance of good results (considering everyone).
>
> Therefore, abortion often is morally permissible.

Here "good results" is most commonly interpreted in terms of pleasure and pain ("hedonistic act utilitarianism") or the satisfaction of desires ("preference act utilitarianism").

The second premise (on the good results of abortion) is controversial. People defending the premise say that abortion often avoids difficulties such as the financial burden of a child on poor parents or on society, the disruption of schooling or a career, and the disgrace of an unwed mother; that where these problems or probable birth defects exist, the child-to-be would have less chance for happiness; and that abortion provides a "second chance" to prevent a birth when contraceptives fail or people want to rethink an earlier choice. But opponents say that we can have equally good results without abortion, by using better social structures (more social support toward unwed mothers and poor families, better adoption practices, wiser use of contraceptives, etc.) and scientific advances (better contraceptives, artificial wombs, etc.); and they say that abortion can harm the woman psychologically and promote callous attitudes toward human life.

I think the weaker link is the first premise—the argument's utilitarian basis. This premise would often justify killing not just fetuses, but also infants and the sick or handicapped or elderly; many utilitarian reasons for not wanting a child around the house would also apply to not wanting grandmother around. And the premise would justify these killings, not just when they have great utilitarian benefits, but even when the utilitarian benefits are slight. Utilitarian says that the killing of an innocent human being is justified whenever it brings even a slight increase in the sum-total of pleasure (or desire satisfaction). This is truly bizarre.

Imagine a town where lynchings give the people pleasure (or satisfy their desires) and the utilitarian sheriff lynches an innocent person each week because the pleasure (or desire) of the masses slightly outweighs the misery (or frustration of desire) of the person to be lynched—and so the action has a slight gain in "good results." If the utilitarian principle is correct then the sheriff's lynchings are morally justified! But could anyone really believe that these lynchings would be morally justified?

I could pile up further examples of strange and unbelievable implications of utilitarianism. Utilitarians try to weasel out of these examples but I think not with ultimate success. So my verdict on utilitarianism is that it would justify so many bizarre actions (including so many killings) that we would not accept this principle if we were consistent and realized its logical consequences.

My second pro-abortion argument is from Michael Tooley.[1] Tooley recognizes that humans have a right to life—presumably a greater right than utilitarians would recognize; but only humans in sense (6) ("rational animals"—or, as he puts it, "persons") have such a right. The human fetus, while it might develop into a being with a right to life, presently has no more right to life than a mouse fetus. A fetus lacks a right to life because "rights" connect with "desires" conceptually—so that you can have rights only if you have desires. Tooley's argument is roughly this:

> A being has a right to *x* only if it desires *x*.
>
> No fetus desires its continued existence [because then the fetus would have to have a concept of itself as a continuing subject of experiences—a concept it cannot as yet have].
>
> Therefore, no fetus has a right to its continued existence.

Tooley claims that the first premise is not correct as it stands; we must add three qualifications to make the premise harmonize with our intuitions regarding rights:

> A being has a right to *x* only if either it desires *x* or else it would desire *x* were it not (a) emotionally unbalanced or (b) temporarily unconscious or (c) conditioned otherwise.

He thinks the revised first premise will serve equally well (assuming obvious changes in the second premise); so he concludes that fetuses (and infants) do not have a right to life.

But we need further exceptions to make the first premise correspond to our intuitions. If we think that the dead have rights (e.g., to have their wills followed), then we need to add "or (d) the being did desire *x* when it was alive." If we think that a child who lacks the concept "hepatitis" (and thus cannot desire not to be given this disease) does not thereby lose his right not to be given hepatitis, then we need to add "or (e) the being would desire *x* if it had the necessary concepts." If we think (as I do) that trees and canyons have the right not to be destroyed without good reason, then we would have to add some exception for this. And if we think that the fetus (or infant) has a right to life, then we need to add something like "or (f) if the being were to grow up to be an adult member of the rational species to which it belongs then it would desire to have had *x*" (presumably if the fetus were to grow up to be an adult member of *Homo sapiens* then it would desire to have had continued life—and this, with (f), allows the fetus to have a right to life).[2] The trouble with Tooley's argument is that disagreements over the main issue of the right to life of the fetus translate into disagreements over how to qualify the first premise to make it mesh with "our" intuitions; so the argument cannot decide the main issue.

The third argument in defense of abortion comes from Judith Jarvis Thomson and presumes that the fetus is a "person" (in some undefined sense):[3]

> One who has voluntarily assumed no special obligation toward another person has no obligation to do anything requiring great personal cost to preserve the life of the other.
>
> Often a pregnant woman has voluntarily assumed no special obligation toward the unborn child (a person), and to preserve its life by continuing to bear the unborn child would require great personal cost.
>
> Therefore, often a pregnant woman has no obligation to continue to bear the unborn child.

The first premise here seems acceptable. Normally you have no obligation to risk your life to save a drowning stranger; if you risk your life then you do more than duty requires. But it is different if you are a lifeguard who has assumed a special obligation—then you have to try to save the person, even at the risk of your own life. Thomson thinks that a woman getting pregnant intending to have a child is voluntarily accepting a special obligation toward the child. However if the pregnancy is accidental (the result of a contraceptive failure or rape) then the woman has assumed no such special obligation and, if continuing to bear the child requires great personal cost, the woman has no obligation to continue to bear it; the woman would do no wrong if she has an abortion—but if she continues to bear the child in spite of personal cost then she is doing something heroic, something beyond what duty requires.

Thomson gives an analogy. Suppose you wake up and find yourself in bed with an unconscious violinist attached to your circulatory system (his friends attached him to you because this was needed to save his life); if you disconnect him before nine months, he will die—otherwise he will live. Even though it might be praiseworthy to make the sacrifice and leave him plugged in for nine months, still you have no obligation to do so; it would be morally right for you to disconnect him, even though he will die. So also if you are pregnant under the conditions mentioned above, then, even though it might be praiseworthy to make the sacrifice and bear the child for nine months, still you have no obligation to do so; it would be morally right for you to have the child removed, even though it will die.

The first premise ofThomson's argument is slightly misstated. A motorist has a special obligation toward a person he has injured in an accident, even though he has not voluntarily assumed this obligation in any clear way (the accident happened against his will and despite all reasonable precautions—just like an accidental pregnancy). Similarly a child has a special obligation toward his parents—even though he has not voluntarily assumed this obligation. Not all special obligations toward others are "voluntarily assumed"—so these two words should he crossed out in the premises.

My main objection to the argument can be put as a dilemma. Utilitarianism is either true or false. If it is *true*, then the first premise is false (because then the person has an obligation to do whatever has the best consequences—despite personal cost); and so the pro-abortion utilitarian Peter Singer rejects this premise, since it conflicts with utilitarianism. But if utilitarianism is *false*, then presumably Sir David Ross was right in claiming it to be morally significant that others:

> . . . stand to me in relation of promisee to promiser, of creditor to debtor, of wife to husband, *of child to parent* [my emphasis], of friend to friend, of fellow countryman to fellow countryman, and the like; and each of these relations is the foundation of a *prima facie* duty, which is more or less incumbent on me according to the circumstances of the case.[4]

If utilitarianism is *false*, then likely a person has greater obligations toward his or her offspring than toward a violinist stranger—and so the second premise, which claims that the pregnant woman has no special responsibility toward her own child, begins to look doubtful (recall that we crossed out the words "voluntarily assumed").

III. A Kantian Argument

My Kantian approach to abortion stresses consistency. In discussing utilitarianism I appealed to simple logical consistency (not accepting a principle without accepting its recognized logical consequences). Here I will use two further consistency requirements (based on the universalizability and prescriptivity principles) and a third consistency requirement derived from these two (a version of the Golden Rule). The following argument displays these three requirements and how the third follows from the first two:

> If you are consistent and think that it would be all right for someone *to do a to a*, then you will think that it would be all right for someone *to do a to you* in similar circumstances.
>
> If you are consistent and think that it would be *all right* for someone to do *a* to you in similar circumstances, then you will *consent* to the idea of someone doing *a* to you in similar circumstances.
>
> Therefore, if you are consistent and think that it would be *all right to do a to x*, then you will *consent* to the idea of someone *doing a to you* in similar circumstances. (GR)

The first premise can be justified by the "universalizability principle," which demands that we make similar ethical judgments about the same sort of situation (regardless of the individuals involved); so if I think it would be all right to rob *Jones* but I don't think it would he all right for someone to rob *me* in an imagined exactly similar situation, then I violate universalizability and am inconsistent. The second premise can be justified by the "prescriptivity principle," which demands that we keep our ethical beliefs in harmony with the rest of our lives (our actions, intentions, desires, and so forth); so if I think an act would be all right but I don't consent to it being done, then I violate prescriptivity and am inconsistent. These and further derived requirements can be formulated and justified in a rigorous way; but I won't do that here. The conclusion GR is a form of the golden rule; if I think it would be all right to rob Jones but yet I don't consent to (or approve of) the idea of someone robbing me in similar circumstances, then I violate GR and am inconsistent.[5]

The following argument combines an instance of GR with an empirical premise about your desires:

> If you are consistent and think that *stealing is normally permissible*, then you will consent to the idea of *people stealing from you* in normal circumstances. (From GR)
>
> You do not consent to the idea of people stealing from you in normal circumstances.
>
> Therefore, if you are consistent then you will not think that stealing is normally permissible.

Most of us do not consent to the idea of people stealing from us in normal circumstances; so we would not be consistent if we held "Stealing is normally permissible" (since then we would violate consistency principle GR). This argument shows that, given that a person has a certain desire (one that most people can be presumed to have), he would not be consistent if he held a given ethical view. The conclusion here concerns the consistency of holding the ethical judgment and not the judgment's truth. A person could escape this conclusion if he did not care if people robbed him; then the second premise would be false. Throughout the rest of this essay I will generally assume that the reader desires not to be robbed or blinded or killed; if you would love people to rob or blind or kill you (or you don't care whether they do this to you)—then most of my further conclusions will not apply to you.

It might seem easy to argue similarly on abortion. How would you like it if someone had aborted you? Should we say that you don't like the idea and so you can't consistently hold that abortion is permissible? Or should we say that as an ignorant fetus you would not have known enough to have been against the abortion—so that this argument won't work?

Let us slow down and try to understand GR more clearly before applying it to abortion. Properly understood, GR has to do with my *present reaction* toward a hypothetical case—not with how I *would react if I were* in the hypothetical case. A few examples may clarify things. Consider this chart:

Issue	*Right Question*	*Wrong Question*
Do I think it permissible to rob x while x is asleep?	Do I now consent to the idea of my being robbed while asleep?	If I were robbed while I was asleep would I then (while asleep) consent to this action?

(In the "Right Question" and "Wrong Question" I presume implicit "in relevantly or exactly similar circumstances" qualifiers). The point of this chart is that, by GR, to be consistent in answering YES to the ISSUE I must also answer *yes* to the *right question*—but I need not answer *yes* to the *wrong question*. Presumably I would answer *no* to the *right questions*; when I consider the hypothetical case of my being robbed while asleep. I find that I now (while awake) do not consent to or approve of this action. But the *wrong question* has to do with what I, if I were robbed while asleep, would consent to or approve of while thus asleep (and thus ignorant of the robbery); GR, correctly understood, has nothing to do with the *wrong question*. Let me give another example:

Issue	*Right Question*	*Wrong Question*
Do I think it permissible to violate *x*'s will after his death?	Do I now consent to the idea of my will being violated after my death?	If my will is violated after my death, would I then (while dead) consent to this action?

Again GR has to do with my *present reaction* toward a hypothetical case in which I may imagine myself as asleep or dead or even a fetus—but not with how I *would* react *while* asleep or dead or a fetus *in* the hypothetical situation.

But is it legitimate to apply the Golden Rule to our treatment of a fetus? Consider a case not involving abortion:

Issue	*Right Question*	*Wrong Question*
Do I think it permissible to blind *x* while *x* is a fetus?	Do I now consent to the idea of my having been blinded while a fetus?	If I were blinded while a fetus, would I then (while a fetus) consent to this action?

Suppose that you had a sadistic mother who, while pregnant with you, contemplated injecting herself with a blindness drug which would have no effect on her but which would cause the fetus (you) to be born blind and remain blind all its (your) life. Your mother could have done this to you. Do you think this would have been all right—and do you consent to the idea of her having done this? The answer is a clear *no*—and an equally clear *no* regardless of the time of pregnancy that we imagine the injection taking place. We could then argue as we did concerning stealing:

> If you are consistent and think that *blinding a fetus is normally permissible*, then you will consent to the idea of *your having been blinded while a fetus* in normal circumstances. (From GR)
>
> You do not consent to the idea of your having been blinded while a fetus in normal circumstances.
>
> Therefore, if you are consistent then you will not think that blinding a fetus is normally permissible.

Again, with most people the second premise will be true—most people can be presumed not to consent to (or approve of) the idea of this act having been done to them.

Is it legitimate to apply the Golden Rule to our treatment of a fetus? Surely it is—the above reasoning makes good sense. If a pregnant woman is about to do something harmful to the fetus (like taking drugs or excessive alcohol or cigarettes), it seems appropriate for her to ask, "How do I now react to the idea of my mother having done this same thing while she was pregnant with me?" Applying the Golden Rule to a fetus raises no special problems.

But someone might object as follows:

> Seemingly your view forces us to accept that the fetus has rights (e.g., not to be blinded by the drug), even though you avoid saying it is human. But your question about "*my* having been blinded *while a fetus*" presupposes that the fetus and my present self are identical—the *same human being*. So aren't you presupposing (despite your earlier discussion on the many senses of "human") that the fetus is "human"?

While my way of phrasing the question may presuppose this, I put my question this way only for the sake of convenience; I could rephrase my question so that it doesn't presuppose this:

Do I now consent to the idea of:

— my having been blinded while a fetus?

— the fetus that developed into my present self having been blinded?

— Helen E. Gensler having taken the blindness drug while pregnant in 1945?

The second and third way to phrase the question do not presuppose that the fetus and my present self are identical or the same human being; if you wish, you may rephrase my comments thusly (I will keep to the first way of speaking for the sake of brevity). I am against the idea of the drug having been given, not because I think that the fetus was in some metaphysical sense the *same human being* as I, but rather because if this drug had been given then I would be blind all my life.

The application of GR to abortion is similar—we need only switch from a blindness drug (which blinds the fetus) to a death drug (which kills the fetus). Your mother could have killed you through such a death drug (or other means of abortion). Do you think this would have been all right—and do you consent to (or approve of) the idea of her having done this? Again the answer is a clear *no*—and an equally clear *no* regardless of the time of pregnancy that we imagine the killing taking place. We can argue as we did concerning blinding:

If you are consistent and think that *abortion is normally permissible*, then you will consent to the idea of *your having been aborted* in normal circumstances. (From GR)

You do not consent to the idea of your having been aborted in normal circumstances.

Therefore, if you are consistent then you will not think that abortion is normally permissible.

Again, with most people the second premise will be true—most people can be presumed not to consent to (or approve of) the idea of this act having been done to them. So insofar as most people take a consistent position they will not think that abortion is normally permissible.

IV. Six Objections

(1) Surely a utilitarian would see your two drug cases as very different—the blindness drug inflicts needless future suffering while the death drug simply eliminates a life. Why wouldn't a utilitarian, moved by the greatest total happiness principle, approve of the death drug having been given to him if this would have led to a greater total happiness? Wouldn't such a person be a consistent upholder of the view that abortion is normally permissible?

My answer is that utilitarianism leads to so many strange moral implications that, even *if* the utilitarian could be consistent on this one case, still he would likely be inconsistent in his overall position. I previously claimed that utilitarianism would justify so many bizarre actions (including so many killings) that we would not accept this principle if we were consistent and realized its logical consequences. But if there are few (if any) consistent utilitarians then there would be few (if any) consistent utilitarian upholders of the view that abortion is normally permissible.

(2) Let us consider a *nonutilitarian* who approves of abortion but not infanticide or the blindness drug. Why couldn't such a person consent to the idea of himself having been aborted under imagined or actual normal circumstances—and hence be consistent?

Such a person could be consistent, but only with bizarre desires about how he himself is to be treated. Let us suppose that someone combined these three judgments (as many are being brought up to do in our society today):

(a) It is wrong to blind an adult or child or infant or fetus.

(b) It is wrong to kill an adult or child or infant.

(c) It is permissible to kill a fetus.

To be consistent the person would have to answer these questions as follows:

Do you consent to the idea of my you *blinding* you now?—NO!	. . . Do you consent to the idea of my *killing* you now?—NO!
Do you consent to the idea of my having *blinded* you yesterday?—NO!	Do you consent to the idea of my having *killed* you yesterday?—NO!
. . . when you were five years old?—NO!	. . . when you were five years old?—NO!
. . . when you were one day old?—NO!	. . . when you were one day old?—NO!
. . . before you were born?—NO!	. . . before you were born?—*YES!!!*

It is strange that the person *disapproves equally* of being *blinded* at the various times—and *disapproves equally* of being *killed* at the first four times—and yet *approves* of being *killed* at the last time. He opposes the blindings because, regardless of their timing, the effect would be the same—he would be blind. He opposes the killings at the first four times because, again, the effect would be the same—he would not be alive; but killing at the fifth time has the same effect—why should he not oppose this killing also? The *yes* here seems rather strange. Of course one who thinks his life not worth living could give a *yes* to the idea of his having been killed while a fetus—but then we would expect *yes* answers to the idea of his being killed at the other times as well (which would make him inconsistent if he held that it is wrong to kill an adult or child or infant). So while a nonutilitarian who combines the three judgments above *could* in principle have such desires and be consistent, still this is unlikely to happen very often—to be consistent the person would have to have very bizarre desires.[6]

(3) Are you saying that the desires that most people have are good while unusual (or "bizarre") desires are bad? How would you establish this?

I am not saying that common desires are good while unusual desires are bad—often the reverse is true; and sometimes when we notice a conflict between our moral beliefs and our desires we come to change our desires and not our moral beliefs. Rather I am appealing to desires that most people have because I am trying to develop a consistency argument to show that most people who adopt the pro-abortion view are inconsistent. In effect I am challenging those who adopt such a view by saying, "Look at what you would have to desire in order to be consistent in your position—go and think about it and see whether you really are consistent!" I claim that most of the times the pro-abortionist will find that he is indeed inconsistent—he is supporting certain moral principles about the treatment of others that he would not wish to have been followed in their actions toward him.

> (4) You question the consistency of one who holds that abortion is permissible but infanticide is wrong. But let us see whether you are consistent. If it would have been wrong for your parents to have aborted you, wouldn't it have been equally wrong for your parents not to have conceived you? The result would have been the same—there would be no YOU!

My answer here is complicated. My first reaction is to disapprove of the idea of my parents not having conceived me—to think it would have been wrong for them to have abstained or used contraceptives; but the universalizing requirement forces me to change my reactions (whereas it doesn't do this in the abortion case). If I hold "It is wrong to have an abortion in this (my) case," then I have to make the same judgment in all similar cases; but I can easily hold (consistently) that it is in general wrong to have an abortion. But if I hold "It is wrong to prevent conception (by, e.g., abstinence or contraceptives) in this (my) case," then I again have to make the same judgment in all similar cases; but I cannot hold (consistently) that it is in general wrong to prevent conception—since this would commit me to desiring a policy which would bring about a greatly overpopulated world of starving people at a very low level of human life. So, in order to be consistent, I change my first reaction and come to judge that it would have been morally permissible for my parents not to have conceived (me) on August 5, 1944—but instead perhaps to have conceived (someone else) on September 5, 1944—and I come, though with hesitation, to consent to the possibility of their having done this. To sum up: the universalizing requirement points to an important difference between *aborting* and *not conceiving*—I can "will as a universal law" a general prohibition against *aborting*, but not one against *nonconceiving*.

> (5) Suppose that reason does force us into thinking that abortion is *normally* wrong. What does "normal" here mean? And aren't the "abnormal" or "unusual" cases the more important and difficult ones to deal with? So isn't your conclusion unimportant?

My claim that abortion is *normally* wrong means that it is wrong in at least the great majority of cases but perhaps not in every conceivable case (e.g., in the imagined case where Dr. Evil will destroy the world if we do not do an abortion). The question of what unusual conditions (if any) would justify abortion is indeed important and difficult. But I think that, in light of the very great number of "convenience abortions" going on today, the issue of the general moral status of abortion is at the present time far more important.

> (6) Suppose that *if I am consistent* I cannot hold that abortion is normally permissible. What if I do not care about being consistent? Can you prove to me that I ought to care? Or can you prove to me that abortion is wrong without appealing to consistency?

You ask too much. Suppose I give you an argument proving that abortion is wrong (or that you ought to care about being consistent). If you do not already care about consistency, why should you not accept the premises of my argument and yet reject the conclusion? This would be inconsistent—but you don't care about this! So you presumably wouldn't care about any argument I might give—in effect you are saying that you have a closed mind. If you don't care about consistency then I am wasting my time when I try to reason with you.

Notes

1. Tooley's original argument was in "Abortion and Infanticide," *Philosophy and Public Affairs* 2 (1972): 37-65. He added refinements to his view in *Philosophy and Public Affairs* 2 (1973): 419-32; in a postscript to a reprint of his article in *The Rights and Wrongs of Abortion*, eds. Marshall Cohen, Thomas Nagel, and Thomas Scanlon (Princeton: Princeton University Press, 1974), pp. 80-84; and in "In Defense of Abortion and Infanticide," in *The Problem of Abortion*, 2d. ed., ed. Joel Feinberg (Belmont, Calif.: Wadsworth, 1984), pp. 120-34. (The weak link in the latest version of the argument seems to be this premise: "An individual existing at one time cannot have desires at other times unless there is at least one time at which it possesses the concept of a continuing self or mental substance," this entails the incredible "Your pet kitten cannot yesterday have had a desire to eat unless at some time it possesses the concept of a continuing self or mental substance.") Peter Singer's defense of abortion and infanticide rests partially on Tooley's earlier argument but mainly on his preference utilitarianism; see chaps. 4 and 6 of his *Practical Ethics* (Cambridge: Cambridge University Press, 1979).

2. Clause (f) was phrased to skirt the issue of Tooley's "superkittens" who become rational if given a certain drug; my intuitions on the superkitten (and Frankenstein) cases are not very clear. Clause (f) may require further refinement.

3. "A Defense of Abortion," in *Philosophy and Public Affairs* 1 (1971): 47-66. [See pp. 197-211 of the present volume.]

4. Sir David Ross, *The Right and the Good* (Oxford: Clarendon Press, 1930), p. 19.

5. In arguing the abortion issue, I use some ideas from the theory of R. M. Hare, as developed in his *Freedom and Reason* (Oxford: Oxford University Press, 1963). Hare once wrote an article on "Abortion and the Golden Rule" (*Philosophy and Public Affairs* 4 [1975]: 201-22); but his approach differs from mine. Hare rests his case on "We should do to others what we are glad was done to us" and on the fact that we are glad that we were conceived, not aborted, and not killed as infants; hence we too ought to conceive, not abort, and not kill infants (but contraception, abortion, and infanticide turn out to have only a weak prima facie wrongness which is easy to override by other considerations). Hare's formulation of the golden rule here is defective; if I am *glad* my parents gave me hundreds of gifts each Christmas, then perhaps to be consistent I must hold that it would be good to do this same thing in similar circumstances—but I need not hold that one *should* do this (that it is a *duty*). Also my conclusions differ from Hare's—I view abortion and infanticide (but not failing to conceive) as seriously wrong; I think my conclusions are what Hare's theory should lead to.

6. On the Tooley/Singer view the cutoff point for killing is not birth but rather when the child comes to desire its continued existence as a continuing subject of experiences. (It is unclear at what age this happens.) My response to this view would he much like the above, except that the killing side of the chart would now have one more *yes*.

25

The Fetus and Fundamental Rights

Joan C. Callahan

The Consistency Problem

Although the 1984 presidential election is history, the campaigns raised a number of questions which have not been resolved, and which need more public discussion. Not the least among these are the questions that surrounded Geraldine Ferraro's position on abortion—a position that significantly disrupted her campaign, and which, during the early fall of 1984, put all liberal Democratic Catholic politicians into political trouble from which they have not yet escaped.[1]

The trouble was focused on the question of abortion, but the problem is deeper than any single issue. The problem is one of consistency: How can a politician believe that something is profoundly morally wrong, yet insist that he or she will not use political power to right the wrong? The reply from the Geraldine Ferraros and Edward Kennedys was that it is not the proper business of the politician to impose his or her religious beliefs on members of a pluralistic society. Although this is surely true, it was an inadequate response. It was inadequate because it missed the point; and it missed the point because it seemed to treat matters like our public policy on abortion as if they were the same in kind as eating meat on Friday or making one's Easter Duty. The Catholic politicians may not have been making a category mistake, but they certainly sometimes sounded as if they were. Bishop James Timlin of Scranton did not have to be a bishop, a Roman Catholic, or even a Christian to say with understandable astonishment that

This is a revised version of an article that appeared in *Commonweal* (April 11, 1986): 203–209. Reprinted by permission of the author and the publisher.

Geraldine Ferraro's position on abortion is like saying "I'm personally opposed to slavery, but I don't care if people down the street want to own slaves."[2] The Catholic liberal Democrats thought and think this analogy fails. But *why* it fails was never made clear. In what follows, I want to address Bishop Timlin's analogy and hence, the particular question of abortion, as well as the larger question of appropriate reasons for a politician's policy choices. My purpose is to get clearer on both the morality of elective abortion and the question of moral consistency in political life.

Religious versus Philosophical Reasons

Bishop Timlin's analogy is faulty in at least three ways. First, refusing to use the law to fight a practice one believes is immoral does not imply that one does not *care* if people engage in that practice. Mario Cuomo, in his thoughtful, if not wholly adequate, speech at Notre Dame made that very clear.[3] There is no doubt that Mr. Cuomo cares deeply about abortion. But we can cite any number of examples (e.g., the selfish breaking of promises, the telling of lies to friends for bad reasons, etc.) of actions we believe are morally wrong and about which we care, but which we do not (and should not) attempt to eradicate by law. Thus, it does not follow from the fact that someone is unwilling to pursue a legal prohibition on some kind of activity that the person does not care if people engage in that activity. Nor does it follow from the fact that one believes that some kind of action is morally wrong that one is morally obligated to seek a legal prohibition on that kind of action.

Bishop Timlin's analogy is also faulty because it fails to recognize that the *reasons* one has for holding something to be wrong are of the utmost importance when one is trying to decide whether to pursue a legal prohibition on individual liberty. In a pluralistic society, the fact that a religious institution, or a religious contingency (no matter how large), holds something to be wrong is simply not a good reason for setting a public policy prohibiting or requiring action on the part of all citizens. Insofar as a Catholic politician's reason for holding that abortion is wrong is that this is church doctrine, there can be no obligation to try to institute a prohibition on abortion on those who do not share the same religious affiliation. Indeed, part of the politician's obligation in a pluralistic society is to guard against just such impositions by religious groups. In the vice-presidential debate, Congresswoman Ferraro made it clear that her reason for being "personally" opposed to abortion is that her church holds this as doctrine. If this is indeed *why* she is opposed to abortion, then it ought to be clear to all of us that she has no more duty (or right) to try to capture her opposition to abortion in law than she has to try to force Americans who do not share her religious affiliation to attend Roman Catholic Mass weekly. And the same is true for any other politician who is opposed to abortion *because* this is a doctrine of his or her faith.[4]

But there are other reasons for being opposed to abortion—philosophical reasons which appeal to the laws of logic and to moral rights—which might be shared by the most ardent atheist. Many who are opposed to abortion have these kinds of reasons for holding that abortion is wrong, and so profoundly wrong that it might be rightly prohibited by law, even in a pluralistic society. We need, then, to make a distinction between those who hold that abortion is wrong simply because their religion says so, and those who think that abortion is wrong because they believe that the philosophical reasons compel us to accept that human fetuses have a right which is comparable to your right and my right not to be killed.

Reasons of the first kind (i.e., purely religious reasons) are excellent reasons for acting or not acting in certain ways in one's own life, but they are bad reasons for imposing legal requirements or legal restraints on those who do not share the same religious commitments. We all know this. If some new, large religious contingency were to come to believe that zero population growth is the will of God, and if the government set out to capture this belief in law, Roman Catholics and other Christians would lead the ranks of civil disobedients. But reasons of the second kind (i.e., reasons appealing to the logic of human rights) are of the appropriate kind to justify or even require someone's working for legal prohibitions on certain actions or practices. The problem in the abortion debate is that there is a profound disagreement about the relative strengths of the philosophical reasons given for and against holding that elective abortion is the killing of an unconsenting innocent person for inadequate moral reasons. If an elective abortion is the killing of an unconsenting innocent person for reasons which would not justify killing an adult person, then it is wrongful killing, and a policy allowing elective abortion cannot be morally justified. But *are* human fetuses persons? The question is a sensible one, and there are responsible philosophical reasons for saying yes and there are responsible philosophical reasons for saying no. And that's the rub.

FETAL RIGHTS AND THE LOGICAL WEDGE

Those who oppose elective abortion often insist that human life begins at conception. But this is just wrong. Human life begins long before conception. The sperm and egg are alive, and they are not bovine or feline or canine—they are living human gametes. To couch the question in terms of the beginning of human life is to muddle the issue. It is to make the question of the morality of abortion sound like one that can be answered by a very clever biologist. But the issue is not when human life begins. Unquestionably, human fetuses are, from the earliest stages, alive. What we *really* want to know is whether the living human fetus should be recognized as a bearer of the same range of fundamental moral rights that you and I have, among them the right not to be killed without *very* good reason. And the most clever biologist in the world cannot answer this for us, since the question is simply not a biological one.

But it might be objected that although some who are opposed to abortion and who have not thought carefully enough about the issue do make the mistake of thinking that the question is when biological life begins, it is also true that not everyone who talks in terms of the beginning of human fife is making this mistake. For surely many who are opposed to elective abortion mean to contend that the life of a *unique* human being, of a distinct *person*, begins at conception, and that is why a policy allowing abortion is wrong.

The problem with this response, however, is that it is not a single claim. For one can grant that the life of a unique human being begins at conception, yet not grant that a distinct person emerges at conception, since the two claims are not equivalent unless one begs the question in favor of fetal personhood. That is, if we mean by "human being" "a member of the biological species *Homo sapiens*," then (if we ignore the problem of identical twins) it is uncontroversially true that the life of a unique human being begins at conception. This is merely a scientific claim, and it is one that can be conclusively defended by scientists as such. But the claim that a distinct *person* emerges at conception is not a scientific one; for to call something "a person" is already to assert that it is a bearer of strongest moral rights—fundamental rights comparable to yours and mine, among them the right not to be killed except for the most compelling of moral reasons. If in asserting that "a human life begins at conception" the opponent of elective abortion means to assert the biological claim, that can be granted immediately. But if he or she means to assert that "a person emerges at conception," that is a very different claim—it is a moral claim. Indeed, it is the very claim that is at issue in the abortion debate. What those who oppose retaining a policy of elective abortion need to tell us is *why* we must accept that the truth of the biological claim commits us to accepting the moral claim.

But those opposed to elective abortion might still respond that those who admit that the life of a unique human being (in the biological sense) begins at conception are indeed committed to granting that (insofar as human fetuses become distinct persons) the life of a distinct person begins here as well. For where did the life of any adult person begin but at conception?

There are, however, at least two responses to this. The first is simply to make the logical point that one can allow that the life of a person begins at conception without allowing that the (biological human) being present at conception is yet a person. That is, just as one can allow that the first tiny bud in an acorn is the beginning of the life of a (future) oak tree without being committed to saying that the bud is already an oak tree, one can allow that conception marks the beginning of the life of a (future) person without being committed to saying that the conceptus is already a person.

This logical point leads to the second, more substantive, response: namely, that we think the tiny bud in the acorn is quite clearly *not* an oak tree. And we think this because the bud does not yet have the characteristics of oak trees. Indeed, acorns with tiny buds are very *unlike* oak trees, even though every oak tree began as a bud in an acorn. In just the same way, the new conceptus is very unlike beings who have the kinds of characteristics which compel us to recognize them as persons. What kinds of characteristics are these? I cannot offer a full account here, but perhaps it will be enough to point out that if we came across a being like [the motion picture character] E.T. (who is not biologically human), we would surely think him a person—a being with fundamental moral rights comparable to yours and mine. And this would be because we would recognize that he has certain characteristics—the capacity to suffer mental and physical pain, the ability to make plans, a sense of himself as an ongoing being, and so on—which are sufficient to compel us to hold that he must (and must not) be treated in certain ways. (And, of course, the film *E.T.* turns on precisely this point.) A conceptus, however, has none of these characteristics. Indeed, like the mystery of the acorn and the oak, what is amazing is that such radically *different* beings emerge from such beginnings. But it needs to be clearly recognized that in the case of the acorn and in the case of the conceptus, at the end of the process, we do have beings *very* unlike those at the beginning of the process.[5]

When, then, must we say of a developing human being that we must recognize it as a person? If we are talking about when we have a being with the kinds of characteristics we take to be relevant to compelling a recognition of human personhood, it seems that persons (at least human persons) are, like oak trees, emergent beings, and that deciding when to classify a developing human being as a person is like deciding when to call a shoot a tree. Young trees do not have all the characteristics of grown trees—for example, children cannot safely swing from them. But when a shoot begins to take on at least some of the characteristics of full-fledged trees, we think we are not confused in beginning to call that shoot a tree. Similarly, there is no clear distinction between where the Mississippi River ends and the Gulf of Mexico begins. But settle the issue by setting a *convention* which does not seem counterintuitive. We are faced with quite the same kind of question when it comes to the matter of persons. Since fetuses do not have the kinds of characteristics which compel us to recognize beings as persons, we must, whether we like it or not, sit down and decide whether fetuses are to be recognized as full-fledged persons as a matter of public policy. And we must decide the question on the basis of the appropriate kinds of reasons. That is, for the purposes of setting public policy in a religiously heterogeneous society, we must decide it on the basis of the nonreligious, philosophical arguments, some of which urge us to accept that we must recognize human fetuses as having the same range of fundamental rights that you and I have, and some of which hold that this is just not so.

One possible convention is to set the recognition of personhood at birth. Still others might be at various stages of prenatality or at various points after birth. Those who oppose elective abortion insist that we *must* recognize personhood at conception, and central to the position is most frequently an argument known as "the logical wedge." This argument holds that if we are going to recognize older children as having the same fundamental rights that you and I have, then logic compels us to recognize that, from the moment of conception, all human beings must have those same rights. The argument proceeds by starting with beings everyone recognizes as having the rights in question and then by pointing out that a child (say) at fifteen is not radically different from one at fourteen and a half; and a child at fourteen and a half is not radically different from one at fourteen; and so on. The argument presses us back from fourteen to thirteen to twelve—to infancy. From infancy, it is a short step to late-term fetuses, because (the argument goes) change in location (from the womb to the wider world) does not constitute an essential change in the being itself. *You* do not lose *your* right not to be killed simply by walking from one room to another. Similarly, it is argued, mere change of place is not philosophically important enough to justify such a radical difference in treatment between infants and late-term fetuses. The argument then presses us back to early-term fetuses—back to conception. Logic and fairness, then, force us to accept that even the new conceptus has the same fundamental right to life that you and I have.

But those who support retaining a policy of elective abortion often point out that this kind of argument for fetal rights is faulty, since if we accept that we can never treat beings who are not radically different from one another in radically different ways, we shall be unable to justify all sorts of public policies which we want to keep and which we all believe are fair. It is argued, for example, that this kind of argument for fetal rights entails that we cannot be justified in setting driving or voting ages, since withholding these privileges until a certain age discriminates against those close to that age: An eighteen-year-old is not radically different from a seventeen-and-a-half-year-old, and so on. Thus, the implication of this kind of argument is that setting ages for the commencement of certain important societal privileges cannot be morally justified. We must give the five-year-old the right to vote, the six-year-old the right to drink, the nine-year-old the right to drive. But these implications, it is argued, show that this kind of argument for fetal rights is unsound.[6]

The response to this criticism of the logical wedge argument, however, is that the granting of societal privileges is not a matter of arbitrariness, even if there is some arbitrariness in selecting ages for the commencement of such privileges. Proper use of these rights, it may be argued, requires a certain degree of maturity—responsibility, background knowledge, experience, independence, and, in the case of driving, a certain degree of developed physical dexterity. Thus, it is because certain changes normally occur as a child matures into an adult that it is appropriate to set policies which acknowledge those changes. But this, it may be argued, is not the case when it comes to recognizing the right to life. That is, those who oppose retaining a policy of elective abortion insist that after conception no changes occur that are relevant to recognizing the personhood (and thus the right to life) of a human being.

But this immediately takes us back to the acorn and the oak. The bud and the tree simply *are* significantly different kinds of beings. And you and I *are* significantly different from a conceptus, which has *none* of the characteristics which morally compel us to recognize it as a being with rights. It will not do simply to deny that there are significant changes between the time of conception and the time when we have a being which we simply *must* recognize as a bearer of rights. Thus, we are once again confronted with the question of deciding where we shall set the convention of recognizing personhood.

At this point, however, there is yet another response open to the opponent of elective abortion—namely, that the kind of reasoning used to defeat the argument for fetal rights cannot be correct, since it will not only rule out our being committed to the rights of fetuses, it also entails that we are not compelled to accept that human infants are beings of a kind which must be recognized as having the full range of fundamental moral rights, since infants are, it might be suggested, more like very young kittens in regard to the characteristics in question than they are like paradigm cases of persons.

But this objection is not devastating. For, again, the question before us is a question of deciding what convention we shall adopt. And one can allow that even if infants do not (yet) have the characteristics which compel us to accept a being as a person, there are other considerations which provide excellent reasons for taking birth as the best place to set the convention of recognizing personhood and the full range of fundamental moral rights, despite the fact that infants as such are far more like very young kittens than they are like beings whose characteristics compel us to accept them as full members of the moral community.

Chief among these considerations are the facts that persons other than an infant's biological mother are able to care for the infant and have an interest in doing so. There is no radical change in the characteristics of a human being just before birth and just after birth. But once a human being emerges from the womb and others are able to care for it, there are radical changes in what is involved in preserving its life. And the crucial change is that sustaining its life violates no right of its biological mother. Thus birth, which marks this change, is not an arbitrary point for commencing recognition of personhood.

It is important to notice here that to hold that a woman has a right to terminate a pregnancy is not to hold that she also has a right to the death of her fetus if that fetus can survive, and quite the same reasons that can justify a proscription on infanticide can justify a requirement to sustain viable fetuses that survive abortion. What we are not entitled to do, it may he argued, is force a woman to complete a pregnancy because others have an interest in having her fetus. But it does not follow from this that a woman may kill a born infant that can be cared for by others. Thus, it does not follow from the kind of reasoning I have sketched above that the defender of a policy allowing elective abortion is committed to a policy allowing infanticide. Indeed, the position is fully consistent with holding that even though infants do not yet possess the kinds of characteristics which compel recognition of a being as a person, the fact that they are now biologically independent beings that can be sustained without forcing an unwilling woman to serve as a life support provides an excellent reason for setting the convention of a right to life at birth, that is, viable emergence.[7]

Perhaps it should be pointed out here that the view I have just sketched can also allow that even kittens have *some* moral rights. I, for one, believe that as sentient beings—beings capable of suffering pain—they have a strong moral right not to be treated cruelly, that is, not to have pain wantonly imposed on them. Insofar as fetuses can suffer pain, the defender of elective abortion must be justified. To say this, however, is not to be committed to holding that fetuses must be recognized as having the same full range of fundamental rights that you and I have. It is, rather, to allow fetuses (at the very least) the moral standing of any being of comparable sentience, and, hence, to hold that there is always a moral obligation not to wantonly impose pain on fetuses. But given the exquisite intimacy of pregnancy, any woman who does not want to bring a child to term has a strong reason for seeking an abortion. Thus, if pain is imposed on the fetus in abortion, it is not wantonly imposed.[8]

But it will surely still be objected that human fetuses and human infants are beings that are potentially like paradigm cases of persons, and this makes them very *unlike* other beings of comparable sentience. Kittens, after all, will never develop the kinds of characteristics that compel us to recognize them as full-fledged members of the moral community, and because of this, we must recognize human fetuses as having a far more significant moral standing than other beings of comparable sentience. Sometimes opponents of elective abortion point this out, saying that from the moment of conception a fetus is a *potential* person, and must, therefore, be granted the right to life. But the problem here is that to say that a being is a potential person is just to say it is a person-not-yet, which is, of course, to deny that it is now a person. And this is to give the defender of the retaining choice in this area the very point that is crucial to his or her argument against the argument for fetal rights, and to thereby turn the question back to the question of deciding on a convention.

ACTUAL AND POTENTIAL PERSONS

The crucial question, then, is whether we should recognize the fetus as a person now or whether we should recognize the fetus as a potential person—as a person-not-yet. If we take the first choice, then the full range of fundamental moral rights attaches to the fetus. If we take the second choice, it remains an open question what moral duties we might have toward the fetus. Either way, our *reasons* for deciding as we do must be more than religious ones if the purpose of deciding is to set policy in a pluralistic society. Bishop Timlin's analogy to slavery fails yet a third time because there are no such open questions about involuntary slavery. Enslaving a person against his or her will is a paradigm case of injustice. But we haven't anything like the same sort of moral certainty about the injustice of abortion. And since we haven't, those who recognize the complexity of the question can hold, without being heartless or inconsistent, that *they* believe abortion is wrong, but also that they are unprepared to impose that view on those who remain reflectively unconvinced by the arguments that the human fetus must be recognized as having the full moral status of a person.

Does it follow from all this that there is some serious doubt about the personhood of fetuses—that is, that the fetus might be a person? Sometimes those who support retaining a policy of elective abortion say things like this—that the fetus *might* be a person, but that the evidence is just not conclusive. But if this is the position one holds, those who oppose allowing elective abortion have a strong response. That response is that we should give the fetus the benefit of the doubt. After all, if a hunter hears a movement in the bushes and shoots without making sure she is not shooting a person, and it turns out that she has killed or injured a person, we charge her with gross recklessness. And her saying that it was possible that what she shot at was not a person is no defense. She simply should not have shot if there were even a remote possibility that she would injure a person. In just the same way, the opponent of allowing elective abortion argues that if there is any possibility that the fetus is a person, we have a duty to act as if it were a person—a duty to avoid acting recklessly. And part of what *that* means is that another person may not kill it for reasons less than self-defense.

This is an interesting argument, but it misses an important point. For the real doubt is not whether a fetus is a person. Rather, if there is a doubt it is about whether we should treat something which is obviously a potential person (in the sense that it has potentially the characteristics of paradigm cases of persons) as if it were a person already. And this is not something that can be decided by going and looking at the fetus, as one might go and look in the bushes. For (again) in looking, we shall find that although fetuses are quite wonderful beings, they lack the kinds of characteristics that morally compel us to accept a being as a person. The question to be resolved, then, is whether we should accept that these beings which will emerge as persons if their lives are supported ought, at this stage of their development, [to] be treated as if [they] were persons already—as beings with a moral right to life comparable to yours and mine, comparably protected by the coercive power of the law.

When we are trying to resolve the real doubt, a large part of what we need to ask is what deciding to treat fetuses as beings with the full range of fundamental moral rights would really involve in practice, and whether our shared moral views about paradigm cases of persons will allow us to accept these things. Let us, then, look for a moment at just two of the implications of deciding to admit human fetuses into the class of full-fledged persons with full-fledged fundamental rights.

Some Implications of Recognizing Fetuses as Persons

If we decide to recognize fetuses as full persons, the first thing that follows (as Mr. Reagan has recognized) is that abortion in cases of rape or incest must be ruled out. Suppose that I were to discover that you are the product of rape or incest. You would not think (and none of us would think) that it followed from this that I could kill you. Fundamental rights are not a consequence of where someone came from. If we allow that human fetuses are persons, we could not consistently allow abortion for (say) an eighteen-year-old woman who had been raped by her father. What is more, if this woman were to perform an abortion on herself and be found out, we must treat her as we treat any murderer. In some jurisdictions, this might lead to life imprisonment or even execution. During the 1984 campaigns, President Reagan was asked in the first debate with Mr. Mondale whether he believed we should treat women who abort for reasons less than self-defense as murderers, with all that might entail. He avoided the question, saying that this would be a matter for the states to decide. But the opponent of elective abortion needs to confront this question squarely and honestly. Precisely what *are* we to do with women who abort? Can we accept that states may decide to imprison them or execute them? Just what are we to do with them? If the proponent of a prohibition on elective abortion confronts this question earnestly and *cannot* comfortably hold that jurisdictions *should* treat these women as they typically treat murderers, then he or she needs to begin to think carefully about *why*. When asked in the first debate to explain his position on abortion, Mr. Mondale (echoing Governor Cuomo) said of the prohibitive policy espoused by Mr. Reagan, "It won't work." This is a woefully inadequate response. But I suspect that what Mr. Mondale had in mind was that accepting the fetus as a full-fledged person commits us to measures in practice that even those who are deeply opposed to elective abortion cannot fully accept, among them that the eighteen-year-old who aborts a fetus resulting from rape by her father is to be treated as any murderer of a helpless, innocent person. We are not, even in this pluralistic society, free to kill others for reasons less than the immediate defense of our own lives, and if we do, we are subject to the most severe legal penalties, including possible execution. If fetuses are to be recognized as full-fledged persons, then justice requires that those who abort them for reasons less than self-defense must be recognized as full-fledged murderers and treated as such. Those who are rigorously opposed to retaining a policy of elective abortion on the ground that fetuses are persons must confront this implication sincerely and sensitively, and they must be explicit on what they are willing to accept as the practical implications of their position. If they are not willing to accept that those who abort should be subject to exactly the same treatments as others who murder innocent persons, then they do not *really* believe that the fetus has precisely the same moral status as you and I.

There is yet another potent implication of recognizing fetuses as full-fledged persons. Mr. Reagan and Mr. Bush would both allow abortion in cases of self-defense—that is, in cases where the woman's life is threatened. But there is a problem with this position that generally goes unnoticed. For if our public policy is to recognize that the fetus is genuinely an innocent person, then its threat to a woman's life is an innocent threat, and the state can have no legitimate reason for systematically preferring the life of the woman to the life of the fetus.[9] That is, the argument from self-defense simply cannot justify the state's allowing a woman the use of medical specialists who will systematically prefer her life to the life of the fetus. If the fetus is a person who has precisely the same moral status as the woman, the state must, as a matter of fairness to the fetus, do nothing that would involve it in giving the woman an unfair advantage over the fetus. And, again, this means that the state should not permit the use of technologically advanced institutions or the use of technologically advanced practitioners which give the woman an unfair advantage in this battle for life between moral equals. The argument from self-defense, then, seems to entail far greater restrictions on abortion than even the most fervent opponents of elective abortion tend to want to allow, Mr. Reagan among them. If opponents of elective abortion want to allow abortions in cases where the woman's life is at stake, then they must realize that implicit in their position is the view that the woman and the fetus are *not* of equal moral stature after all.

MORAL SENSITIVITY AND SETTING PUBLIC POLICY

My own view is that there are insurmountable difficulties to finding an argument for the recognition of fetuses as persons which is cogent and compelling enough to justify imposing on women the exquisitely intimate burden of bearing an unwanted child. But even if this view is correct, it does not follow that we can do just anything to human fetuses. Kittens are not persons, but we are not at moral liberty to wantonly impose pain on them. Natural resources are not persons, but we are not at moral liberty to wantonly destroy them. Several years ago, Patrick Buchanan wrote of an experiment on human fetuses, discussed in *The Second American Revolution*, by John Whitehead. Six months after *Roe* v. *Wade*, Dr. A. J. Adam of Case Western Reserve University reported to the American Pediatric Research Society that he and his associates had conducted an experiment on twelve fetuses, up to twenty weeks old, delivered alive by hysterectomy abortion. Adam and his associates cut the heads off these fetuses and cannulated the internal carotid arteries. They kept the heads alive, much as the Russians kept dogs' heads alive during the 1950s. When challenged, Dr. Adam's response was that society had decided that these fetuses would die, thus they had no rights. Said Adam, "I don't see any ethical problem." I find Dr. Adam's failure to see any ethical problem chilling and morally repugnant, even though these fetuses had no real chance of long-term survival *ex utero*. One of the legitimate worries of those who are opposed to abortion is that this kind of ghoulish insensitivity will become more and more prevalent in our society, spilling over to a cavalier attitude toward human life in general. One need not be absolutely opposed to allowing elective abortion to share that worry, and one need not think nonviable fetuses are persons to be astonished at Dr. Adam's failure to see *any* ethical problem.

When asked in the 1984 campaign debate about his position on abortion, Vice President Bush replied that he had changed his view (which previously had been more liberal) because of the number of legal abortions that have taken place in this country. But the problem with this reason for disallowing elective abortion is that it misses the very point of those who have traditionally opposed abortion; for if fetuses have the same range of moral rights that you and I have, then even one abortion for reasons less than those which would justify killing an adult person is too many. Determining moral rights is not a numbers game. We don't have laws against murder because there are too many murders—we have laws against murder because every single person has a compelling moral right not to be murdered. Because that right is so compelling, the state comes forward to protect it. When one understands that persons have a compelling moral right not to be murdered, one also understands that numbers of murders are irrelevant to the question of whether society should have laws against murder. One murder is simply one too many. Mr. Bush's position, then, misses the very strong position on fundamental fetal rights that has been the moral centerpiece of the movement against elective abortion.

Still, there is much to be said for Mr. Bush's discomfort with the use of abortion as a form of birth control. Although I believe that defenders of retaining a policy of elective abortion who have thought carefully and sensitively about the issue are more than willing to admit that abortion, however well-justified, is never a happy moral choice, some who favor elective abortion angrily talk about fetuses as being, like tumors, morally equivalent to parasites. Such talk is inexcusably cavalier; and those who believe that the human fetus is of significant moral worth are understandably infuriated when they hear it or read it. Language like that does not help get us to reasonable, sensitive discussion. And it is precisely reasonable, sensitive discussion that we now most need on this difficult question of morality and public policy.

It should go without saying that public policy should not be set by those who shout the loudest—that it should not be set by those who carry the most emotively charged posters, or by those who use the most emotively charged language. But neither should it be carelessly set by an unreflective commitment to a woman's right to self-direction which fails to take into serious account the genuine moral costs of giving absolute priority to such a right. Public policy must be set by sitting down and coining to understand the legitimate concerns on both sides of hard issues. It must be set with an eye toward what *all* morally sensitive persons in a pluralistic society can live with.

The abortion issue is one about which reasonable people can disagree. We all need to realize this, and we need to do more talking instead of shouting. Deliberation in the philosophy of moral rights involves much more than repeating bumper sticker slogans; and rational agreement in such deliberation is often hard-won, and will only succeed when each side can see clearly why the other side begins from the position it does. It will not do, then, for those who are opposed to retaining a policy of elective abortion to call themselves "pro-life" and to call fetuses "babies" and take the issue to be settled. And it will not do for those who believe we must retain abortion as an option for women to call fetuses "parasites" and take the issue to be settled. Trying to decide public policy must involve refusing to use language which implies that the opposition is against something that any morally reasonable person would support or which simply begs the question against the other side. It must involve sensitive deliberation which takes carefully into account the deeply felt and morally reasonable concerns of a variety of perspectives. And the effort must lead to decisions that thoughtful persons in a pluralistic society can respect, no matter what policies they would prefer to see. Defenders and opponents of a policy of elective abortion must realize that we share a large common moral ground. We must begin to work from that common ground to come to an agreement on policies that can respectfully govern us all.

The liberal Catholic politicians are in trouble, and they will stay in trouble until they more adequately explain their reasons for not seeking a moratorium on elective abortion. Mario Cuomo began that explanation at Notre Dame. But there is much more to be said if all morally concerned Americans are to understand why politicians like Geraldine Ferraro and Mario Cuomo are neither necessarily inconsistent, nor rabid moral relativists, nor insensitive moral thugs.

Notes

1. An edited version of this essay appeared in *Commonweal* 11 (April 1986): 203–209. 1 am deeply indebted to Peter Steirifels for his extensive and enormously helpful comments and questions on an earlier draft. For an expanded discussion of fetal rights, see James W. Knight and Joan C. Callahan, *Preventing Birth: Contemporary Methods and Related Moral Controversies* (Salt Lake City: University of Utah Press, 1989), chaps. 7 and 9.

2. *Newsweek*, Sept. 24, 1984.

3. Governor Cuomo's speech was given on Sept. 13, 1984.

4. I offer a more detailed account of what it means to be "personally" opposed to some kind of action in "Religion and Moral Consistency in Politics," in progress.

5. For a fuller discussion of the kinds of characteristics morally relevant to compelling a recognition of beings (including nonhuman beings) as persons see, e.g., Mary Anne Warren, "On the Moral and Legal Status of Abortion," in *Today's Moral Problems*, ed. Richard Wasserstrom (New York: Macmillan, 1975), pp. 120–36 [see pages 272–79 of the present volume]. See also Jane English, "Abortion and the Concept of a Person," *Canadian Journal of Philosophy* 5, no. 2 (1975): 233–43, for an even more detailed discussion of the cluster of features that enter into our concept of a person.

6. For a more detailed treatment of this response to the logical wedge, see, e.g., Jonathan Glover, *Causing Death and Saving Lives* (New York: Penguin, 1977), chap. 12.

7. Again, see Warren for a version of this line of reasoning.

8. I deal with this question of fetal sentience (as well as several related issues) in more detail in "*The Silent Scream*: A New, Conclusive Argument Against Abortion?" *Philosophy Research Archives* 11 (1986): 181–95. On the question of fetal sentience, see also L. W. Sumner, *Abortion and Moral Theory* (Princeton: Princeton University Press, 1981), chap. 4. A revised version of that chapter appears as "A Third Way," in *The Problem of Abortion*, 2d ed., ed. Joel Feinberg (Belmont, Calif.: Wadsworth, 1984), pp. 71–93.

9. This point is argued in detail by Nancy Davis in "Abortion and Self-Defense," *Philosophy, and Public Affairs* 13, no. 3 (summer 1984): 175–207,

26

WHY ABORTION IS IMMORAL

Don Marquis

The view that abortion is, with rare exceptions, seriously immoral has received little support in the recent philosophical literature. No doubt most philosophers affiliated with secular institutions of higher education believe that the antiabortion position is either a symptom of irrational religious dogma or a conclusion generated by seriously confused philosophical argument. The purpose of this essay is to undermine this general belief. This essay sets out an argument that purports to show, as well as any argument in ethics can show, that abortion is, except possibly in rare cases, seriously immoral, that it is in the same moral category as killing an innocent adult human being.

The argument is based on a major assumption. Many of the most insightful and careful writers on the ethics of abortion—such as Joel Feinberg, Michael Tooley, Mary Anne Warren, H. Tristram Engelhardt Jr., L. W. Sumner, John T. Noonan Jr., and Philip Devine[1]—believe that whether or not abortion is morally permissible stands or falls on whether or not a fetus is the sort of being whose life it is seriously wrong to end. The argument of this essay will assume, but not argue, that they are correct.

Also, this essay will neglect issues of great importance to a complete ethics of abortion. Some antiabortionists will allow that certain abortions, such as abortion before implantation or abortion when the life of a woman is threatened by a pregnancy or abortion after rape, may be morally permissible. This essay will not explore the casuistry of these hard cases. The purpose of this essay is to develop a general argument for the claim that the overwhelming majority of deliberate abortions are seriously immoral.

From *Journal of Philosophy* 86, no. 4 (April 1989). Reprinted with permission.

I

A sketch of standard antiabortion and pro-choice arguments exhibits how those arguments possess certain symmetries that explain why partisans of those positions are so convinced of the correctness of their own positions, why they are not successful in convincing their opponents, and why, to others, this issue seems to be unresolvable. An analysis of the nature of this standoff suggests a strategy for surmounting it.

Consider the way a typical antiabortionist argues. She will argue or assert that life is present from the moment of conception or that fetuses look like babies or that fetuses possess a characteristic such as a genetic code that is both necessary and sufficient for being human. Antiabortionists seem to believe that (1) the truth of all of these claims is quite obvious, and (2) establishing any of these claims is sufficient to show that abortion is morally akin to murder.

A standard pro-choice strategy exhibits similarities. The pro-choicer will argue or assert that fetuses are not persons or that fetuses are not rational agents or that fetuses are not social beings. Pro-choicers seem to believe that (1) the truth of any of these claims is quite obvious, and (2) establishing any of these claims is sufficient to show that an abortion is not a wrongful killing.

In fact, both the pro-choice and the antiabortion claims do seem to be true, although the "it looks like a baby" claim is more difficult to establish the earlier the pregnancy. We seem to have a standoff. How can it be resolved?

As everyone who has taken a bit of logic knows, if any of these arguments concerning abortion is a good argument, it requires not only some claim characterizing fetuses, but also some general moral principle that ties a characteristic of fetuses to having or not having the right to life or to some other moral characteristic that will generate the obligation or the lack of obligation not to end the life of a fetus. Accordingly, the arguments of the antiabortionist and the pro-choicer need a bit of filling in to be regarded as adequate.

Note what each partisan will say. The antiabortionist will claim that her position is supported by such generally accepted moral principles as "It is always prima facie seriously wrong to take a human life" or "It is always prima facie seriously wrong to end the life of a baby." Since these are generally accepted moral principles, her position is certainly not obviously wrong. The pro-choicer will claim that her position is supported by such plausible moral principles as "Being a person is what gives an individual intrinsic moral worth" or "It is only seriously prima facie wrong to take the life of a member of the human community." Since these are generally accepted moral principles, the pro-choice position is certainly not obviously wrong. Unfortunately, we have again arrived at a standoff.

Now, how might one deal with this standoff? The standard approach is to try to show how the moral principles of one's opponent lose their plausibility under analysis. It is easy to see how this is possible. On the one hand, the antiabortionist will defend a moral principle concerning the wrongness of killing which tends to be broad in scope in order that even fetuses at an early stage of pregnancy will fall under it. The problem with broad principles is that they often embrace too much. In this particular instance, the principle "It is always prima facie wrong to take a human life" seems to entail that it is wrong to end the existence of a living human cancer-cell culture, on the grounds that the culture is both living and human. Therefore, it seems that the antiabortionist's favored principle is too broad.

On the other hand, the pro-choicer wants to find a moral principal concerning the wrongness of killing which tends to be narrow in scope in order that fetuses will not fall under it. The problem with narrow principles is that they often do not embrace enough. Hence, the needed principles such as "It is prima facie seriously wrong to kill only persons" or "It is prima facie wrong to kill only rational agents" do not explain why it is wrong to kill infants or young children or the severely retarded or even perhaps the severely mentally ill. Therefore, we seem again to have a standoff: The antiabortionist charges, not unreasonably, that pro-choice principles concerning killing are too narrow to be acceptable; the pro-choicer charges, not unreasonably, that antiabortionist principles concerning killing are too broad to be acceptable.

Attempts by both sides to patch up the difficulties in their positions run into further difficulties. The antiabortionist will try to remove the problem in her position by reformulating her principle concerning killing in terms of human beings. Now we end up with: "It is always prima facie seriously wrong to end the life of a human being." This principle has the advantage of avoiding the problem of the human cancer-cell culture counterexample. But this advantage is purchased at a high price. For although it is clear that a fetus is both human and alive, it is not, it all clear that a fetus is a human *being*. There is at least something to be said for the view that something becomes a human being only after a process of development, and that therefore first-trimester fetuses and perhaps all fetuses are not yet human beings. Hence, the antiabortionist, by this move, has merely exchanged one problem for another.[2]

The pro-choicer fares no better. She may attempt to find reasons why killing infants, young children, and the severely retarded is wrong which are independent of her major principle that is supposed to explain the wrongness of taking human life, but which will not also make abortion immoral. This is no easy task. Appeals to social utility will seem satisfactory only to those who resolve not to think of the enormous difficulties with a utilitarian account of the wrongness of killing and the significant social costs of preserving the lives of the unproductive.[3] A pro-choice strategy that extends the definition of "person" to infants or even to young children seems just as arbitrary as an antiabortion strategy that extends the definition of "human being" to fetuses. Again, we find symmetries in the two positions and we arrive at a standoff.

There are even further problems that reflect symmetries in the two positions. In addition to counterexample problems, or the arbitrary application problems that can be exchanged for them, the standard anti-abortionist principle "It is prima facie seriously wrong to kill a human being," or one of its variants, can be objected to on the grounds of ambiguity. If "human being" is taken to be a *biological* category, then the antiabortionist is left with the problem of explaining why a merely biological category should make a moral difference. Why, it is asked, is it any more reasonable to base a moral conclusion on the number of chromosomes in one's cells than on the color of one's skin?[4] If "human being," on the other hand, is taken to be a *moral* category, then the claim that a fetus is a human being cannot be taken to be a premise in the antiabortion argument, for it is precisely what needs to be established. Hence, either the antiabortionist's main category is a morally irrelevant, merely biological category, or it is of no use to the antiabortionist in establishing (noncircularly, of course) that abortion is wrong.

Although this problem with the antiabortionist position is often noticed, it is less often noticed that the pro-choice position suffers from an analogous problem. The principle "Only persons have the right to life" also suffers from an ambiguity. The term "person" is typically defined in terms of psychological characteristics, although there will certainly be disagreement concerning which characteristics are most important. Supposing that this matter can be settled, the pro-choicer is left with the problem of explaining why *psychological* characteristics should make a *moral* difference. If the pro-choicer should attempt to deal with this problem by claiming that an explanation is not necessary, that in fact we do treat such a cluster of psychological properties as having moral significance, the sharp-witted antiabortionist should have a ready response. We do treat being both living and human as having moral significance. If it is legitimate for the pro-choicer to demand that the antiabortionist provide an explanation of the connection between the biological character of being a human being and the wrongness of being killed (even though people accept this connection), then it is legitimate for the antiabortionist to demand that the pro-choicer provide an explanation of the connection between psychological criteria for being a person and the wrongness of being killed (even though that connection is accepted).[5]

Feinberg has attempted to meet this objection (he calls psychological personhood "commonsense personhood"):

> The characteristics that confer commonsense personhood are not arbitrary bases for rights and duties, such as race, sex or species membership; rather they are traits that make sense out of rights and duties and without which those moral attributes would have no point or function. It is because people are conscious; have a sense of their personal identities have plans, goals, and projects; experience emotions; are liable to pains

> anxieties, and frustrations; can reason and bargain, and so on—it is because of these attributes that people have values and interests, desires and expectations of their own, including a stake in their own futures and a personal well-being of a sort we cannot ascribe to unconscious or nonrational beings. Because of their developed capacities they can assume duties and responsibilities and can have and make claims on one another. Only because of their sense of self, their life plans, their value hierarchies, and their stakes in their own futures can they be ascribed fundamental rights. There is nothing arbitrary about these linkages.[6]

The plausible aspects of this attempt should not be taken to obscure its implausible features. There is a great deal to be said for the view that being a psychological person under some description is a necessary condition for having duties. One cannot have a duty unless one is capable of behaving morally, and a being's capability of behaving morally will require having a certain psychology. It is far from obvious, however, that having rights entails consciousness or rationality, as Feinberg suggests. We speak of the rights of the severely retarded or the severely mentally ill, yet some of these persons are not rational. We speak of the rights of the temporarily unconscious. The New Jersey Supreme Court based their decision in the Quinlan case on Karen Ann Quinlan's right to privacy, and she was known to be permanently unconscious at that time. Hence, Feinberg's claim that having rights entails being conscious is, on its face, obviously false.

Of course, it might not make sense to attribute rights to a being that would never in its natural history have certain psychological traits. This modest connection between psychological personhood and moral personhood will create a place for Karen Ann Quinlan and the temporarily unconscious. But then it makes a place for fetuses also. Hence, it does not serve Feinberg's pro-choice purposes. Accordingly, it seems that the pro-choicer will have as much difficulty bridging the gap between psychological personhood and personhood in the moral sense as the antiabortionist has bridging the gap between being a biological human being and being a human being in the moral sense.

Furthermore, the pro-choicer cannot any more escape her problem by making person a purely moral category than the anti-abortionist could escape by the analogous move. For if person is a moral category, then the pro-choicer is left without the resources for establishing (noncircularly, of course) the claim that a fetus is not a person, which is an essential premise in her argument. Again, we have both a symmetry and a standoff between pro-choice and antiabortion views.

Passions in the abortion debate run high. There are both plausibilities and difficulties with the standard positions. Accordingly, it is hardly surprising that partisans of either side embrace with fervor the moral generalizations that support the conclusions they preanalytically favor, and reject with disdain the moral generalizations of their opponents as being subject to inescapable difficulties. It is easy to believe that the counterexamples to one's own moral principles are merely temporary difficulties that will dissolve in the wake of further philosophical research, and that the counterexamples to the principles of one's opponents are as straightforward as the contradiction between *A* and *O* propositions in traditional logic. This might suggest to an impartial observer (if there are any) that the abortion issue is unresolvable.

There is a way out of this apparent dialectical quandary. The moral generalizations of both sides are not quite correct. The generalizations hold for the most part, for the usual cases. This suggests that they are all *accidental* generalizations, that the moral claims made by those on both sides of the dispute do not touch on the *essence* of the matter.

This use of the distinction between essence and accident is not meant to invoke obscure metaphysical categories. Rather, it is intended to reflect the rather atheoretical nature of the abortion discussion. If the generalization a partisan in the abortion dispute adopts were derived from the reason why ending the life of a human being is wrong, then there could not be exceptions to that generalization unless some special case obtains in which there are even more powerful countervailing reasons. Such generalizations would not be merely accidental generalizations; they would point to, or be based upon, the essence of the wrongness of killing, what it is that makes killing wrong. All this suggests that a necessary condition of resolving the abortion controversy is a more theoretical account of the wrongness of killing. After all, if we merely believe, but do not understand, why killing adult human beings such as ourselves is wrong how could we conceivably show that abortion is either immoral or permissible?

II

In order to develop such an account, we can start from the following unproblematic assumption concerning our own case: it is wrong to kill *us*. Why is it wrong? Some answers can be easily eliminated. It might be said that what makes killing us wrong is that a killing brutalizes the one who kills. But the brutalization consists of being inured to the performance of an act that is hideously immoral; hence, the brutalization does not explain the immorality. It might be said that what makes killing us wrong is the great loss others would experience due to our absence. Although such hubris is understandable, such an explanation does not account for the wrongness of killing hermits, or those whose lives are relatively independent and whose friends find it easy to make new friends.

A more obvious answer is better. What primarily makes killing wrong is neither its effect on the murderer nor its effect on the victim's friends and relatives, but its effect on the victim. The loss of one's life is one of the greatest losses one can suffer. The loss of one's life deprives one of all the experiences, activities, projects, and enjoyments that would otherwise have constituted one's future. Therefore, killing someone is wrong, primarily because the killing inflicts (one of) the greatest possible losses on the victim. To describe this as the loss of life can be misleading, however. The change in my biological state does not by itself make killing me wrong. The effect of the loss of my biological life is the loss to me of all those activities, projects, experiences, and enjoyments which would otherwise have constituted my future personal life. These activities, projects, experiences, and enjoyments are either valuable for their own sakes or are means to something else that is valuable for its own sake. Some parts of my future are not valued by me now, but will come to be valued by me as I grow older and as my values and capacities change. When I am killed, I am deprived both of what I now value which would have been part of my future personal life, but also what I would come to value. Therefore, when I die, I am deprived of all of the value of my future. Inflicting this loss on me is ultimately what makes killing me wrong. This being the case, it would seem that what makes killing *any* adult human being prima facie seriously wrong is the loss of his or her future.[7]

How should this rudimentary theory of the wrongness of killing be evaluated? It cannot be faulted for deriving an "ought" from an "is," for it does not. The analysis assumes that killing me (or you, reader) is prima facie seriously wrong. The point of the analysis is to establish which natural property ultimately explains the wrongness of the killing, given that it is wrong. A natural property will ultimately explain the wrongness of killing, only if (1) the explanation fits with our intuitions about the matter and (2) there is no other natural property that provides the basis for a better explanation of the wrongness of killing. This analysis rests on the intuition that what makes killing a particular human or animal wrong is what it does to that particular human or animal. What makes killing wrong is some natural effect or other of the killing. Some would deny this. For instance, a divine-command theorist in ethics would deny it. Surely this denial is, however, one of those features of divine-command theory which renders it so implausible.

The claim that what makes killing wrong is the loss of the victim's future is directly supported by two considerations. In the first place, this theory explains why we regard killing as one of the worst of crimes. Killing is especially wrong, because it deprives the victim of more than perhaps any other crime. In the second place, people with AIDS or cancer who know they are dying believe, of course, that dying is a very bad thing for them. They believe that the loss of a future to them that they would otherwise have experienced is what makes their premature death a very bad thing for them. A better theory of the wrongness of killing would require a different natural property associated with killing which better fits with the attitudes of the dying. What could it be?

The view that what makes killing wrong is the loss to the victim of the value of the victim's future gains additional support when some of its implications are examined. In the first place, it is incompatible with the view that it is wrong to kill only beings who are biologically human. It is possible that there exists a different species from another planet whose members have a future like ours. Since having a future like that is what makes killing someone wrong, this theory entails that it would be wrong to kill members of such a species. Hence, this theory is opposed to the claim that only life that is biologically human has great moral worth, a claim which many antiabortionists have seemed to adopt. This opposition, which this theory has in common with personhood theories, seems to be a merit of the theory.

In the second place, the claim that the loss of one's future is the wrong-making feature of one's being killed entails the possibility that the futures of some actual nonhuman mammals on our own planet are sufficiently like ours that it is seriously wrong to kill them also. Whether some animals do have the same right to life as human beings depends on adding to the account of the wrongness of killing some additional account of just what it is about my future or the futures of other adult human beings which makes it wrong to kill us. No such additional account will be offered in this essay. Undoubtedly, the provision of such an account would be a very difficult matter. Undoubtedly, any such account would be quite controversial. Hence, it surely should not reflect badly on this sketch of an elementary theory of the wrongness of killing that it is indeterminate with respect to some very difficult issues regarding animal rights.

In the third place, the claim that the loss of one's future is the wrong-making feature of one's being killed does not entail, as sanctity of human life theories do, that active euthanasia is wrong. Persons who are severely and incurably ill, who face a future of pain and despair, and who wish to die will not have suffered a loss if they are killed. It is, strictly speaking, the value of a human's future which makes killing wrong in this theory. This being so, killing does not necessarily wrong some persons who are sick and dying. Of course, there may be other reasons for a prohibition of active euthanasia, but that is another matter. Sanctity-of-human-life theories seem to hold that active euthanasia is seriously wrong even in an individual case where there seems to be good reason for it independently of public policy considerations. This consequence is most implausible, and it is a plus for the claim that the loss of a future of value is what makes killing wrong that it does not share this consequence.

In the fourth place, the account of the wrongness of killing defended in this essay does straightforwardly entail that it is prima facie seriously wrong to kill children and infants, for we do presume that they have futures of value. Since we do believe that it is wrong to kill defenseless little babies it is important that a theory of the wrongness of killing easily account for this. Personhood theories of the wrongness of killing on the other hand cannot straightforwardly account for the wrongness of killing infants and young children.[8] Hence, such theories must add special ad hoc accounts of the wrongness of killing the young. The plausibility of such ad hoc theories seems to be a function of how desperately one wants such theories to work. The claim that the primary wrong-making feature of a killing is the loss to the victim of the value of its future accounts for the wrongness of killing young children and infants directly; it makes the wrongness of such acts as obvious as we actually think it is. This is a further merit of this theory. Accordingly it seems that this value of a future-like-ours theory of the wrongness of killing shares strengths of both sanctity-of-life and personhood accounts while avoiding weaknesses of both. In addition it meshes with a central intuition concerning what makes killing wrong.

The claim that the primary wrong-making feature of a killing is the loss to the victim of the value of its future has obvious consequences for the ethics of abortion. The future of a standard fetus includes a set of experiences, projects, activities, and such, which are identical with the futures of adult human beings and are identical with the futures of young children. Since the reason that is sufficient to explain why it is wrong to kill human beings after the time of birth is a reason that also applies to fetuses it follows that abortion is prima facie seriously morally wrong.

This argument does not rely on the invalid inference that since it is wrong to kill persons, it is wrong to kill potential persons also. The category that is morally central to this analysis is the category of having a valuable future like ours; it is not the category of personhood. The argument to the conclusion that abortion is prima facie seriously morally wrong proceeded independently of the notion of person or potential person or any equivalent. Someone may wish to start with this analysis in terms of the value of a human future, conclude that abortion is, except perhaps in rare circumstances, seriously morally wrong, infer that fetuses have the right to life and then call fetuses "persons" as a result of their having the right to life. Clearly, in this case the category of person is being used to state the *conclusion* of the analysis rather than to generate the *argument of* the analysis.

The structure of this antiabortion argument can be both illuminated and defended by comparing it to what appears to be the best argument for the wrongness of the wanton infliction of pain on animals. This latter argument is based on the assumption that it is prima facie wrong to inflict pain on me (or you reader). What is the natural property associated with the infliction of pain which makes such infliction wrong? The obvious answer seems to be that the infliction of pain causes suffering and that suffering is a misfortune. The suffering caused by the infliction of pain is what makes the wanton infliction of pain on me wrong. The wanton infliction of pain on other adult humans causes suffering. The wanton infliction of pain on animals causes suffering. Since causing suffering is what makes the wanton infliction of pain wrong and since the wanton infliction of pain on animals causes suffering it follows that the wanton infliction of pain on animals is wrong.

This argument for the wrongness of the wanton infliction of pain on animals shares a number of structural features with the argument for the serious prima facie wrongness of abortion. Both arguments start with an obvious assumption concerning what it is wrong to do to me (or you reader). Both then look for the characteristic or the consequence of the wrong action which makes the action wrong. Both recognize that the wrong-making feature of these immoral actions is a property of actions sometimes directed at individuals other than postnatal human beings. If the structure of the argument for the wrongness of the wanton infliction of pain on animals is sound, then the structure of the argument for the prima facie serious wrongness of abortion is also sound, for the structure of the two arguments is the same. The structure common to both is the key to the explanation of how the wrongness of abortion can be demonstrated without recourse to the category of person. In neither argument is that category crucial.

This defense of an argument for the wrongness of abortion in terms of a structurally similar agreement for the wrongness of the wanton infliction of pain on animals succeeds only if the account regarding animals is the correct account. Is it? In the first place, it seems plausible. In the second place, its major competition is Kant's account. Kant believed that we do not have direct duties to animals at all, because they are not persons. Hence Kant had to explain and justify the wrongness of inflicting pain on animals on the grounds that "he who is hard in his dealings with animals becomes hard also in his dealing with men."[9] The problem with Kant's account is that there seems to be no reason for accepting this latter claim unless Kant's account is rejected. If the alternative to Kant's account is accepted, then it is easy to understand why someone who is indifferent to inflicting pain on animals is also indifferent to inflicting pain on humans, for one is indifferent to what makes inflicting pain wrong in both cases. But, if Kant's account is accepted, there is no intelligible reason why one who is hard in his dealings with animals (or crabgrass or stones) should also be hard in his dealings with men. After all, men are persons: animals are no more persons than crabgrass or stones. Persons are Kant's crucial moral category. Why, in short, should a Kantian accept the basic claim in Kant's argument?

Hence, Kant's argument for the wrongness of inflicting pain on animals rests on a claim that, in a world of Kantian moral agents, is demonstrably false. Therefore, the alternative analysis, being more plausible anyway, should be accepted. Since this alternative analysis has the same structure as the antiabortion argument being defended here, we have further support for the argument for the immorality of abortion being defended in this essay.

Of course, this value of a future-like-ours argument, if sound, shows only that abortion is prima facie wrong, not that it is wrong in any and all circumstances. Since the loss of the future to a standard fetus, if killed, is, however, at least as great a loss as the loss of the future to a standard adult human being who is killed, abortion, like ordinary killing, could be justified only by the most compelling reasons. The loss of one's life is almost the greatest misfortune that can happen to one. Presumably abortion could be justified in some circumstances, only if the loss consequent on failing to abort would be at least as great. Accordingly, morally permissible abortions will be rare indeed unless, perhaps, they occur so early in pregnancy that a fetus is not yet definitely an individual. Hence, this argument should be taken as showing that abortion is presumptively very seriously wrong, where the presumption is very strong—as strong as the presumption that killing another adult human being is wrong.

III

How complete an account of the wrongness of killing does the value of a future-like-ours account have to be in order that the wrongness of abortion is a consequence? This account does not have to be an account of the necessary conditions for the wrongness of killing. Some persons in nursing homes may lack valuable human futures, yet it may be wrong to kill them for other reasons. Furthermore, this account does not obviously have to be the sole reason killing is wrong where the victim did have a valuable future. This analysis claims only that, for any killing where the victim did have a valuable future like ours, having that future by itself is sufficient to create the strong presumption that the killing is seriously wrong.

One way to overturn the value of a future-like-ours argument would be to find some account of the wrongness of killing which is at least as intelligible and which has different implications for the ethics of abortion. Two rival accounts possess at least some degree of plausibility. One account is based on the obvious fact that people value the experience of living and wish for that valuable experience to continue. Therefore, it might be said, what makes killing wrong is the discontinuation of that experience for the victim. Let us call this the *discontinuation account*.[10] Another rival account is based upon the obvious fact that people strongly desire to continue to live. This suggests that what makes killing us so wrong is that it interferes with the fulfillment of a strong and fundamental desire, the fulfillment of which is necessary for the fulfillment of any other desires we might have. Let us call this the *desire account*.[11]

Consider first the desire account as a rival account of the ethics of killing which would provide the basis for rejecting the antiabortion position. Such an account will have to be stronger than the value of a future-like-ours account of the wrongness of abortion if it is to do the job expected of it. To entail the wrongness of abortion, the value of a future-like-ours account has only to provide a sufficient, but not a necessary, condition for the wrongness of killing. The desire account, on the other hand, must provide us also with a necessary conclusion for the wrongness of killing in order to generate a pro-choice conclusion on abortion. The reason for this is that presumably the argument from the desire account moves from the claim that what makes killing wrong is interference with a very strong desire to the claim that abortion is not wrong because the fetus lacks a strong desire to live. Obviously, this inference fails if someone's having the desire to live is not a necessary condition of its being wrong to kill that individual.

One problem with the desire account is that we do regard it as seriously wrong to kill persons who have little desire to live or who have no desire to live or, indeed, have a desire not to live. We believe it is seriously wrong to kill the unconscious, the sleeping, those who are tired of life, and those who are suicidal. The value-of-a-human-future account renders standard morality intelligible in these cases; these cases appear to be incompatible with the desire account.

The desire account is subject to a deeper difficulty. We desire life, because we value the goods of this life. The goodness of life is not secondary to our desire for it. If this were not so, the pain of one's own premature death could be done away with merely by an appropriate alteration in the configuration of one's desires. This is absurd. Hence, it would seem that it is the loss of the goods of one's future, not the interference with the fulfillment of a strong desire to live, which accounts ultimately for the wrongness of killing.

It is worth noting that, if the desire account is modified so that it does not provide a necessary, but only a sufficient, condition for the wrongness of killing, the desire account is compatible with the value of a future-like-ours account. The combined accounts will yield an antiabortion ethic. This suggests that one can retain what is intuitively plausible about the desire account without a challenge to the basic argument of this paper.

It is also worth noting that, if future desires have moral force in a modified desire account of the wrongness of killing, one can find support for an antiabortion ethic even in the absence of a value of a future-like-ours account. If one decides that a morally relevant property, the possession of which is sufficient to make it wrong to kill some individual, is the desire at some future time to live—one might decide to justify one's refusal to kill suicidal teenagers on these grounds, for example—then, since typical fetuses will have the desire in the future to live, it is wrong to kill typical fetuses. Accordingly, it does not seem that a desire account of the wrongness of killing can provide a justification of a pro-choice ethic of abortion which is nearly as adequate as the value of a human-future justification of anti-abortion ethic.

The discontinuation account looks more promising as an account of the wrongness of killing. It seems just as intelligible as the value of a future-like-ours account, but it does not justify an antiabortion position. Obviously, if it is the continuation of one's activities, experiences, and projects, the loss of which makes killing wrong, then it is not wrong to kill fetuses for that reason, for fetuses do not have experiences, activities, and projects to be continued or discontinued. Accordingly, the discontinuation account does not have the antiabortion consequences that the value of a future-like-ours account has. Yet, it seems as intelligible as the value of a future-like-ours account, for when we think of what would be wrong with our being killed, it does seem as if it is the discontinuation of what makes our lives worthwhile which makes killing us wrong.

Is the discontinuation account just as good an account as the value of a future-like-ours account? The discontinuation account will not be adequate at all, if it does not refer to the *value* of the experience that may be discontinued. One does not want the discontinuation account to make it wrong to kill a patient who begs for death and who is in severe pain that cannot be relieved short of killing. (I leave open the question of whether it is wrong for other reasons.) Accordingly the discontinuation account must be more than a bare discontinuation account. It must make some reference to the positive value of the patent's experiences. But, by the same token, the value of a future-like-ours account cannot be a bare future account either. Just having a future surely does not itself rule out killing the above patient. This account must make some reference to the value of the patient's future experiences and projects also. Hence both accounts solve the value of experiences, projects, and activities. So far we still have symmetry between the accounts.

The symmetry fades, however, when we focus on the time period of the value of the experiences, etc., which has moral consequences. Although both accounts leave open the possibility that the patient in our example may be killed, this possibility is left open only in virtue of the utterly bleak future for the patient. It makes no difference whether the patient's immediate past contains intolerable pain, or consists of being in a coma (which we can imagine is a situation of indifference), or consists in a life of value. If the patient's future is a future of value, we want our account to make it wrong to kill the patient. If the patient's future is intolerable, whatever his or her immediate past, we want our account to allow killing the patient. Obviously, then, it is the value of that patient's future which is doing the work in rendering the morality of killing the patient intelligible.

This being the case, it seems clear that whether one has immediate past experiences or not does no work in the explanation of what makes killing wrong. The addition the discontinuation account makes to the value of a human future account is otiose. Its addition to the value-of-a-future account plays no role at all in rendering intelligible the wrongness of killing. Therefore, it can be discarded with the discontinuation account of which it is a part.

IV

The analysis of the previous section suggests that alternative general accounts of the wrongness of killing are either inadequate or unsuccessful in getting around the anti-abortion consequences of the value of a future-like-ours argument. A different strategy for avoiding these antiabortion consequences involves limiting the scope of the value of a future argument. More precisely, the strategy involves arguing that fetuses lack a property that is essential for the value-of-a-future argument (or for any antiabortion argument) to apply to them.

One move of this sort is based upon the claim that a necessary condition of one's future being valuable is that one values it. Value implies a valuer. Given this one might argue that, since fetuses cannot value their futures, their futures are not valuable to them. Hence, it does not seriously wrong them deliberately to end their lives.

This move fails, however, because of some ambiguities. Let us assume that something cannot be of value unless it is valued by someone. This does not entail that my life is of no value unless it is valued by me. I may think, in a period of despair, that my future is of no worth whatsoever, but I may be wrong because others rightly see value—even great value—in it. Furthermore, my future can be valuable to me even if I do not value it. This is the case when a young person attempts suicide, but is rescued and goes on to significant human achievements. Such young people's futures are ultimately valuable to them, even though such futures do not seem to be valuable to them at the moment of attempted suicide. A fetus's future can be valuable to it in the same way. Accordingly, this attempt to limit the antiabortion argument fails.

Another similar attempt to reject the anti-abortion position is based on Tooley's claim that an entity cannot possess the right to live unless it has the capacity to desire its continued existence. It follows that, since fetuses lack the conceptual capacity to desire to continue to live, they lack the right to life. Accordingly, Tooley concludes that abortion cannot be seriously prima facie wrong.[12]

What could be the evidence for Tooley's basic claim? Tooley once argued that individuals have a prima facie right to what they desire and that the lack of the capacity to desire something undercuts the basis of one's right to it.[13] This argument plainly will not succeed in the context of the analysis of this essay, however, since the point here is to establish the fetus's right to life on other grounds. Tooley's argument assumes that the right to life cannot be established in general on some basis other than the desire for life. This position was considered and rejected in the preceding section of this paper.

One might attempt to defend Tooley's basic claim on the grounds that, because a fetus cannot apprehend continued life as a benefit, its continued life cannot be a benefit or cannot be something it has a right to or cannot be something that is in its interest. This might be defended in terms of the general proposition that, if an individual is literally incapable of caring about or taking an interest in some *X*, then one does not have a right to *X* or *X* is not a benefit or *X* is not something that is in one's interest.[14]

Each member of this family of claims seems to be open to objections. As John C. Stevens[15] has pointed out, one may have a right to be treated with a certain medical procedure (because of a health insurance policy one has purchased), even though one cannot conceive of the nature of the procedure. And, as Tooley himself has pointed out, persons who have been indoctrinated, or drugged, or rendered temporarily unconscious may be literally incapable of caring about or taking an interest in something that is in their interest or is something to which they have a right, or is something that benefits them. Hence, the Tooley claim that would restrict the scope of the value of a future-like-ours argument is undermined by counterexamples.[16]

Finally, Paul Bassen[17] has argued that, even though the prospects of an embryo might seem to be a basis for the wrongness of abortion, an embryo cannot be a victim and therefore cannot be wronged. An embryo cannot be a victim, he says, because it lacks sentience. His central argument for this seems to be that, even though plants and the permanently unconscious are alive, they clearly cannot be victims. What is the explanation of this? Bassen claims that the explanation is that their lives consist of mere metabolism and mere metabolism is not enough to ground victimizability. Mentation is required.

The problem with this attempt to establish the absence of victimizability is that both plants and the permanently unconscious clearly lack what Bassen calls "prospects" or what I have called "a future life like ours." Hence, it is surely open to one to argue that the real reason we believe plants and the permanently unconscious cannot be victims is that killing them cannot deprive them of a future life like ours; the real reason is not their absence of present mentation.

Bassen recognizes that his view is subject to this difficulty, and he recognizes that the case of children seems to support this difficulty for "much of what we do for children is based on prospects." He argues, however, that in the case of children and in other such cases "potentiality comes into play only where victimizability has been secured on other grounds."[18]

Bassen's defense of his view is patently question-begging since what is adequate to secure victimizability is exactly what is at issue. His examples do not support his own view against the thesis of this essay. Of course, embryos can be victims: when their lives are deliberately terminated, they are deprived of their futures of value, their prospects. This makes them victims, for it directly wrongs them.

The seeming plausibility of Bassen's view stems from the fact that paradigmatic cases of imagining someone as a victim involve empathy, and empathy requires mentation of the victim. The victims of flood, famine, rape, or child abuse are all persons with whom we can empathize. That empathy seems to be part of seeing them as victims.[19]

In spite of the strength of these examples, the attractive intuition that a situation in which there is victimization requires the possibility of empathy is subject to counterexamples. Consider a case that Bassen himself offers: "Posthumous obliteration of an author's work constitutes a misfortune for him only if he had wished his work to endure."[20] The conditions Bassen wishes to impose upon the possibility of being victimized here seem far too strong. Perhaps this author, due to his unrealistic standards of excellence and his low self-esteem, regarded his work as unworthy of survival, even though it possessed genuine literary merit. Destruction of such work would surely victimize its author. In such a case, empathy with the victim concerning the loss is clearly impossible

Of course, Bassen does not make the possibility of empathy a necessary condition of victimizability; he requires only mentation. Hence, on Bassen's actual view this author, as I have described him, can be a victim. The problem is that the basic intuition that renders Bassen's view plausible is missing in the author's case. In order to attempt to avoid counterexamples, Bassen has made his thesis too weak to be supported by the intuitions that suggested it.

Even so, the mentation requirement on victimizability is still subject to counterexamples. Suppose a severe accident renders me totally unconscious for a month after which I recover. Surely killing me while I am unconscious victimizes me even though I am incapable of mentation during that time. It follows that Bassen's thesis fails. Apparently, attempts to restrict the value of a future-like-ours argument so that fetuses do not fall within its scope do not succeed.

V

In this essay it has been argued that the correct ethic of the wrongness of killing can be extended to fetal life and used to show that there is a strong presumption that any abortion is morally impermissible. If the ethic of killing adopted here entails, however, that contraception is also seriously immoral, then there would appear to be a difficulty with the analysis of this essay.

But this analysis does not entail that contraception is wrong. Of course, contraception prevents the actualization of a possible future of value. Hence, it follows from the claim that futures of value should be maximized that contraception is prima facie immoral. This obligation to maximize does not exist, however; furthermore, nothing in the ethics of killing in this paper entails that it does. The ethics of killing in this essay would entail that contraception is wrong only if something were denied a human future of value by contraception. Nothing at all is denied such a future by contraception however.

Candidates for subject of harm by contraception fall into four categories: (1) some sperm or other, (2) some ovum or other, (3) a sperm and an ovum separately, and (4) a sperm and an ovum together. Assigning the harm to some sperm is utterly arbitrary, for no reason can be given for making a sperm the subject of harm rather than an ovum. Assigning the harm to some ovum is utterly arbitrary for no reason can be given for making an ovum the subject of harm rather than a sperm. One might attempt to avoid these problems by insisting that contraception deprives both the sperm and the ovum separately of a valuable future like ours. On this alternative, too many futures are lost. Contraception was supposed to be wrong, because it deprived us of one future of value, not two. One might attempt to avoid this by holding that contraception deprives the combination of sperm and ovum of a valuable future like ours. But here the definite article misleads. At the time of contraception there are hundreds of millions of sperm, one (released) ovum and millions of possible combinations of all of these. There is no actual combination at all. Is the subject of the loss to be a merely possible combination? Which one? This alternative does not yield an actual subject of harm either. Accordingly, the immorality of contraception is not entailed by the loss of a future-like-ours argument simply because there is no nonarbitrarily identifiable subject of the loss in the case of contraception.

VI

The purpose of this essay has been to set out an argument for the serious presumptive wrongness of abortion subject to the assumption that the moral permissibility of abortion stands or falls on the moral status of the fetus. Since a fetus possesses a property, the possession of which in adult human beings is sufficient to make killing an adult human being wrong, abortion is wrong. This way of dealing with the problem of abortion seems superior to other approaches to the ethics of abortion, because it rests on an ethics of killing which is close to self-evident, because the crucial morally relevant property clearly applies to fetuses, and because the argument avoids the usual equivocations on "human life," "human being," or "person." The argument rests neither on religious claims nor on papal dogma. It is not subject to the objection of "speciesism." Its soundness is compatible with the moral permissibility of euthanasia and contraception. It deals with our intuitions concerning young children.

Finally, this analysis can be viewed as resolving a standard problem—indeed, *the* standard problem—concerning the ethics of abortion. Clearly, it is wrong to kill adult human beings. Clearly, it is not wrong to end the life of some arbitrarily chosen single human cell. Fetuses seem to be like arbitrarily chosen human cells in some respects and like adult humans in other respects. The problem of the ethics of abortion is the problem of determining the fetal property that settles this moral controversy. The thesis of this essay is that the problem of the ethics of abortion, so understood, is solvable.

NOTES

1. Joel Feinberg, "Abortion," in *Matters of Life and Death: New Introductory Essays in Moral Philosophy*, ed. Tom Regan (New York: Random House, 1986), pp. 256-93; Michael Tooley, "Abortion and Infanticide," *Philosophy and Public Affairs,* 2, n. 1 (1972): 37-65, *Abortion and Infanticide* (New York: Oxford, 1984); Mary Anne Warren, "On the Moral and Legal Status of Abortion," *Monist* 1/7, no. 1 (1973): 43-61; H. Tristram Engelhardt Jr., "The Ontology of Abortion," *Ethics* 1/34, no. 3 (1974): 217-34; L. W. Sumner, *Abortion and Moral Theory* (Princeton: University Press, 1981); John T. Noonan Jr., "An Almost Absolute Value in History," in *The Morality of Abortion: Legal and Historical Perspectives* (Cambridge: Harvard, 1970); and Philip Devine, *The Ethics of Homicide* (Ithaca: Cornell, 1978).

2. For interesting discussions of this issue see Warren Quinn, "Abortion: Identity and Loss," *Philosophy and Public Affairs* 13, no. 1 (1984): 24-54; and Lawrence C. Becker "Human Being: The Boundaries of the Concept," *Philosophy and Public Affairs* 4, no. 4 (1975): 334-59.

3. For example, see my "Ethics and The Elderly: Some Problems," in *Aging and the Elderly: Humanistic Perspectives in Gerontology*, eds. Stuart Spicker, Kathleen Woodward, and David van Tassel (Atlantic Highlands, N.J.: Humanities, 1978), pp. 341-355.

4. See Warren, "On the Moral and Legal Status of Abortion," and Tooley, "Abortion and Infanticide."

5. This seems to be the fatal flaw in Warren's treatment of this issue.

6. Feinberg, "Abortion," p. 270.

7. I have been most influenced on this matter by Jonathan Glover, *Causing Death and Saving Lives* (New York: Penguin, 1977), chap. 3; and Robert Young, "What Is So Wrong with Killing People?" *Philosophy,* 1/4, no. 210 (1979): 515-28

8. Feinberg, Tooley, Warren, and Engelhardt have all dealt with this problem.

9. Immanuel Kant, "Duties to Animals and Spirits," in *Lectures on Ethics*, trans. Louis Infeld (New York: Harper, 1963), p. 239.

10. I am indebted to Jack Bricke for raising this objection.

11. Presumably a preference utilitarian would press such an objection. Tooley once suggested that his account has such a theoretical underpinning. See his "Abortion and Infanticide," pp. 44–45.

12. Ibid., pp. 46–47.

13. Ibid., pp. 44–45.

14. Donald VanDeVeer seems to think this is self-evident. See his "Whither Baby Doe?" in *Matters of Life and Death,* p. 233.

15. John C. Stevens, "Must the Bearer of a Right Have the Concept of That To Which He Has a Right?" *Ethics* 95, no. 1 (1984):68-74.

16. See Tooley again in "Abortion and Infanticide," pp. 47–49.

17. Paul Bassen, "Present Sakes and Future Prospects: The Status of Early Abortion," *Philosophy and Public Affairs* 11, no. 4 (1982): 322–26.

18. Ibid., p. 333.

19. Note carefully the reasons he gives on the bottom of p. 316.

20. Bassen, "Present Sakes and Future Prospects," p. 318.

27

ASYMMETRIC VALUE AND ABORTION, WITH A REPLY TO DON MARQUIS

Jeffrey H. Reiman

A powerful clue to the solution of the moral problem of abortion has been largely ignored. I call it the *asymmetric value of human life.* This value, which we commonly attribute to human beings when we think it is morally wrong to kill them, is so unusual that it points us to the solution to the moral problem of abortion, as the shape of a keyhole points us to the key that will open it.

. . .

Let us assume what all pro-lifers and many pro-choicers believe, namely, that the fetus living inside a pregnant woman is a human being, at least in the biological sense. We can think of the normal career of such a (biological) human being as stretching from conception through the stages of pregnancy to birth and beyond into childhood and adulthood. Both pro-lifers and pro-choicers agree that, somewhere along this career, killing this human being (in the absence of excusing conditions, such as self-defense, war, legitimate punishment, or ignorance, insanity, duress, and so on) is *murder.* I use this term in a strictly moral, not legal, sense. Morally speaking, murder is the gravely immoral killing of a human being, whether or not it meets the specific legal criteria for criminal homicide. Pro-choicers and pro-lifers, then, disagree on when the killing of a biological human being is murder—but they agree that at some point it is.

Let us focus on this agreement: At some point, it is morally murder to kill a human being. Now, whenever we think it is murder to kill a human

This essay originally appeared as the introduction to *Abortion and the Ways We Value Human Life* by Jeffrey Reiman (1999). Reprinted with permission of Rowman & Littlefield Publishers, Inc.

being, we are valuing human life in a special way. We can see the "shape" of this special valuing by considering the judgments that it normally implies. For example, though murder is gravely immoral, it is not immoral, at least not seriously immoral, to refuse to procreate. Nor can the immorality of murder be made up for or canceled out if the killer adds another human being to the human population.

What these judgments reveal is that when we think it is morally murder to kill a human being, we are not simply valuing human life as such. If human life were valued as such, then there would be no net loss in value if one human being were killed and replaced with another, or there would be just as much loss from not procreating as from murder. So, murder could be made up for—its evil canceled out—by adding a new life to the population, and intentional contraception or abstinence by fertile couples would be as great an evil as murder—or murder would be as little an evil as contraception or abstinence. Such valuing, so to speak, values existing life and future possible life alike, or, as I shall say, *symmetrically*.[1]

Since we do not think that murder can be made up for by replacing the victim with another or that refusal to procreate is as great an evil as murder, it is evident that the valuing that underlies our views about the wrongness of murder is not symmetrical valuing. It is not a valuing of human life as such. Rather, it is a valuing of existing particular human lives *asymmetrically,* that is, far above the value of the lives of possible future human beings.

That we (pro-lifers and pro-choicers included) value human life or lives asymmetrically is a clue that can lead us to a solution to the moral problem of abortion. This clue works because asymmetric valuing is unusual enough to rule out a large number of common bases for valuing human life. Usually that we value something is about equally a reason for creating new ones and a reason for not destroying existing ones. This is not just a description of our conventional valuing practice. It is that, but it is also a claim about the nature of value itself. Normally, when we value something, we think this thing is good, and its goodness exercises a pull on our rational judgments and actions in all temporal directions. The goodness of something is roughly equally a reason for preserving existing ones and for producing new ones. Thus the normal way we value things is symmetric between existing ones and future ones. Such valuing will imply that killing one human and replacing her with a new one yields no net loss in value and that refusing to procreate deprives the world of as much value as does killing. To account for the valuing of life that underlies our common beliefs about the wrongness of murder, then, we need to find a reasonable way of valuing human life asymmetrically.

It is no solution to this problem to say that human life has intrinsic worth, or that human beings are ends-in-themselves, and therefore human life has asymmetric value. That merely asserts that human life has asymmetric value; it does not show that it does or explain how it even could.

Moreover, though I speak roughly about how much value the world is deprived of by killing one human and replacing her with another, or by killing versus refusing to procreate, my argument is in no way limited to a utilitarian ethical framework or even to one that thinks of value as quantifiable or maximizable. For example, a deontologist may think that killing a human is worse than refusing to procreate because killing is a greater violation of duty, and a virtue-ethicist may think that killing is worse because it manifests a more evil character.[2] However, both kinds of theorist will have to explain why killing a human is a greater violation of duty or manifests a worse character than refusing to procreate, *when both acts result in there being one less human being.* Thus, both kinds of moral theorists will have to find a reasonable way of valuing human life asymmetrically. It is this problem, which I believe haunts all moral approaches, that I am trying to speak of generally in terms of value added or taken from the world. So as not to have to continually translate this into the specific lingo of each moral approach, I ask the reader to keep in mind this larger purpose.

If we value human life by imputing goodness or intrinsic value to human beings because of their distinctive properties—rationality, creativity, capacity for loving attachment, and the like—such valuing is symmetric. It implies that one human with these properties could be killed and replaced without loss. Some may object that, even if we value something because of the goodness of its properties, our valuation need not imply that the valued one could acceptably be replaced by another with similar properties. For example, though you value Van Gogh's painting *Wheat Field With Crows* for its properties—its fantastic color, its careful composition, its overwhelming sense of foreboding, you would nevertheless object to someone destroying *Crows* and replacing it with another painting with equally impressive color, composition, and foreboding.[3]

This suggestion allows us to say more precisely what asymmetric valuing is by comparing a close look-alike. Note, to start, that we would object to the destruction of *Crows,* not because of properties that it shares with all paintings, but because of the very special constellation of properties that makes it a special painting. But nothing like this can be the basis of the value of human life, since that value is attributed to human beings generally, not just to special ones. I suspect that just about anything we value because of its properties and that we think is irreplaceable will have a similar specialness and thus not correspond to the way we value human beings. But, more importantly, even in such special cases, we are still not valuing asymmetrically. To see this, suppose that it was Van Gogh himself who destroyed *Crows,* and who then painted an identical duplicate as a replacement—so that the same special constellation of properties was present in the new painting. Surely there would be no loss of value when the first *Crows* was replaced by the second.

Compare this to the way in which we think about human beings. When we think it is gravely immoral to kill a human being, we think it would remain gravely immoral even if that human being were replaced by an identical duplicate with all the properties of the first one. *That is asymmetric valuing.* And, although, for it to have a rational foundation, asymmetric valuing will have to be based on some special properties of human beings, it cannot be based on imputing goodness to those properties (or to their possessors), since that is symmetric valuing: It implies the goodness of both existing and future possible human beings with those properties.

Since imputing goodness or intrinsic value to human traits (or to humans because of their traits) is not asymmetric valuing, I will argue that the object of asymmetric valuing must be human beings' own subjective awareness of, and caring about, their own lives. Note, as a first step toward understanding this claim, that, unlike traits like rationality, which in principle is as much a reason for valuing existing as future rational humans, human beings' conscious caring about their own lives pertains only to the particular lives that are theirs. This gives us, so to speak, a foot in the asymmetric door. Conscious beings care about their particular lives asymmetrically. Their caring about their own lives does not imply that it would be about equally good to preserve them as to produce new beings, or equally bad to murder them as not to procreate. For them, nothing is comparable to the loss of the particular lives they care about.

However, this is only part of the story. Since it is we who are valuing human beings when we think it seriously immoral to kill them, *we* must be valuing consciously caring beings in a way that implies the asymmetric wrongness of killing them. Thus, our valuing cannot take the form of imputing goodness to consciously cared about lives. Such valuing is symmetric; it implies that we think that one cared about life is about as good as any other, even a future one.

To arrive at the asymmetric valuing of human life, then, we must value consciously cared about lives in a distinctive way. Instead of imputing goodness to consciously cared about lives, we must, I contend, value *that beings who consciously care about the continuation of their lives get what they care about.* This is an asymmetric way of valuing human life. We can value life in this way without thinking it good that there be, or come into existence, beings who care about their lives continuing, much as we can value that starving beings get fed without thinking it good that starving beings come into existence. Such valuing does not imply that it would be about equally good to create new beings as to preserve existing ones, since what we are valuing is that existing caring be satisfied. Nor does it imply that new caring beings should be brought into existence, for it implies nothing about whether it is better to care and be satisfied than never to have cared at all. Of course, I believe that it is almost always better to care and be satisfied than never to have cared at all. But that is a separate judgment. As long as this judgment is not implied by "valuing that caring beings get what they care about," the latter is an asymmetric way of valuing human life.

This much shows how we *can* value human life asymmetrically. But, if we are to account for asymmetric valuing as more than an irrational quirk, we must also see how it is *reasonable* to value life this way. Valuing that individuals who consciously care about the continuation of their lives get to continue is reasonable because, once conscious caring has come on the scene, the ending of the life that is cared about causes a loss that cannot be made good by replacing that life with another. Though this is a loss to a conscious being, I am not talking about a conscious loss, such as the anguish of a person who knows that he is about to die. Rather, once self-consciousness begins, our cares, desires, and reasons attach themselves to the ongoing "point of view" that constitutes our self, and that continues as our self even during periods of sleep or unconsciousness. It is the loss to this self—with or without consciousness of the loss or its approach—that I have in mind here. (You don't have to be aware of a loss to suffer it: If your house burned down while you were away, you underwent a loss at that very moment even if you didn't learn about the fire until your return.) This does not, however, amount to saying that there can be a loss to a being who is never conscious of her cares and desires. Rather, once conscious cares and desires come on the scene, they become abiding properties of the individual's self, against which a disappointment counts as a loss.

The loss of life to a being who has begun to care about living on cannot be made up for or made good by replacing the dead being with a new one. Consequently, to value that beings vulnerable to this loss be protected against suffering it implies that we believe that ending a life is far worse than not creating a new one, and thus it implies the asymmetric value of human life. But the only kind of being who can suffer this loss is a conscious being. For us to value life in a way that implies the appropriateness of protecting it against this loss, we must value *that* a consciously valuing being gets what she values. In a wide sense of the term, we can think of this kind of valuing as a form of *respect* because respect is a kind of indirect valuing, a valuing of another's valuing. Wrote Kant, "When I observe the duty of respect, I . . . keep myself within my own bounds in order not to deprive another of any of the value which he as a human being is entitled to put upon himself."[4]

Bear in mind the "direction" in which my argument moves. I start with features of the value that people ascribe to human life at whatever stage of development they think that it is morally murder to kill a human being. Though people on opposing sides of the abortion dispute differ on when this stage is reached, they agree that, once it is reached, the life of particular living human beings has asymmetric value compared to the life of future possible human beings. I use this fact as a keyhole from which we can trace the shape of the sought-after key to the abortion problem. I look for some property that characterizes human beings (at some point) and that can reasonably be valued asymmetrically. I identify this property as people's subjective valuation of their lives, and I characterize the valuing of this property as respect. But note that my argument does not hinge on proving that we should respect people's subjective valuation of their lives. Rather, my main claim is that *only* our respect for people's subjective valuation of their lives can account for the way in which we normally think murder is immoral. Since such an account will only succeed if it shows our thinking about the immorality of murder to be reasonable, I try to show that we have good reason to respect people's subjective valuation of their lives.[5]

Since fetuses are not conscious that they are alive, they do not possess the property that is the object of asymmetric valuing, and thus there is no ground for according them the special protection to which we think human life (at some point) is entitled. Neither, of course, are infants conscious that they are alive. I claim in that case that the indirect valuing of respect is also at work; however, the respect is aimed, not at the infants, but at the people who love them. People generally (not just parents or relatives) do (and I contend that it is good that they do) love infants—a love I link to the sentiment that Hume called "humanity" and that he understood as a general affection for our conspecifics. Respect for this love gives us a strong reason not to kill infants. I think that a similar ground will provide a strong reason not to kill severely retarded individuals or victims of senile dementia.

Moreover, I shall argue that, as humans develop into children and then adults, they are rightly granted autonomy rights which further imply the wrongness of killing them. Indeed, my argument about abortion is set within a larger analysis of the ways in which our valuation and protection of human life changes in appropriate response to changes in the development of humans themselves, so that the lives of infants, of young children, of older children and adults, and of severely retarded or demented humans are appropriately valued—and appropriately protected—in different ways. In fact, this argument can be extended before birth and after death to account for the special treatment to be accorded to aborted fetuses and human corpses.

. . .

For this reason, my argument is not vulnerable to a criticism that Don Marquis has leveled, which may also have occurred to some readers: "If what makes killing us wrong is that we care about our future lives, then because suicidal teenagers, some of the clinically depressed, and some of the brainwashed don't care about the continuation of their lives, killing them is morally permissible."[6] This objection appears to have considerable force until one realizes that it assumes that there is one and only one continuing reason for the (asymmetric) wrongness of killing us. Once this much is clear, the answer to Marquis's objection is that depressed or suicidal teens, as well as brainwashed adults, have *autonomy* rights that entitle them to protection of their lives even if they have stopped caring positively about going on living. So we protect depressed and suicidal teens because we believe that their lives are theirs to make of what they wish—and we try to treat their psychological problems precisely because such problems undermine their ability to live the lives they want. As for victims of brainwashing, their autonomy rights have already been violated by the brainwashing, and that can surely not justify depriving them of the rights (which they can exercise or which others can exercise in their name) that they would have had without the brainwashing.

. . .

Persons and Ends-in-Themselves

We have seen that it is common to think that human beings have special moral rights either because they are *persons* or because they are *ends-in-themselves*. However, there is a striking absence of satisfactory accounts of what property qualifies human beings for these statuses and of how having that property makes it appropriate to grant humans special moral rights. So, while Mary Anne Warren gives a list of the properties conventionally associated with personhood (consciousness, reasoning, self-motivated activity, and so on), she fails to explain why any or all of these elements make it appropriate to hold a being that possesses the elements to be asymmetrically valuable.[7] After all, these properties will be replicated in any human being that comes of age, and thus it seems that one human with these properties can be killed and replaced by another, with no loss in value. Likewise, Kant holds that ends-in-themselves cannot be substituted for, but provides neither a clear idea of what about humans makes them ends in-themselves nor why being an end-in-itself implies nonsubstitutability. Here, too, it seems, on the contrary, that one end-in-itself is as good as another and so substitutable for the other without net loss. In this section, I shall suggest what it is about persons and ends-in-themselves that makes it appropriate to value them asymmetrically.

Take personhood first. I have argued that the only reasonable basis for asymmetrically valuing human life is that humans are aware of, and counting on, the continuation of the particular lives they already have. This is possible only for a being who is aware of his self as the same self enduring over time. A hallowed philosophical tradition defines personhood by this very awareness. Locke defined a *person* as "a thinking intelligent being, that . . . can consider itself as itself . . . in different times and places."[8] Kant wrote, "That which is conscious of the numerical identity of itself at different times is in so far a *person*."[9]

Not only does this argument rescue the idea that it is persons who are morally entitled to protection against killing; it also reinforces my claim that the asymmetric value of human life is based on our respect for our fellows as beings who care about their lives. Persons are commonly thought to be proper objects of respect.

Consider now ends-in-themselves. Two features characterize ends in-themselves. First, they have value that does not depend on their being means to some value beyond them. Second, they are the sources of the value of things that are valued only as a means to something beyond them. That is, as I seek some end, say, my paycheck, I do so for some end to which it is a means, say, shelter. If shelter is yet a means to something else, say, comfort, it is not an end-in-itself. However, as Aristotle long ago pointed out, unless I have some end that I desire for its own sake and not as a means to something beyond it, my striving will be futile and pointless, since nothing will really have value for me.[10] Each goal will be valued as a means to another, which is valued as a means to another, and so on, without ever arriving at something capable of sending value back down the line to the things that are means to it. On the other hand, if I have some end that I value for its own sake, say, comfort again, then it is an end-in-itself. Its value does not depend on its being a means to something else. This end-in itself will give value to all the means that were sought to get to it. In short, ends-in-themselves are the unmoved movers of the valuable. This suggests that we should think of ends-in-themselves less as things of very great value than as *sources of value.*[11]

Recall that, when we respect human beings, that which is the object of our respect is precisely their capacity to set values for themselves. If, then, we take being an end-in-itself as being capable of bestowing value on things, we have the trait of human beings that is the object of respect. Since that respect amounts to valuing that such beings get what they value, respecting ends-in-themselves will lead to protecting the things they value, such as their ongoing life.

What links ends-in-themselves to personhood is that being a source of values and being able to recognize oneself as the same particular at different points in time are features of rational beings. This, then, is what we ultimately respect when we treat human beings as asymmetrically valuable. Kant tied it all together: "Rational beings are called 'persons' inasmuch as their nature already marks them out as ends-in-themselves . . . , which are thus objects of respect."[12]

Love, Infanticide, and Fetuses

The newborn infant's level of awareness is more like a fetus's than like an adult's or a child's. It does not yet have awareness that it is alive, much less that it is the selfsame person enduring over time.[13] If being aware of one's life is the necessary condition of the objection to killing human beings, what follows about the moral status of infanticide? This question is important because some philosophers (and many nonphilosophers) take their intuition that infanticide is as wrong as killing adults or children so seriously as to rule out any account of the wrongness of killing that doesn't apply equally to infants.[14]

The attitude that we have when we think it wrong to kill children or adults because they care about their lives going on is a form of respect. We respect their property of being aware of, and caring about, their lives (and all this brings in its wake), and we respect them for having this attribute. We show this respect by protecting their ability to get what they care about. We are not (necessarily) either caring about them independently of what they care about or directly caring about what they care about, either of which would characterize love, rather than respect.[15]

The normal reaction to infants is a loving one (though, of course, it is not the only reaction, or the only normal one). This has surely been built into us as a result of evolution. Human babies are born at a very early stage of their development and must therefore be tended to by their parents (primarily their mothers, at least until recently) for a long time before they can get along on their own, and surely for a long time before they can begin to pay their own way.[16] There are numerous evolutionary advantages of the long extrauterine development of humans. Most importantly, this long development allows adult human beings to have larger brains than could pass through a human female's birth canal. It is inconceivable that adults would have provided the necessary care for their helpless offspring over the hundreds of thousands of years of human evolution if they had not developed a strong tendency to love infants. This is love, rather than respect, precisely because it must happen automatically, before the infant can do anything to deserve or be worthy of it.

Moreover, since we are all products of this evolutionary development, the tendency to love infants is not limited to their parents or relatives. It is a general tendency in all adults, as can be testified to by the virtually universal human vulnerability to tears and to cuteness. Thus, the love of which I am talking is virtually a universal human phenomenon. Human beings generally love infants, not just their own. This love is directed at infants generally, even neglected or abandoned ones. Because this love is natural, virtually universally felt, and felt for all infants, I liken it to the sentiment that

Hume called that of "humanity," by which he meant a natural, universal, and generalized affection for our conspecifics.

Not only is this love natural and virtually universal; it is good. Some of the infants will become children and adults, and loving them as infants is a condition of their future psychological well-being. Stanley Benn acknowledges our "instinctual tenderness and protectiveness toward babies," but contends that "there is a better reason . . . for not treating infants as expendable; namely, that some infants grow up into persons. And if as infants *they* are not treated with at least some minimal degree of tenderness and consideration, they will suffer for it later, as persons."[17]

Moreover, the love that we naturally direct toward infants is arguably a necessary condition of their development into beings worthy of respect. In any event, it contributes importantly to that development. This is so for at least two reasons, and probably more. First, by loving infants, we are moved to devote the energy and attention necessary to bring them to awareness of their lives, which is a necessary condition of their caring about their lives and our respecting them for that.[18] (The *Oxford English Dictionary* gives the root of *infant* as *infans,* Latin for "unable to speak.") Second, by loving infants, we convey to them a positive valuation of their sheer existence, which, in turn, underlies and reinforces their valuation of their own particular lives once they are capable of it. Because people's own valuation of their lives is the condition of our respect for them, we can say that our loving infants is part of the process by which infants develop into worthy objects of respect.

Love is respect's pioneer. It goes on ahead and prepares the soil where respect will take root. Respect is what infants will get once they qualify for full membership in the human moral community, but love is what reaches out and brings them into that community and necessarily does so before they qualify. And this love is not compatible with treating infants as expendable, as "trial babies" who may or may not be kept. The love of infants must be genuine and must start early to do its work and that in turn implies that the naturalness of this love counts toward its goodness.

This gives us enough to characterize the special status that infants have as natural objects of adults' love. As I suggested earlier, love cherishes the sheer existence of its object. Thus, love makes us want very much to protect existing infants and to make sure that they survive. On the other hand, since love is given rather than deserved, it is not based on anything that makes the infants worthy of it. Thus, we find ourselves strongly inclined to believe that it is wrong to kill infants, yet unable to point to some property of infants (not shared by human fetuses, or even by animals that many people think may be acceptably killed) that justifies this belief.

If this is correct, then we can say that the strong belief in the wrongness of killing infants is the product of our natural love for them, coupled with (or strengthened by) our respect for our fellows' love of them. And this love is worth supporting because it is respect's pioneer. By loving infants, we treat them as asymmetrically valuable before they really deserve it, but as part of the process by which they come really to deserve it. Then, it is wrong to kill infants because it is wrong generally to block or frustrate this love for two reasons: (1) because we and our fellows naturally and virtually universally feel this love, and (2) because it is good that we feel it inasmuch as it is important to infants' development into children and adults worthy of respect.

Insofar as respect is a valuation of other people's valuing, we can say that we protect infants out of respect, not for them, but for those who love them. We value that those people—just about everyone—get what they value. And we are supported in this by the general goodness of the love that just about everyone has for infants.

This will not apply to fetuses. They may be objects of love, but not of such love as can play a role in their psychomoral development. That requires a real, interactive social relation that can occur only after birth. Except for the pregnant woman herself, anyone who loves the fetus inside a woman's uterus is loving the object of his imagination, not a being with whom he has interacted. Though this may be an extension of our natural love for infants, it is not the spontaneous emotion itself that became part of us as a result of natural selection. Thus it lacks the warrant of naturalness and virtual universality that characterizes the love of infants. More importantly, since it cannot contribute to the psychomoral development of the fetus, it lacks the warrant of goodness that characterizes the love of infants. This is not to say that the fact that many people love fetuses counts for nothing. Much as respect for our fellows' love for infants justifies protecting infants' lives, I think that respect for those who love fetuses calls for treating aborted fetuses with special care. But, since this is a matter of other people's love rather than fetuses' own worthiness for respect, it surely will not be enough to justify requiring women to stay pregnant against their wills.

. . .

This account denies that the reasons that make it wrong to kill infants are the same as those that make it wrong to kill children or adults. Quite the contrary. Killing children or adults is wrong because it violates the respect they are due as creatures aware of, and caring about, their lives; killing infants, because it violates the love we give them as a means of making them into creatures aware of, and caring about, their lives. Killing children or adults is wrong because of properties *they* possess; killing infants, because of an emotion that *we* naturally and rightly have toward infants. Infants, for the moment, do not possess in their own right a property that makes it wrong to kill them. For this reason, there will be permissible exceptions to the rule against killing them that will not apply to the rule against killing adults or children. In particular, I think (as do many philosophers, doctors, and parents) that ending the lives of severely handicapped newborns will be acceptable. It does not take from the newborns a life that they yet care about, and it is arguably compatible with, rather than violative of, our natural love for infants. Other than that room should be left for the possibility of such exceptions, my argument is compatible with the idea that *legally* we ought to protect infants from being killed by including them under the same laws against homicide that protect children and adults. Nonetheless, my argument does imply that killing infants is not, morally speaking, murder.

. . .

A Reply to Marquis

Don Marquis holds that "loss of a future life" is what makes killing human adults and human fetuses equally wrong: "Since the loss of the future to a standard fetus, if killed, is . . . at least as great a loss as the loss of the future to a standard adult human being who is killed, abortion . . . is presumptively very seriously wrong, where that presumption is very strong—as strong as the presumption that killing another adult human being is wrong."[19]

Consider, however, that we do not view every premature stopping of a natural process as a loss. If a rose seed is planted but not watered and thus dies, we do not say that the seed has *lost* its rose-future. More accurate would be to say that its rose-future failed to occur. On the other hand, if an adult human being is murdered, we say that he *lost* the future life he would have otherwise had. A pro-choicer thinks that an aborted fetus is like the seed and not like the murdered adult. Marquis has simply assumed the reverse. He has not provided an argument for why the fetus should count as a being that can *lose its* future, as opposed to merely as a being whose future phases may fail to occur.

Marquis appears to deal with this problem when he responds to the objection that an embryo cannot be a victim, as put forth in an article by Paul Bassen. Bassen contends that embryos cannot be victims because they lack sentience or other mental activity, and he poses the counterexample of plants, which, though living, cannot be victims.[20] Against this, Marquis argues that plants cannot be victims because "killing them cannot deprive them of a future like ours." But notice that this makes the issue of whether a being can be a victim hinge on *what* it can be deprived of, rather than on whether it can be *deprived* of anything at all. What I said about loss applies equally to deprivation. The unwatered rose seed is not deprived of its rose-future; a rose seed is not the sort of thing that can be deprived of anything. To think it is, is to impute victimizability to it and thereby to beg the question. Which is precisely what Marquis does when he says against Bassen, "Of course, embryos can be victims: when their lives are deliberately terminated, they are *deprived* of their futures of value, their prospects. This makes them victims, for it directly wrongs them."[21] This puts the cart before the horse. To assert that cutting short their lives deprives embryos of something, as opposed to merely causing some future phase not to occur, is to assume in advance that embryos can be victims of morally relevant losses. Since what the embryo is thought capable of losing in a morally relevant way is its life, this is tantamount to ascribing moral vulnerability to murder to embryos. And, since that is what is at issue in the argument about abortion, Marquis has begged the question by assuming precisely what he must prove.

NOTES

1. Of course, most of us do value human life in this way. This gives us a good reason to want to reproduce the human race—perhaps even a duty to do so. However, unless we are thought to be morally required to produce as many new human beings as we physically can (which no serious moral view recommends), the value of human life as such is a reason only for maintaining some optimal number of human beings alive. Since the optimal number can be maintained even though some are killed and replaced, this way of valuing human life cannot account for the way in which we think murder is immoral.

2. A *utilitarian ethic is* one that aims at the maximization of some good, normally, happiness. *A deontologist is* a moral theorist who stresses duty or right conduct over the maximization of any good. A *virtue-ethicist is* a moral theorist who stresses the goodness of character over duty, right conduct, or the maximization of any good. The most important of utilitarian moral theorists are Jeremy Bentham and John Stuart Mill. The most important deontologist is Immanuel Kant. The most important virtue-ethicist is Aristotle. All of these approaches have contemporary representatives.

3. I owe this example to David Luban, who has pushed me hard and helpfully to clarify and defend my claims about the nature of valuing.

4. Immanuel Kant, "The Metaphysical Principles of Virtue," part 2 of *The Metaphysics of Morals*, in *Ethical Philosophy,* trans. James W. Ellington (1797; Indianapolis, Ind.: Hackett, 1983), p. 114.

5. Some readers will have noted that the notion of asymmetric value is close to what moral philosophers call the *inviolability of persons,* according to which it is wrong to violate people's rights even as a means to produce a net reduction of such violations generally. This has posed a problem for recent moral theorists, since it seems that, if such violations are bad, then it is better to produce fewer than to allow more. What inviolability shares with asymmetry is a rejection of the moral fungibility of human beings. Asymmetry rejects the moral fungibility of human beings by denying that evil done to existing human beings can be canceled out by good done to (or derived from) future possible ones, whereas inviolability rejects fungibility by denying that evil done to existing human beings can be canceled out by good done to other existing ones. Inviolability is a stronger restriction than asymmetry, because

existing humans have stronger claims on us than possible ones, but inviolability presupposes asymmetry. One could hardly believe that the fates of existing human beings are not fungible with each other while believing that the fates of existing humans are fungible with the fates of future possible humans. Consequently, if my solution to the problem of asymmetry is correct, it will be part of the solution to the problem of inviolability. For a sampling of comments on inviolability, see Robert Nozick, *Anarchy, State, and Utopia* (New York: Basic Books, 1974), p. 30; Samuel Scheffler, *The Rejection of Consequentialism* (Oxford: Oxford University Press, 1982), pp. 88–89; F. M. Kamm, "Non-Consequentialism the Person as an End-in-Itself, and the Significance of Status," *Philosophy and Public Affairs* 21, no. 4 (fall 1992): 383; Thomas Nagel, *Equality and Partiality* (New York: Oxford University Press, 1991), pp. 148–49.

6. Don Marquis, "Reiman on Abortion," *Journal of Social Philosophy* 29, no. 1 (spring 1998):143.

7. Mary Anne Warren, "On the Moral and Legal Status of Abortion," in *The Problem of Abortion*, 2d ed., ed. Joel Feinberg (Belmont, Calif.: Wadsworth, 1984), pp. 110–14.

8. John Locke, *An Essay concerning Human Understanding,* ed. and abridged by John Yolton (1690; London: Everyman, 1994), book 2, chap. 27, sec. 9, p. 180.

9. Kant, *Critique of Pure Reason*, p. 341 (emphasis in original).

10. Aristotle, *Nicomachean Ethics* 1.2.1094a, in *Complete Works of Aristotle,* ed. Barnes, vol. 2, p. 1729.

11. Allan Wood has proposed an interpretation of Kant's notion of rational agents as ends-in-themselves based on the idea that ends-in-themselves are sources of value: "Rational volition is what makes it the case that other things are good. . . . " See Allan Wood, "Humanity as As End in Itself," in *Kant's Groundwork of the Metaphysics of Morals: Critical Essays,* ed. Paul Guyer (Lanham, Md.: Rowman & Littlefield, 1998), pp. 165–87 (quotation from p. 176).

12. Kant, *Groundwork of the Metaphysics of Morals*, p. 36.

13. According to one expert on infant cognitive development:

> [I]t is a most un-Proustian life, not thought, only lived. Sensorimotor schemata . . . enable a child to walk a straight line but not to think about a line in its absence, to recognize his or her mother but not to think about her when she is gone. It is a world difficult for us to conceive, accustomed as we are to spend much of our time ruminating about the past and anticipating the future. Nevertheless, this is the state that Piaget posits for the child before one-and-a-half, that is, an ability to recognize objects and events but an inability to recall them in their absence. Because of this inability . . . the child cannot even remember what he or she did a few minutes ago. . . . These observations have been made by others as well, but more recently there have been occasional suggestions that recall may occur considerably earlier than Piaget believed, perhaps in the second 6 months of life.

Jean M. Mandler, "Representation and Recall in Infancy," in *Infant Memory: Its Relation to Normal and Pathological Memory in Humans and Other Animals,* ed. Morris Moscovitch (New York: Plenum Press, 1984), pp. 75-76.

14. See, for example, Michael Lockwood, "Warnock versus Powell (and Harradine): When Does Potentiality Count?" *Bioethics* 2, no. 3 (1988): 187-213; Richard Werner, "Abortion: The Moral Status of the Unborn," *Social Theory and Practice* 3, no. 2 (fall 1974): 201-22; John T. Noonan Jr., "An Almost Absolute Value in History," in *The Problem of Abortion,* pp. 9-14; Philip E. Devine, "The Scope of the Prohibition against Killing," in *The Problem of Abortion,* pp. 21-42; see also Loren E. Lomasky, "Being a Person: Does It Matter?" in *The Problem of Abortion,* pp. 161-72.

15. Of course, we will normally care in these ways, too. The point is that our doing so is not necessary to the way we value the lives of children or adults. For that, all that is necessary is that we respect their caring about their lives.

16. "Human babies are the most helpless in the animal kingdom; they require many years of care before they can survive on their own" (Mary Batten, *Sexual Strategies: How Females Choose Their Mates* [New York: G. P. Putnam's Sons, 1992], p. 142).

17. Stanley I. Benn, "Abortion, Infanticide, and Respect for Persons," in *The Problem of Abortion,* p. 143.

18. "When infants become *attached* to their mothers many language-critical processes are encouraged: the desire to engage in playful vocalization, including vocal exploration, the emergence of turn taking and dialogue structure, and the desire to imitate vocal patterns. In turn, mothers who are attached to and feeling nurturant toward their infants provide them with a number of opportunities to learn. Among the other processes encouraged by attachment are the use of eye gaze and manual gestures to signal attentional focus and convey labels, and the use of voice to designate and convey" (John L. Locke, *The Child's Path to Spoken Language* [Cambridge, Mass.: Harvard University Press, 1993], p. 107 [emphasis in original]). Elsewhere Locke points out that infants who do not find this emotional responsiveness in their mothers seek it from others. Ibid., pp. 109-10.

19. Don Marquis, "Why Abortion Is Immoral," *Journal of Philosophy* 86, no. 4 (April 1989): 183-202 (quotation from p. 194). Also see pp. 309-29 in this volume.

20. See Paul Bassen, "Present Sakes and Future Prospects: The Status of Early Abortion," *Philosophy and Public Affairs* 11, no. 4 (1982): 314-37, esp. pp. 322-26.

21. Marquis, "Why Abortion Is Immoral," p. 200 (emphasis in original).

28

ABORTION AND BRAIN WAVES

Gregg Easterbrook

No other issue in American politics stands at such an impasse. Decades after *Roe* v. *Wade*, the abortion debate remains a clash of absolutes: one side insists that all abortions be permitted, the other that all be prohibited. The stalemate has many and familiar causes, but a critical and little-noticed one is this: Public understanding has not kept pace with scientific discovery. When *Roe* was decided in 1973, medical knowledge of the physiology and neurology of the fetus was surprisingly scant. Law and religion defined our understanding, because science had little to say. That is now changing, and it is time for the abortion debate to change in response.

Quietly, without fanfare, researchers have been learning about the gestational phases of human life, and the new information fits neither the standard pro-choice position nor the standard pro-life position. As far as science can tell, what happens early in the womb looks increasingly like cold-hearted chemistry, with the natural termination of potential life far more common than previously assumed. But science also shows that by the third trimester the fetus has become much more human than once thought—exhibiting, in particular, full brain activity. In short, new fetal research argues for keeping abortion legal in the first two trimesters of pregnancy and prohibiting it in the third.

This is a message neither side wants to hear. But, as the Supreme Court prepares to take up the abortion issue for the first time in nearly a decade, new fetal science may provide a rational, nonideological foundation on which to ground the abortion compromise that currently proves so elusive. And, curiously enough, by supporting abortion choice early in pregnancy while arguing against it later on, the science brings us full circle—to the forgotten original reasoning behind *Roe*. Many religious interpretations today hold that life begins when sperm meets egg. But this has not always been so; until 1869, for example, the Catholic Church maintained that life commenced forty days after conception. Derived from interpretation rather than from Scripture—the Bible says nothing about when the spark of life is struck—the notion that sacredness begins when sperm meets egg hinges on the assumption that it is God's plan that each act of conception should lead to a baby.

But new science shows that conception usually does not produce a baby. "The majority of cases in which there is a fertilized egg result in the nonrealization of a person," says Dr. Machelle Seibel, a reproductive endocrinologist at the Boston University School of Medicine. What exists just after conception is called a zygote. Research now suggests that only about half of all zygotes implant in the uterine wall and become embryos; the others fail to continue dividing and expire. Of those embryos that do trigger pregnancy, only around 65 percent lead to live births, even with the best prenatal care. The rest are lost to natural miscarriage. All told, only about one-third of sperm-egg unions result in babies, even when abortion is not a factor.

This new knowledge bears particularly on such controversies as the availability of "morning after" birth-control pills, which some pharmacy chains will not stock. "Morning after" pills prevent a zygote from implanting in the uterine wall. If half of all fertilized eggs naturally do not implant in the uterine wall, it is hard to see why a woman should not be allowed to produce the same effect using artificial means.

More generally, the evidence that two-thirds of conceptions fail regardless of abortion provides a powerful new argument in favor of choice in the early trimesters. Perhaps it is possible that God ordains, for reasons we cannot know, that vast numbers of souls be created at conception and then naturally denied the chance to become babies. But science's new understanding of the tenuous link between conception and birth makes a strong case that what happens early in pregnancy is not yet life in the constitutional sense.

Yet, if new science buttresses the pro-choice position in the initial trimesters, at the other end of pregnancy it delivers the opposite message. Over the past two decades it has become increasingly clear that by the third trimester many fetuses are able to live outside the mother, passing a basic test of personhood. Now research is beginning to show that by the beginning of the third trimester the fetus has sensations and brain activity and exhibits other signs of formed humanity.

Until recently most physicians scoffed at the idea of fetal "sentience." Even newborns were considered incapable of meaningful sensation: until this generation, many doctors assumed that it would be days or weeks before a newly delivered baby could feel pain. That view has been reversed, with the medical establishment now convinced that newborns experience complex sensations. The same thinking is being extended backward to the third-trimester fetus.

Over the past decade, pediatric surgeons have learned to conduct within-womb operations on late-term fetuses with correctable congenital conditions. As they operated within the womb, doctors found that the fetus is aware of touch, responds to sound, shows a hormonal stress reaction, and exhibits other qualities associated with mental awareness. "The idea that the late-term fetus cannot feel or sense has been overturned by the last fifteen years of research," says Dr. Nicholas Fisk, a professor of obstetrics at the Imperial College School of Medicine in London.

Most striking are electroencephalogram (EEG) readings of the brain waves of the third-trimester fetus. Until recently, little was known about fetal brain activity because EEG devices do not work unless electrodes are attached to the scalp, which is never done while the fetus is in the womb. But the past decade has seen a fantastic increase in doctors' ability to save babies born prematurely. That in turn has provided a supply of fetal-aged subjects who are out of the womb and in the neonatal intensive care ward, where their EEG readings can be obtained.

EEGs show that third-trimester babies display complex brain activity similar to that found in full-term newborns. The legal and moral implications of this new evidence are enormous. After all, society increasingly uses cessation of brain activity to define when life ends. Why not use the onset of brain activity to define when life begins?

Here is the developmental sequence of human life as suggested by the latest research. After sperm meets egg, the cells spend about a week differentiating and dividing into a zygote. One to two weeks later the zygote implants in the uterine wall, commencing the pregnancy. It is during this initial period that about half of the "conceived" sperm-egg pairings die naturally. Why this happens is not well-understood: one guess is that genetic copying errors occur during the incipient stages of cellular division.

The zygotes that do implant soon transform into embryos. During its early growth, an embryo is sufficiently undifferentiated that it is impossible to distinguish which tissue will end up as part of the new life and which will be discarded as placenta. By about the sixth week the embryo gives way to the fetus, which has a recognizable human shape. (It was during the embryo-fetus transition, Augustine believed, that the soul is acquired, and this was Catholic doctrine for most of the period from the fifth century until 1869.) Also around the sixth week, faint electrical activity can be detected from the fetal nervous system. Some pro-life commentators say this means that brain activity begins during the sixth week, but, according to Dr. Martha Herbert, a neurologist at Massachusetts General Hospital, there is little research to support that claim. Most neurologists assume that electrical activity in the first trimester represents random neuron firings as nerves connect—basically, tiny spasms.

The fetus's heart begins to beat, and by about the twentieth week the fetus can kick. Kicking is probably a spasm, too, at least initially, because the fetal cerebral cortex, the center of voluntary brain function, is not yet "wired," its neurons still nonfunctional. (Readings from twenty- to twenty-two-week-old premature babies who died at birth show only very feeble EEG signals.) From the twenty-second week to the twenty-fourth week, connections start to be established between the cortex and the thalamus, the part of the brain that translates thoughts into nervous-system commands. Fetal consciousness seems physically "impossible" before these connections form, says Fisk, of the Imperial College School of Medicine.

At about the twenty-third week the lungs become able to function, and, as a result, twenty-three weeks is the earliest date at which premature babies have survived. At twenty-four weeks the third trimester begins, and at about this time, as the cerebral cortex becomes "wired," fetal EEG readings begin to look more and more like those of a newborn. It may be a logical consequence, either of natural selection or of divine creation, that fetal higher brain activity begins at about the time when life outside the mother becomes possible. After all, without brain function, prematurely born fetuses would lack elementary survival skills, such as the ability to root for nourishment.

At about twenty-six weeks the cell structure of the fetal brain begins to resemble a newborn's, though many changes remain in store. By the twenty-seventh week, according to Dr. Phillip Pearl, a pediatric neurologist at Children's Hospital in Washington, D.C., the fetal EEG reading shows well-organized activity that partly overlaps with the brain activity of adults, although the patterns are far from mature and will continue to change for many weeks. By the thirty-second week, the fetal brain pattern is close to identical to that of a full-term baby.

Summing up, Paul Grobstein, a professor of neurology at Bryn Mawr University, notes, "I think it can be comfortably said that by the late term the brain of the fetus is responding to inputs and generating its own output. The brain by then is reasonably well-developed. But we still don't know what within the fetal brain corresponds to the kind of awareness and experience that you and I have." The fetus may not know it is a baby or have the language-ordered thoughts of adults. But Grobstein points out that from the moment in the third trimester that the brain starts running, the fetus can experience the self/other perceptions that form the basis of human consciousness—since the womb, to it, represents the outside world.

In 1997, the Royal College of Obstetricians and Gynecologists, Britain's equivalent to a panel of the National Academy of Sciences, found that, because new research shows that the fetus has complex brain activity from the third trimester on, "we recommend that practitioners who undertake termination of pregnancy at 24 weeks or later should consider the requirements for feticide or fetal analgesia and sedation." In this usage, "feticide" means killing the fetus the day before the abortion with an injection of potassium that stops the fetus's heart, so that death comes within the womb. Otherwise, the Royal College suggests that doctors anesthetize the fetus before a third-trimester termination—because the fetus will feel the pain of death and may even, in some sense, be aware that it is being killed.

If a woman's life is imperiled, sacrificing a third-trimester fetus may be unavoidable. But the American Medical Association (AMA) says late-term abortions to save the mother's life are required only under "extraordinary circumstances"; almost all late-term abortions are elective. In turn, the best estimates suggest that about 750 late-term abortions occur annually in the United States, less than one percent of total abortions. (An estimated 89 percent of U.S. abortions occur in the first trimester, ethically the least perilous time.) Pro-choice advocates sometimes claim that, because less than 1 percent of abortions are late-term, the issue doesn't matter. But moral dilemmas are not attenuated by percentages: no one would claim that 750 avoidable deaths of adults did not matter.

On paper the whole issue would seem moot, because Supreme Court decisions appear to outlaw late-term abortion except when the woman's life is imperiled. But in practice the current legal regime allows almost any abortion at anytime, which turns out to be a corruption of *Roe*.

In its 1973 opinions in *Roe* and a companion case called *Bolton*, the Supreme Court established an abortion hierarchy: during the first trimester, there would be essentially no restrictions; during the second trimester, states could regulate abortion, but only to insure that procedures were carried out by qualified practitioners; during the third trimester, states could prohibit abortion, except when necessary "to preserve the life or health of the mother." (In abortion law, the Supreme Court sets ground rules, but states enact the regulations; Congress can sometimes intervene.) *Roe*'s third-trimester standard was considered largely theoretical, because in 1973 doctors were generally unable to perform safe late-term abortions. That would change.

Roe was premised on the idea that the Constitution protects medical privacy, an important concept in law for everyone, not just women. But even constitutional rights may be regulated, as, for example, libel laws regulate free speech. *Roe* did not grant an unqualified privilege: it held that a woman's claim to make her own medical choices is strong in the first trimester of pregnancy, moderate in the second, and weak in the third, at which point the state acquires a "compelling" interest in the protection of new life. The court's inclination to permit abortion in the first two trimesters and all but ban it in the third was both morally defensible and helpful to physicians and regulators, because the beginning of the third trimester can be objectively determined within a week or so. Whatever one thinks of the legal reasoning in *Roe*—the opinion is sometimes attacked even by liberal scholars for its shaky use of precedent—its attempts at rights-balancing are a model of conscientious jurisprudence.

The problem is that *Roe*'s third-trimester protections were brushed aside by two descendant Supreme Court cases, *Danforth* in 1976 and *Colautti* in 1979. *Danforth* tossed out *Roe*'s clear, comprehensible third-trimester distinction and substituted a "viability" standard so vague it was impossible to make heads or tails of it. Unlike the third trimester, which can be objectively delineated, viability is subjective. Some babies are viable at the biological frontier of twenty-three weeks; others die even if carried to term; there is no way to know in advance. *Danforth* went so far as to prohibit states from drawing clear lines at the third trimester—that is, it forbade states from using the logic of *Roe*.

Three years later, *Colautti* essentially said that, since no one could understand *Danforth*, it would henceforth be up to each woman's physician to determine whether a fetus was viable and thus legally protected. Here a misjudgment was poised atop an error, given that no doctor can ever be sure that a fetus is viable. Since the person making the determination may also perform the abortion, all a physician has to do under *Colautti* is hazard a guess that the fetus is not viable, and a late-term abortion may proceed. There is no accountability for, or review of, the physician's judgment. And, if an abortion occurs, no disproof of the doctor's judgment is possible, since the chance of viability ends.

The blurry viability standard was reinforced in the 1992 Supreme Court case called *Casey*. Again the Court appeared to outlaw late-term abortion, saying that a viable fetus should be constitutionally protected. But it rejected bright-line definitions of the onset of life, specifically forbidding states to employ the third trimester as a clear, enforceable standard. Instead the Court cryptically declared that viability confers protection "whenever it may occur"—medically close to meaningless, since there is no sure means to determine viability. Under *Casey*, as under *Colautti,* it is the abortion provider who deems whether a third-trimester fetus is viable, which makes almost any late-term abortion permissible. That is the status quo today.

Casey appeared to grant states the authority to restrict late-term abortion so long as they do not "unduly" burden women seeking early abortions. Thirty states proceeded to enact third-trimester restrictions, but most of these have been struck down, either for being too vague to enforce or for containing Trojan-horse language meant to erode *Roe* itself.

Recently, some states have opted for legislation intended solely to prevent a form of late-term abortion called D & X in which delivery is induced, the fetus is partly born, feet first, and then the skull is crushed and the brains vacuumed out. There is no moral distinction between aborting a late-term fetus via D & X and doing the same via the D & E procedure, in which death occurs within the womb: either both are defensible or neither is. Yet D & X is undeniably barbaric. The AMA has recommended that its members not perform this procedure, adding that "there does not appear to be any identified situation" in which it is required for the health of the mother. In many nations, the technique is unthinkable: Fisk, of the Imperial College School of Medicine, notes, "I've never known a respectable physician who has done a D & X."

This fall, the U.S. Court of Appeals for the Seventh Circuit upheld a Wisconsin statute that prohibited D & X abortion but allowed D & E. (The opinion was by my brother Frank, an appellate judge, who had no connection to the writing of this article.) Editorialists declared that, for the first time, a federal court had "banned" late-term abortion, though the decision did nothing of the kind—it simply found that Wisconsin could regulate types of late-term procedures, so long as women retained the rights delineated under *Roe.* Also this fall, the U.S. Court of Appeals for the Eighth Circuit overturned a Nebraska law that restricted D & X but made no provisions for threats to the life of the mother. Faced with conflicting opinions among the appellate circuits, the Supreme Court said last week that it would hear the late-term abortion issue again, setting the stage for the first important abortion ruling of this generation.

Meanwhile, each year since 1995, Congress has enacted legislation to restrict late-term abortion, and each year President Clinton has either vetoed or threatened to veto it. During the sequence of votes and vetoes, each side has gone out of its way to make itself look bad. Pro-life members of Congress have proposed absolute bans that make no provision for protecting the life of the mother, which undermines their claim to revere life. Senator Diane Feinstein of California, in what was surely one of the all-time lows for American liberalism, brought to the Senate floor a bill intended to affirm a woman's right to terminate a healthy, viable late-term fetus. Both sides have opposed a reasonable middle ground. In 1996, for example, Representative Steny Hoyer of Maryland, a liberal Democrat, offered a bill to ban late-term abortions except when necessary to avert "serious adverse health consequences" to the woman. Rather than rally around this compromise, pro-lifers and pro-choicers mutually assailed it.

In 1997, the AMA declared that third-trimester abortions should not be performed "except in cases of serious fetal anomalies incompatible with life," meaning when the fetus appears fated to die anyway. The AMA supports *Roe,* backs public funding of abortions, and favors availability of RU 486; it simply thinks that, once a fetus can draw its own breath, a new life exists and must be protected. The AMA declaration had a strong influence on centrists such as Democratic Representative Tim Roemer of Indiana, who has called the D & X procedure "inches from infanticide," and Senate Minority Leader Tom Daschle, who in 1997 switched from supporting late-term abortion to opposing it.

Daschle offered a bill that would have prohibited third-trimester abortions except to avoid "grievous injury" to the mother and would have required any physician performing a late-term abortion to certify that the fetus was not viable. Under pressure from pro-choice lobbyists, Clinton offered only tepid, pro forma support for the Daschle bill. Pro-life activists rallied against it, asserting that the "grievous injury" clause could justify abortions based upon a woman's mental rather than physical health. Gridlock has prevailed since.

The issue of mental health is an example of how absolutist thinking cripples both pro-life and pro-choice advocacy. Pro-life forces find it repugnant that a woman might be allowed to terminate a pregnancy to preserve her emotional state, yet it is fair to assume that no man will ever understand the mental-health consequences to a woman of unwanted motherhood. Conversely, pro-choice theory concerns itself only with a woman's mental health during pregnancy, not afterward. A woman who carries an unwanted child to term and then offers the baby for adoption may suffer physical and psychological hardship and social opprobrium—but, for the rest of her life, her conscience will be clear. Pro-choice absolutism takes no account of the mental health of the woman who aborts a viable child and then suffers remorse for an act she cannot undo.

If women's health and freedom represent the blind spot of the pro-life side, the moral standing of the third-trimester fetus—the baby, by that point—is the blind spot of pro-choicers. Pro-choice adherents cite the slippery slope, but that apprehension is an artifact of lobbying and fundraising, not of law. Clinton, reflecting the absolutist line, has said that late-term abortion is "a procedure that appears inhumane" but that restrictions "would be even more inhumane" because they would lead to the overturning of *Roe*. For those who know what's actually in *Roe*—a trimester system whose very purpose is to allow early choice while protecting late-term babies—this claim is more than a little ironic.

Women are right to fear that political factions are working to efface their rights. Late-term abortion is simply not the ground on which to stage the defense—because, unless the mother's life is at stake, late-term abortion is wrong.

It is time to admit what everyone knows and what the new science makes clear: that third-trimester abortion should be very tightly restricted. The hopelessly confusing viability standard should be dropped in favor of a bright line drawn at the start of the third trimester, when complex fetal brain activity begins. Restricting abortion after that point would not undermine the rights granted by *Roe,* because there is no complex brain activity before the third trimester and thus no slippery slope to start down. Scientifically based late-term abortion restrictions would not enter into law poignant but unprovable spiritual assumptions about the spark of life but would simply protect lives whose humanity is now known.

To be sure, restrictions on late-term abortion would harm the rights of American women, but the harm would be small, while the moral foundation of abortion choice overall would be strengthened by removing the taint of late-term abortion. By contrast, restrictions on early abortions would cause tremendous damage to women's freedom while offering only a hazy benefit to the next generation, since so many pregnancies end naturally anyway. There are costs to either trade-off, but they are costs that a decent society can bear.

Western Europe is instructive in this regard. In most European Union nations, early abortion is not only legal but far less politically contentious than it is here. Yet, in those same countries, late-term abortion is considered infanticide. All European Union nations except France and the United Kingdom ban abortion in the third trimester, except to save the mother's life. And, even where allowed, late-term abortion occurs at one-third the U.S. rate. Western European countries have avoided casting abortion as a duel between irresolvable absolutes. They treat abortion in the first two trimesters as a morally ambiguous private matter, while viewing it in the third trimester as public and morally odious. We should follow their lead. All it requires is knowledge of the new fetal science and a return to the true logic of *Roe.*

CONTRIBUTORS

Joan C. Callahan is assistant professor of philosophy at the University of Kentucky.

Sidney Callahan is associate professor of psychology at Mercy College, Dobbs Ferry, New York.

Gregg Easterbrook is a senior editor for the *New Republic*.

Harry J. Gensler is professor of philosophy at Loyola University of Chicago.

Rick Hampson is an Associated Press journalist.

Jack Hitt is a contributing writer for several publications, including *Harpers* and *Lingua Franca*.

Miriam Jordan is a staff reporter for the *Wall Street Journal*.

Gary Leber is director of Operation Rescue in Binghamton, New York.

Daniel C. Maguire is professor of moral theology at Marquette University and a member of Catholics for Free Choice.

Don Marquis is professor of philosophy at the University of Kansas.

Kathryn E. May is a psychotherapist and coauthor of *Back Rooms: Voices from the Illegal Abortion Era* (1988).

Michael E. McConnell is professor of constitutional law at the University of Utah.

Ellen Messer is a social worker and coauthor of *Back Rooms: Voices from the Illegal Abortion Era* (1988).

Roger A. Paynter, former pastor of Lake Shore Baptist Church, Waco, Texas, is now pastor of First Baptist Church, Austin, Texas.

Anna Quindlen is a columnist for the *Los Angeles Times*.

Jeffrey H. Reiman is the William Fraser McDowell Professor of Philosophy at the American University.

Richard Selzer, a surgeon, is a member of the faculty of the Yale School of Medicine.

Richard Schoenig is professor of philosophy at San Antonio College.

Paul D. Simmons is clinical professor of medical ethics at the University of Louisville School of Medicine and is adjunct professor in the department of philosophy.

Judith Jarvis Thomson is professor of philosophy at the Massachusetts Institute of Technology.

Mary Anne Warren is associate professor of philosophy, San Francisco State University.

John T. Wilcox is retired professor of philosophy, State University of New York at Binghamton.

Naomi Wolf is an author, lecturer, and social critic representing a feminist perspective.

Melvin L. Wulf is an attorney in New York City. He was legal director of the American Civil Liberties Union from 1962 to 1977.